T0017295

CONTINENTAL
DRIFTER

CONTINENTAL DRIFTER

KATHY MACLEOD

:01

First Second
New York

For my family

1

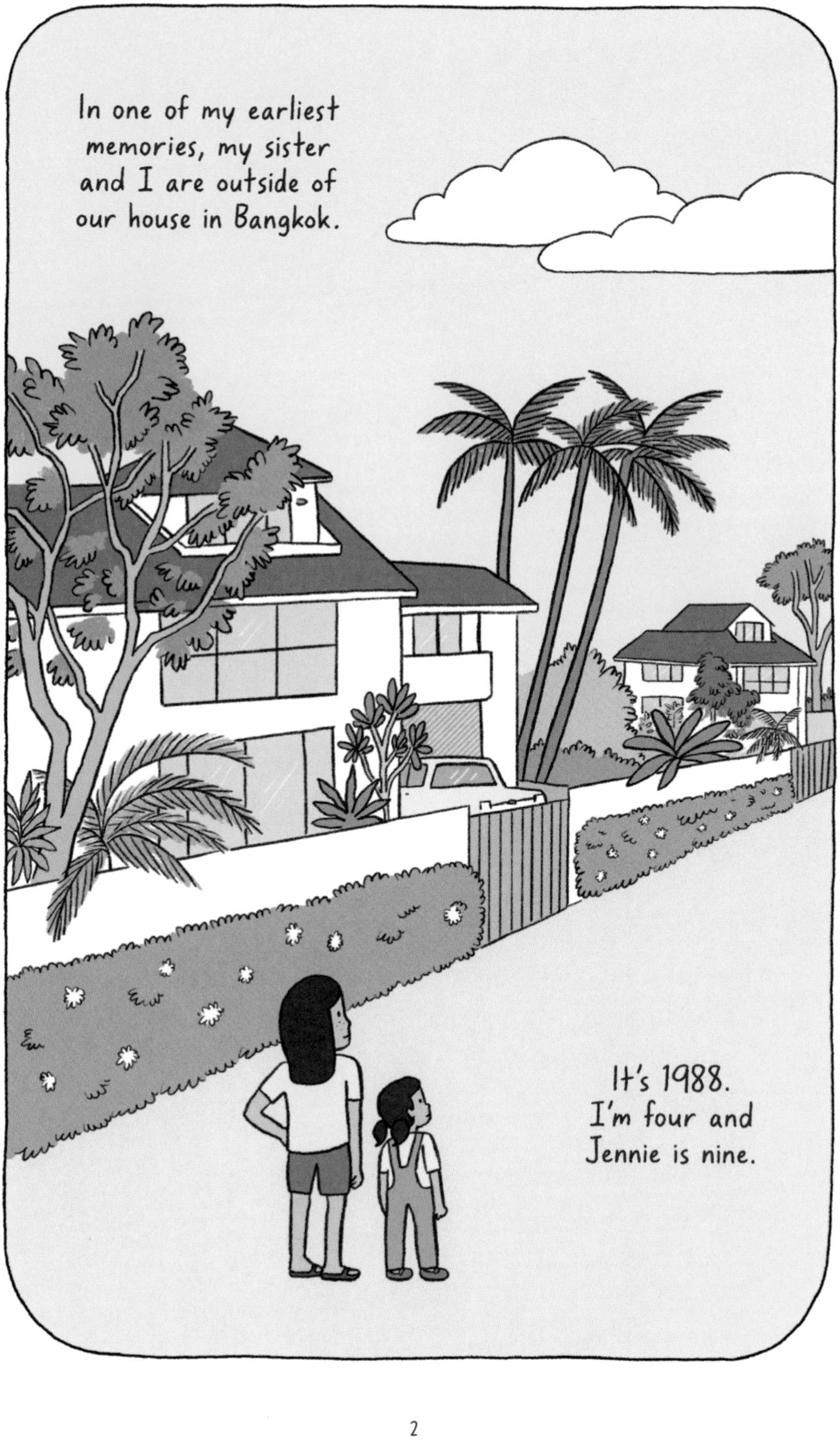
In one of my earliest memories, my sister and I are outside of our house in Bangkok.
It's 1988. I'm four and Jennie is nine.

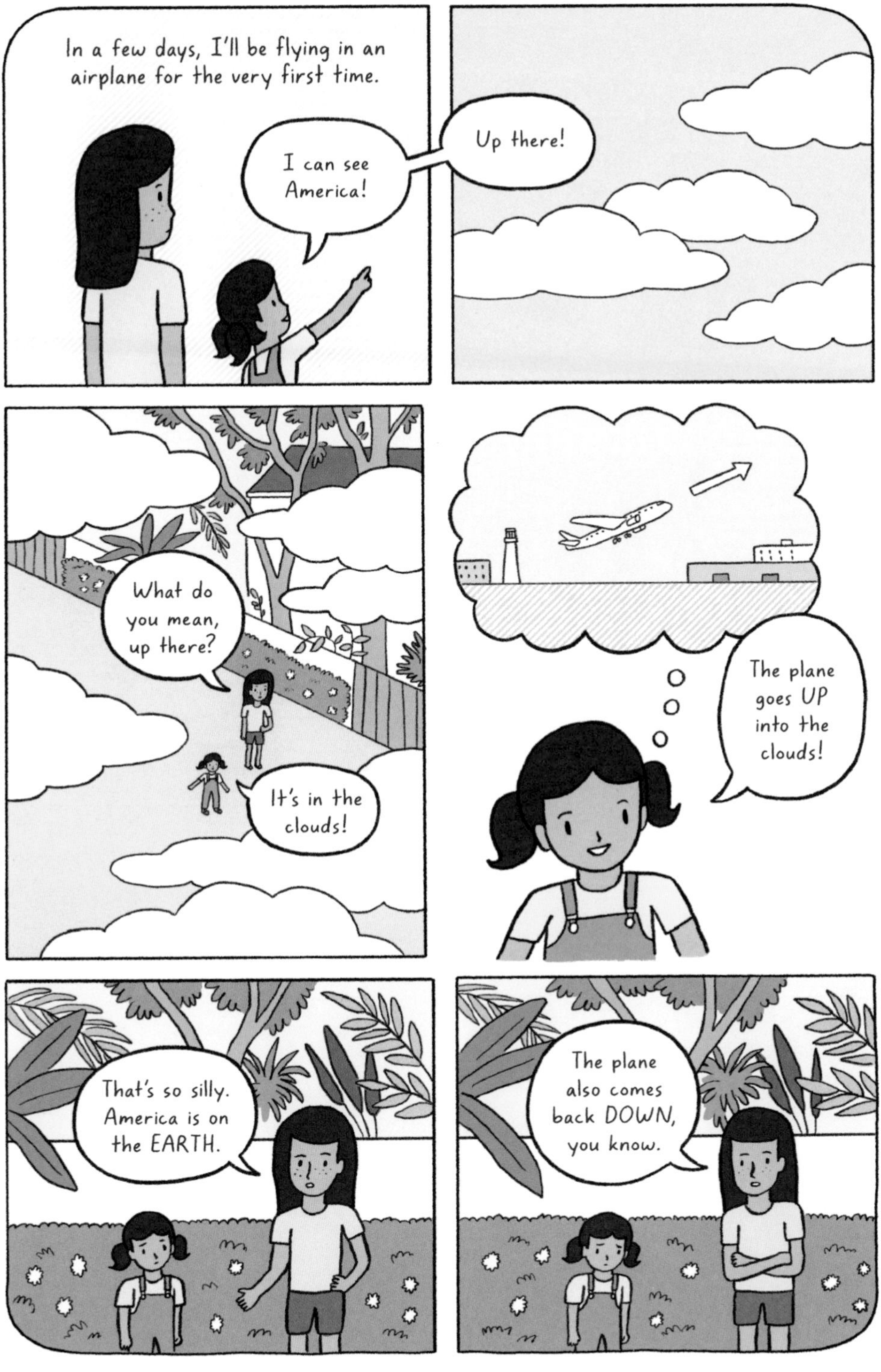
In a few days, I'll be flying in an airplane for the very first time.
I can see America!
Up there!
What do you mean, up there?
It's in the clouds!
The plane goes UP into the clouds!
That's so silly. America is on the EARTH.
The plane also comes back DOWN, you know.

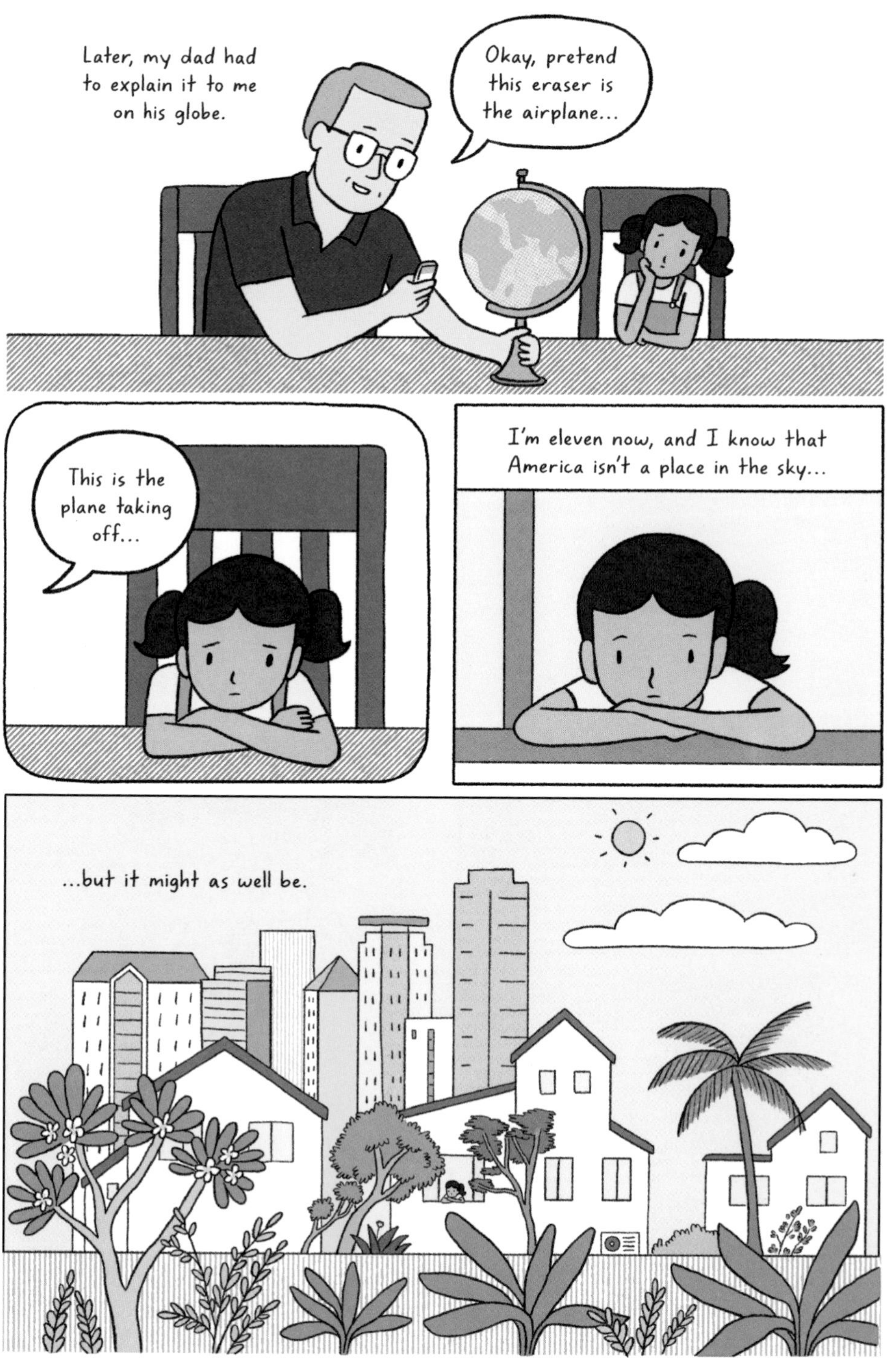
Later, my dad had to explain it to me on his globe.
Okay, pretend this eraser is the airplane...
This is the plane taking off...
I'm eleven now, and I know that America isn't a place in the sky...
...but it might as well be.

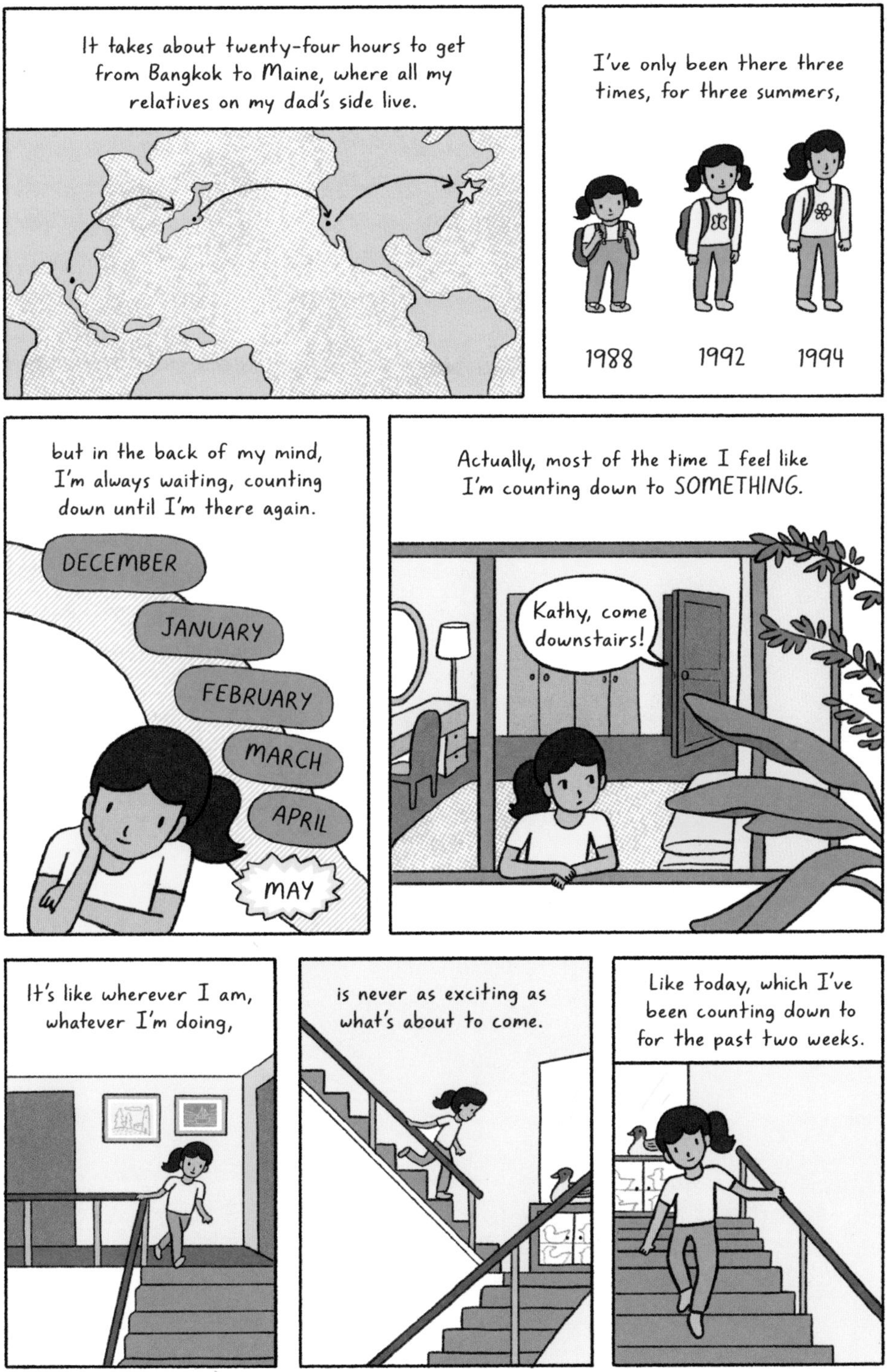
It takes about twenty-four hours to get from Bangkok to Maine, where all my relatives on my dad's side live.
I've only been there three times, for three summers,
1988
1992
1994
but in the back of my mind, I'm always waiting, counting down until I'm there again.
DECEMBER
JANUARY
FEBRUARY
MARCH
APRIL
MAY
Actually, most of the time I feel like I'm counting down to SOMETHING.
Kathy, come downstairs!
It's like wherever I am, whatever I'm doing,
is never as exciting as what's about to come.
Like today, which I've been counting down to for the past two weeks.

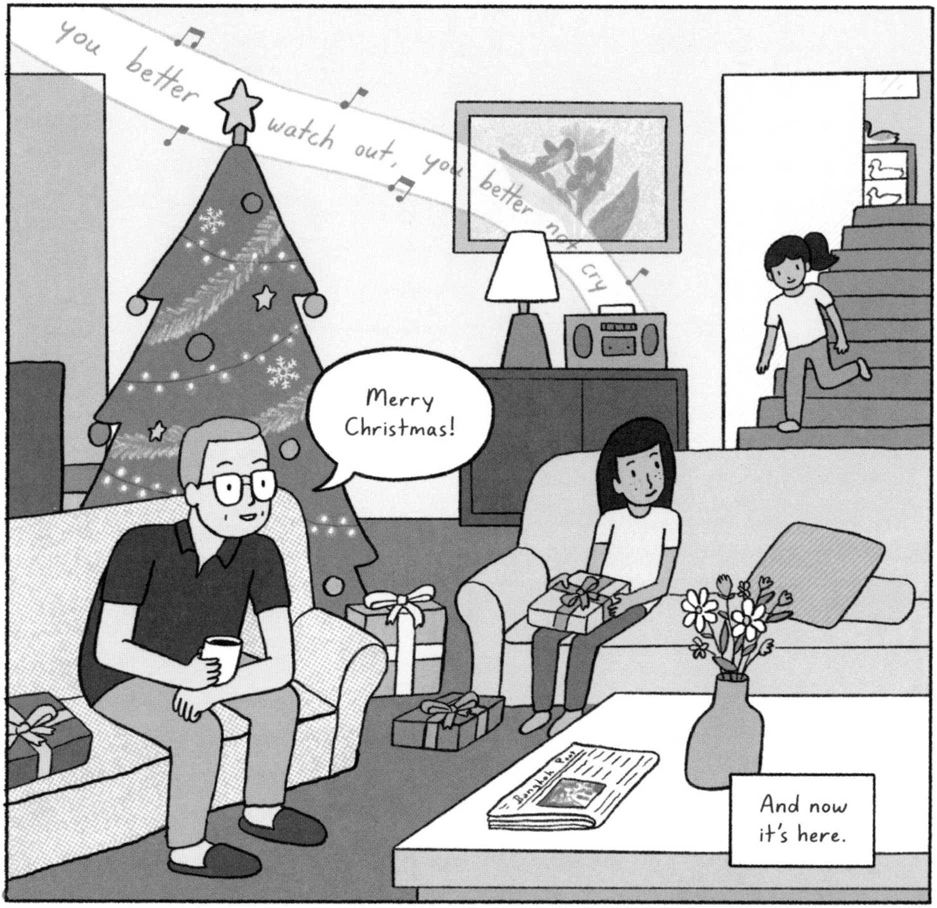
you better watch out, you better not cry
Merry Christmas!
And now it's here.

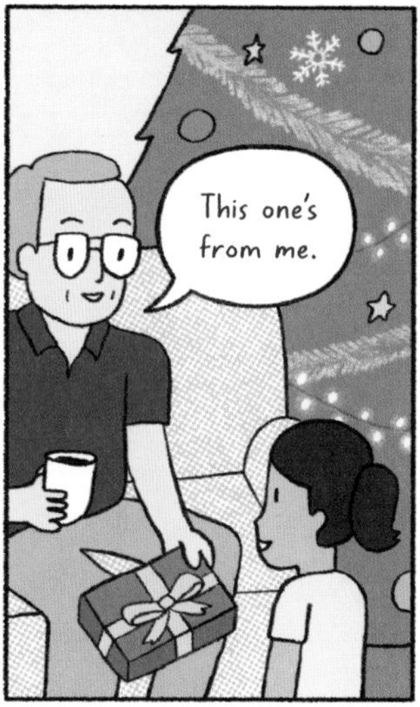
This one's from me.

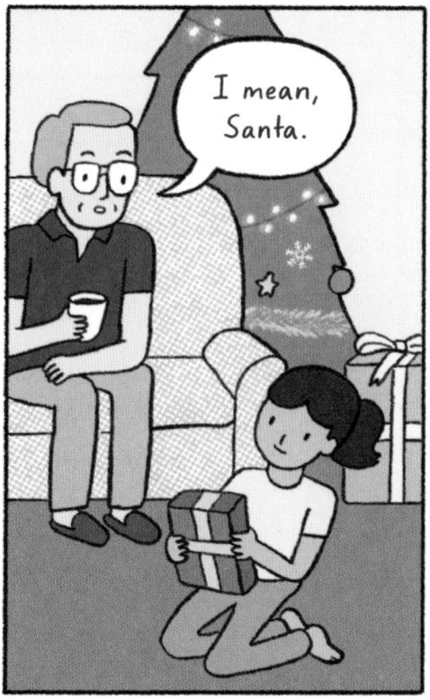
I mean, Santa.

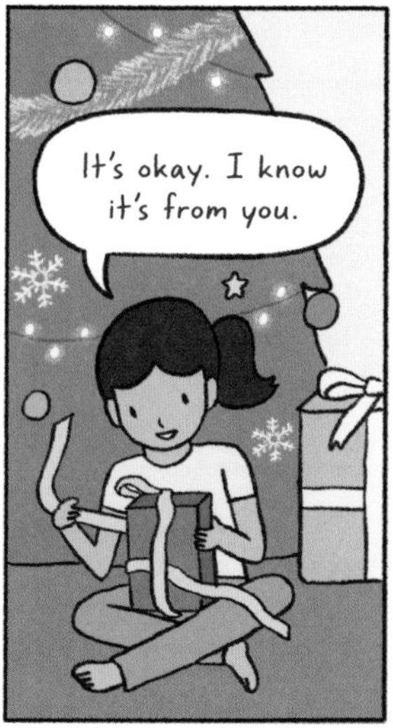
It's okay. I know it's from you.

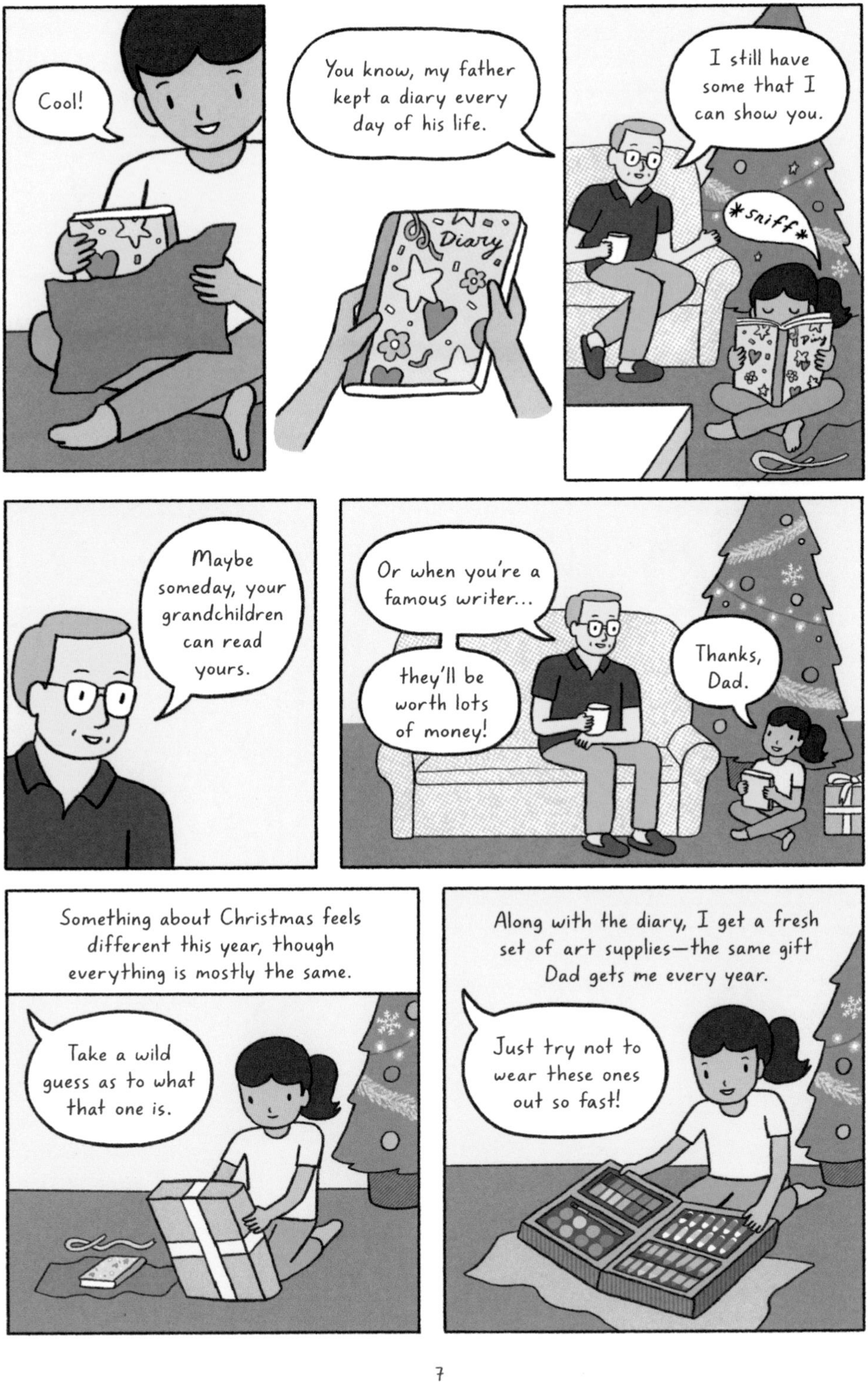
Cool!
You know, my father kept a diary every day of his life.
Diary
I still have some that I can show you.
sniff
Diary
Maybe someday, your grandchildren can read yours.
Or when you're a famous writer...
they'll be worth lots of money!
Thanks, Dad.
Something about Christmas feels different this year, though everything is mostly the same.
Take a wild guess as to what that one is.
Along with the diary, I get a fresh set of art supplies—the same gift Dad gets me every year.
Just try not to wear these ones out so fast!

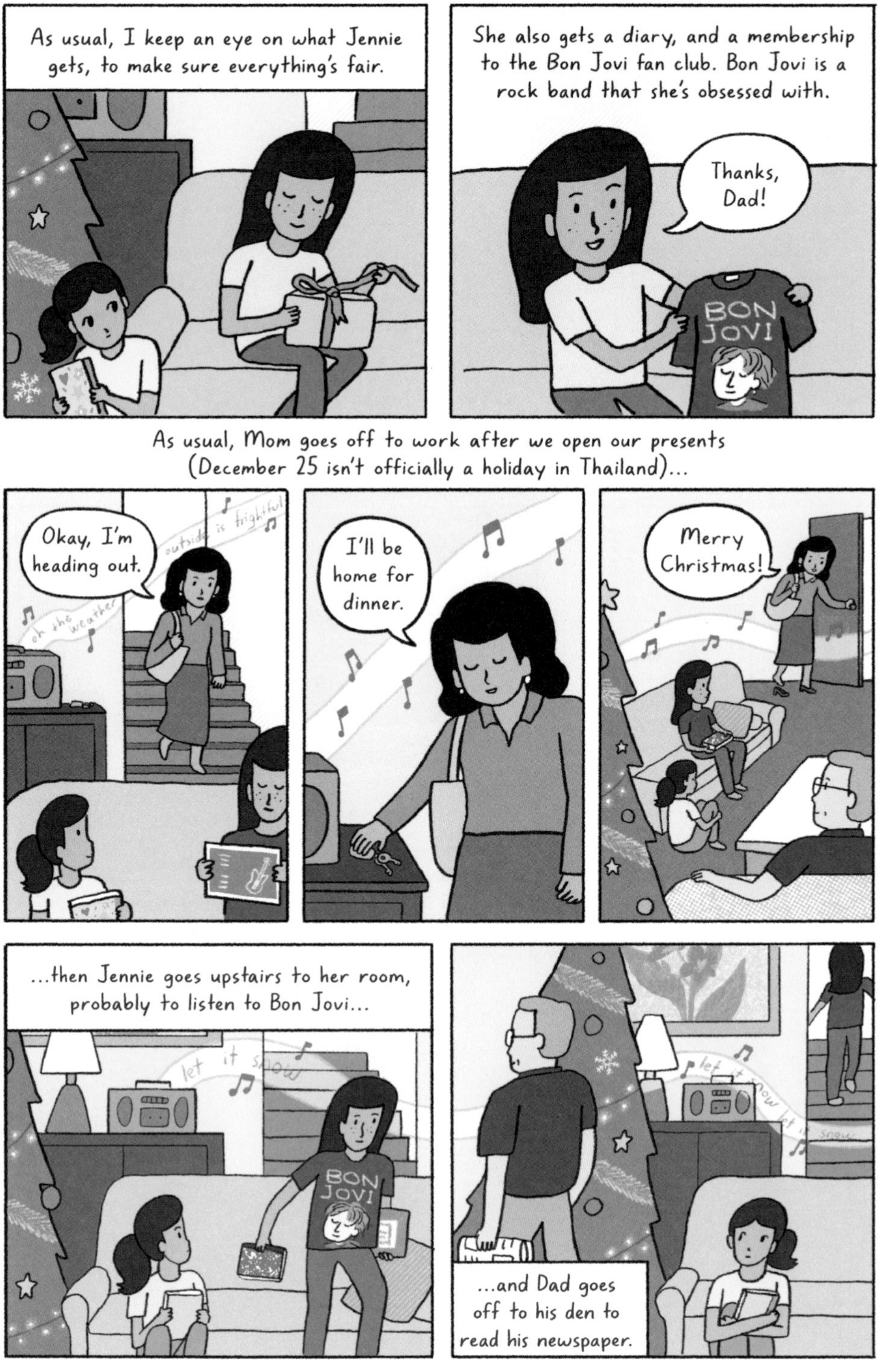
As usual, I keep an eye on what Jennie gets, to make sure everything's fair.
She also gets a diary, and a membership to the Bon Jovi fan club. Bon Jovi is a rock band that she's obsessed with.
Thanks, Dad!
BON JOVI
As usual, Mom goes off to work after we open our presents (December 25 isn't officially a holiday in Thailand)...
Okay, I'm heading out.
oh the weather outside is frightful
I'll be home for dinner.
Merry Christmas!
...then Jennie goes upstairs to her room, probably to listen to Bon Jovi...
let it snow
BON JOVI
let it snow let it snow let it snow
...and Dad goes off to his den to read his newspaper.

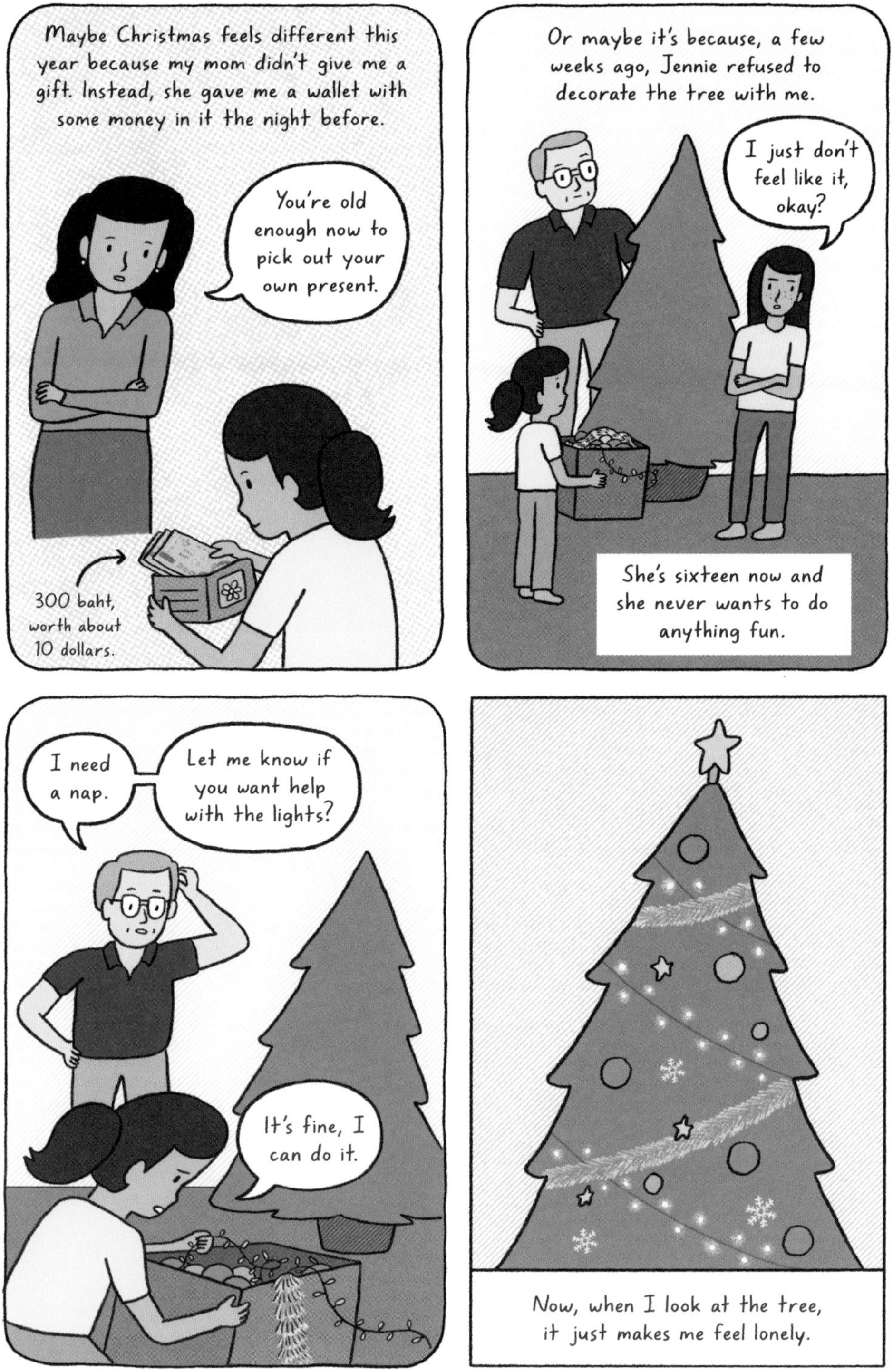
Maybe Christmas feels different this year because my mom didn't give me a gift. Instead, she gave me a wallet with some money in it the night before.
You're old enough now to pick out your own present.
300 baht, worth about 10 dollars.
Or maybe it's because, a few weeks ago, Jennie refused to decorate the tree with me.
I just don't feel like it, okay?
She's sixteen now and she never wants to do anything fun.
I need a nap.
Let me know if you want help with the lights?
It's fine, I can do it.
Now, when I look at the tree, it just makes me feel lonely.

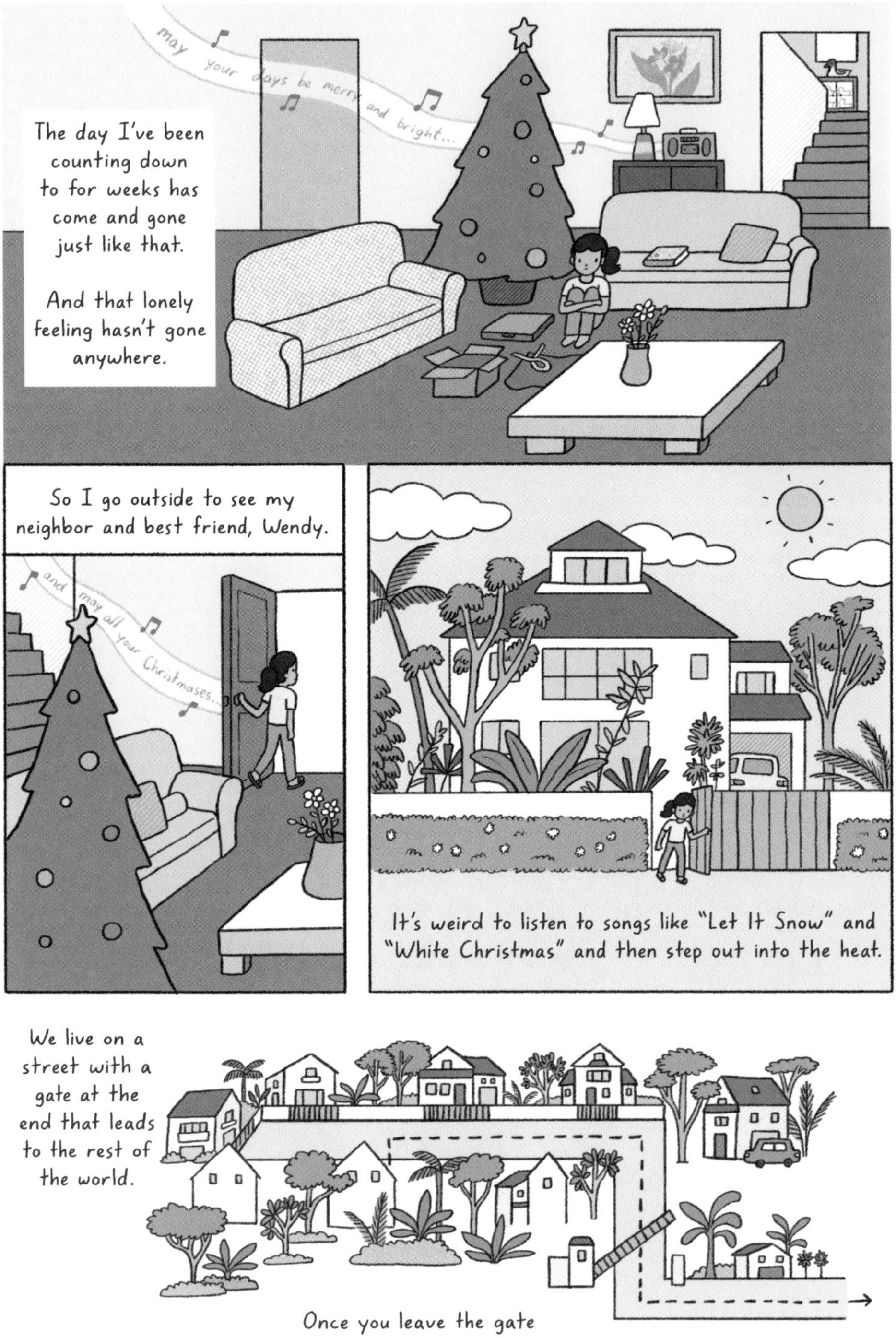
may your days be merry and bright...
The day I've been counting down to for weeks has come and gone just like that.
And that lonely feeling hasn't gone anywhere.
So I go outside to see my neighbor and best friend, Wendy.
and may all your Christmases...
It's weird to listen to songs like "Let It Snow" and "White Christmas" and then step out into the heat.
We live on a street with a gate at the end that leads to the rest of the world.
Once you leave the gate and turn a corner...

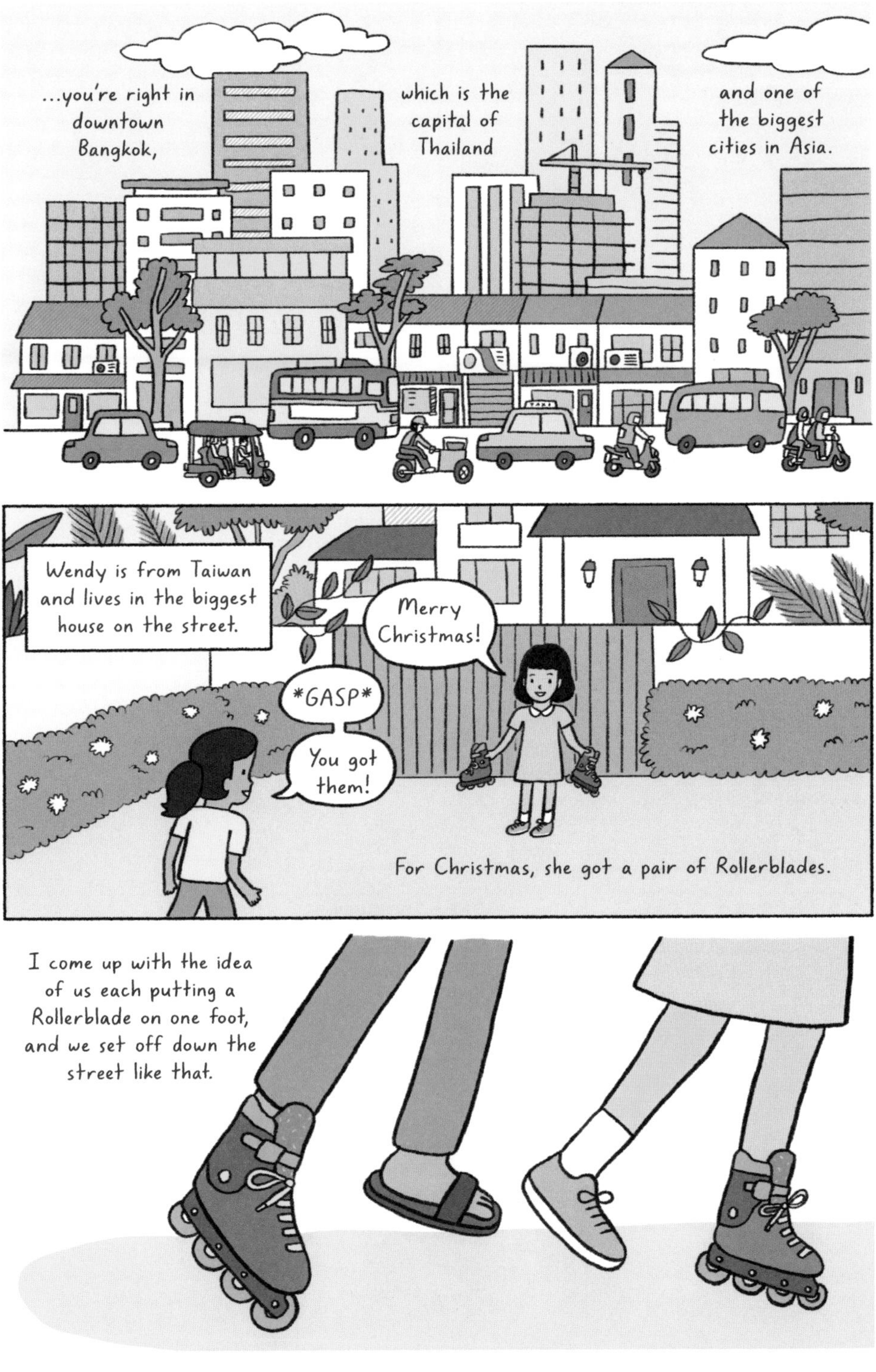

...you're right in downtown Bangkok,
which is the capital of Thailand
and one of the biggest cities in Asia.
Wendy is from Taiwan and lives in the biggest house on the street.
Merry Christmas!
GASP
You got them!
For Christmas, she got a pair of Rollerblades.
I come up with the idea of us each putting a Rollerblade on one foot, and we set off down the street like that.

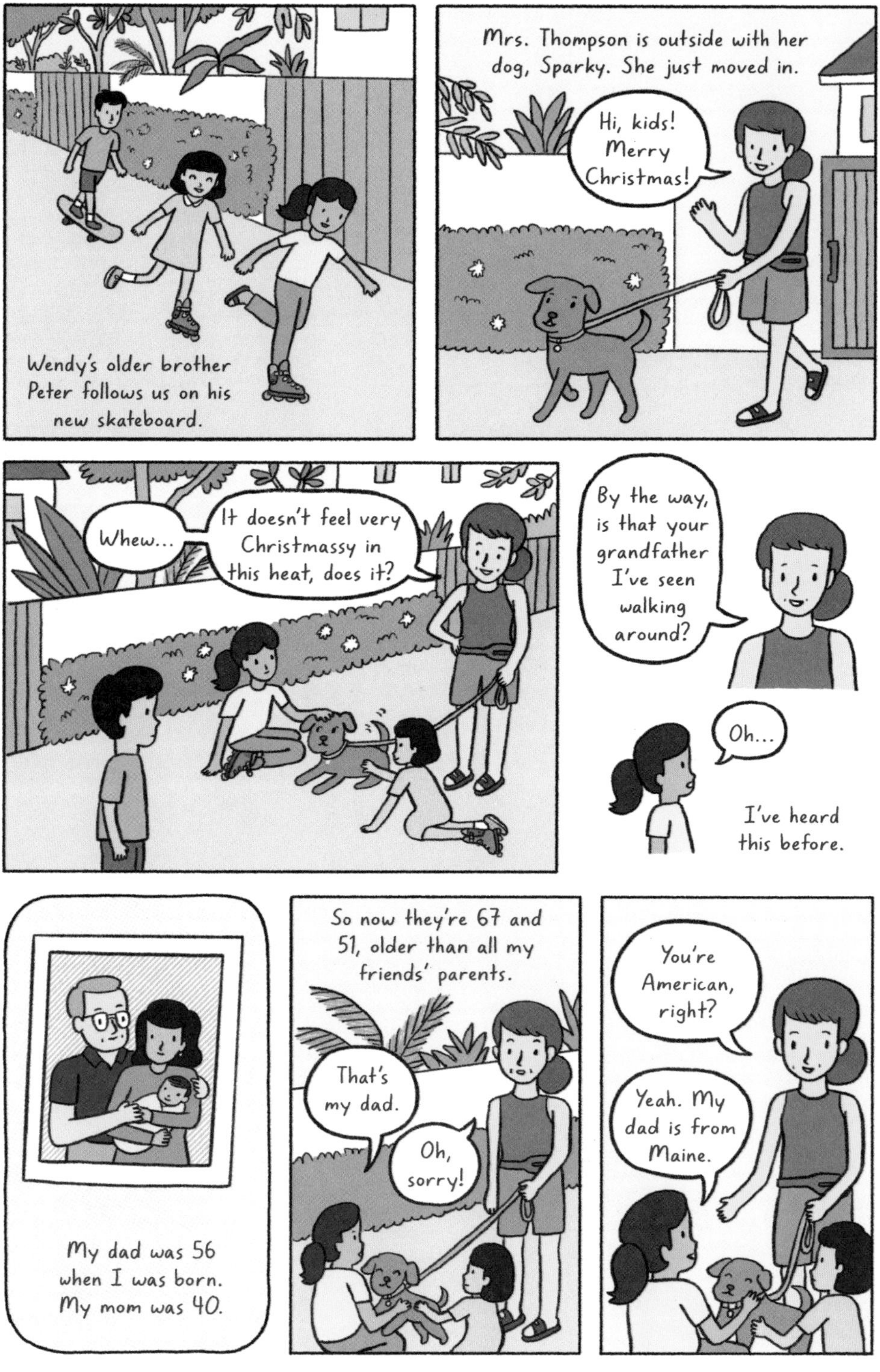

Wendy's older brother Peter follows us on his new skateboard.
Mrs. Thompson is outside with her dog, Sparky. She just moved in.
Hi, kids! Merry Christmas!
Whew...
It doesn't feel very Christmassy in this heat, does it?
By the way, is that your grandfather I've seen walking around?
Oh...
I've heard this before.
My dad was 56 when I was born. My mom was 40.
So now they're 67 and 51, older than all my friends' parents.
That's my dad.
Oh, sorry!
You're American, right?
Yeah. My dad is from Maine.

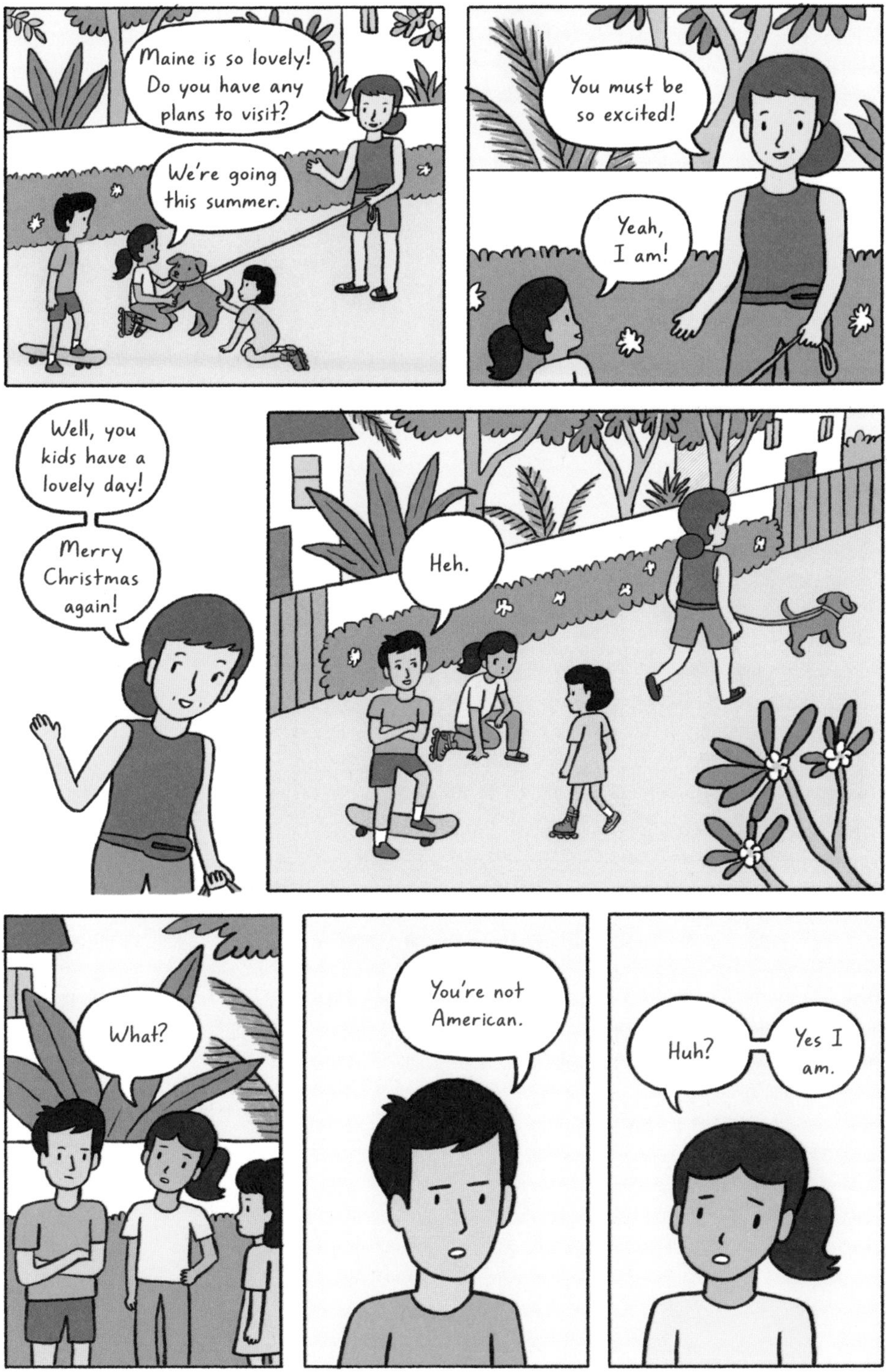
Maine is so lovely! Do you have any plans to visit?
We're going this summer.
You must be so excited!
Yeah, I am!
Well, you kids have a lovely day!
Merry Christmas again!
Heh.
What?
You're not American.
Huh?
Yes I am.

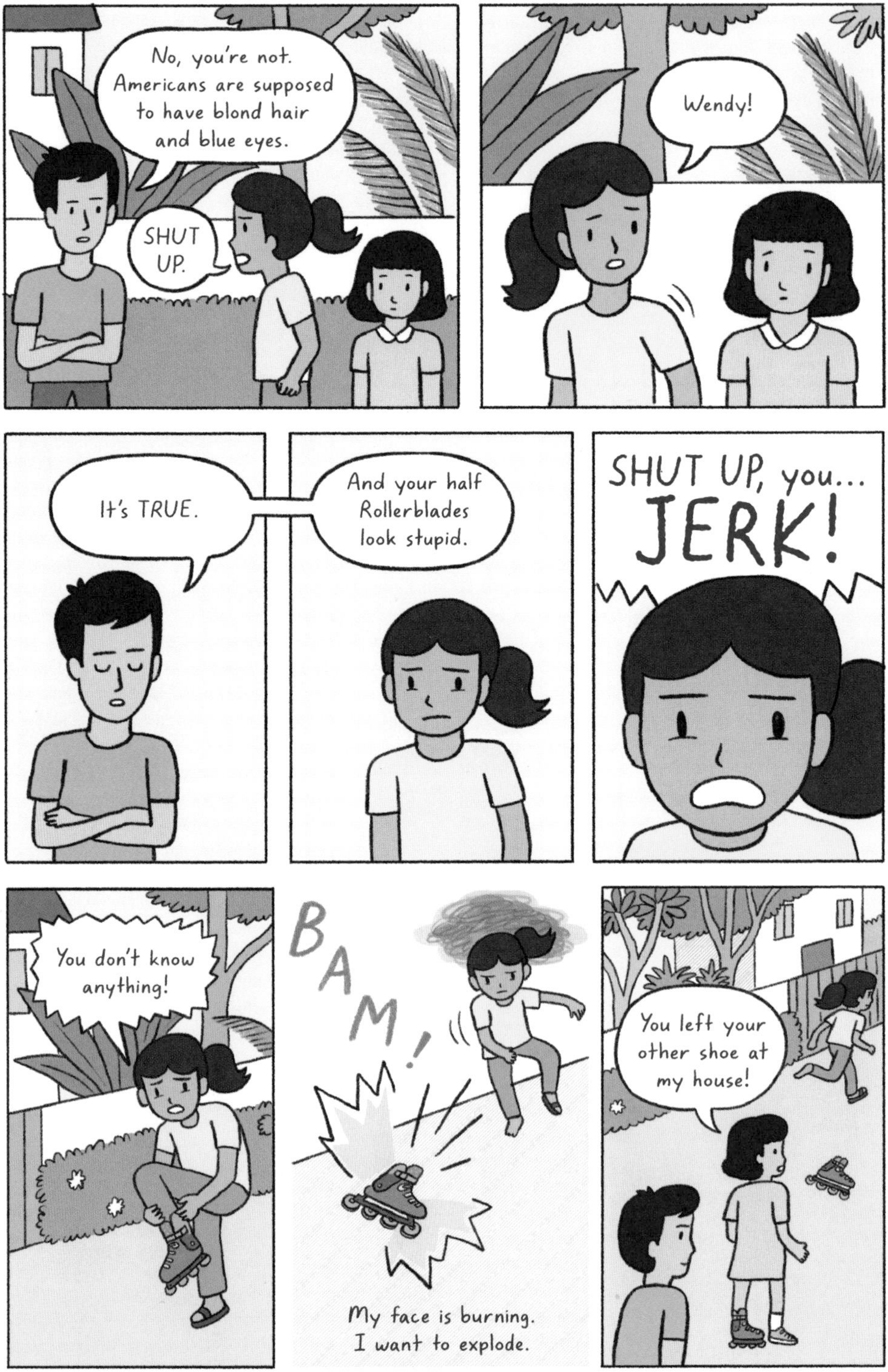
No, you're not. Americans are supposed to have blond hair and blue eyes.
SHUT UP.
Wendy!
It's TRUE.
And your half Rollerblades look stupid.
SHUT UP, you... JERK!
You don't know anything!
BAM!
My face is burning. I want to explode.
You left your other shoe at my house!

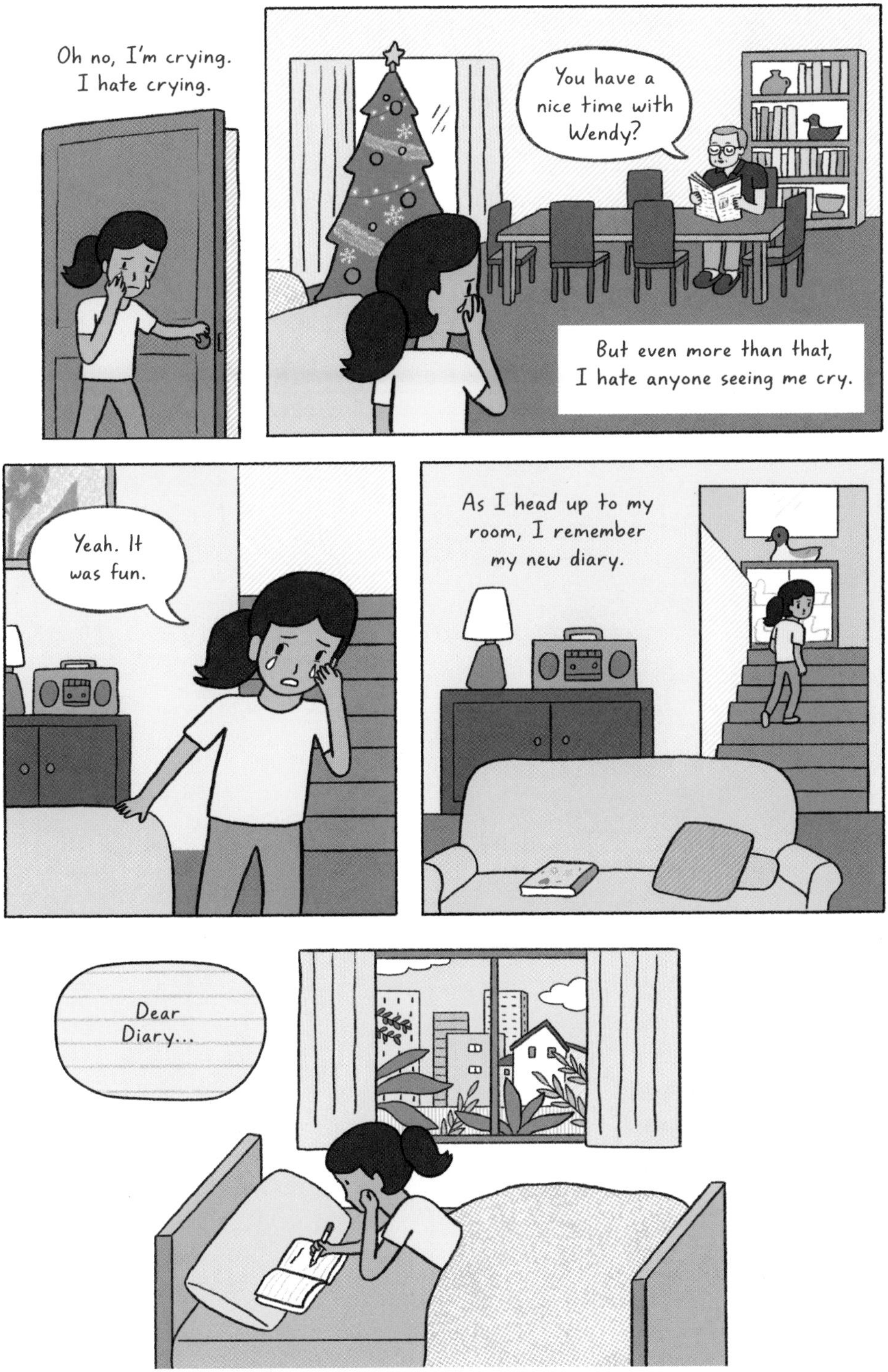
Oh no, I'm crying. I hate crying.
You have a nice time with Wendy?
But even more than that, I hate anyone seeing me cry.
Yeah. It was fun.
As I head up to my room, I remember my new diary.
Dear Diary...

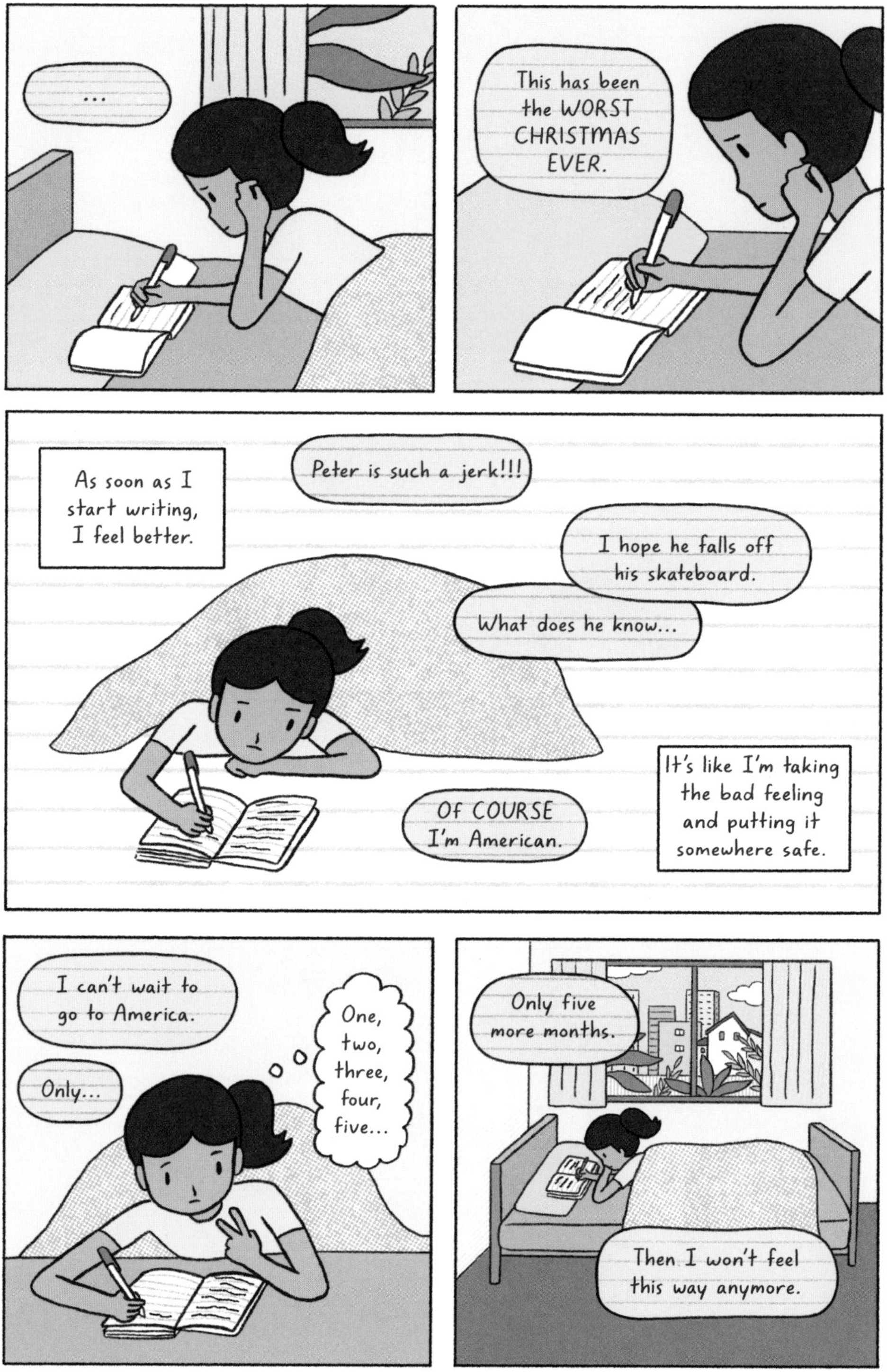
...
This has been the WORST CHRISTMAS EVER.
As soon as I start writing, I feel better.
Peter is such a jerk!!!
I hope he falls off his skateboard.
What does he know...
OF COURSE I'm American.
It's like I'm taking the bad feeling and putting it somewhere safe.
I can't wait to go to America.
Only...
One, two, three, four, five...
Only five more months.
Then I won't feel this way anymore.

2

There's a word in Thai for kids like me, who have parents from two different backgrounds:

Luk khrueng, which translates to "half child."

There are lots of other luk khruengs at my school.

My friend Eileen is also half Thai and half American. Her mom is my math teacher.

Justin is half Thai, half British, and he's the cutest boy in my grade.

Then there's Camille, who's half Thai, half French, and already a famous actress.

I go to an international school, which means that classes are taught in English.

Aside from singing the national anthem every morning...

ประเทศไทย รวมเลือดเนื้อชาติเชื้อไทย

...you're not allowed to speak Thai at all.

ไปกินข้าว กันไหม

In fact, you have to pay a fine if you're caught.

You know the rule, Nirun!

That'll be five baht.*

*25 cents

Most of my classmates, like me, speak perfect English, even though they come from lots of different countries.

Is that fried chicken, Arti?

It's chicken pakora, want some?

My mom made it.

My school is so international that this year we're celebrating Culture Day, where we come dressed in traditional costumes.

She's letting me wear one of her fancy saris tomorrow!

I've been dreading it for weeks.

I have an idea—

Mom helped me put together an "American" costume.

You can be a cowgirl!

19

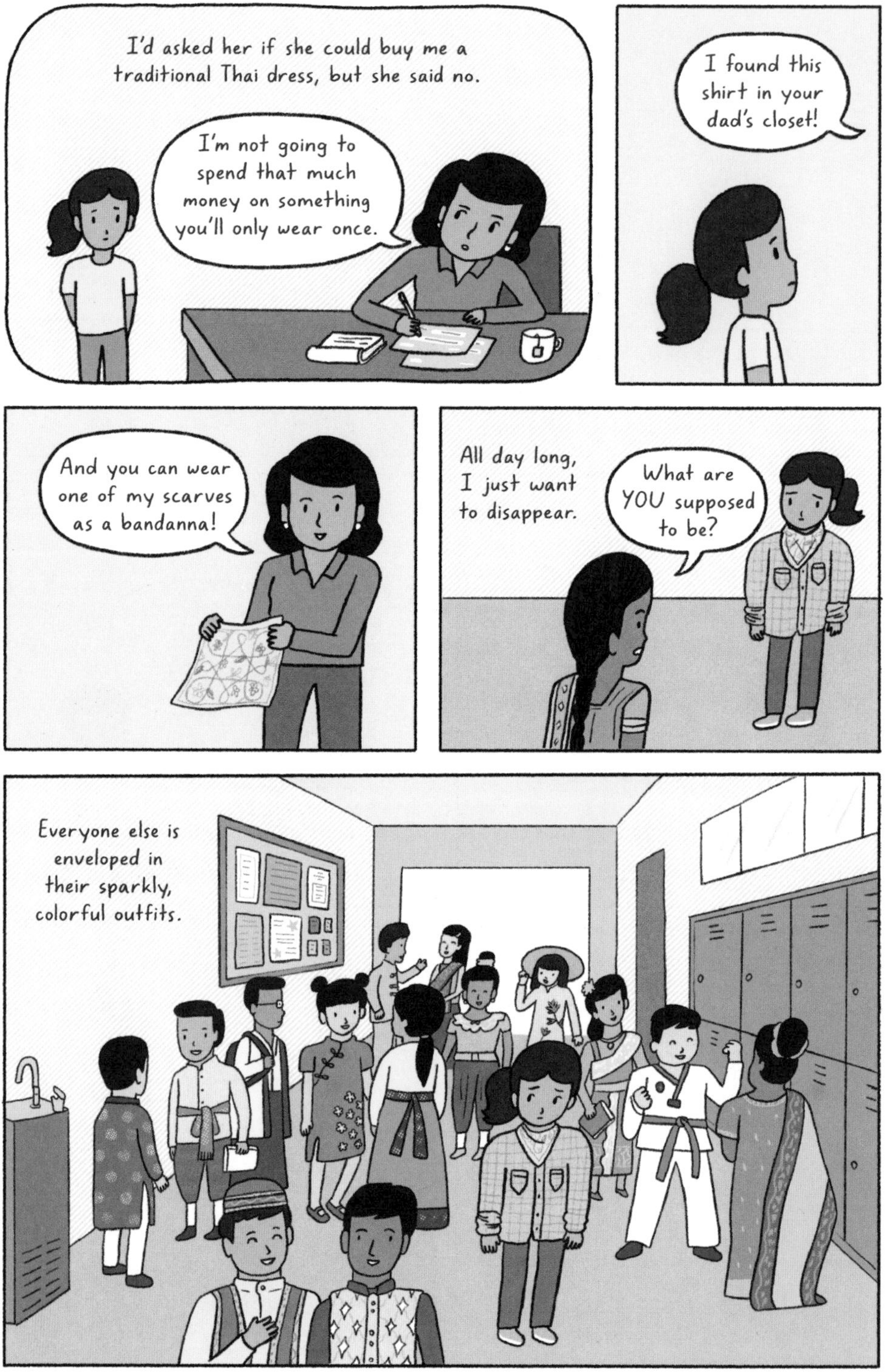
I'd asked her if she could buy me a traditional Thai dress, but she said no.
I'm not going to spend that much money on something you'll only wear once.
I found this shirt in your dad's closet!
And you can wear one of my scarves as a bandanna!
All day long, I just want to disappear.
What are YOU supposed to be?
Everyone else is enveloped in their sparkly, colorful outfits.

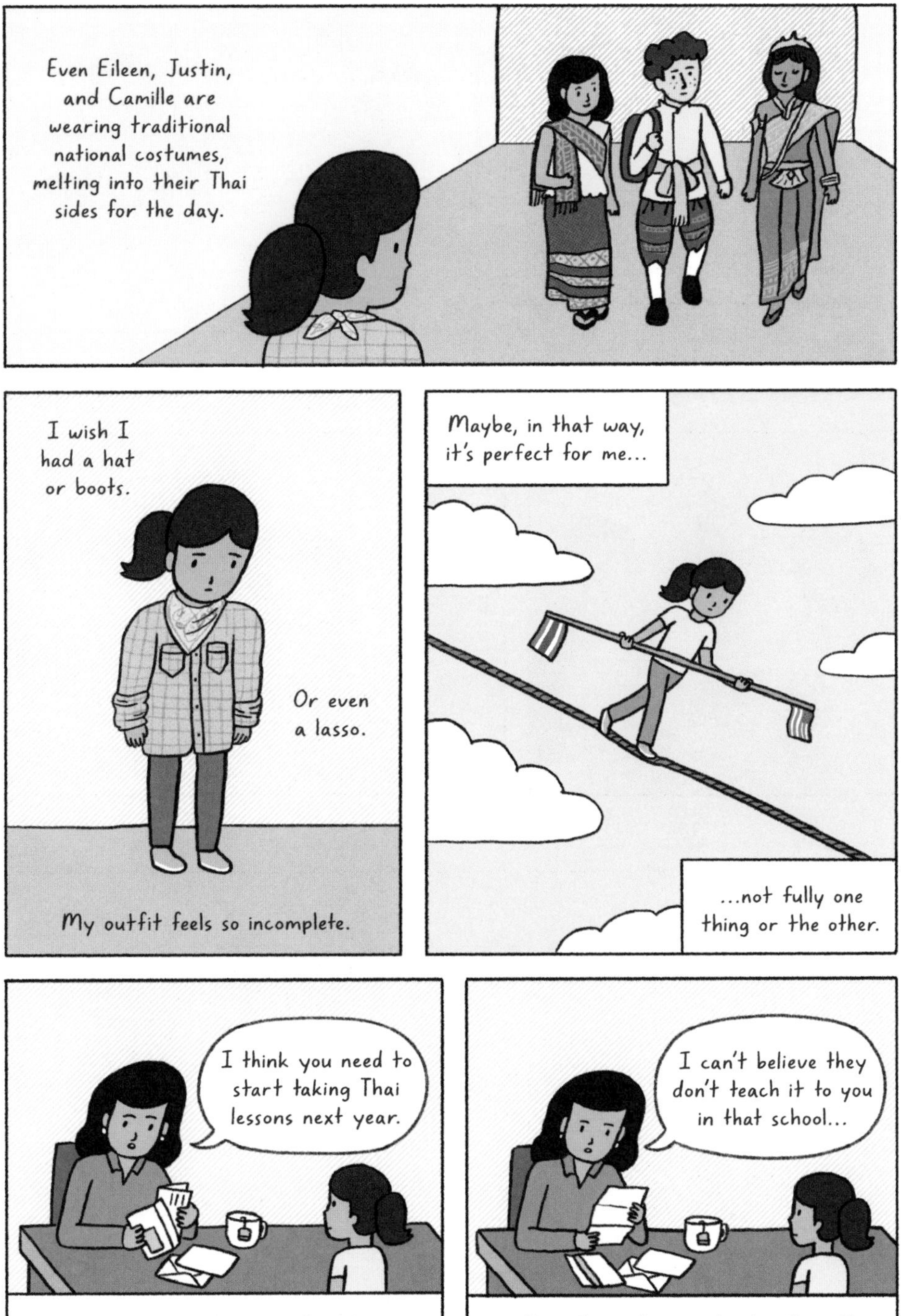

Even Eileen, Justin, and Camille are wearing traditional national costumes, melting into their Thai sides for the day.
I wish I had a hat or boots.
Or even a lasso.
My outfit feels so incomplete.
Maybe, in that way, it's perfect for me...
...not fully one thing or the other.
I think you need to start taking Thai lessons next year.
My mom gets frustrated with me because I don't speak Thai very well.
I can't believe they don't teach it to you in that school...
I can't read or write it, either. I think she's a little ashamed of that.

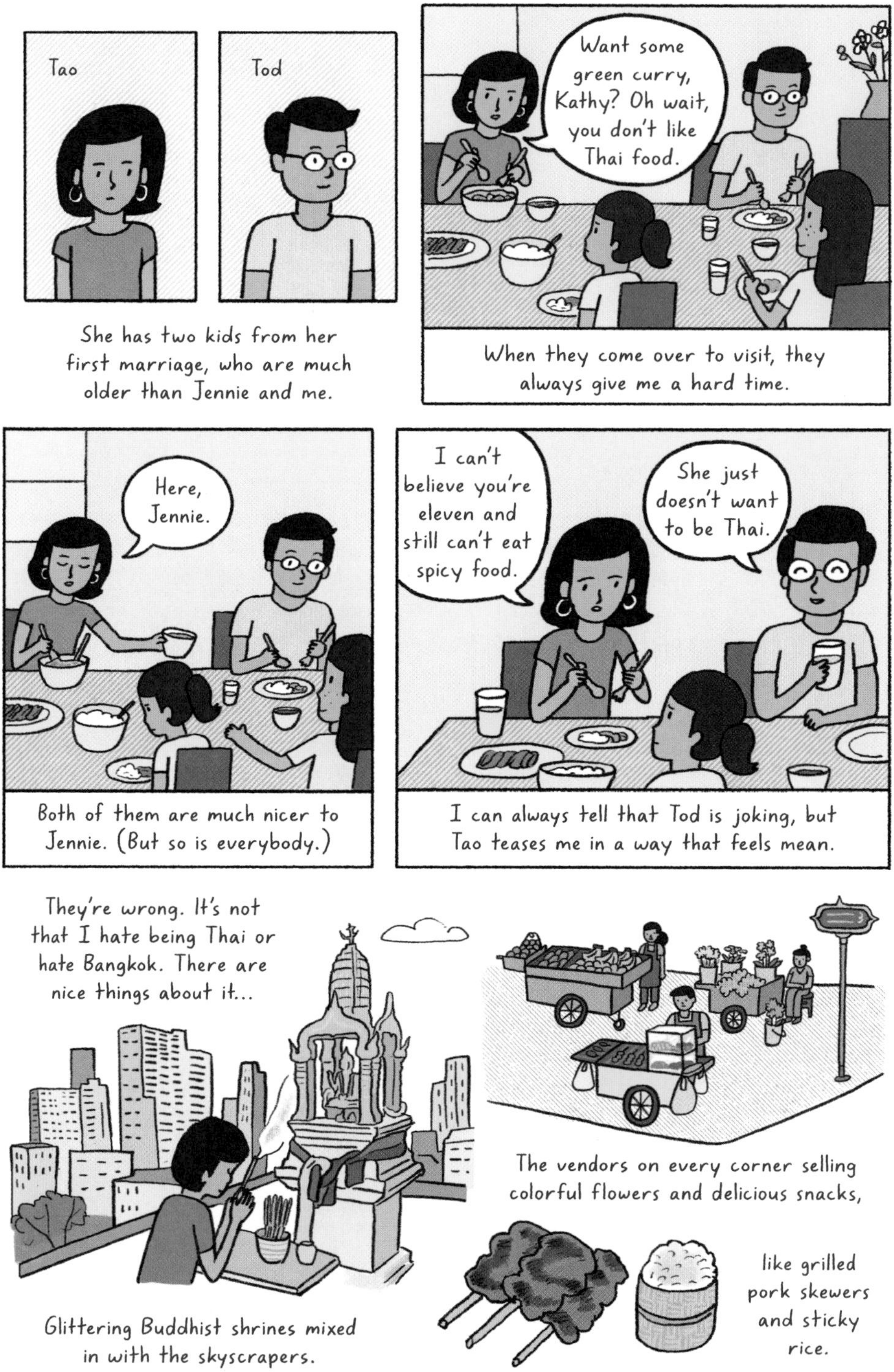
Tao
Tod
She has two kids from her first marriage, who are much older than Jennie and me.
Want some green curry, Kathy? Oh wait, you don't like Thai food.
When they come over to visit, they always give me a hard time.
Here, Jennie.
Both of them are much nicer to Jennie. (But so is everybody.)
I can't believe you're eleven and still can't eat spicy food.
She just doesn't want to be Thai.
I can always tell that Tod is joking, but Tao teases me in a way that feels mean.
They're wrong. It's not that I hate being Thai or hate Bangkok. There are nice things about it...
Glittering Buddhist shrines mixed in with the skyscrapers.
The vendors on every corner selling colorful flowers and delicious snacks,
like grilled pork skewers and sticky rice.

There are some fun traditions, like Songkran, the celebration of the Thai New Year in April, where everyone has water fights in the street.

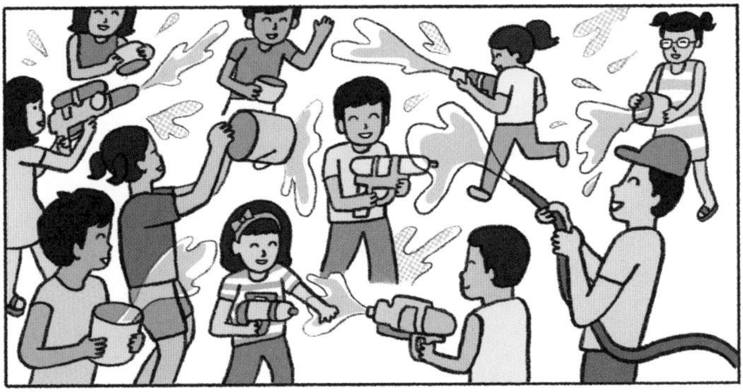

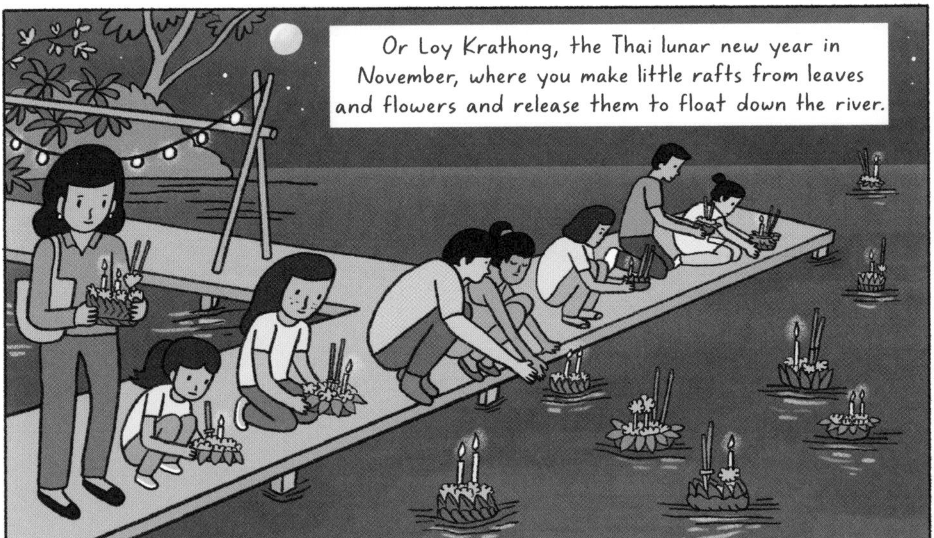

Or Loy Krathong, the Thai lunar new year in November, where you make little rafts from leaves and flowers and release them to float down the river.

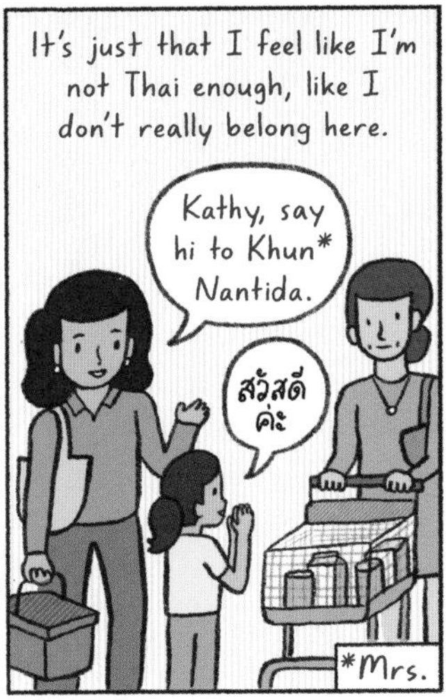

It's just that I feel like I'm not Thai enough, like I don't really belong here.
Kathy, say hi to Khun* Nantida.
สวัสดี ค่ะ
*Mrs.

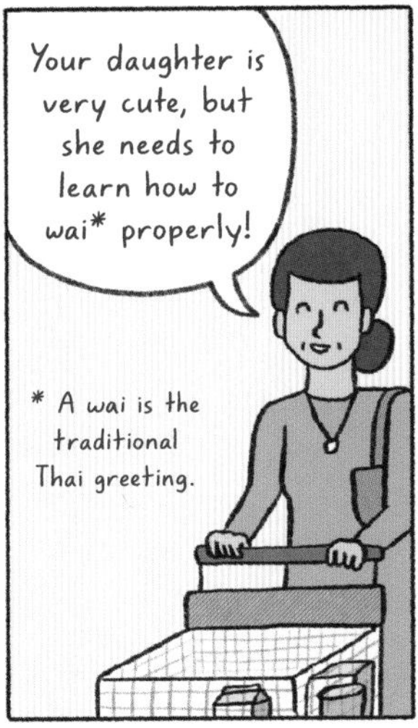

Your daughter is very cute, but she needs to learn how to wai* properly!
* A wai is the traditional Thai greeting.

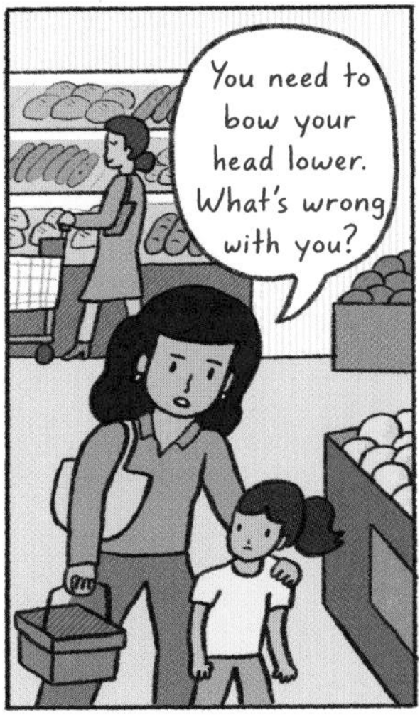

You need to bow your head lower. What's wrong with you?

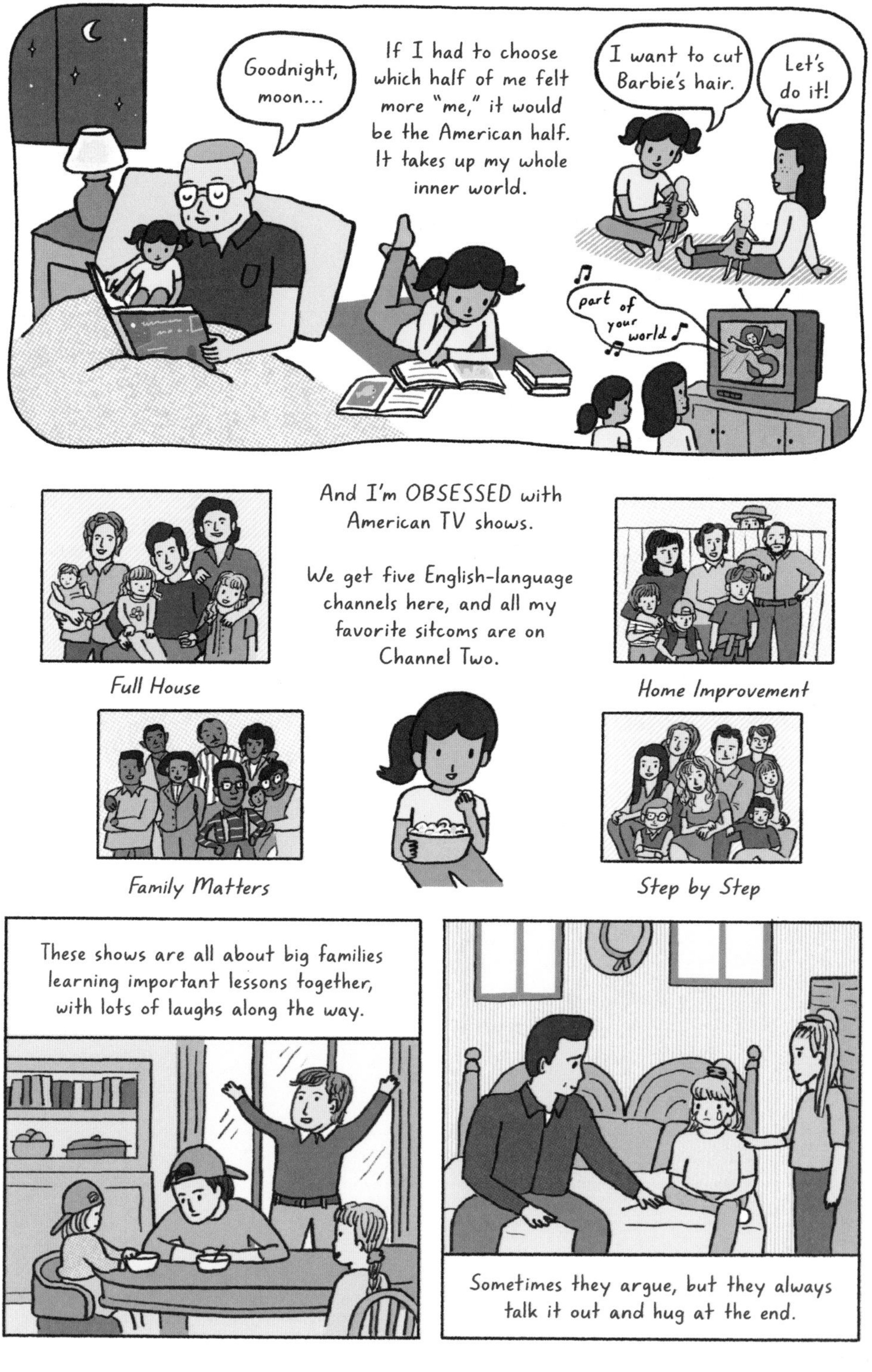

Goodnight, moon...
If I had to choose which half of me felt more "me," it would be the American half. It takes up my whole inner world.
I want to cut Barbie's hair.
Let's do it!
part of your world
And I'm OBSESSED with American TV shows.
We get five English-language channels here, and all my favorite sitcoms are on Channel Two.
Full House
Home Improvement
Family Matters
Step by Step
These shows are all about big families learning important lessons together, with lots of laughs along the way.
Sometimes they argue, but they always talk it out and hug at the end.

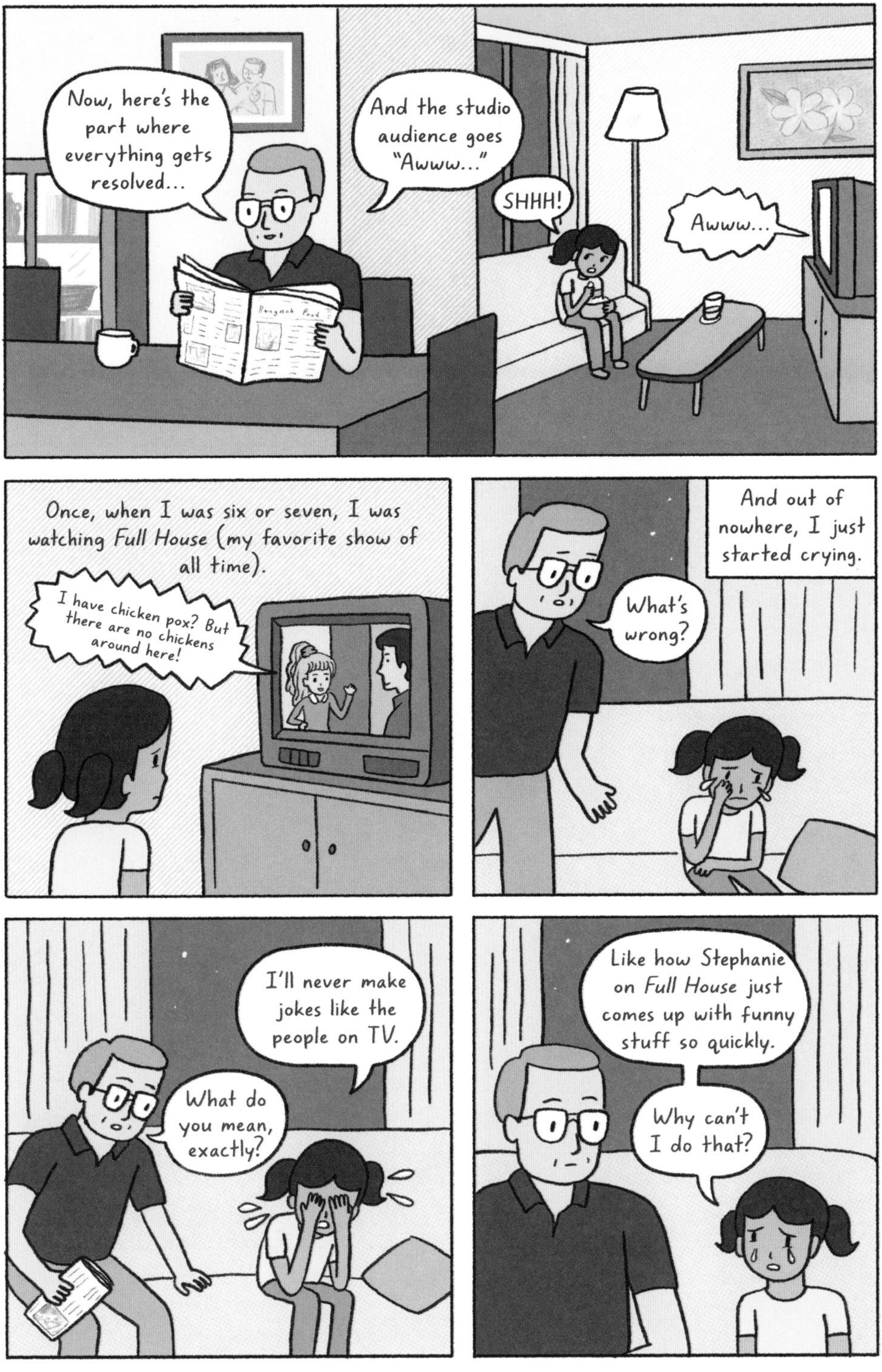
Now, here's the part where everything gets resolved...
And the studio audience goes "Awww..."
SHHH!
Awww...
Once, when I was six or seven, I was watching *Full House* (my favorite show of all time).
I have chicken pox? But there are no chickens around here!
And out of nowhere, I just started crying.
What's wrong?
I'll never make jokes like the people on TV.
What do you mean, exactly?
Like how Stephanie on *Full House* just comes up with funny stuff so quickly.
Why can't I do that?

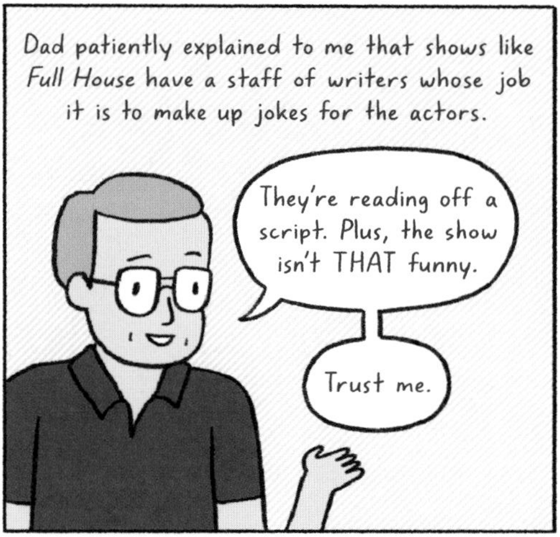
Dad patiently explained to me that shows like *Full House* have a staff of writers whose job it is to make up jokes for the actors.
They're reading off a script. Plus, the show isn't THAT funny.
Trust me.

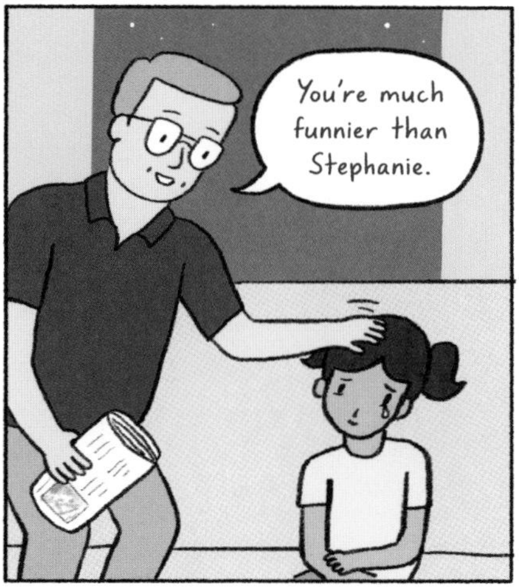
You're much funnier than Stephanie.

This year, I'm extra excited about our trip to America.

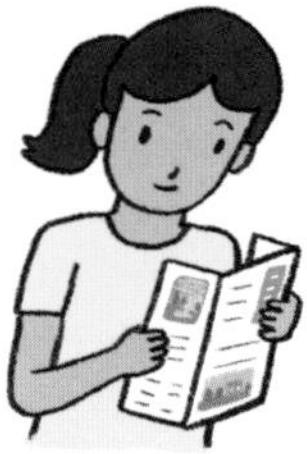

For the first time, my parents are letting me go to SUMMER CAMP.

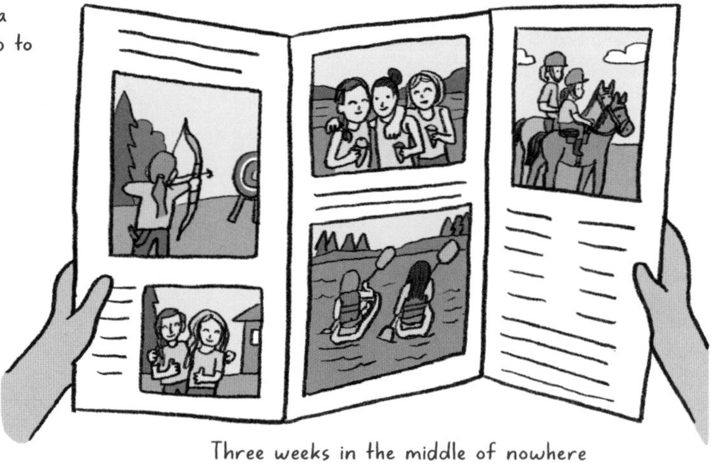

Three weeks in the middle of nowhere with about a hundred other girls.

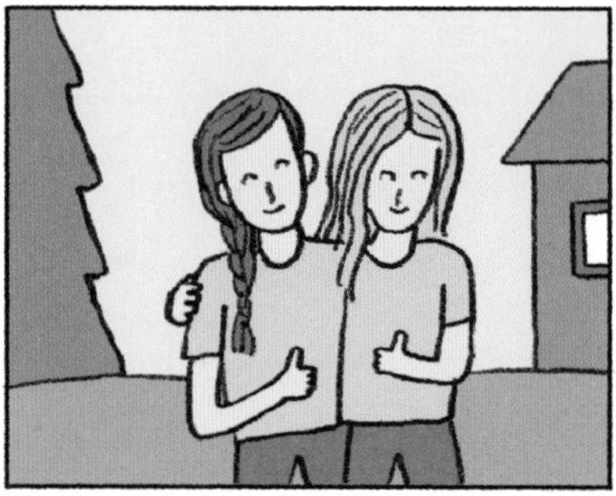

But what if the girls at camp are all like the girls on TV?

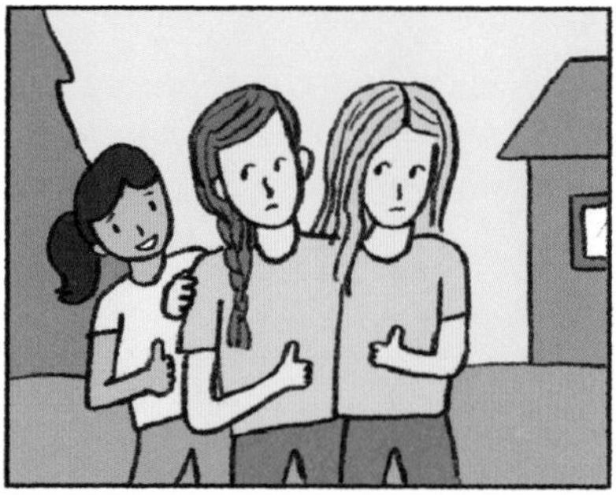

How do I prove that deep down inside, I'm just like them? That I like the same things and can make the same jokes?

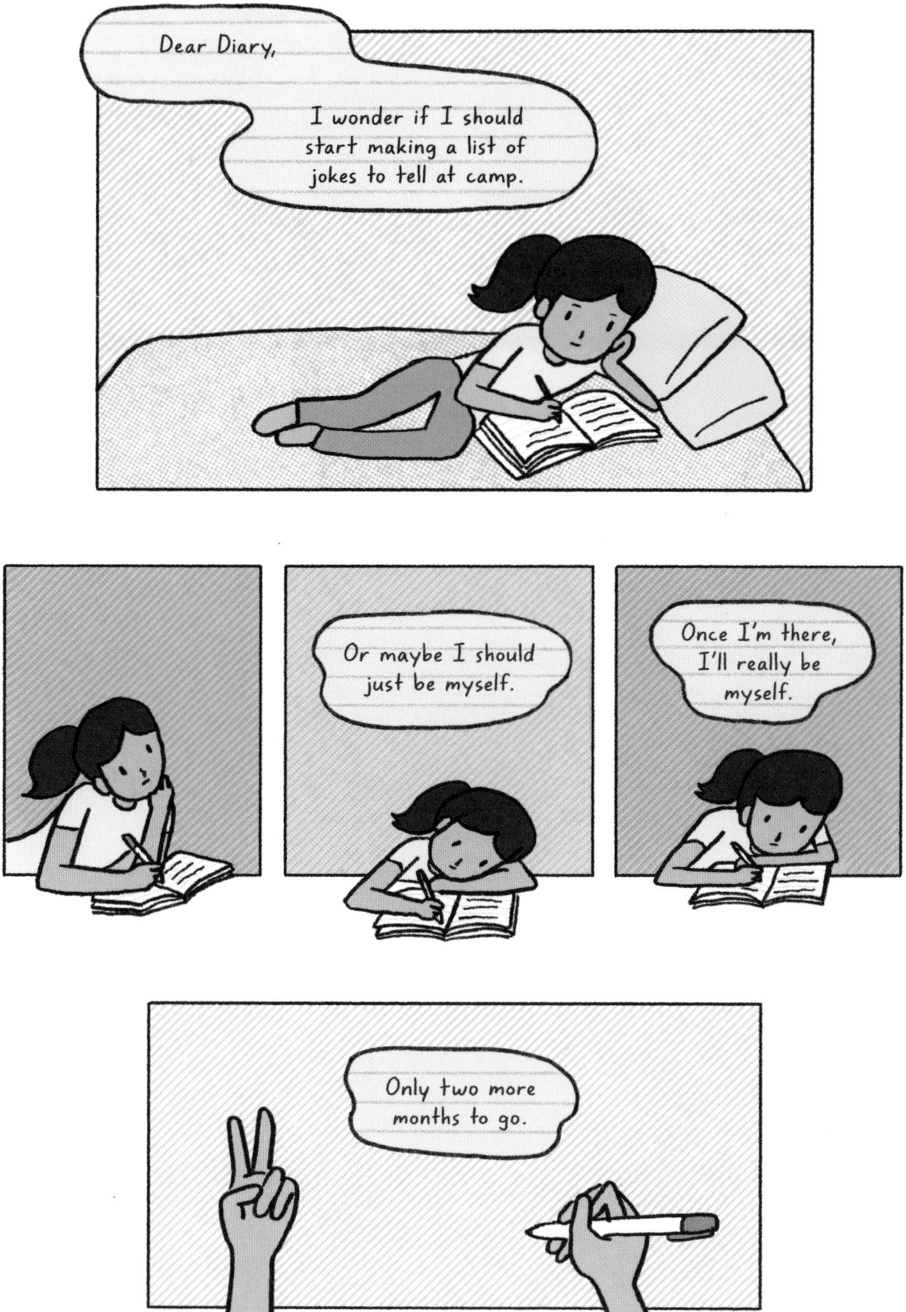
Dear Diary,
I wonder if I should start making a list of jokes to tell at camp.
Or maybe I should just be myself.
Once I'm there, I'll really be myself.
Only two more months to go.

3

My family is not like the ones on TV.

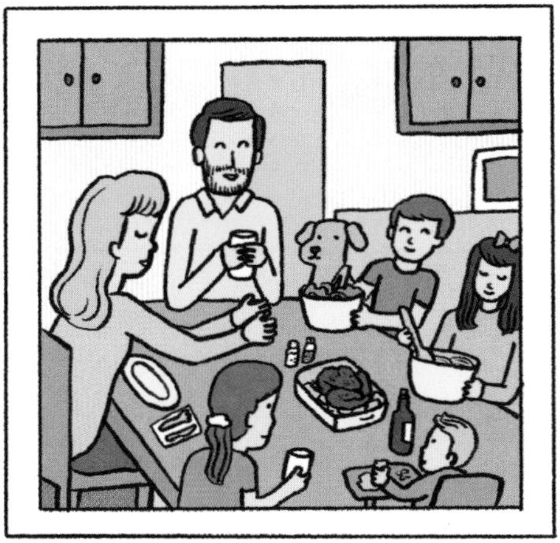

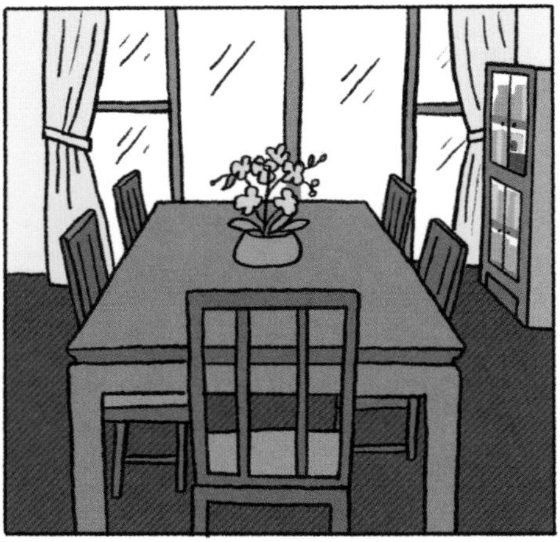

For one thing, we don't sit around the table eating dinner together every night.

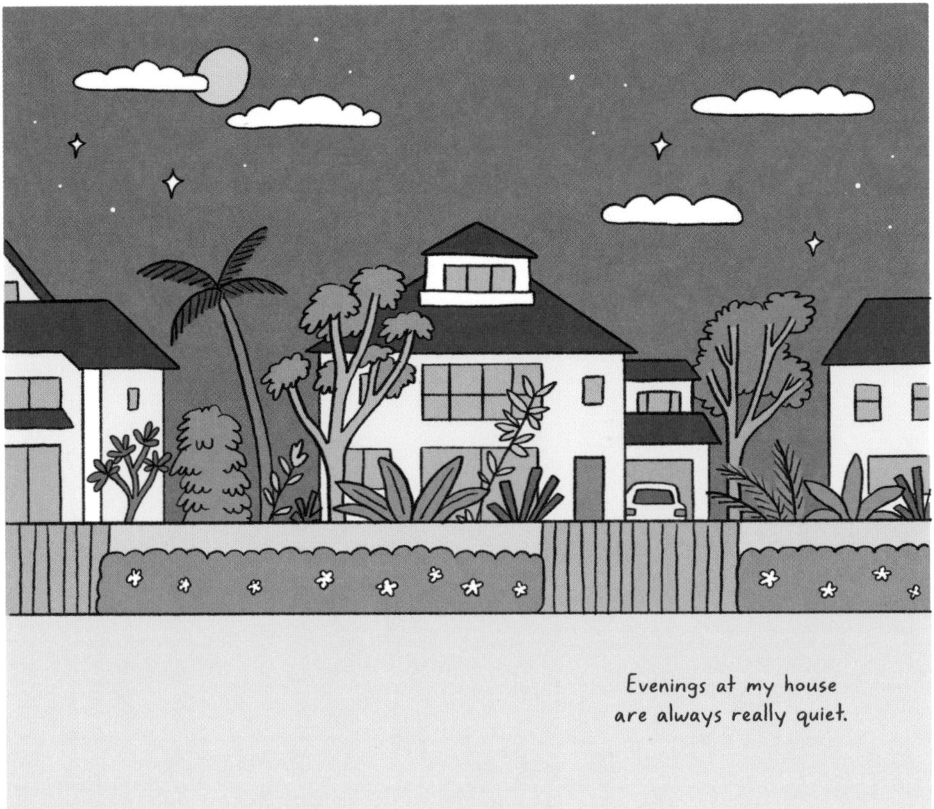
Evenings at my house
are always really quiet.

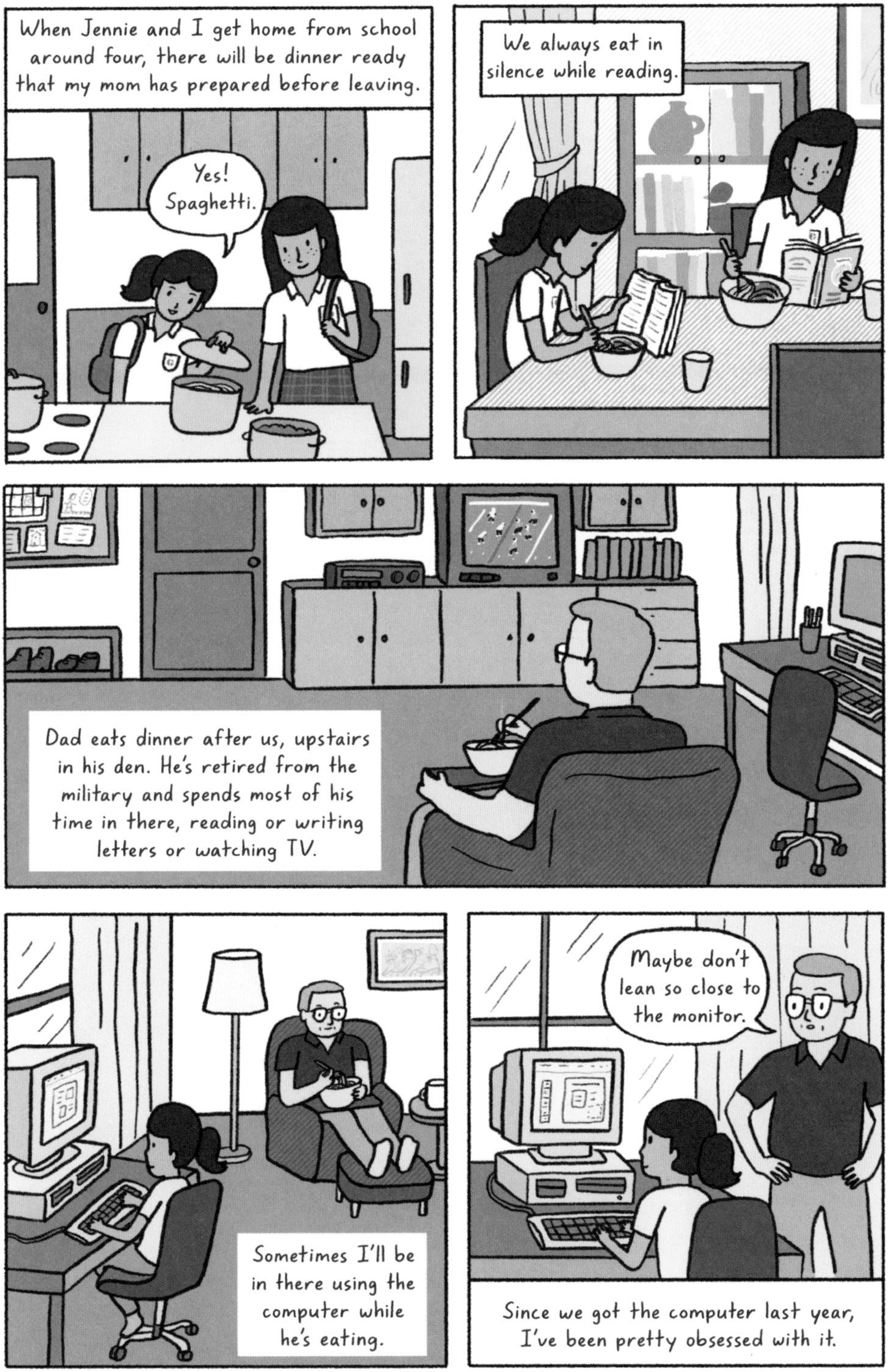
When Jennie and I get home from school around four, there will be dinner ready that my mom has prepared before leaving.
Yes! Spaghetti.
We always eat in silence while reading.
Dad eats dinner after us, upstairs in his den. He's retired from the military and spends most of his time in there, reading or writing letters or watching TV.
Sometimes I'll be in there using the computer while he's eating.
Maybe don't lean so close to the monitor.
Since we got the computer last year, I've been pretty obsessed with it.

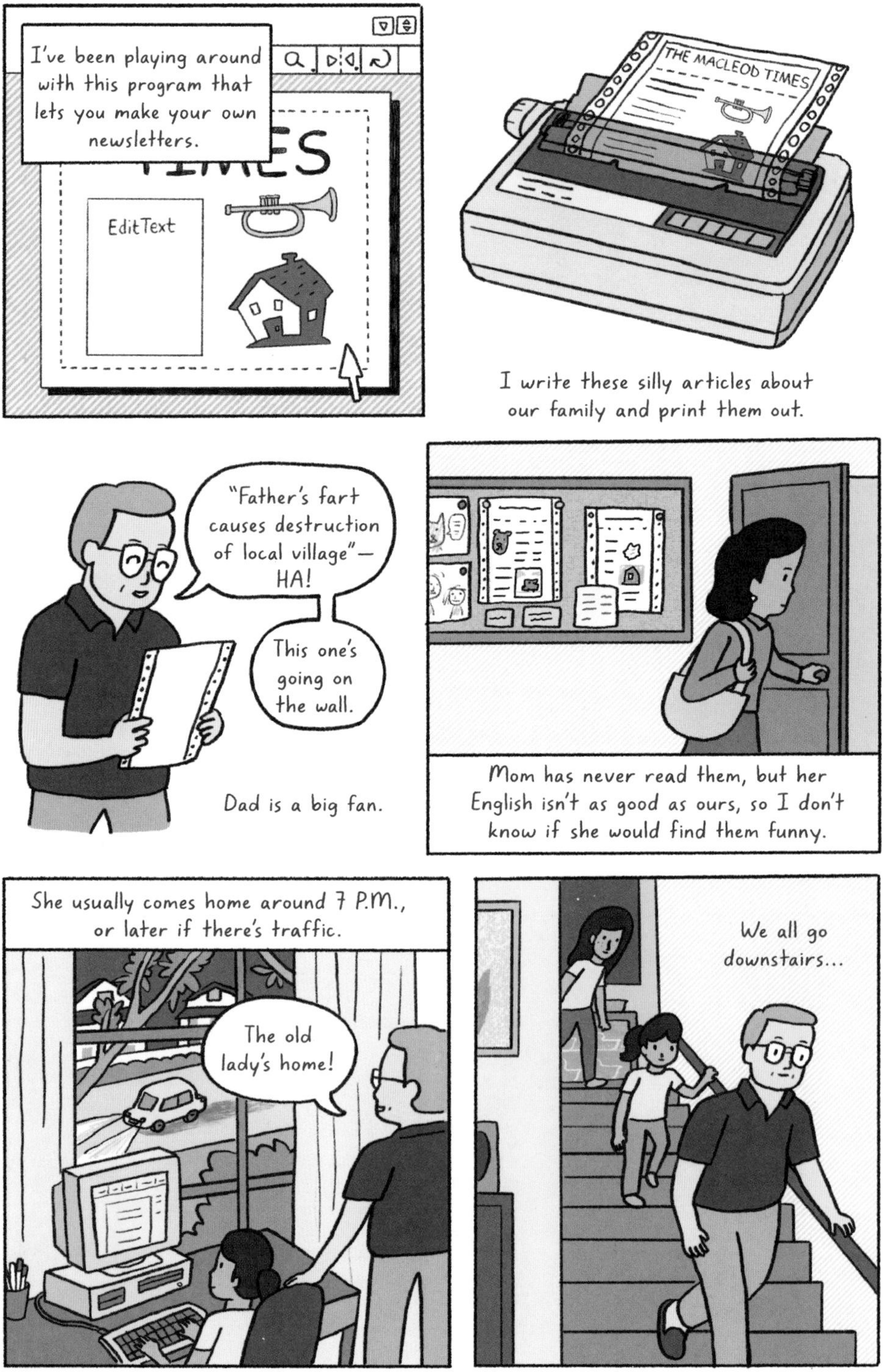

I've been playing around with this program that lets you make your own newsletters.
EditText
THE MACLEOD TIMES
I write these silly articles about our family and print them out.
"Father's fart causes destruction of local village"— HA!
This one's going on the wall.
Dad is a big fan.
Mom has never read them, but her English isn't as good as ours, so I don't know if she would find them funny.
She usually comes home around 7 P.M., or later if there's traffic.
The old lady's home!
We all go downstairs...

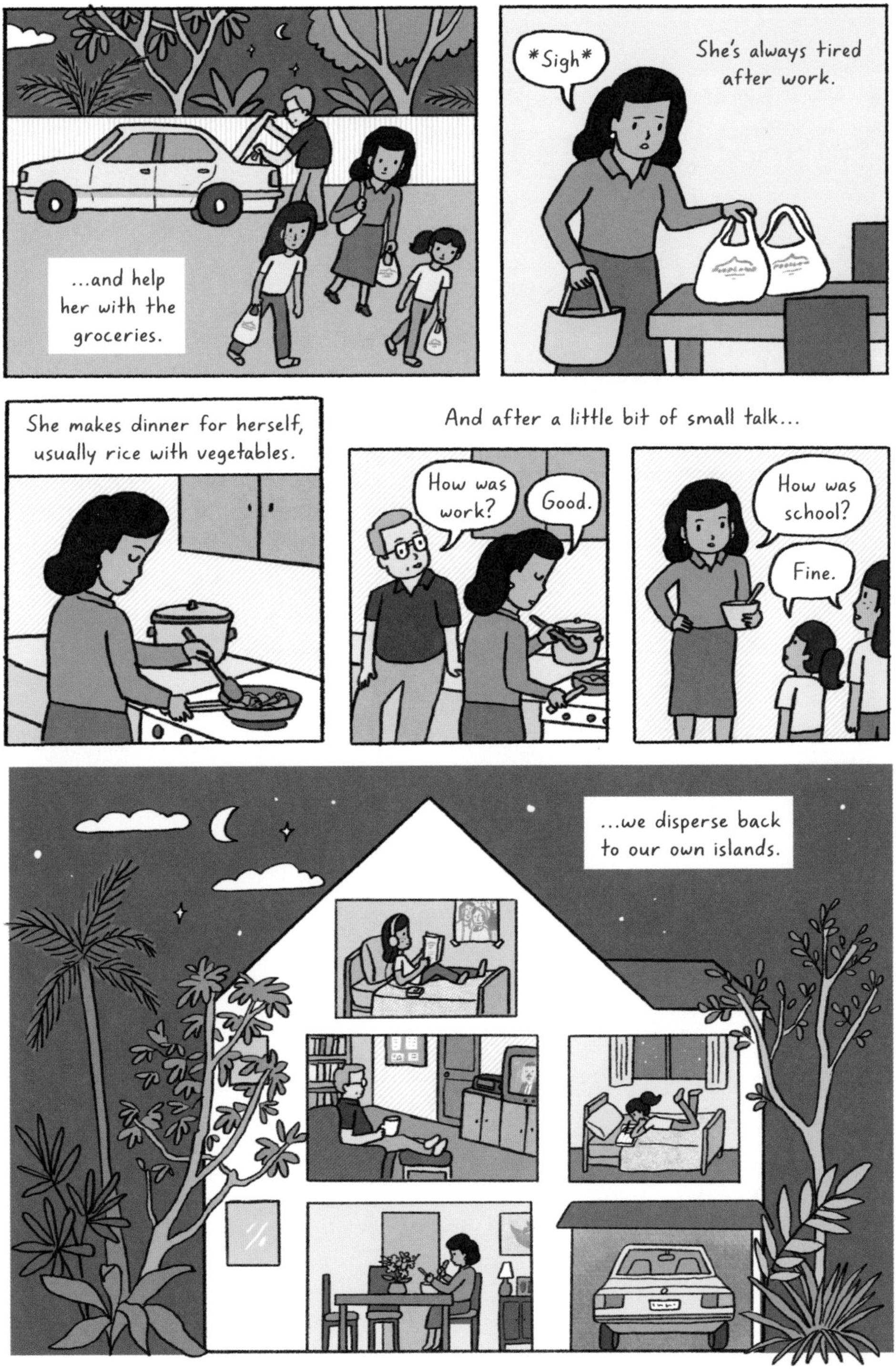
...and help her with the groceries.
Sigh
She's always tired after work.
She makes dinner for herself, usually rice with vegetables.
And after a little bit of small talk...
How was work?
Good.
How was school?
Fine.
...we disperse back to our own islands.

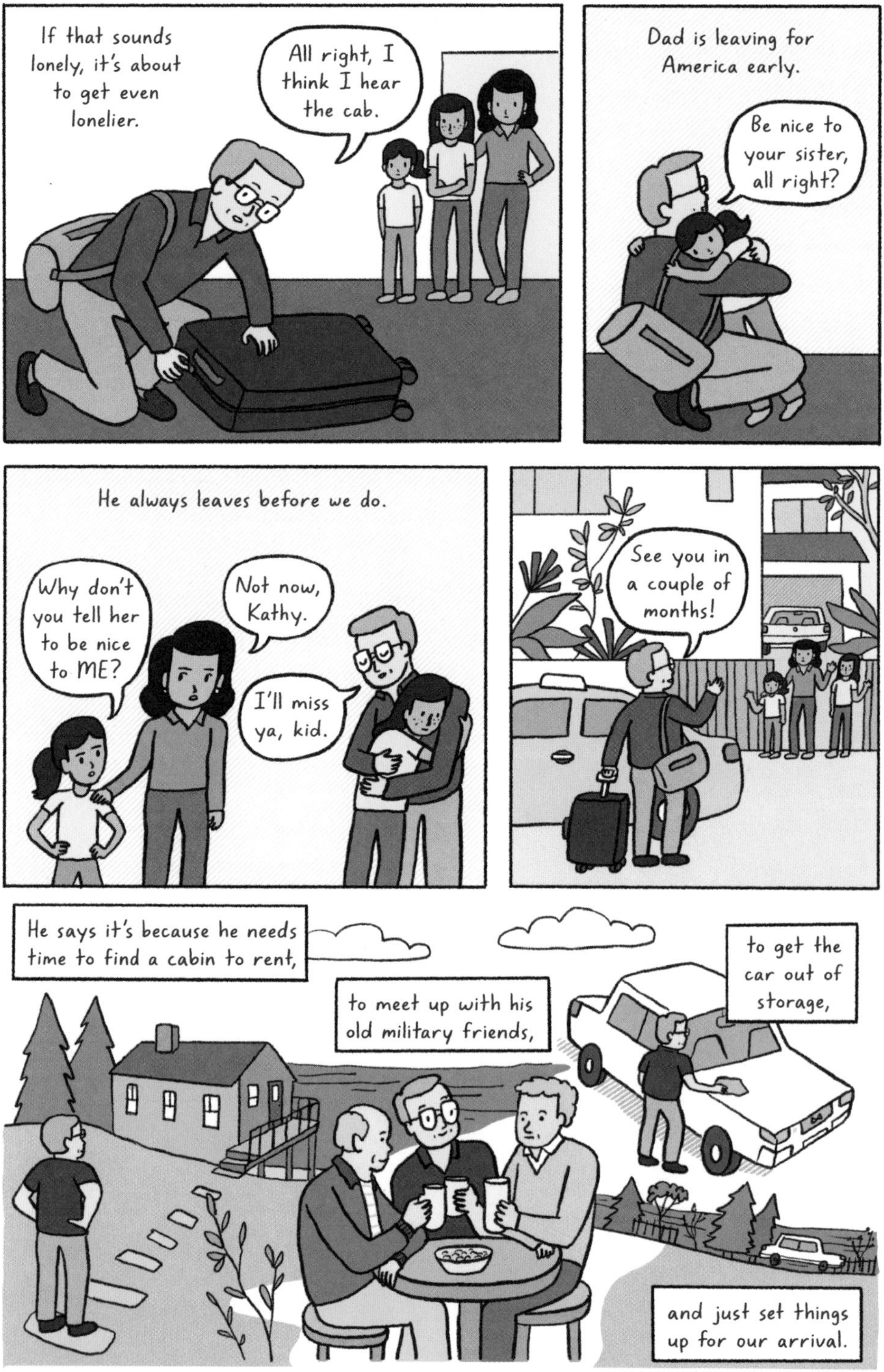
If that sounds lonely, it's about to get even lonelier.
All right, I think I hear the cab.
Dad is leaving for America early.
Be nice to your sister, all right?
He always leaves before we do.
Why don't you tell her to be nice to ME?
Not now, Kathy.
I'll miss ya, kid.
See you in a couple of months!
He says it's because he needs time to find a cabin to rent,
to meet up with his old military friends,
to get the car out of storage,
and just set things up for our arrival.

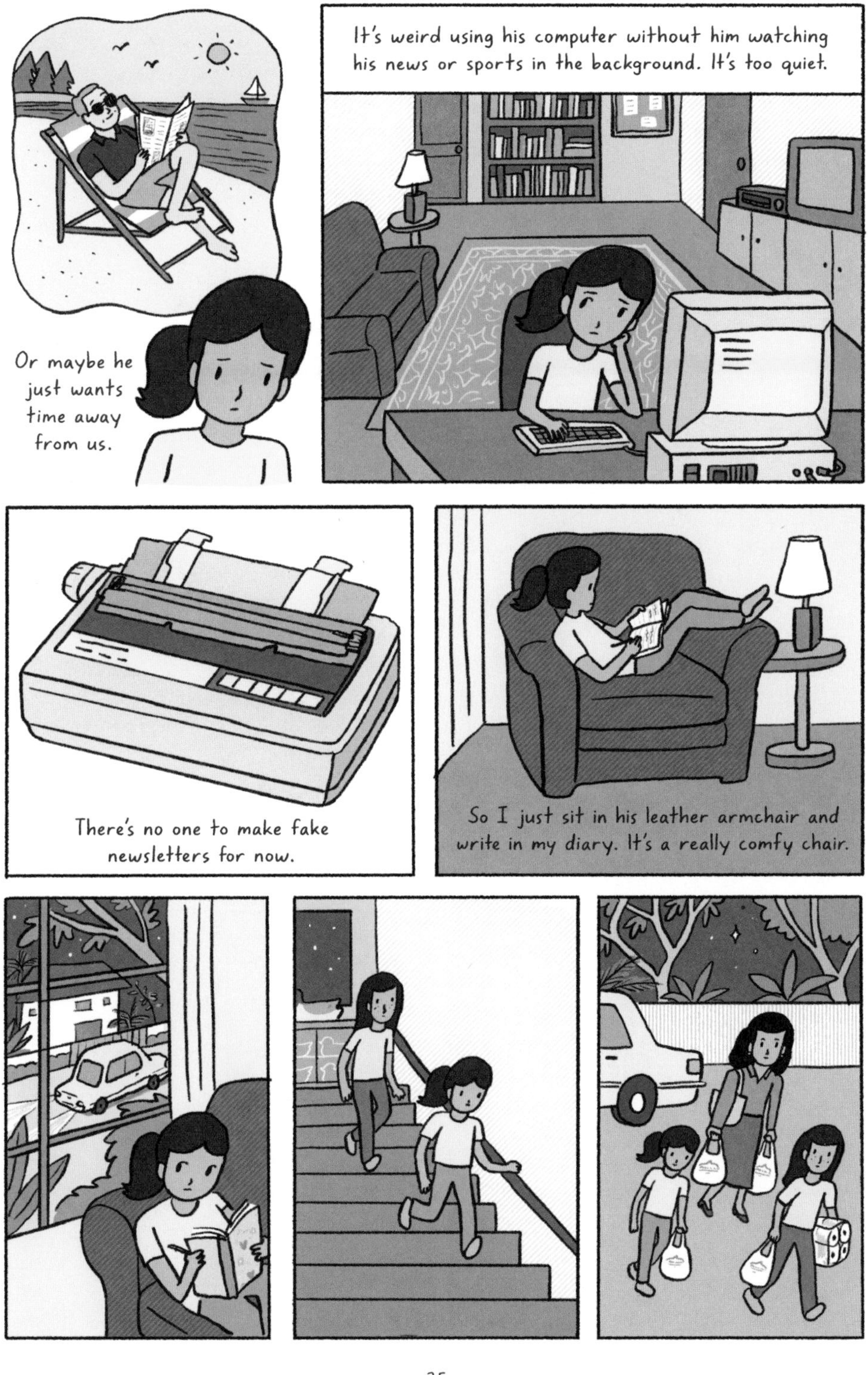
Or maybe he just wants time away from us.
It's weird using his computer without him watching his news or sports in the background. It's too quiet.
There's no one to make fake newsletters for now.
So I just sit in his leather armchair and write in my diary. It's a really comfy chair.

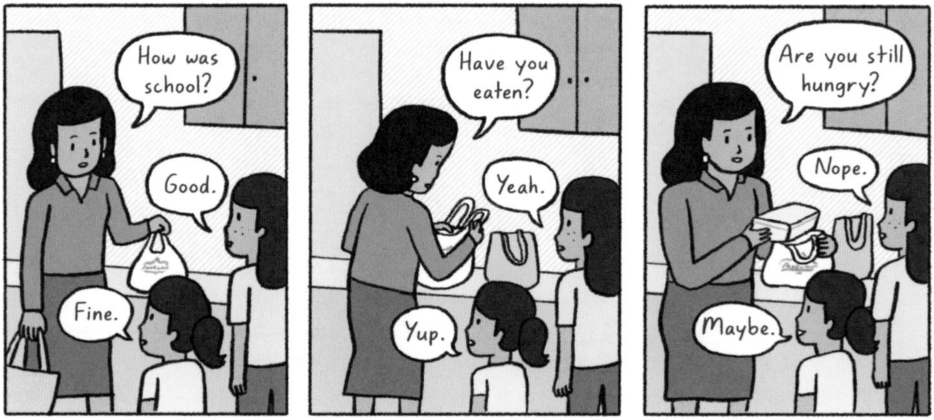
How was school?
Good.
Fine.
Have you eaten?
Yeah.
Yup.
Are you still hungry?
Nope.
Maybe.

Without Dad around, it's even more obvious how little
I really talk to Mom—or how little she talks to us.

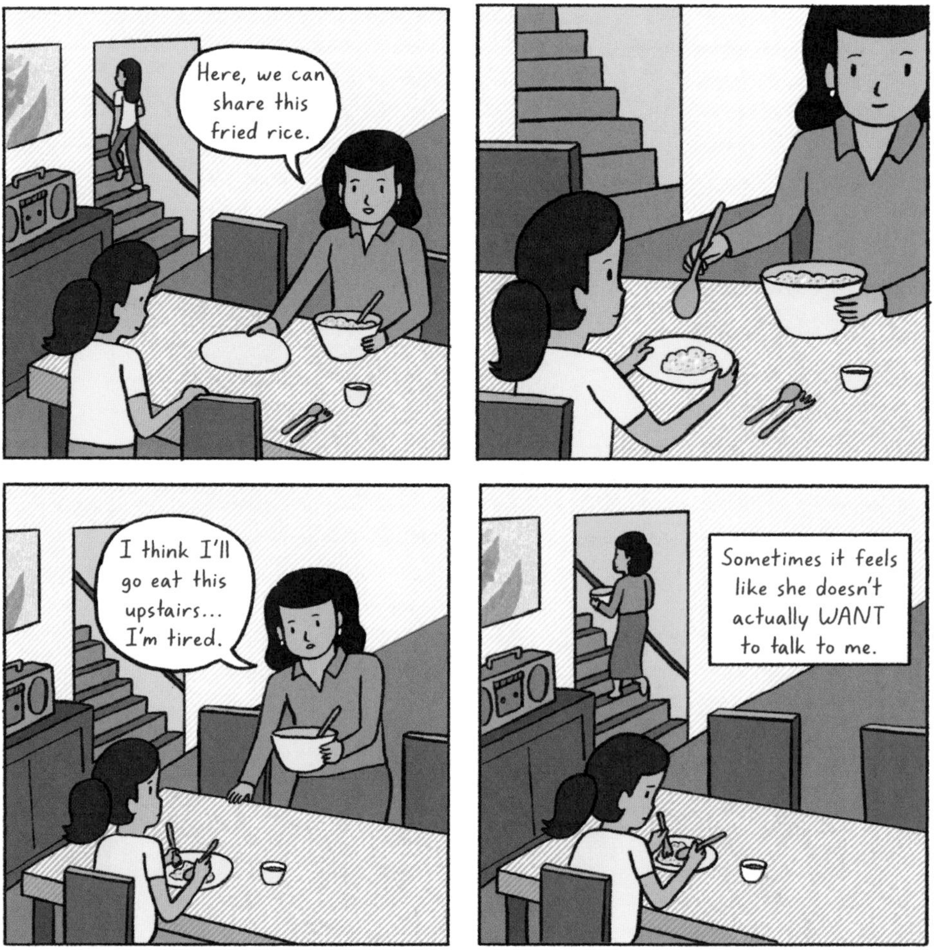
Here, we can share this fried rice.
I think I'll go eat this upstairs... I'm tired.
Sometimes it feels like she doesn't actually WANT to talk to me.

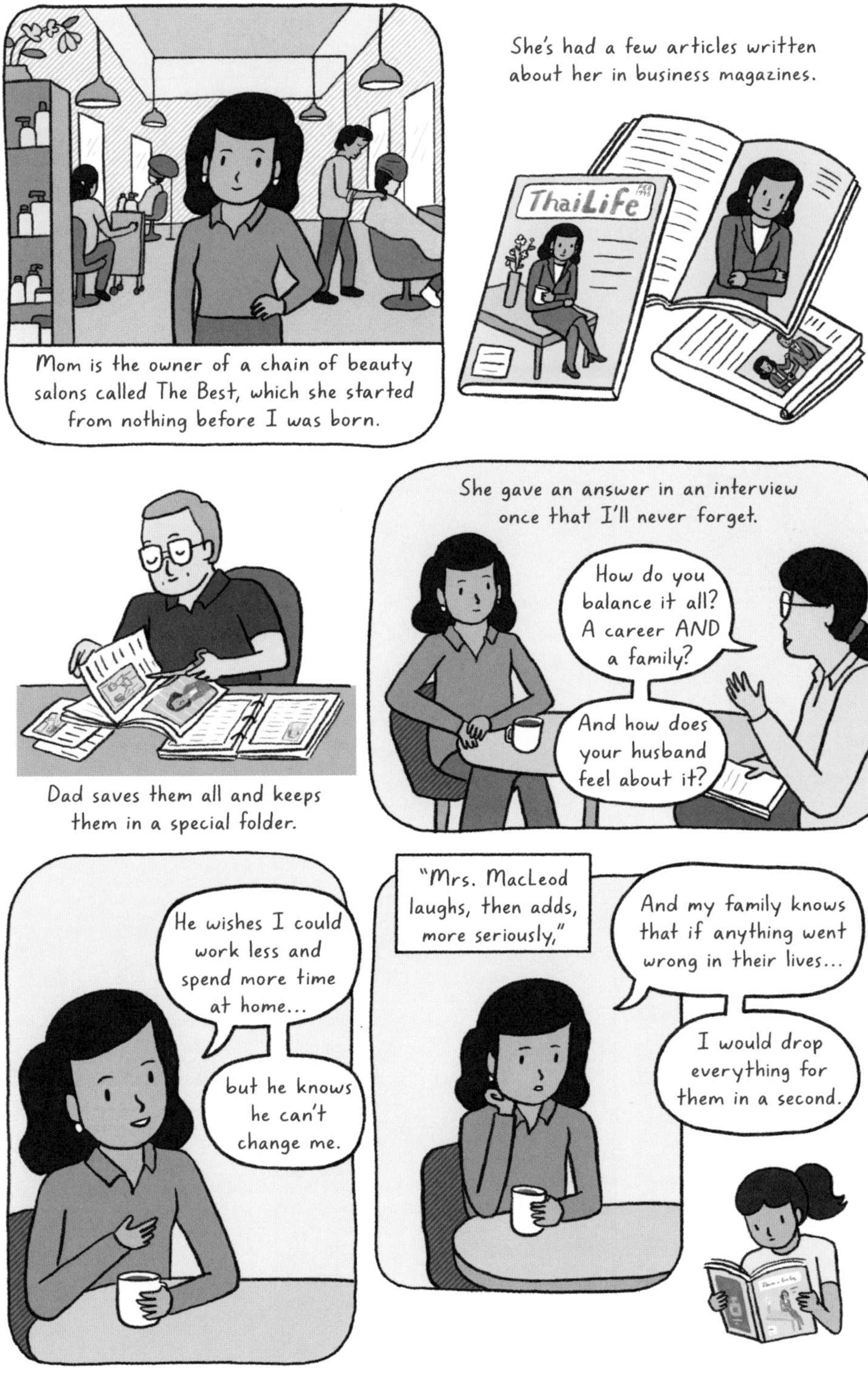
Mom is the owner of a chain of beauty salons called The Best, which she started from nothing before I was born.
She's had a few articles written about her in business magazines.
ThaiLife
Dad saves them all and keeps them in a special folder.
She gave an answer in an interview once that I'll never forget.
How do you balance it all? A career AND a family?
And how does your husband feel about it?
He wishes I could work less and spend more time at home...
but he knows he can't change me.
"Mrs. MacLeod laughs, then adds, more seriously,"
And my family knows that if anything went wrong in their lives...
I would drop everything for them in a second.

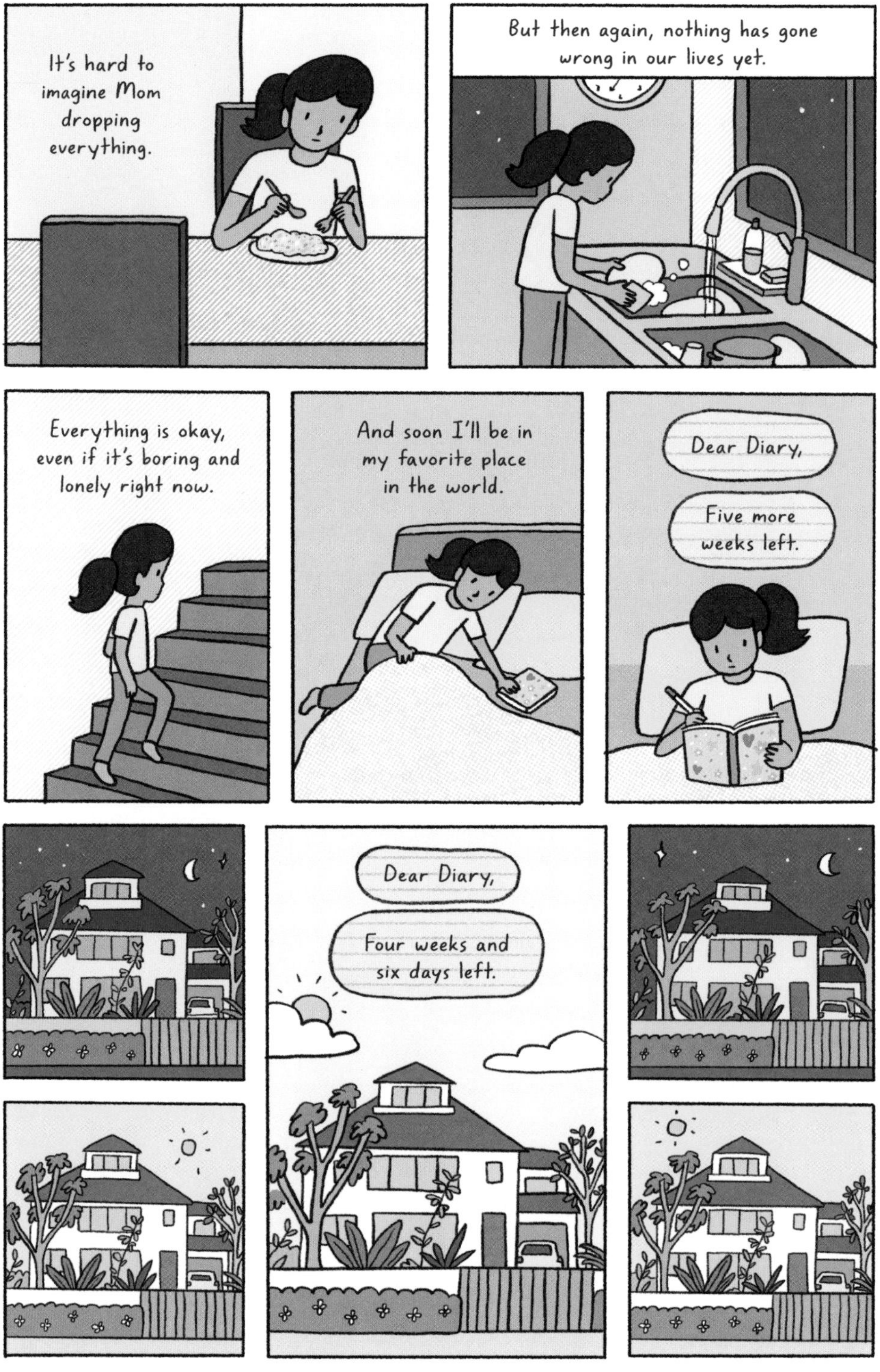
It's hard to imagine Mom dropping everything.
But then again, nothing has gone wrong in our lives yet.
Everything is okay, even if it's boring and lonely right now.
And soon I'll be in my favorite place in the world.
Dear Diary,
Five more weeks left.
Dear Diary,
Four weeks and six days left.

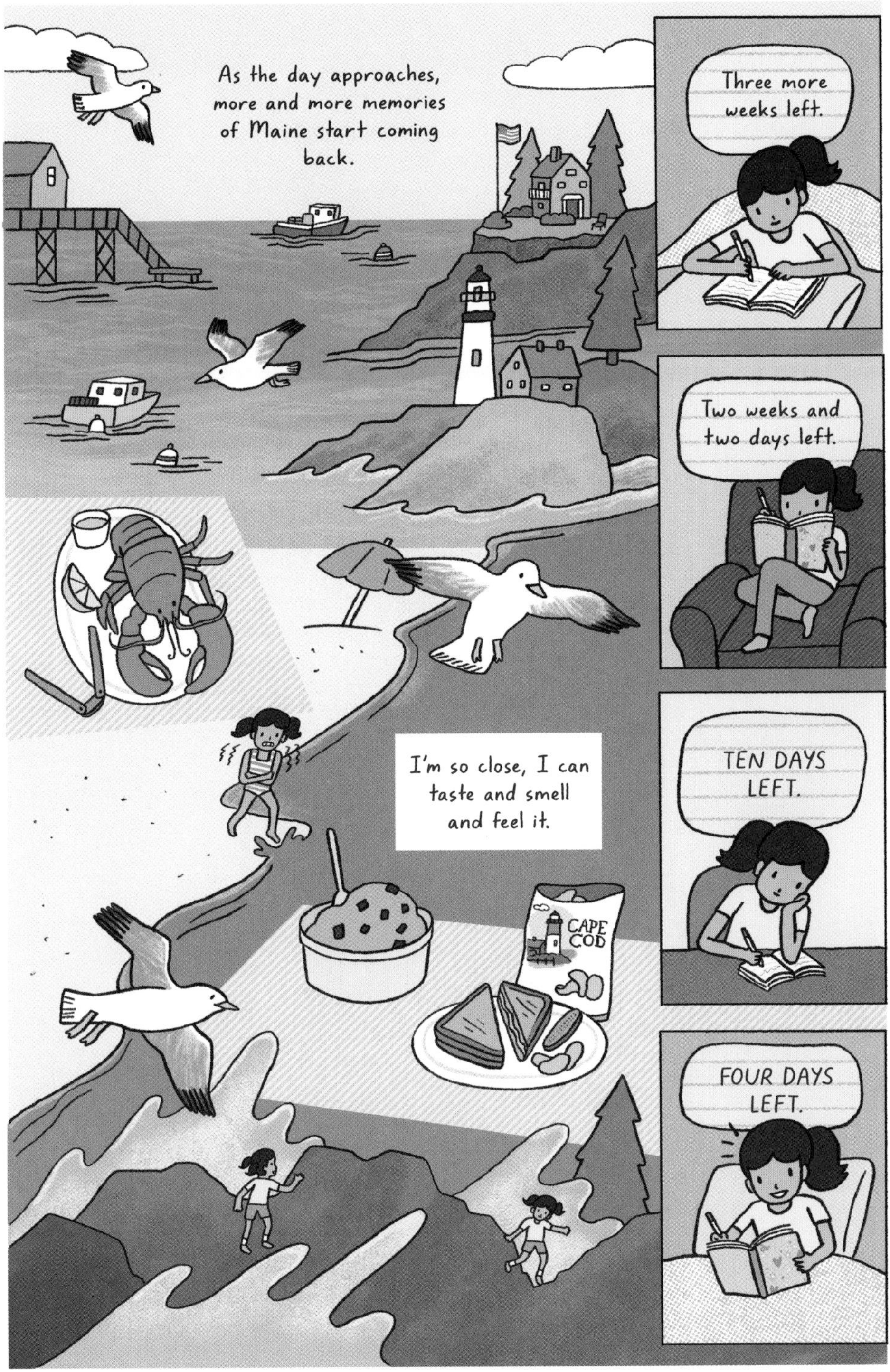
As the day approaches, more and more memories of Maine start coming back.
Three more weeks left.
Two weeks and two days left.
I'm so close, I can taste and smell and feel it.
TEN DAYS LEFT.
CAPE COD
FOUR DAYS LEFT.

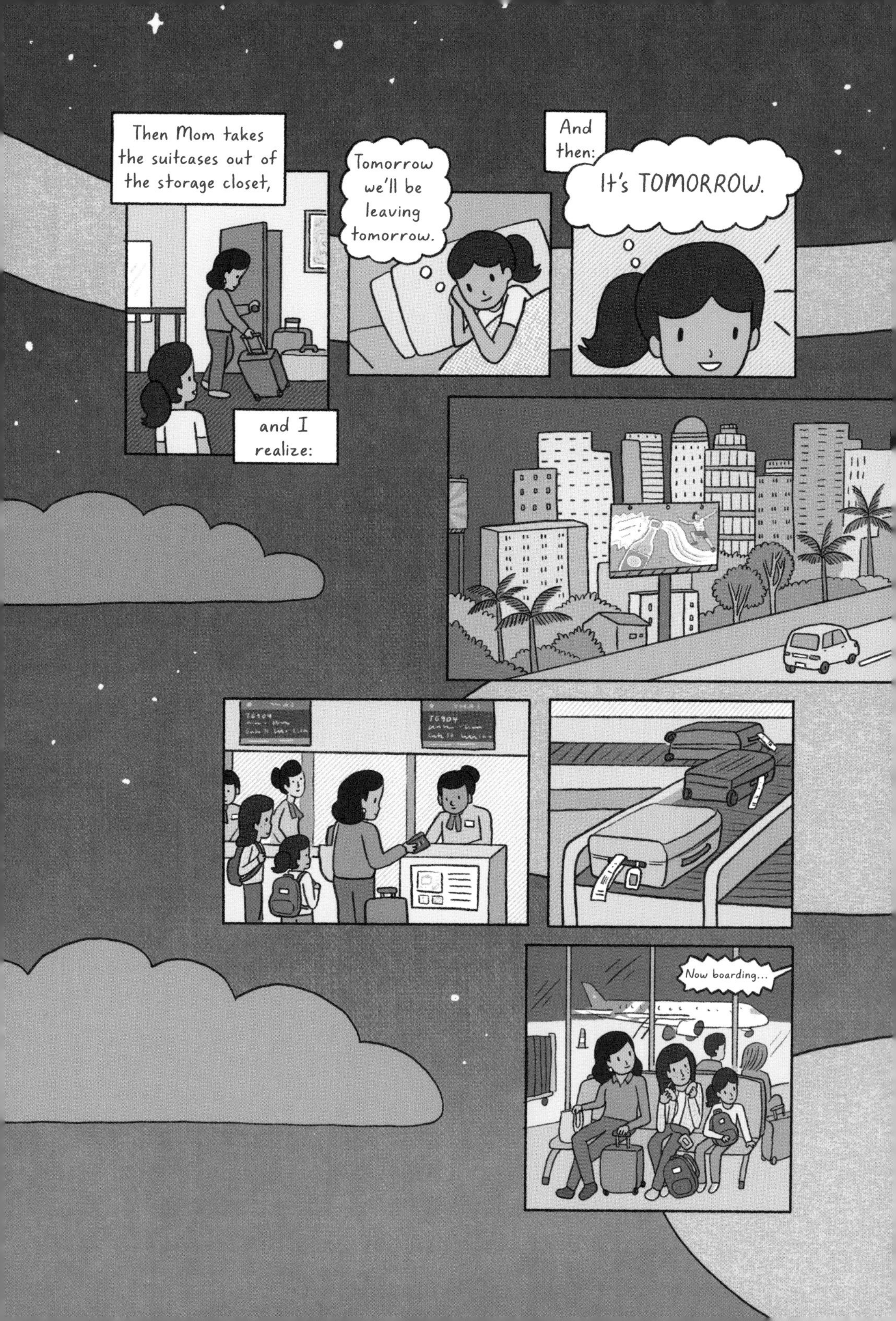

Then Mom takes the suitcases out of the storage closet,
and I realize:
Tomorrow we'll be leaving tomorrow.
And then:
It's TOMORROW.
Now boarding...

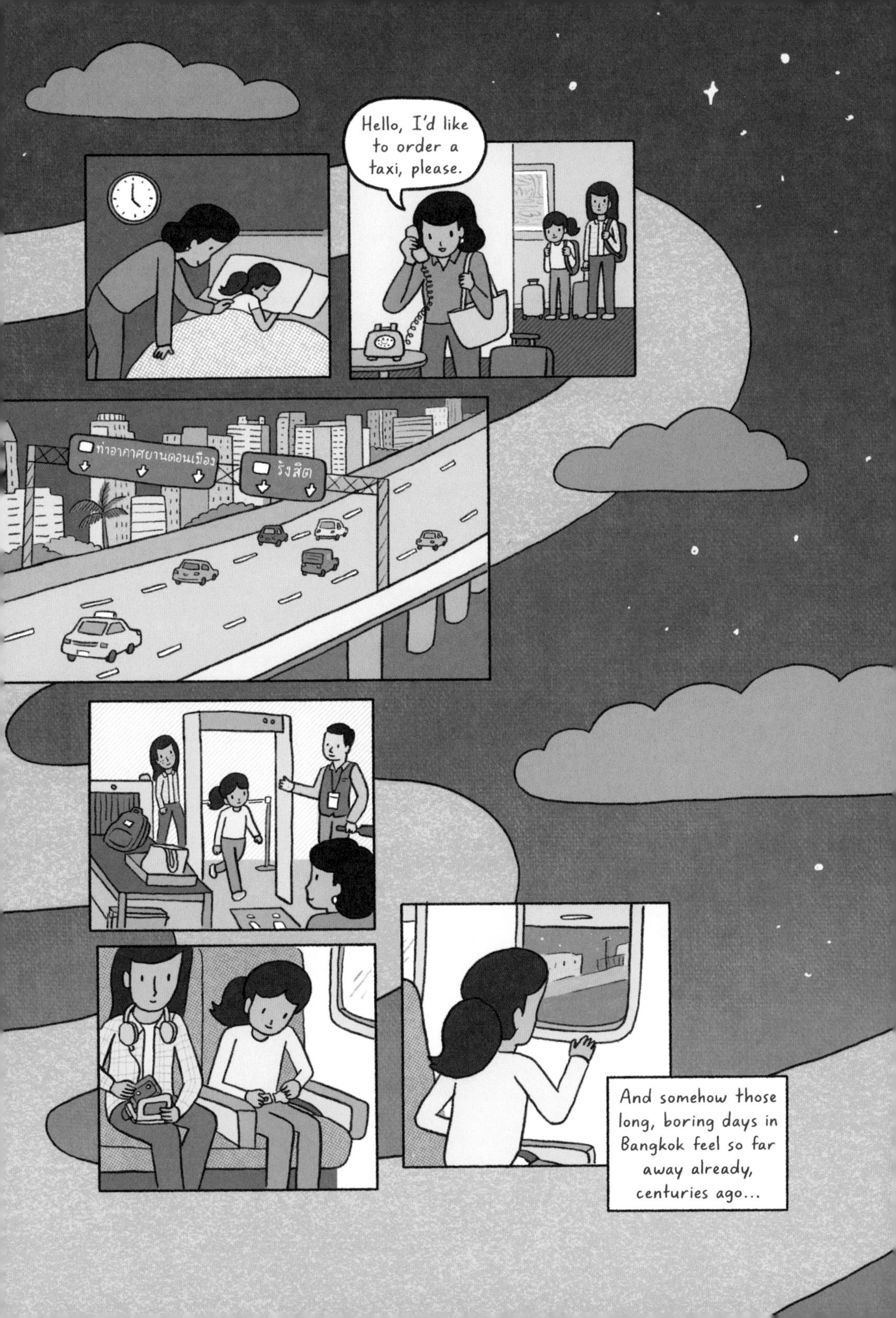
Hello, I'd like to order a taxi, please.
ท่าอากาศยานดอนเมือง
รังสิต
And somehow those long, boring days in Bangkok feel so far away already, centuries ago...

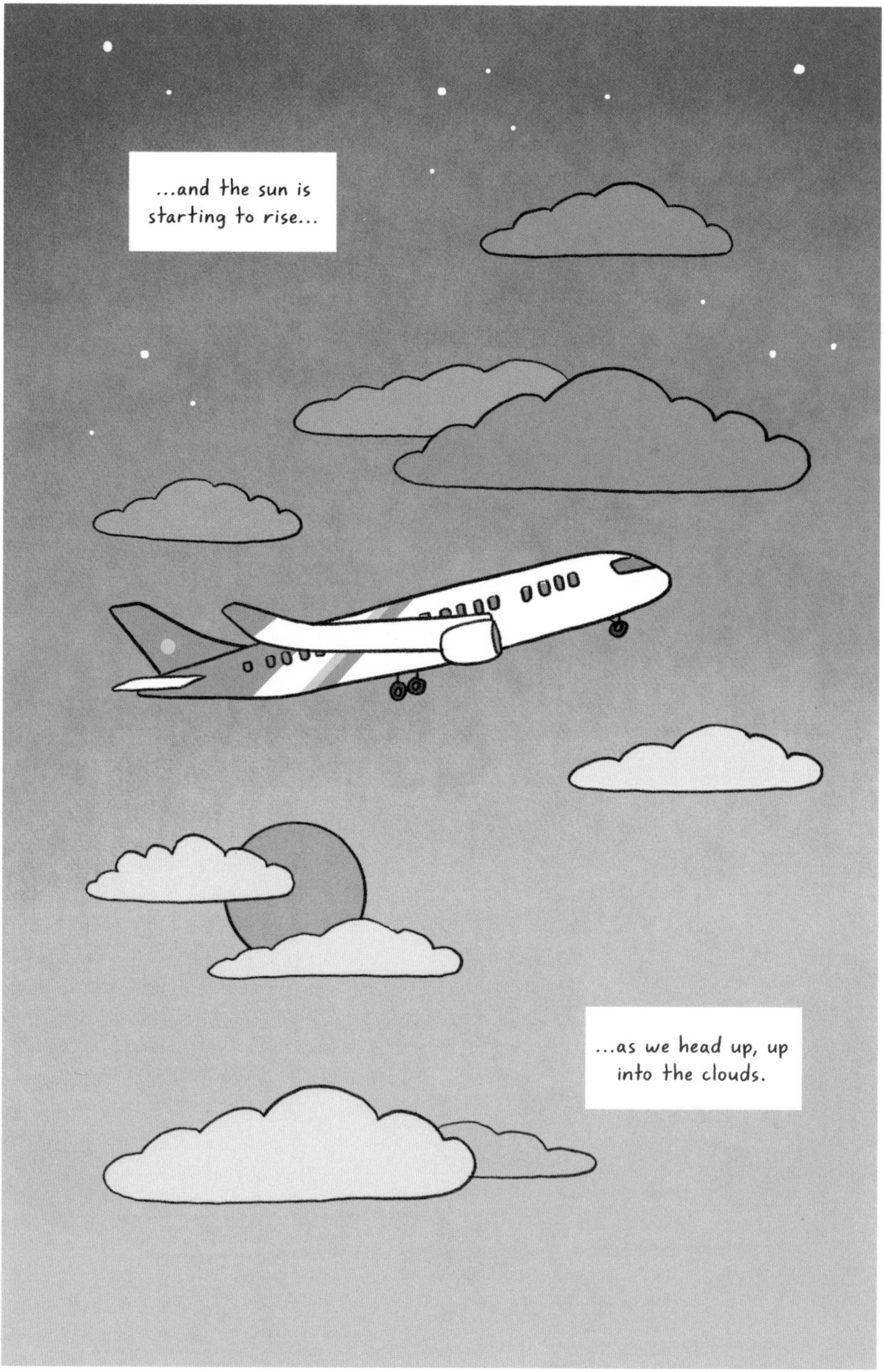
...and the sun is starting to rise...
...as we head up, up into the clouds.

4

Even though my home is in Bangkok, I feel like
I've always lived in this American bubble.

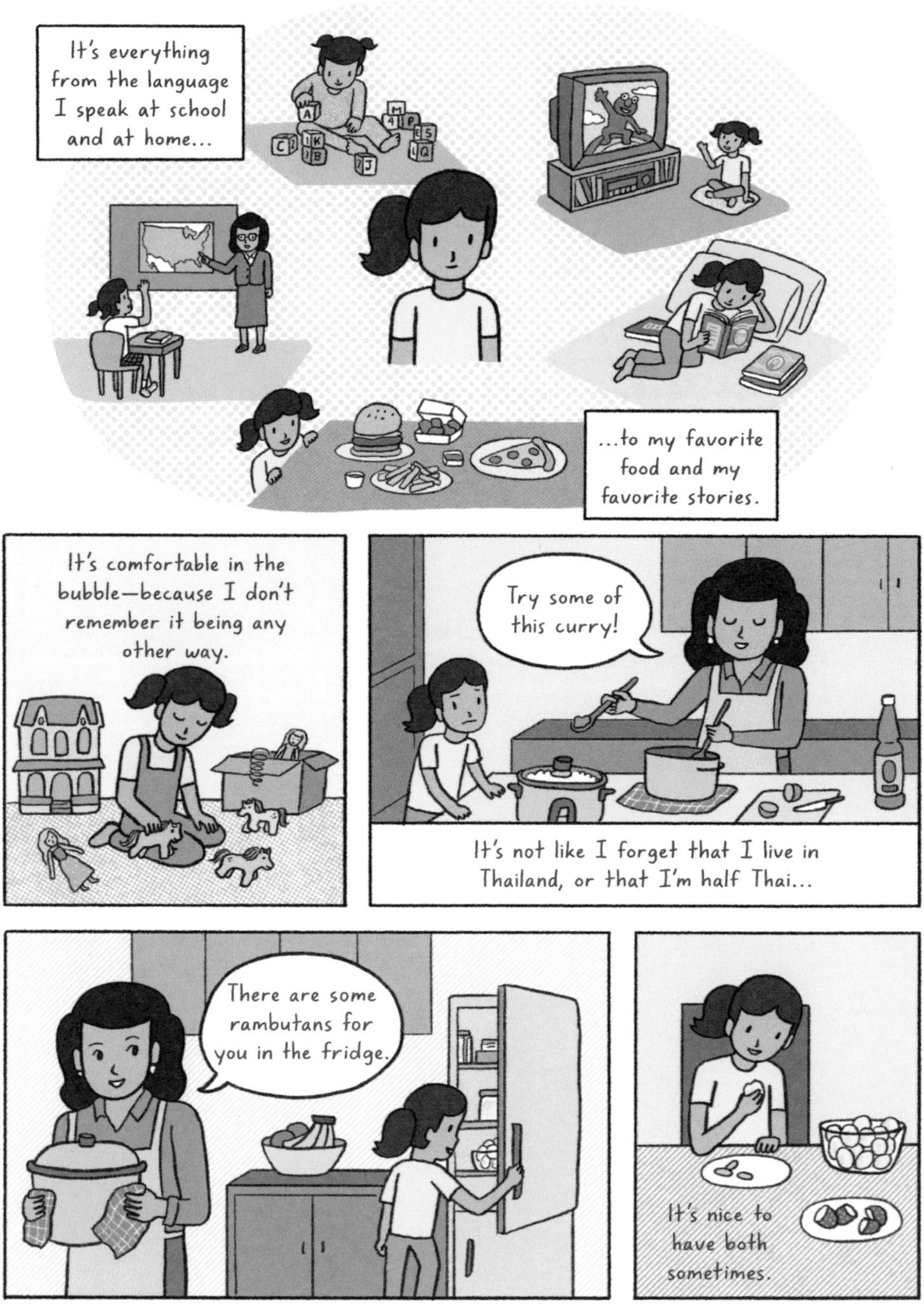
It's everything from the language I speak at school and at home...
...to my favorite food and my favorite stories.
It's comfortable in the bubble—because I don't remember it being any other way.
Try some of this curry!
It's not like I forget that I live in Thailand, or that I'm half Thai...
There are some rambutans for you in the fridge.
It's nice to have both sometimes.

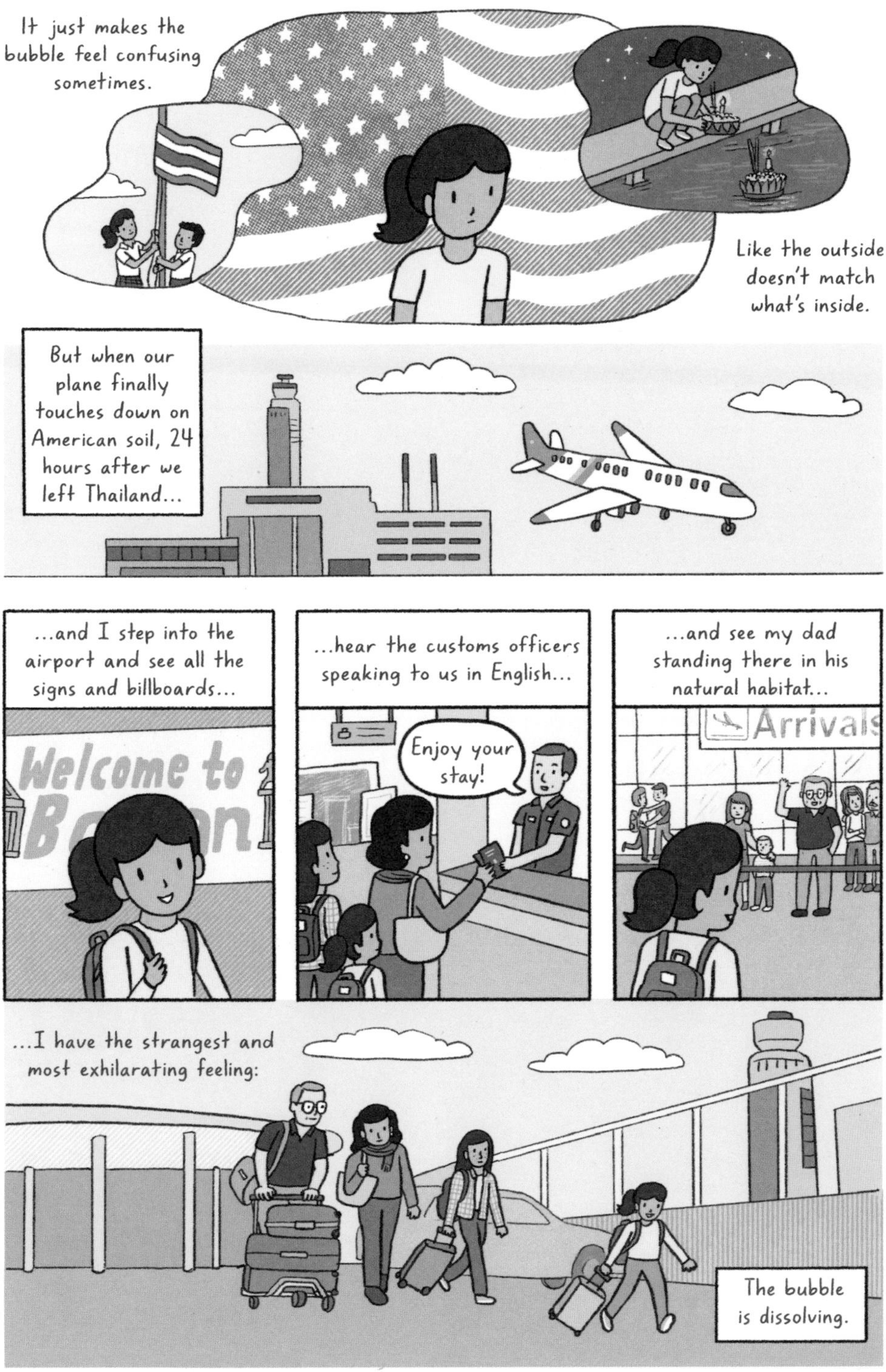
It just makes the bubble feel confusing sometimes.
Like the outside doesn't match what's inside.
But when our plane finally touches down on American soil, 24 hours after we left Thailand...
...and I step into the airport and see all the signs and billboards...
Welcome to B
...hear the customs officers speaking to us in English...
Enjoy your stay!
...and see my dad standing there in his natural habitat...
Arrivals
...I have the strangest and most exhilarating feeling:
The bubble is dissolving.

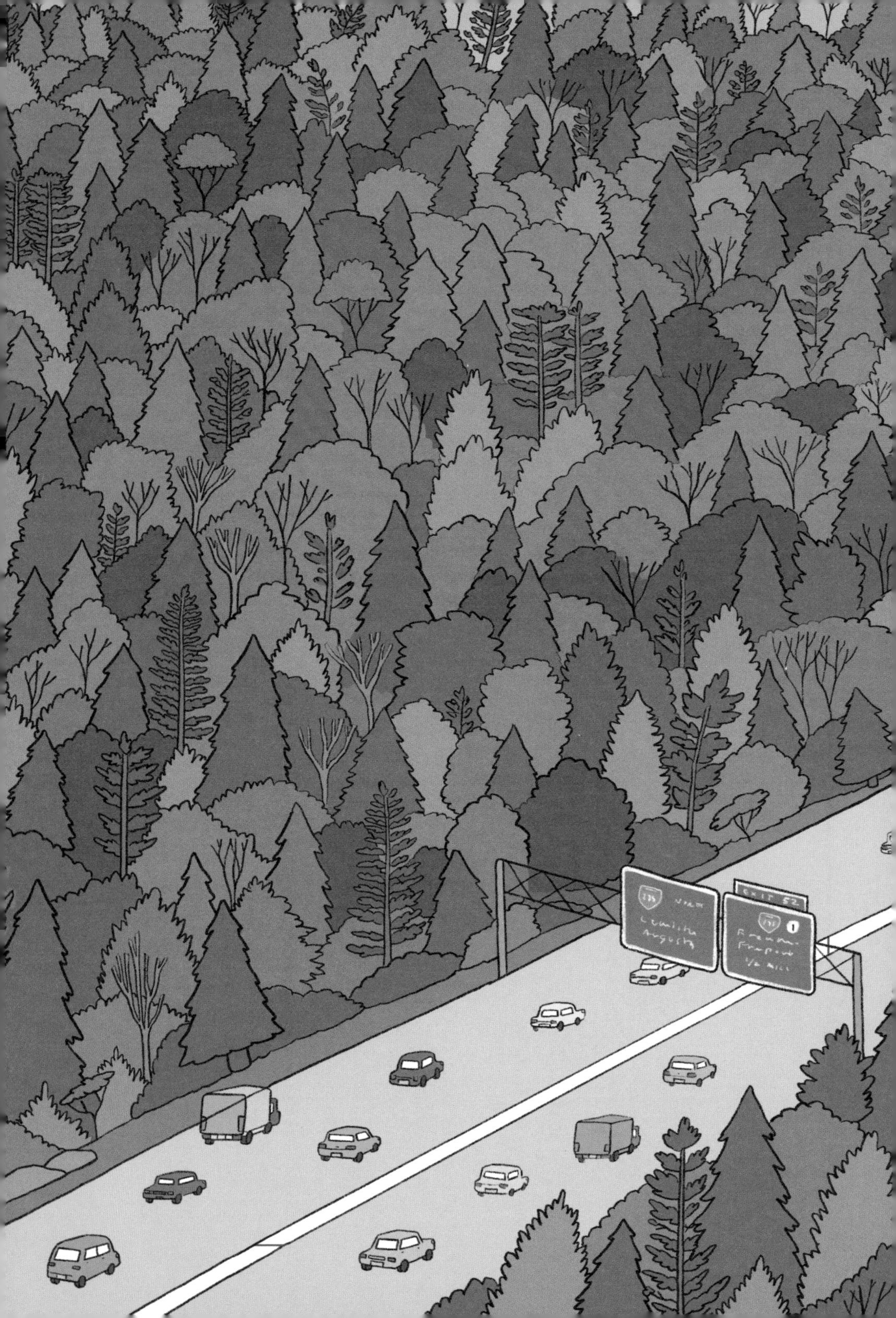
EXIT 52
1

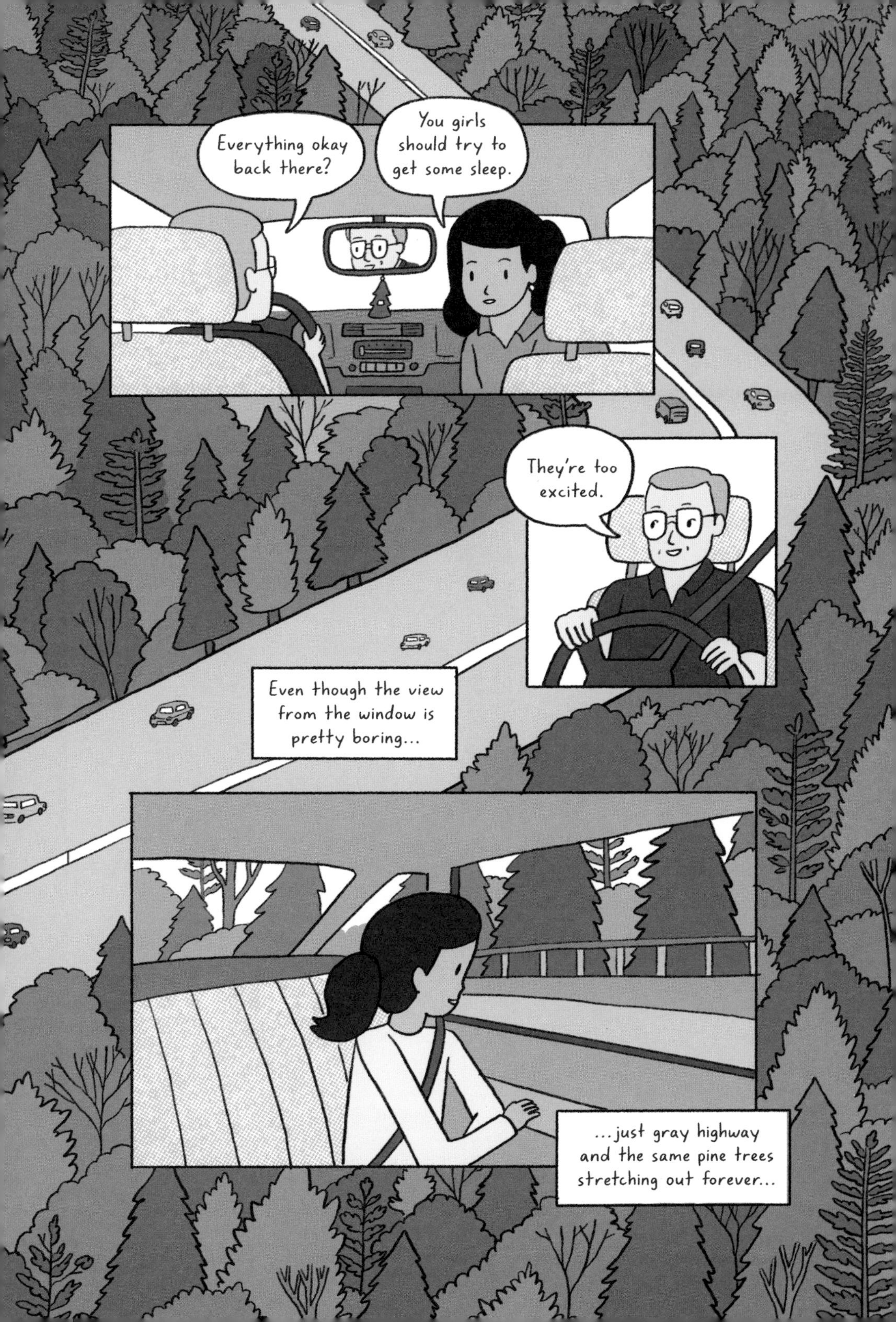
Everything okay back there?
You girls should try to get some sleep.
They're too excited.
Even though the view from the window is pretty boring...
...just gray highway and the same pine trees stretching out forever...

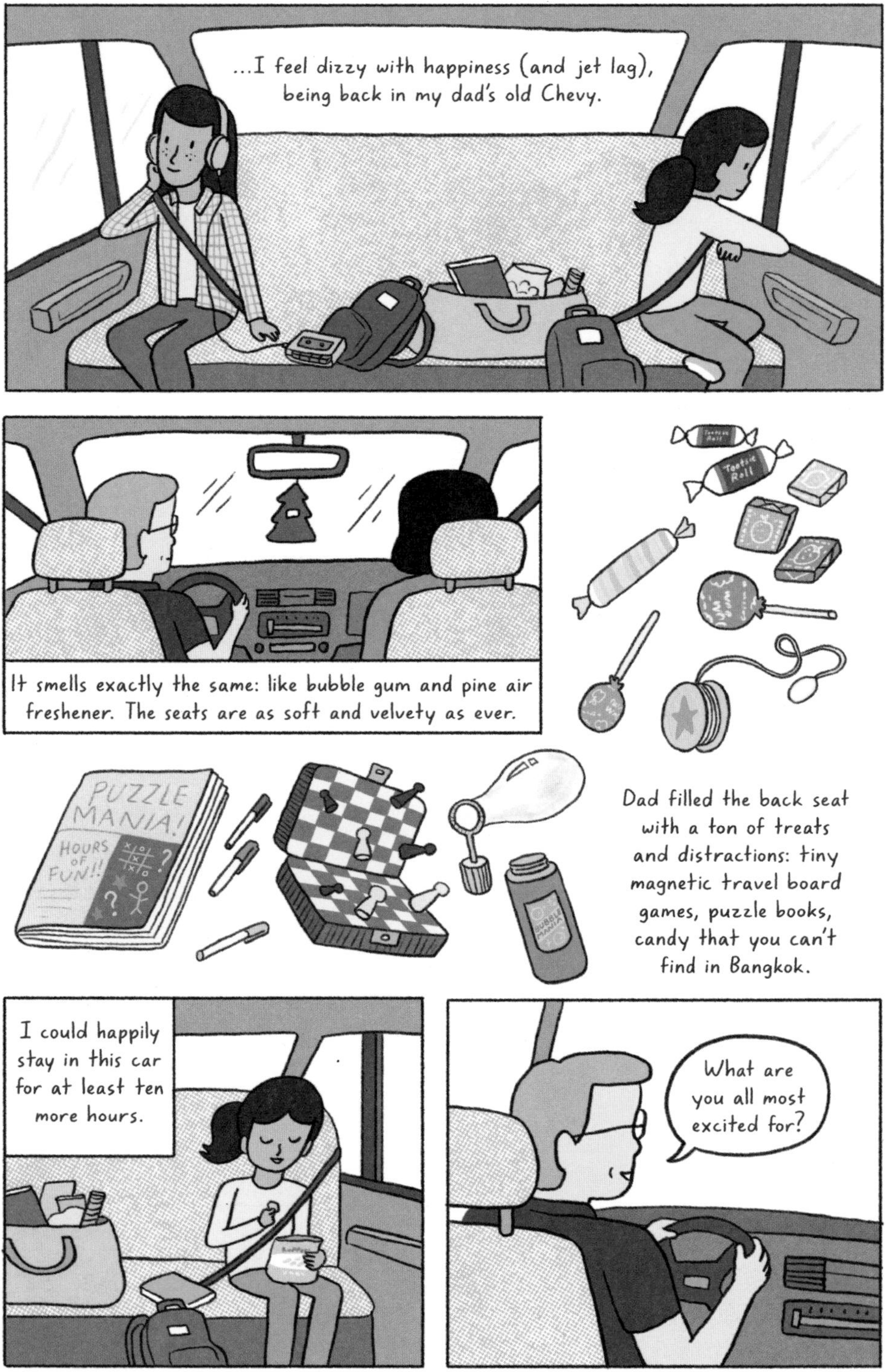
...I feel dizzy with happiness (and jet lag), being back in my dad's old Chevy.
It smells exactly the same: like bubble gum and pine air freshener. The seats are as soft and velvety as ever.
Tootsie Roll
PUZZLE MANIA!
HOURS OF FUN!!
BUBBLE MANIA
Dad filled the back seat with a ton of treats and distractions: tiny magnetic travel board games, puzzle books, candy that you can't find in Bangkok.
I could happily stay in this car for at least ten more hours.
What are you all most excited for?

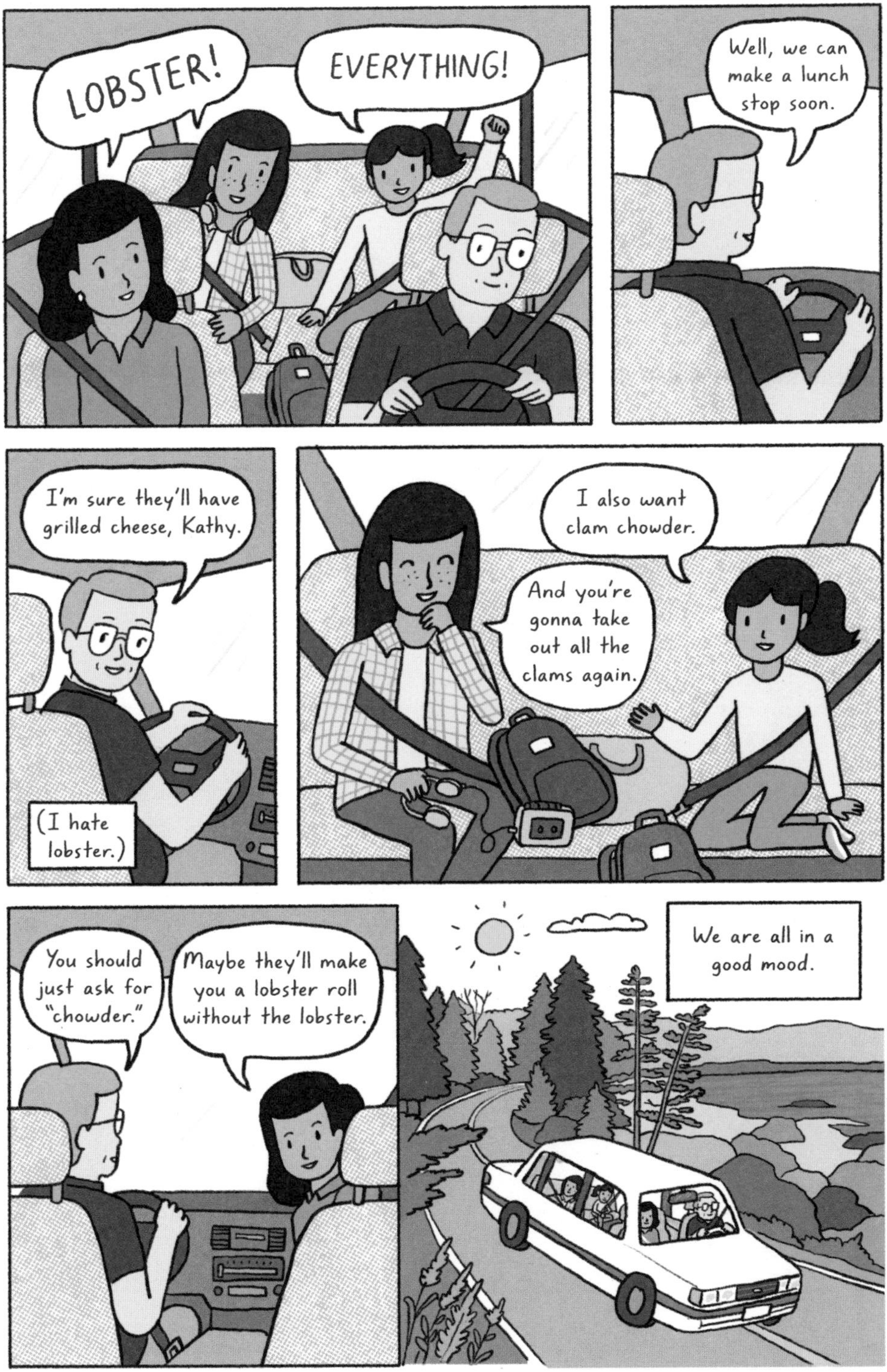
LOBSTER!
EVERYTHING!
Well, we can make a lunch stop soon.
I'm sure they'll have grilled cheese, Kathy.
(I hate lobster.)
I also want clam chowder.
And you're gonna take out all the clams again.
You should just ask for "chowder."
Maybe they'll make you a lobster roll without the lobster.
We are all in a good mood.

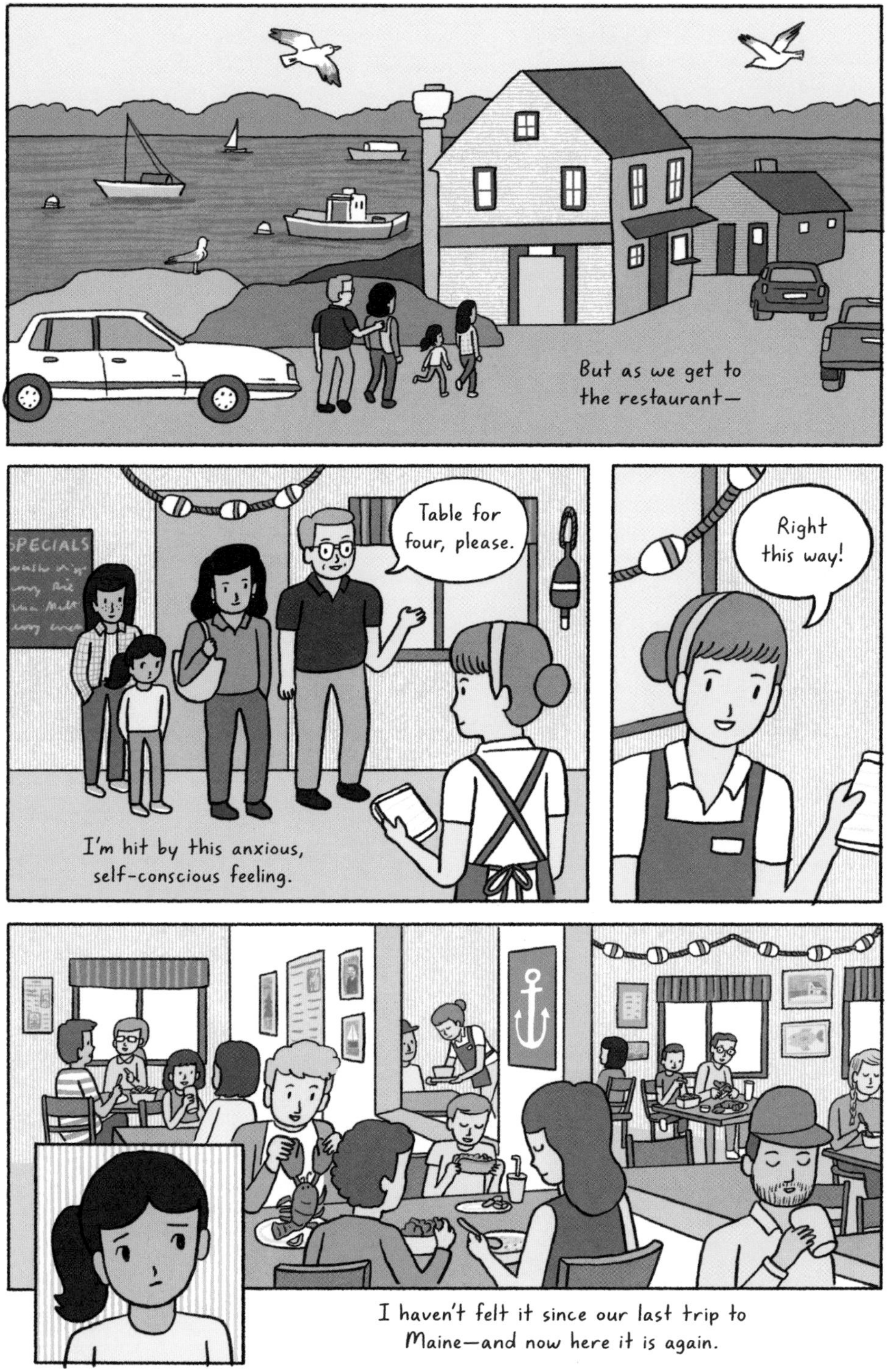
But as we get to the restaurant—
SPECIALS
Table for four, please.
I'm hit by this anxious, self-conscious feeling.
Right this way!
I haven't felt it since our last trip to Maine—and now here it is again.

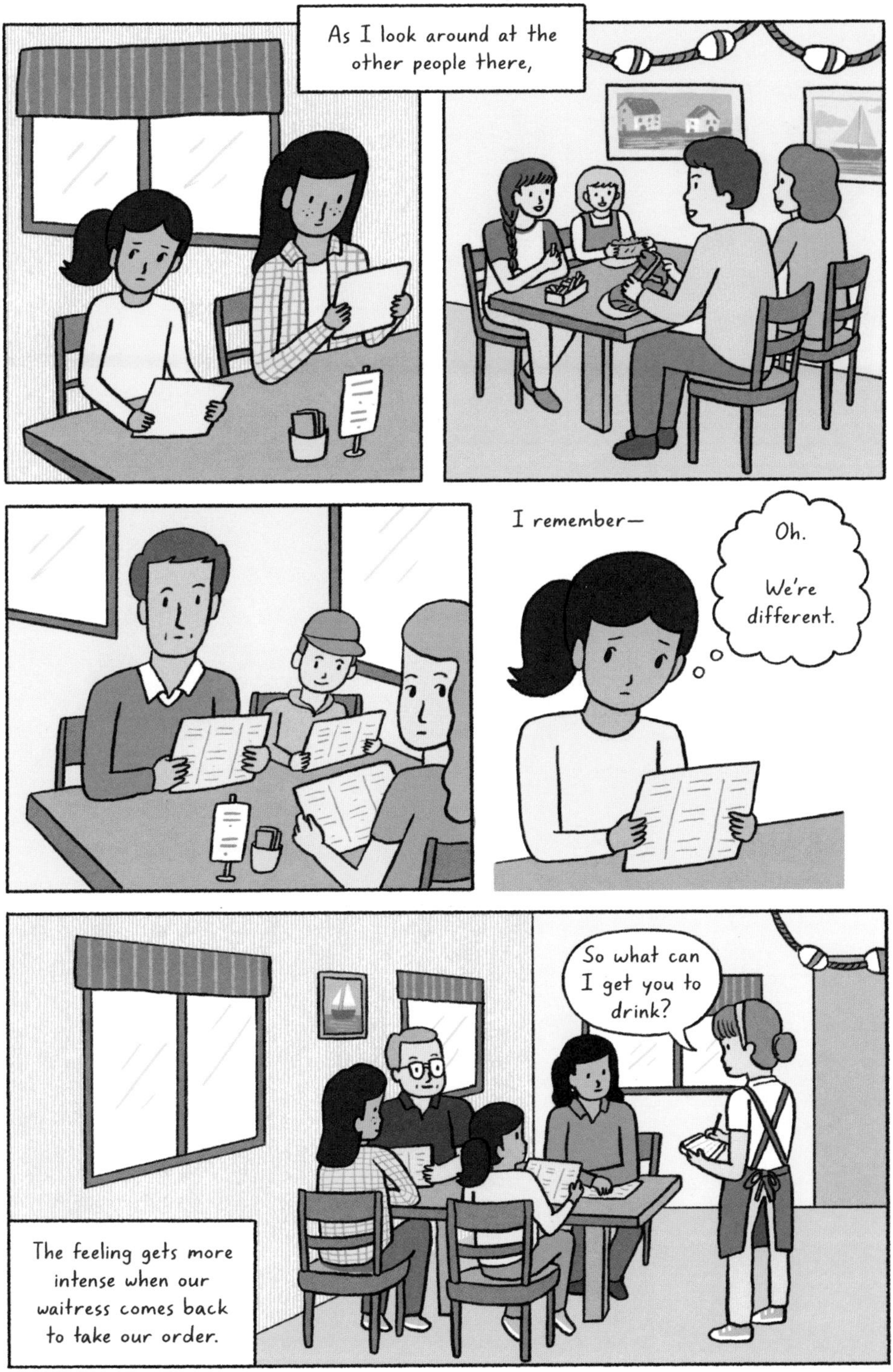
As I look around at the other people there,
I remember—
Oh.
We're different.
So what can I get you to drink?
The feeling gets more intense when our waitress comes back to take our order.

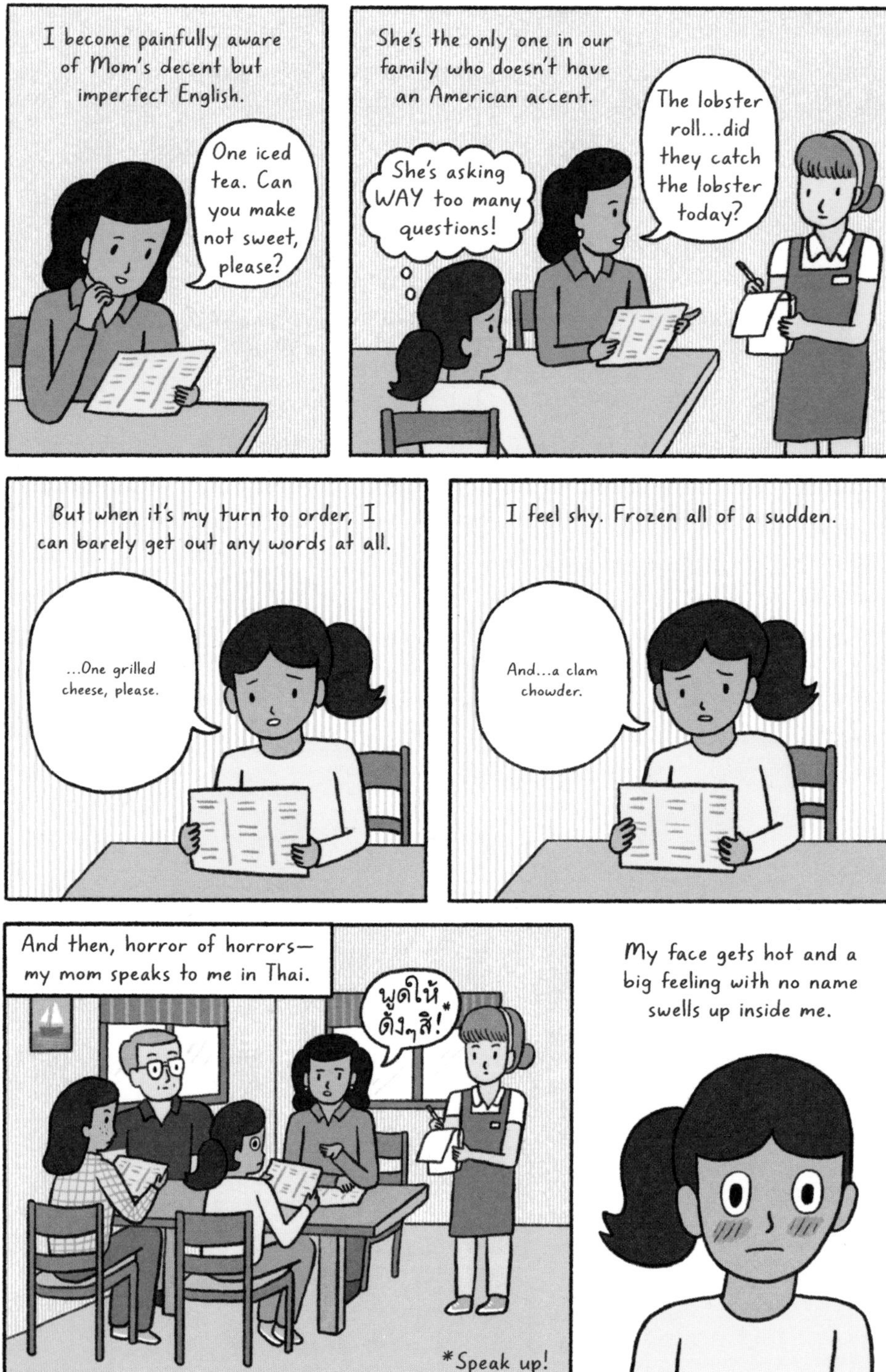
I become painfully aware of Mom's decent but imperfect English.
One iced tea. Can you make not sweet, please?
She's the only one in our family who doesn't have an American accent.
She's asking WAY too many questions!
The lobster roll...did they catch the lobster today?
But when it's my turn to order, I can barely get out any words at all.
...One grilled cheese, please.
I feel shy. Frozen all of a sudden.
And...a clam chowder.
And then, horror of horrors—my mom speaks to me in Thai.
พูดให้ดังๆสิ!*
*Speak up!
My face gets hot and a big feeling with no name swells up inside me.

A GRILLED CHEESE AND A CLAM CHOWDER.

PLEASE!

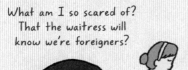

What am I so scared of? That the waitress will know we're foreigners?

Isn't it already clear—from Mom's face, and Jennie's, and mine—

—that we're not from this town, or from any town in Maine?

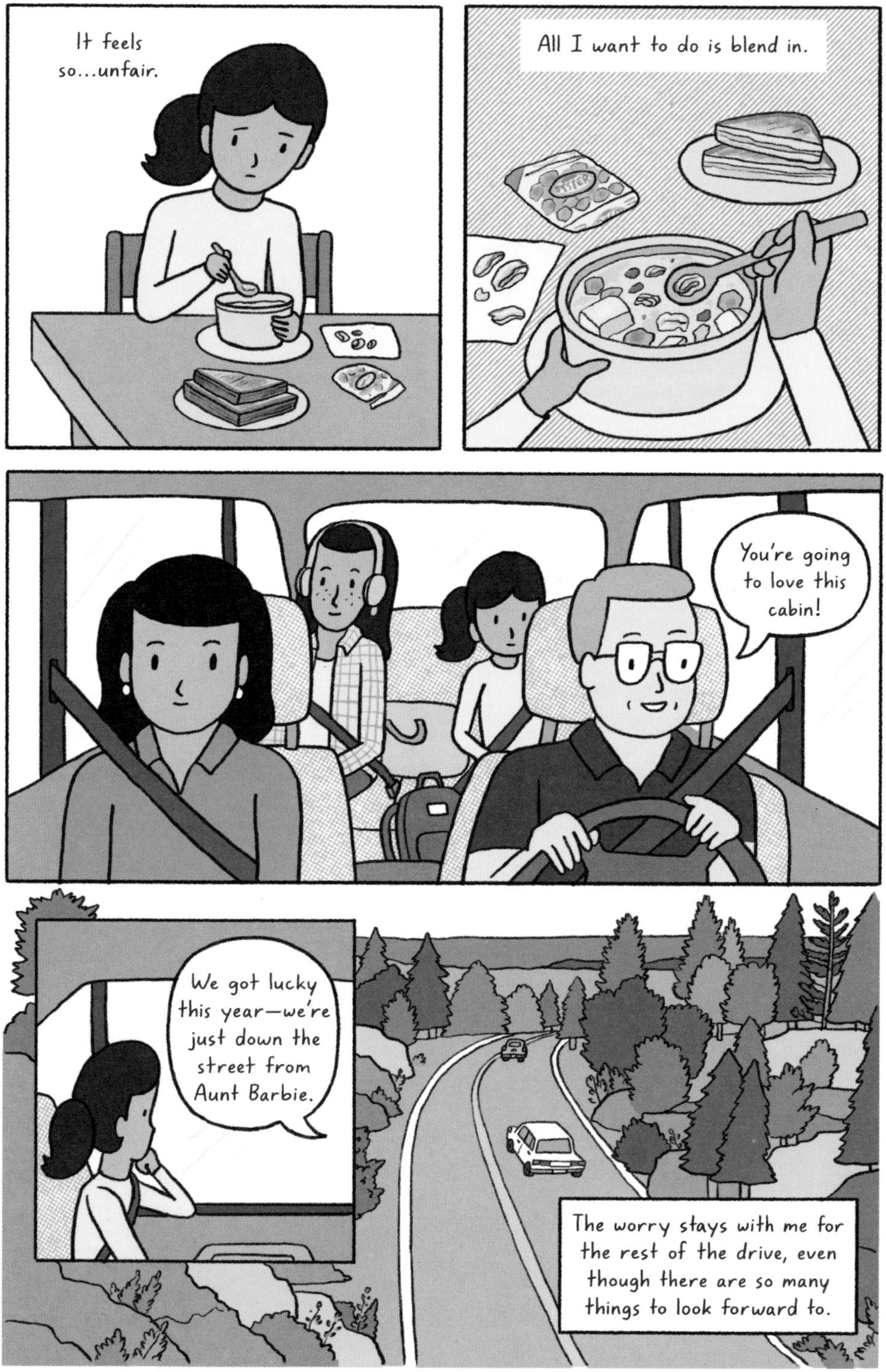
It feels so...unfair.
All I want to do is blend in.
You're going to love this cabin!
We got lucky this year—we're just down the street from Aunt Barbie.
The worry stays with me for the rest of the drive, even though there are so many things to look forward to.

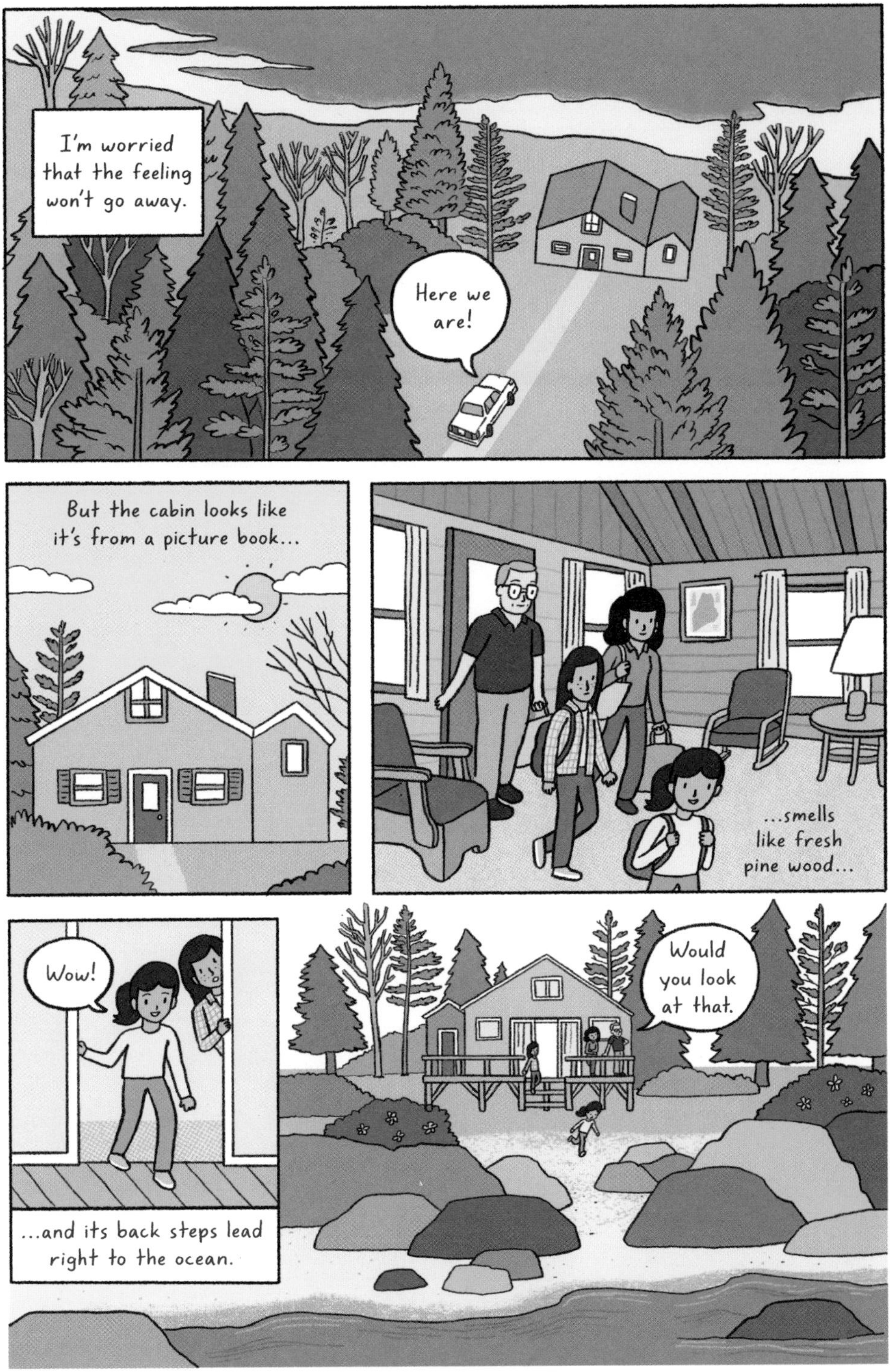
I'm worried that the feeling won't go away.
Here we are!
But the cabin looks like it's from a picture book...
...smells like fresh pine wood...
Wow!
...and its back steps lead right to the ocean.
Would you look at that.

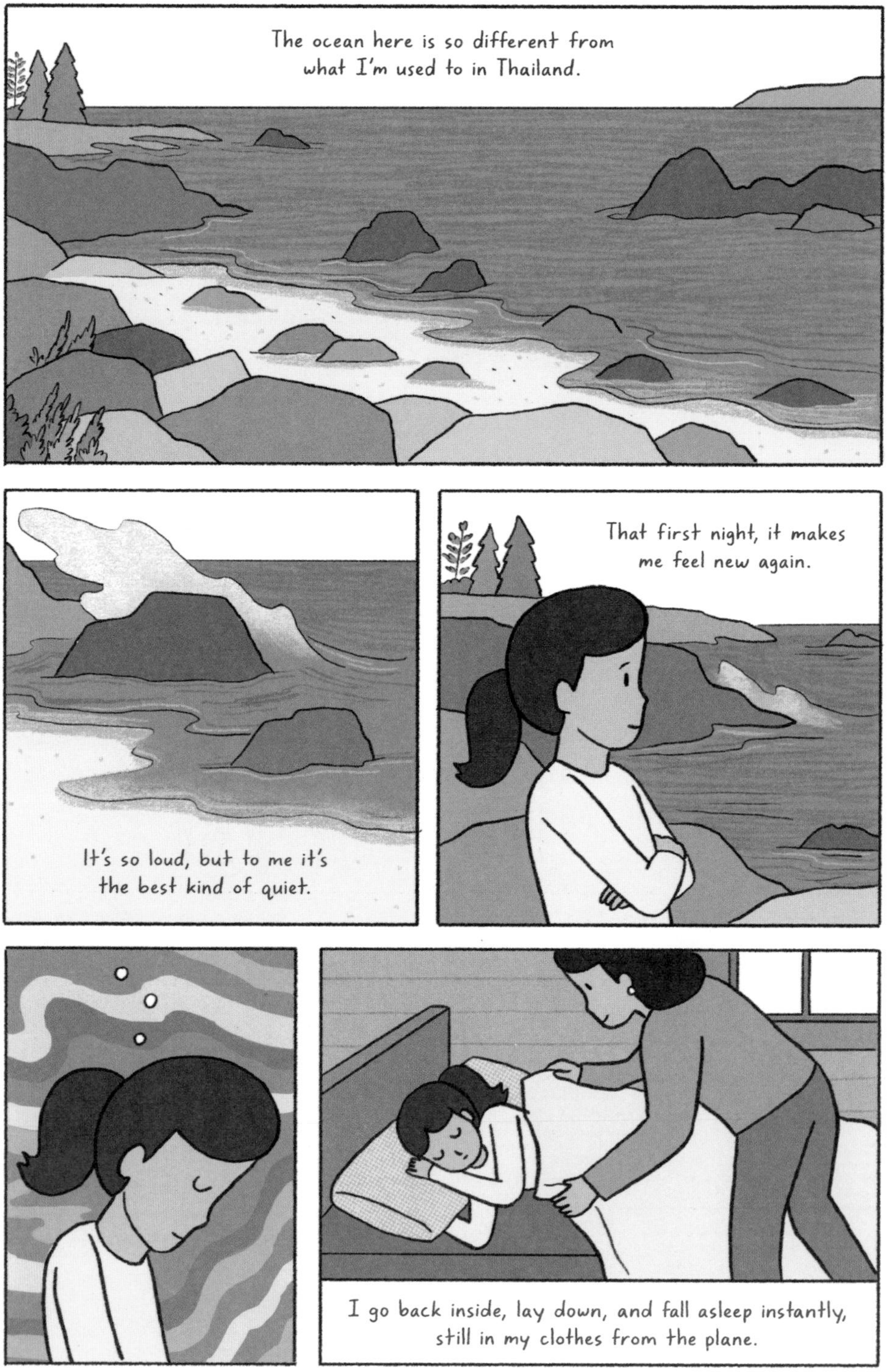
The ocean here is so different from what I'm used to in Thailand.
It's so loud, but to me it's the best kind of quiet.
That first night, it makes me feel new again.
I go back inside, lay down, and fall asleep instantly, still in my clothes from the plane.

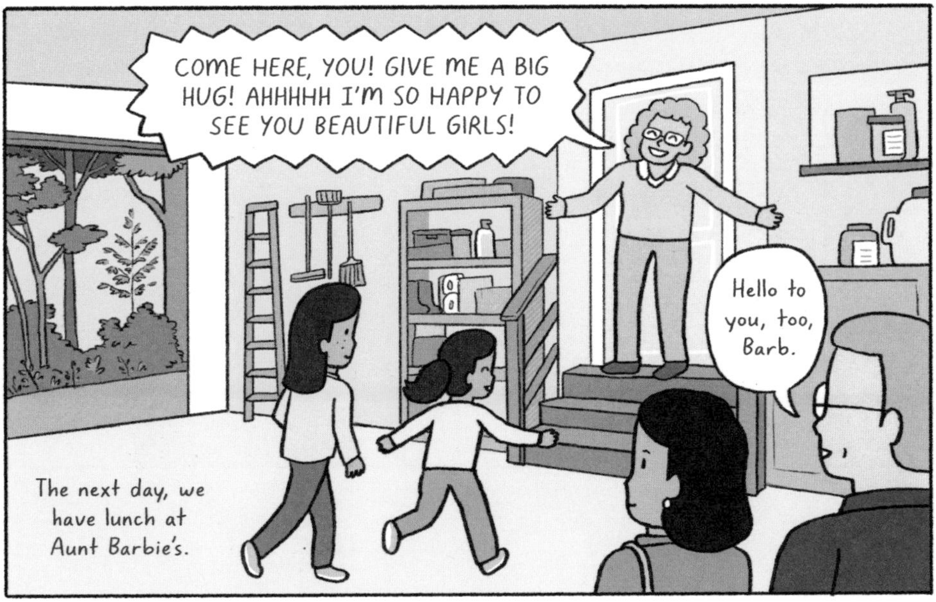
COME HERE, YOU! GIVE ME A BIG HUG! AHHHHH I'M SO HAPPY TO SEE YOU BEAUTIFUL GIRLS!
Hello to you, too, Barb.
The next day, we have lunch at Aunt Barbie's.

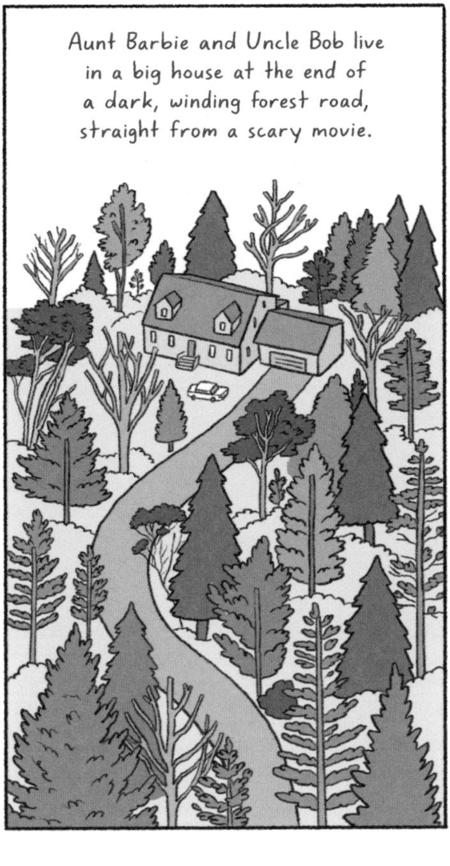
Aunt Barbie and Uncle Bob live in a big house at the end of a dark, winding forest road, straight from a scary movie.

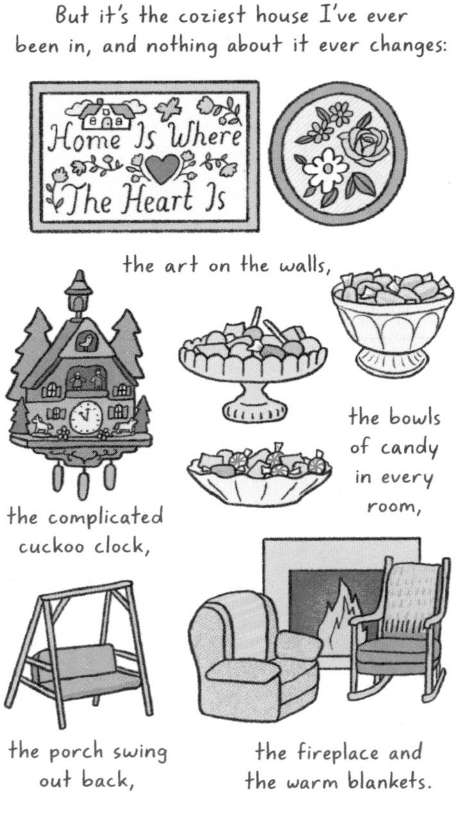
But it's the coziest house I've ever been in, and nothing about it ever changes:
Home Is Where The Heart Is
the art on the walls,
the complicated cuckoo clock,
the bowls of candy in every room,
the porch swing out back,
the fireplace and the warm blankets.

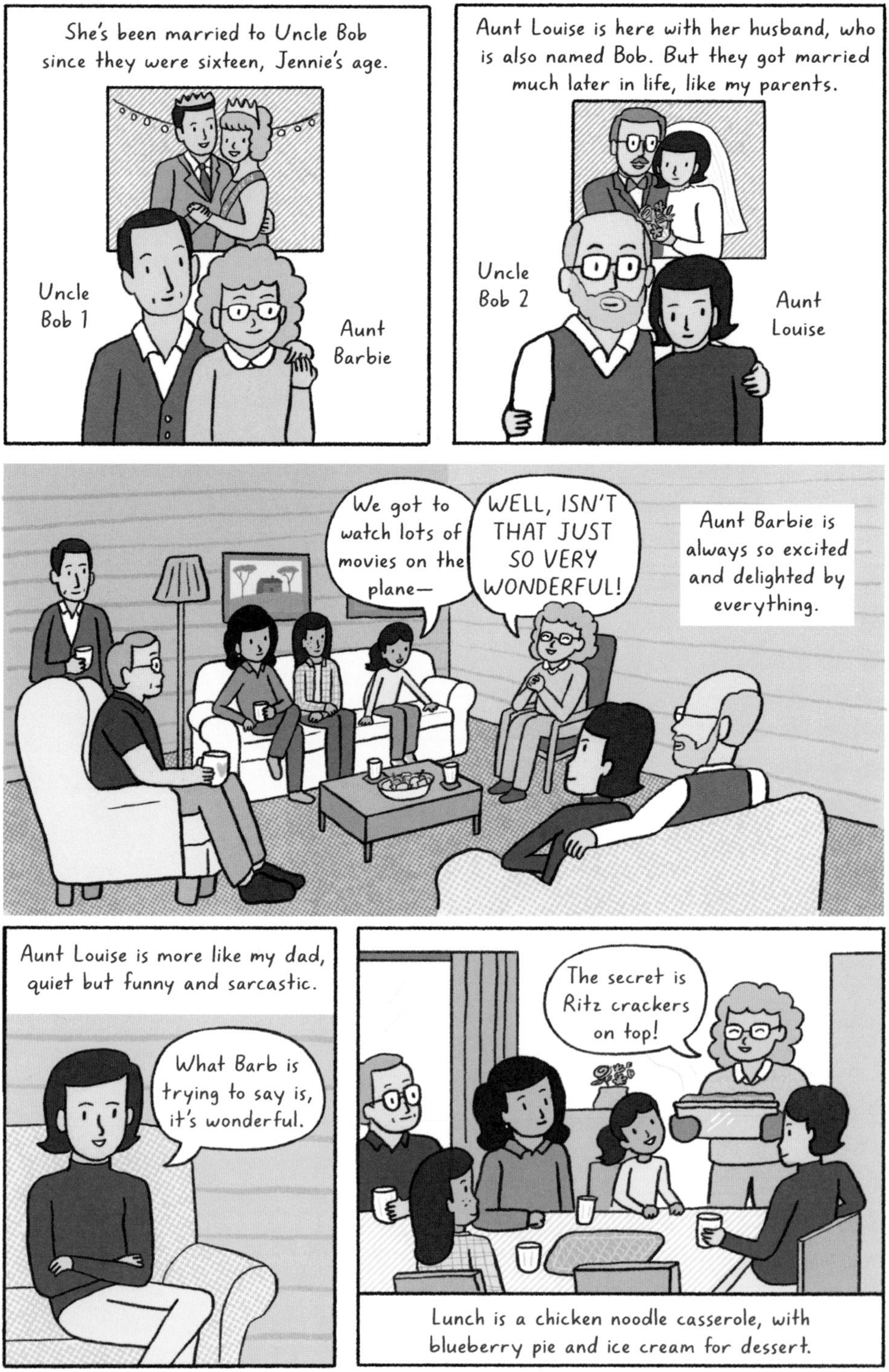
She's been married to Uncle Bob since they were sixteen, Jennie's age.
Uncle Bob 1
Aunt Barbie
Aunt Louise is here with her husband, who is also named Bob. But they got married much later in life, like my parents.
Uncle Bob 2
Aunt Louise
We got to watch lots of movies on the plane—
WELL, ISN'T THAT JUST SO VERY WONDERFUL!
Aunt Barbie is always so excited and delighted by everything.
Aunt Louise is more like my dad, quiet but funny and sarcastic.
What Barb is trying to say is, it's wonderful.
The secret is Ritz crackers on top!
Lunch is a chicken noodle casserole, with blueberry pie and ice cream for dessert.

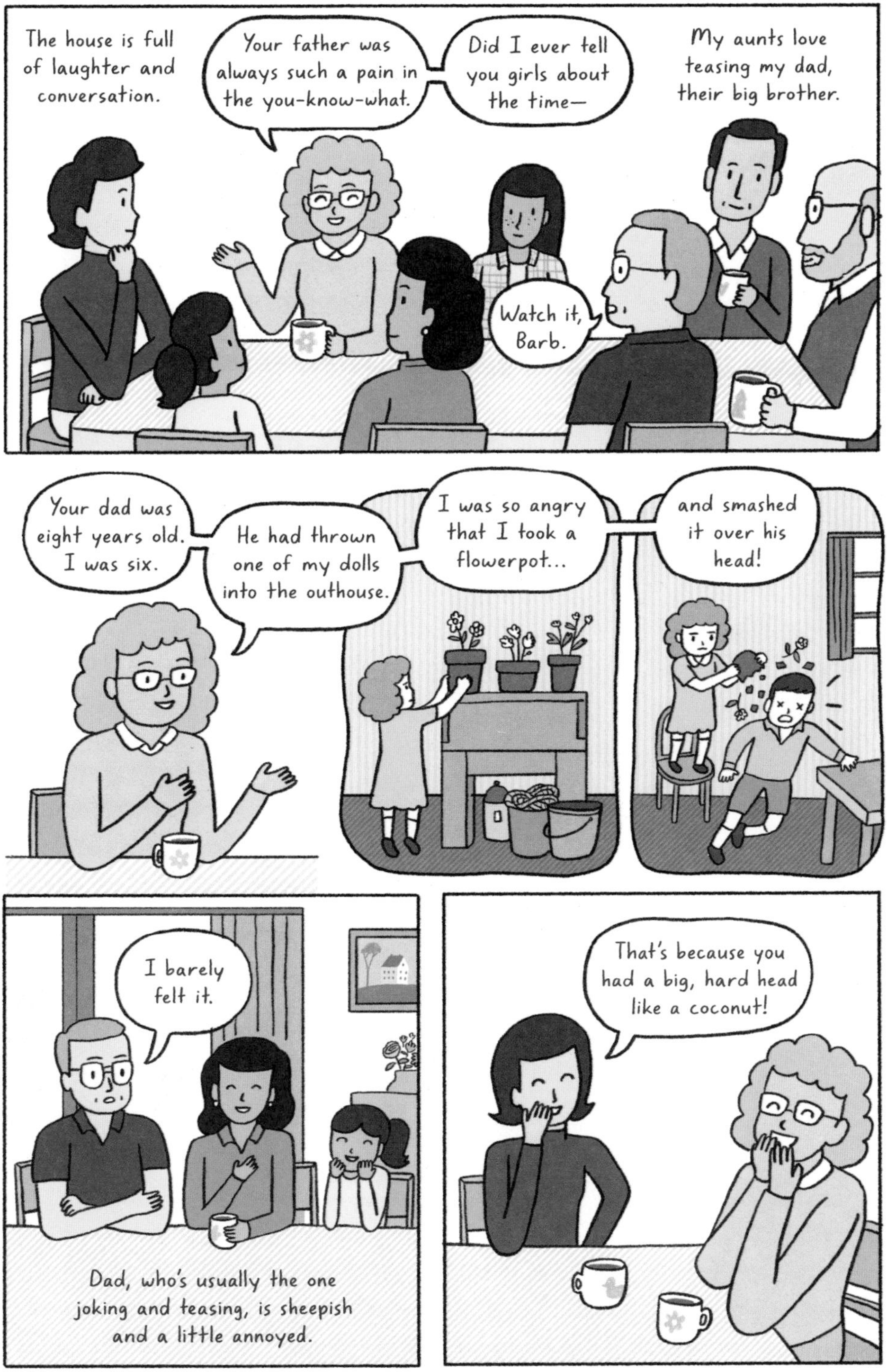

The house is full of laughter and conversation.
Your father was always such a pain in the you-know-what.
Did I ever tell you girls about the time—
My aunts love teasing my dad, their big brother.
Watch it, Barb.
Your dad was eight years old. I was six.
He had thrown one of my dolls into the outhouse.
I was so angry that I took a flowerpot...
and smashed it over his head!
I barely felt it.
Dad, who's usually the one joking and teasing, is sheepish and a little annoyed.
That's because you had a big, hard head like a coconut!

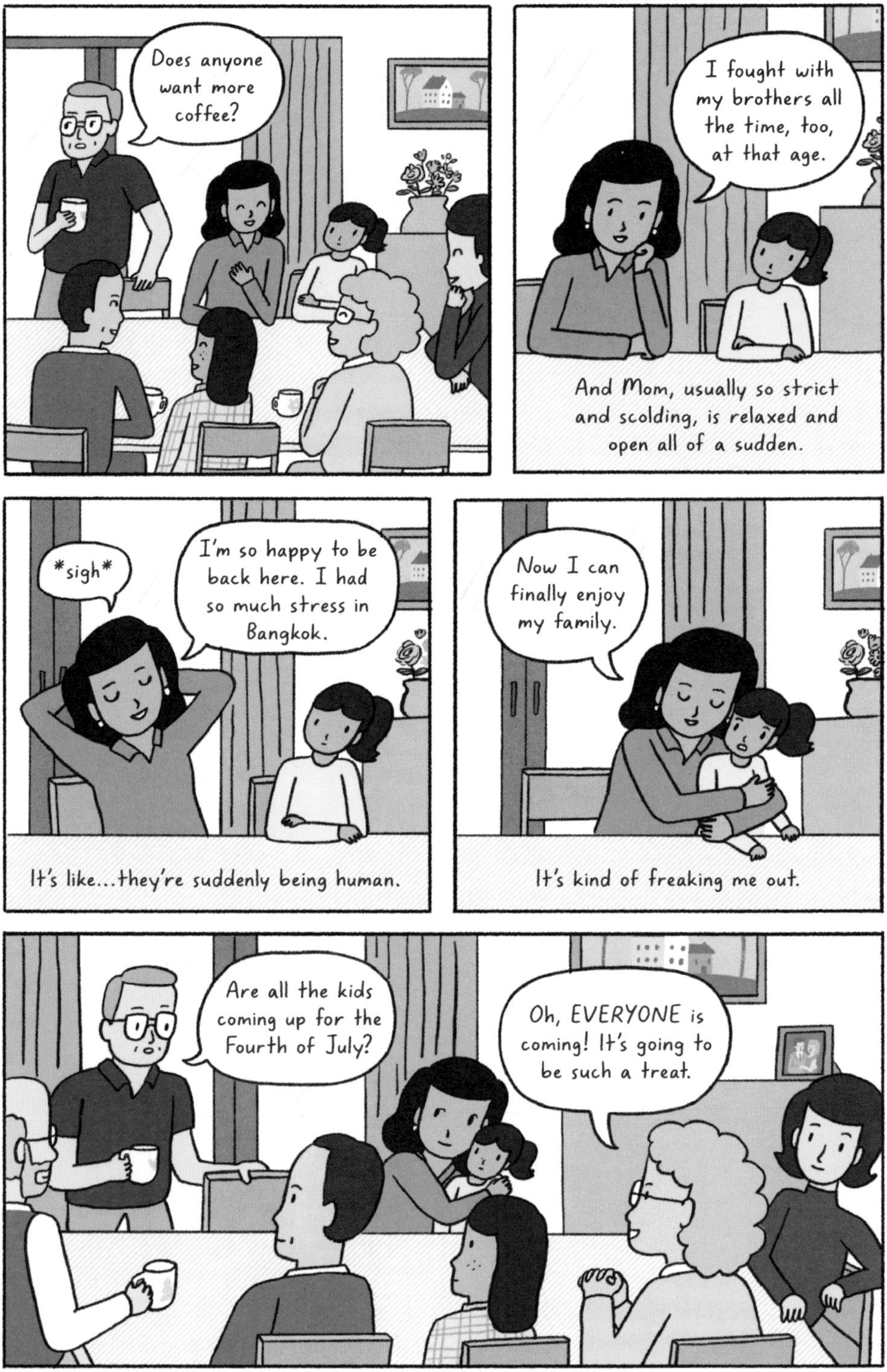
Does anyone want more coffee?
I fought with my brothers all the time, too, at that age.
And Mom, usually so strict and scolding, is relaxed and open all of a sudden.
sigh
I'm so happy to be back here. I had so much stress in Bangkok.
It's like...they're suddenly being human.
Now I can finally enjoy my family.
It's kind of freaking me out.
Are all the kids coming up for the Fourth of July?
Oh, EVERYONE is coming! It's going to be such a treat.

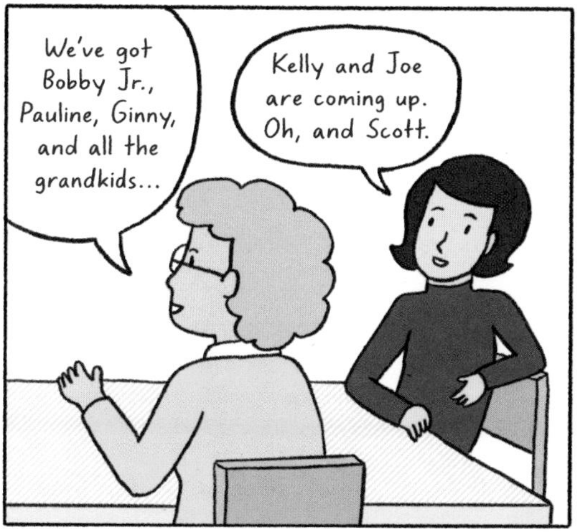
We've got Bobby Jr., Pauline, Ginny, and all the grandkids...
Kelly and Joe are coming up. Oh, and Scott.

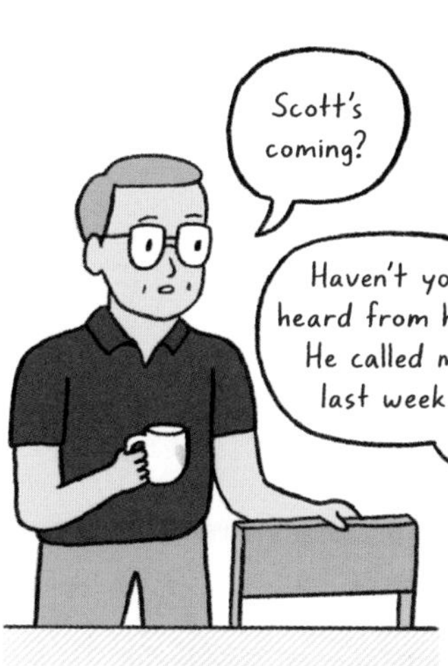
Scott's coming?
Haven't you heard from him? He called me last week.

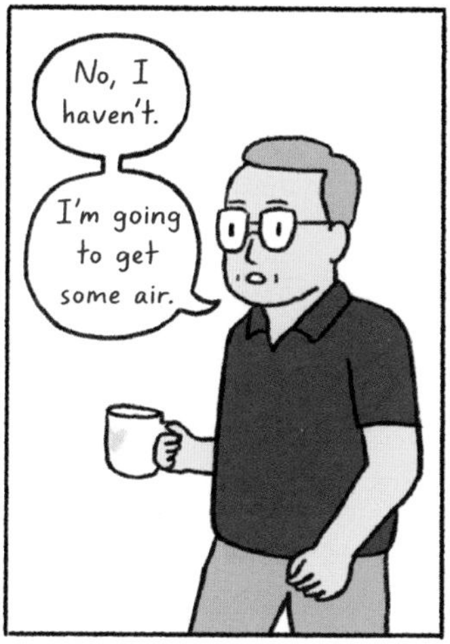
No, I haven't.
I'm going to get some air.

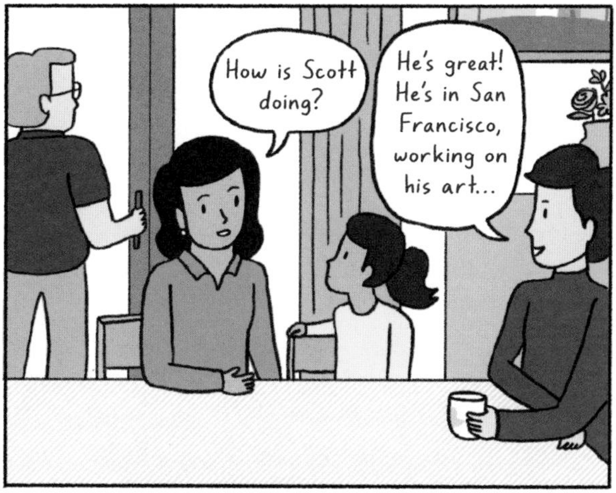
How is Scott doing?
He's great! He's in San Francisco, working on his art...

Scott is my dad's son from his previous marriage. My half brother.

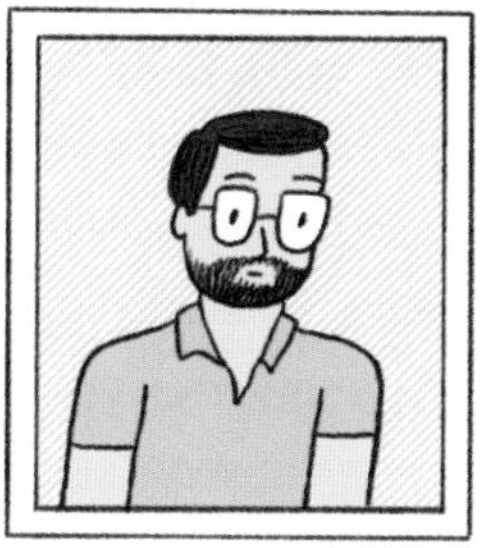

I've never met him or spoken to him—only seen pictures. He's forty. He looks just like my dad.

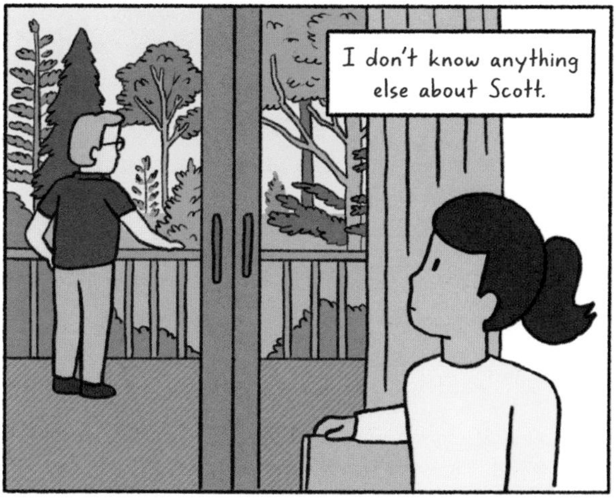
I don't know anything else about Scott.

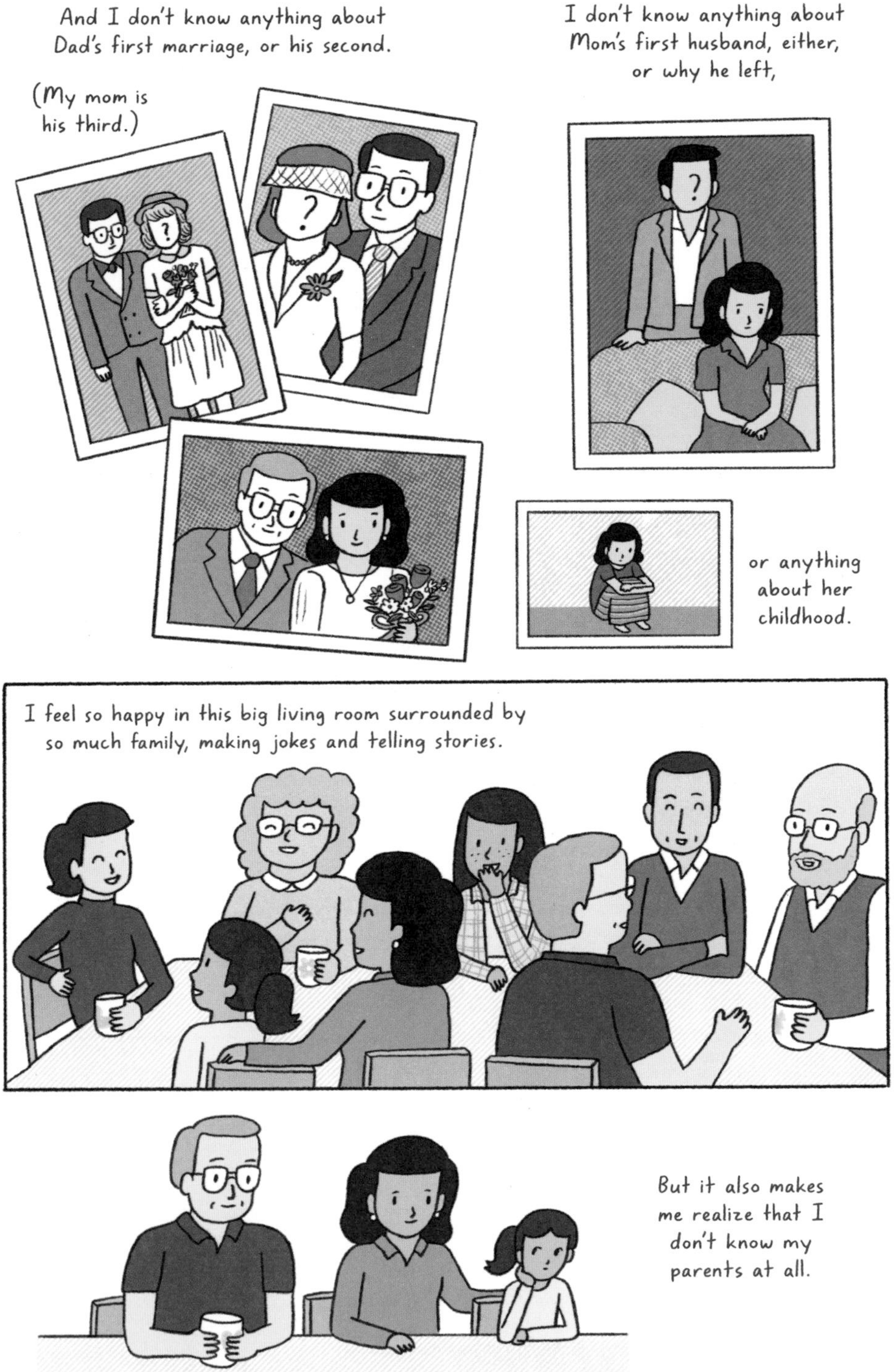
And I don't know anything about Dad's first marriage, or his second.
(My mom is his third.)
I don't know anything about Mom's first husband, either, or why he left,
or anything about her childhood.
I feel so happy in this big living room surrounded by so much family, making jokes and telling stories.
But it also makes me realize that I don't know my parents at all.

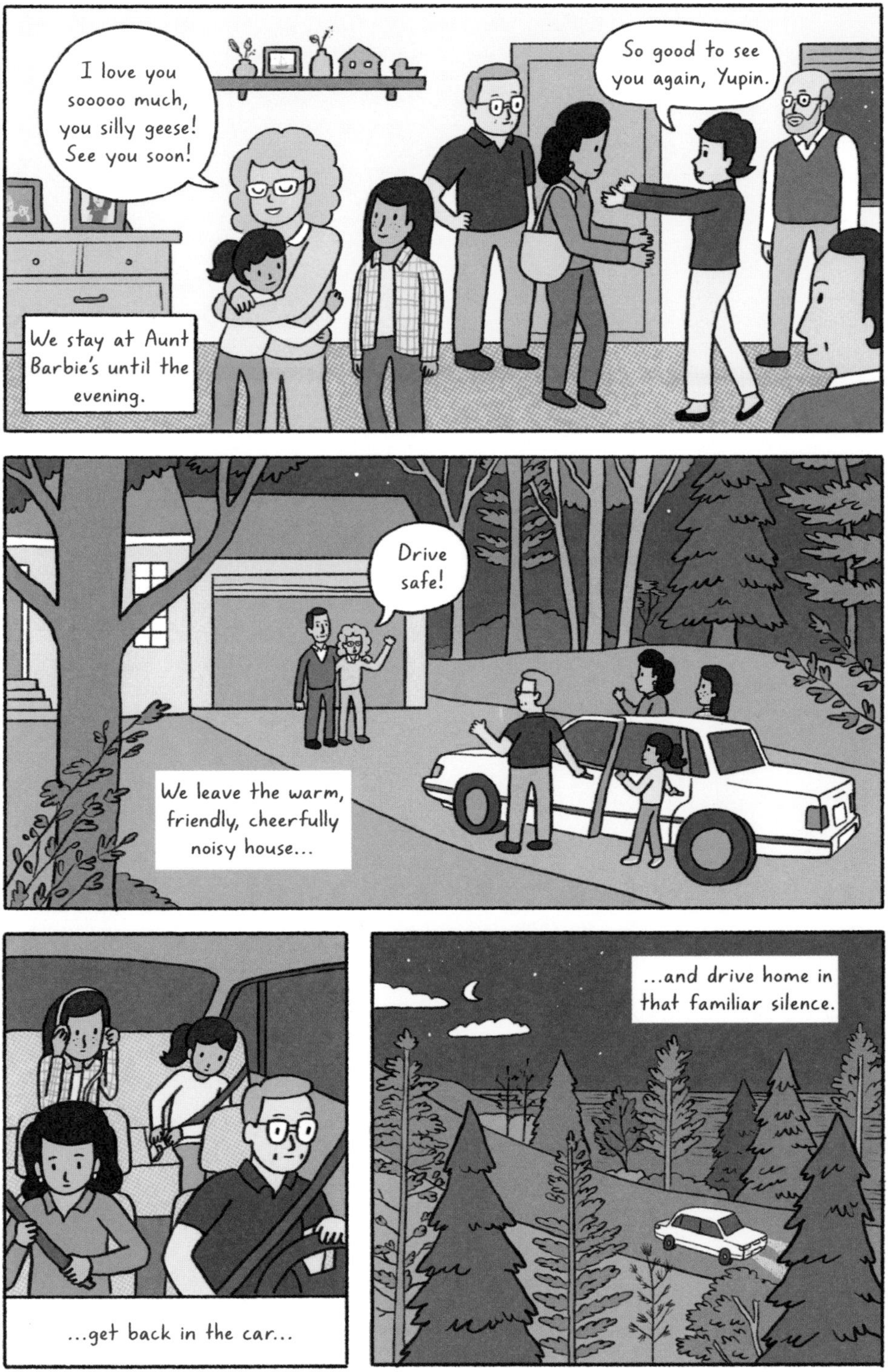
I love you sooooo much, you silly geese! See you soon!
So good to see you again, Yupin.
We stay at Aunt Barbie's until the evening.
Drive safe!
We leave the warm, friendly, cheerfully noisy house...
...get back in the car...
...and drive home in that familiar silence.

5

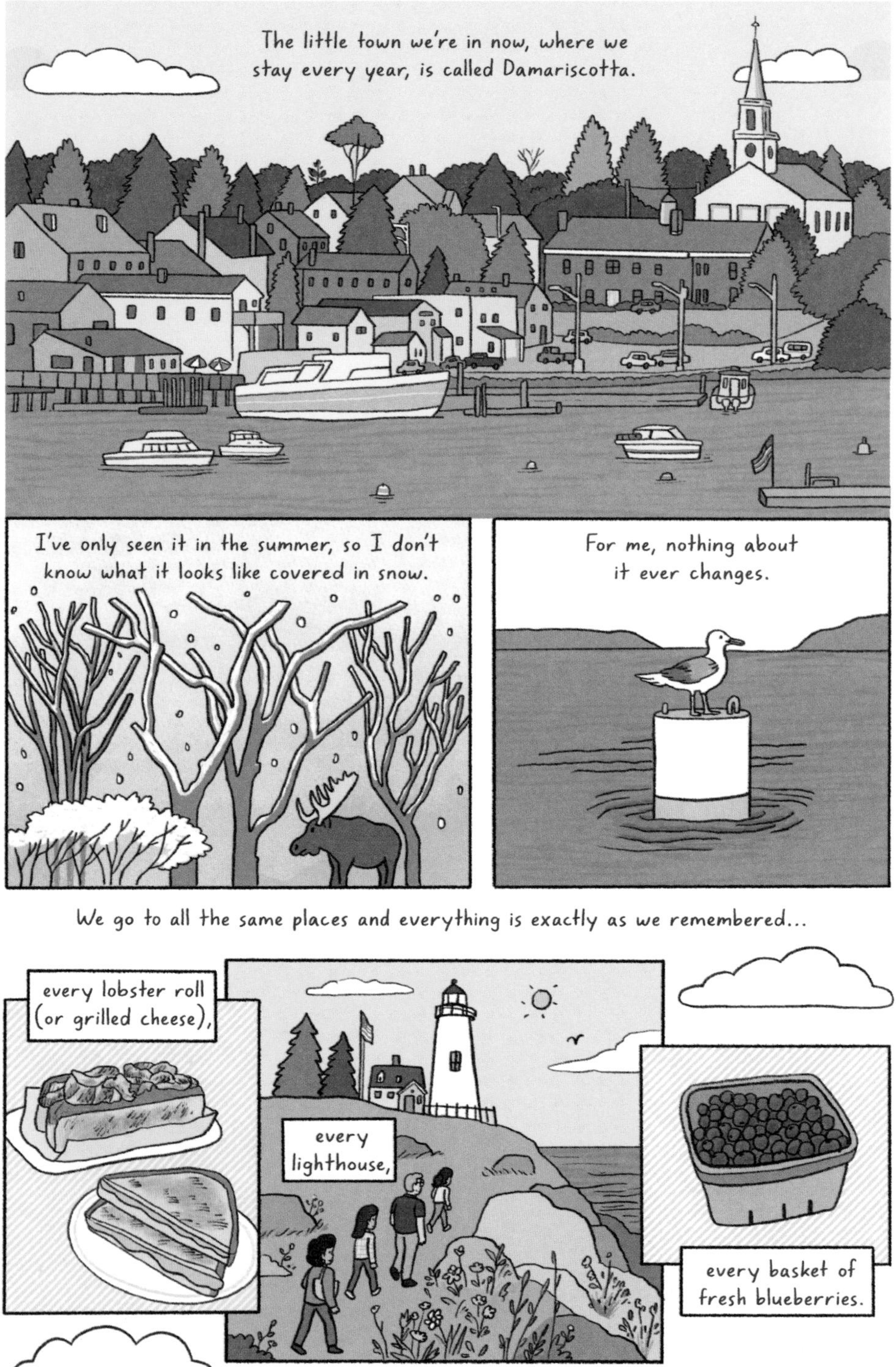
The little town we're in now, where we stay every year, is called Damariscotta.
I've only seen it in the summer, so I don't know what it looks like covered in snow.
For me, nothing about it ever changes.
We go to all the same places and everything is exactly as we remembered...
every lobster roll (or grilled cheese),
every lighthouse,
every basket of fresh blueberries.

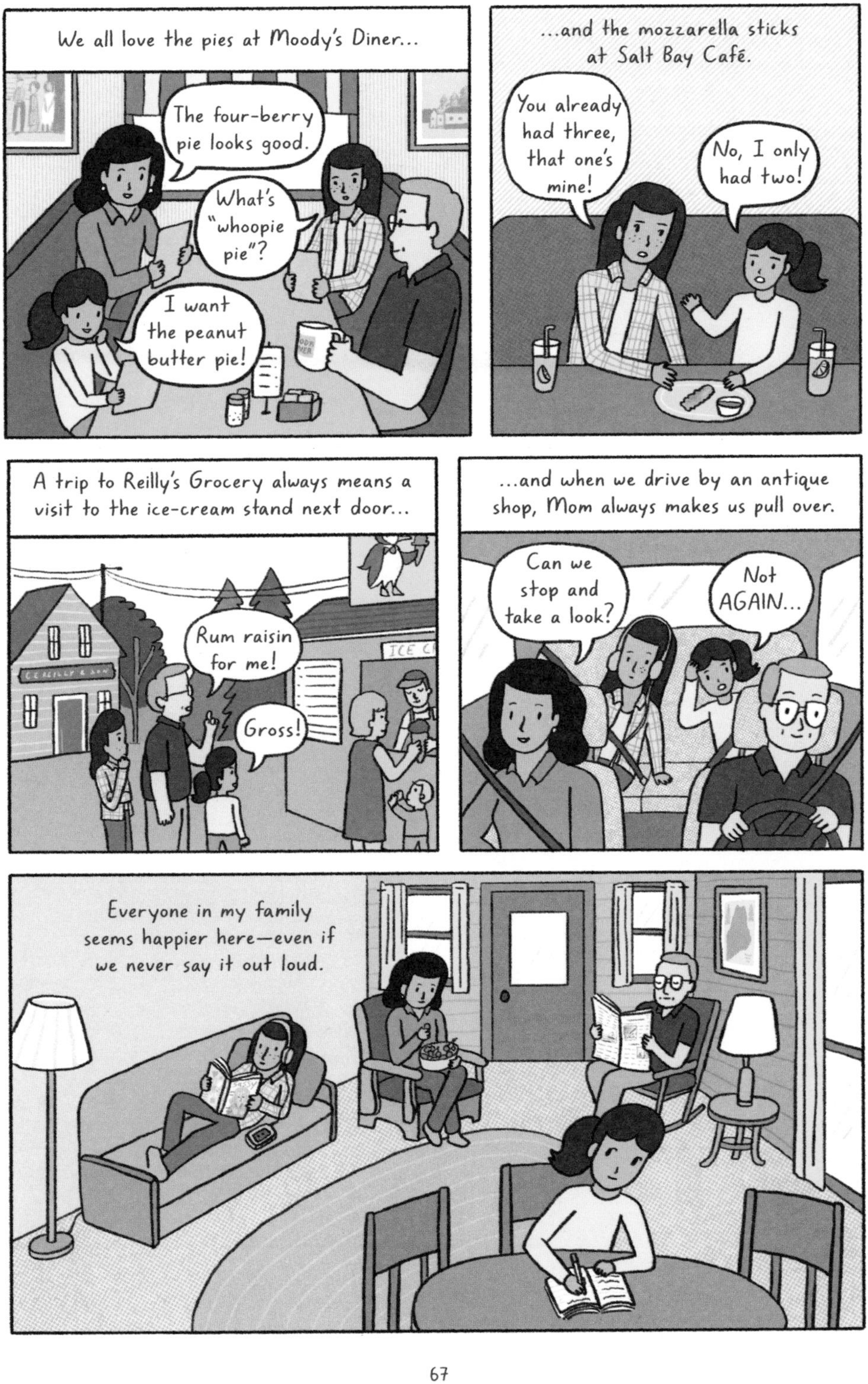
We all love the pies at Moody's Diner...
The four-berry pie looks good.
What's "whoopie pie"?
I want the peanut butter pie!
...and the mozzarella sticks at Salt Bay Café.
You already had three, that one's mine!
No, I only had two!
A trip to Reilly's Grocery always means a visit to the ice-cream stand next door...
Rum raisin for me!
Gross!
ICE C
...and when we drive by an antique shop, Mom always makes us pull over.
Can we stop and take a look?
Not AGAIN...
Everyone in my family seems happier here—even if we never say it out loud.

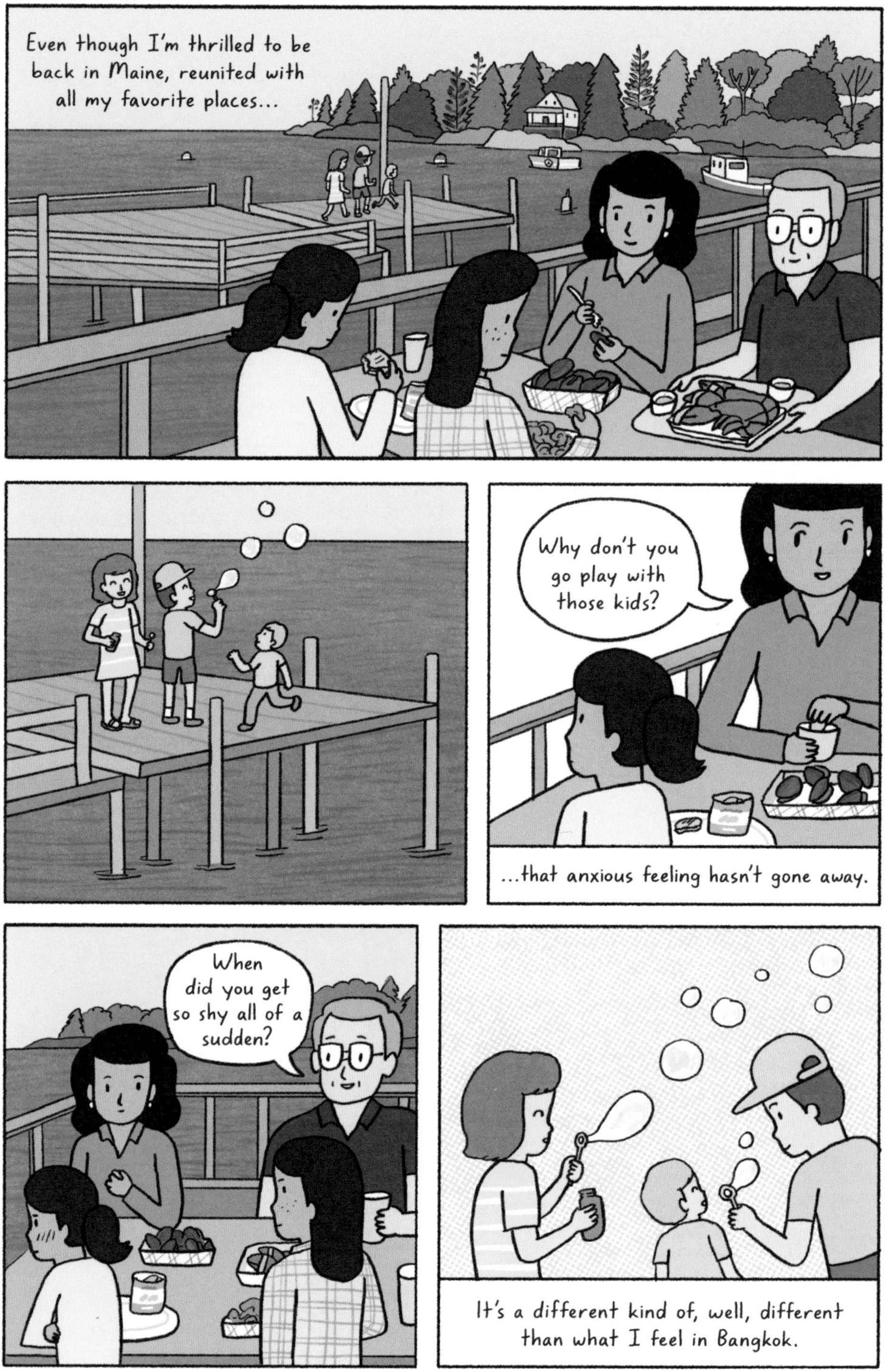
Even though I'm thrilled to be back in Maine, reunited with all my favorite places...
Why don't you go play with those kids?
...that anxious feeling hasn't gone away.
When did you get so shy all of a sudden?
It's a different kind of, well, different than what I feel in Bangkok.

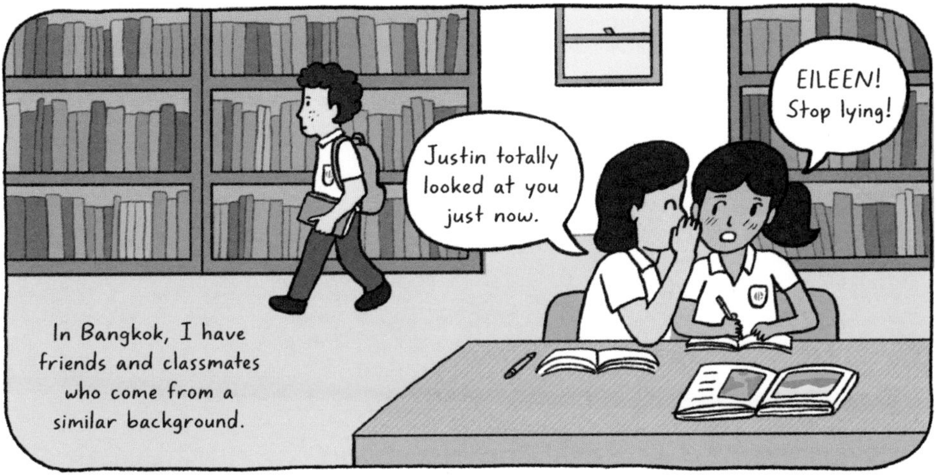
Justin totally looked at you just now.
EILEEN! Stop lying!
In Bangkok, I have friends and classmates who come from a similar background.

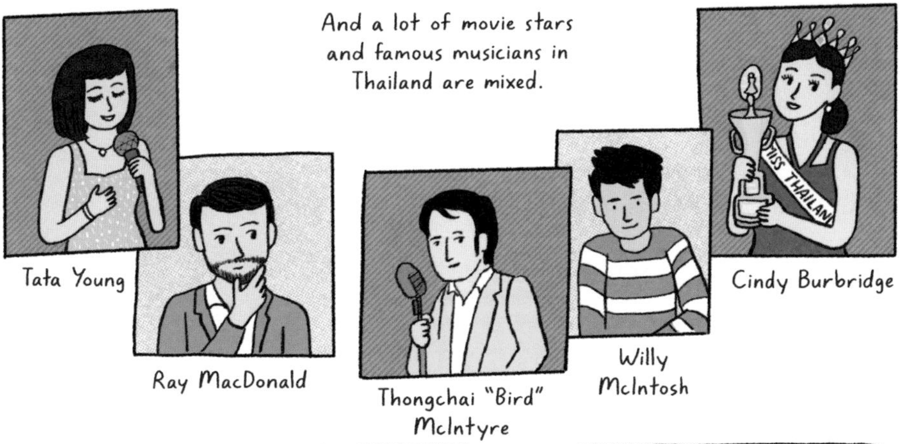
And a lot of movie stars and famous musicians in Thailand are mixed.
MISS THAILAND
Tata Young
Ray MacDonald
Thongchai "Bird" McIntyre
Willy McIntosh
Cindy Burbridge

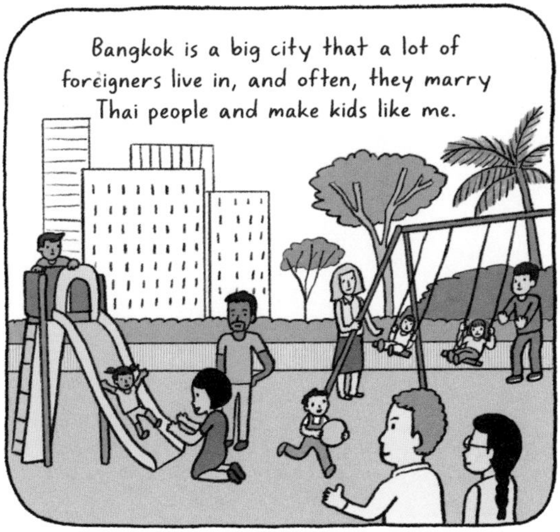
Bangkok is a big city that a lot of foreigners live in, and often, they marry Thai people and make kids like me.

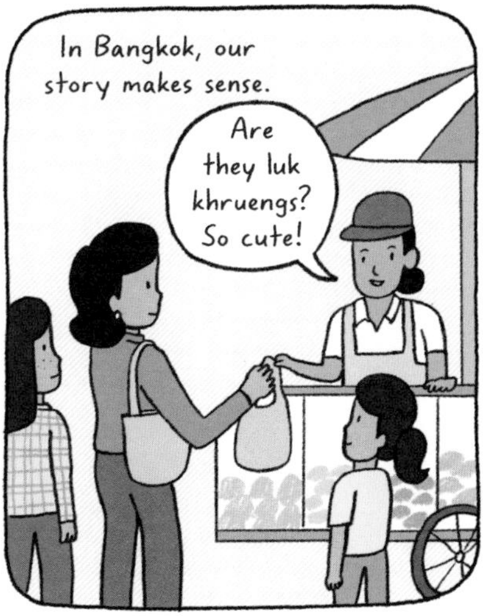
In Bangkok, our story makes sense.
Are they luk khruengs? So cute!

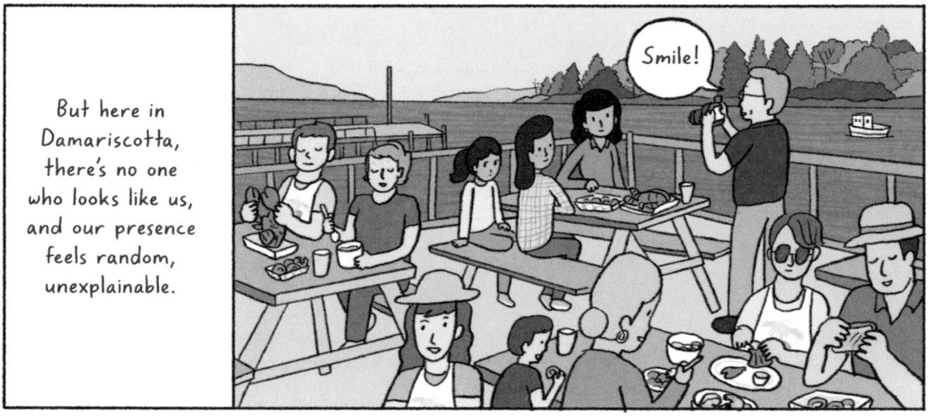
But here in Damariscotta, there's no one who looks like us, and our presence feels random, unexplainable.
Smile!

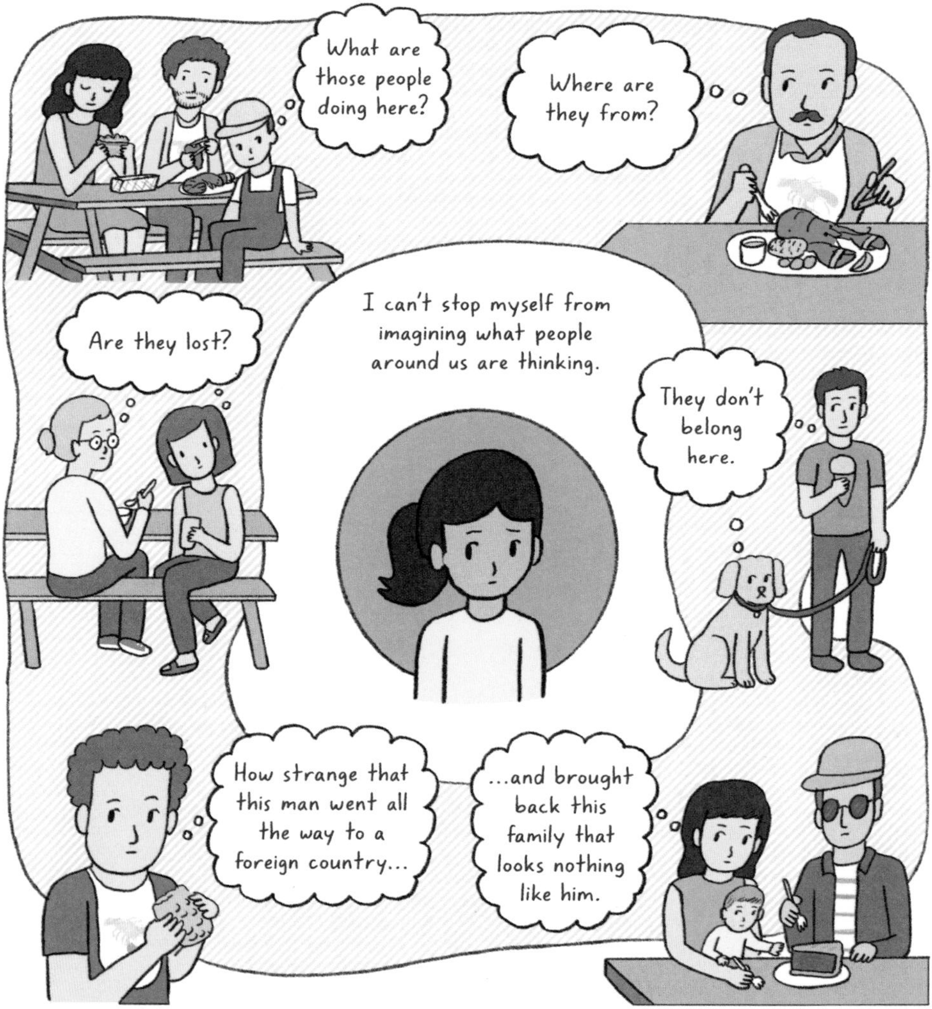
What are those people doing here?
Where are they from?
Are they lost?
I can't stop myself from imagining what people around us are thinking.
They don't belong here.
How strange that this man went all the way to a foreign country...
...and brought back this family that looks nothing like him.

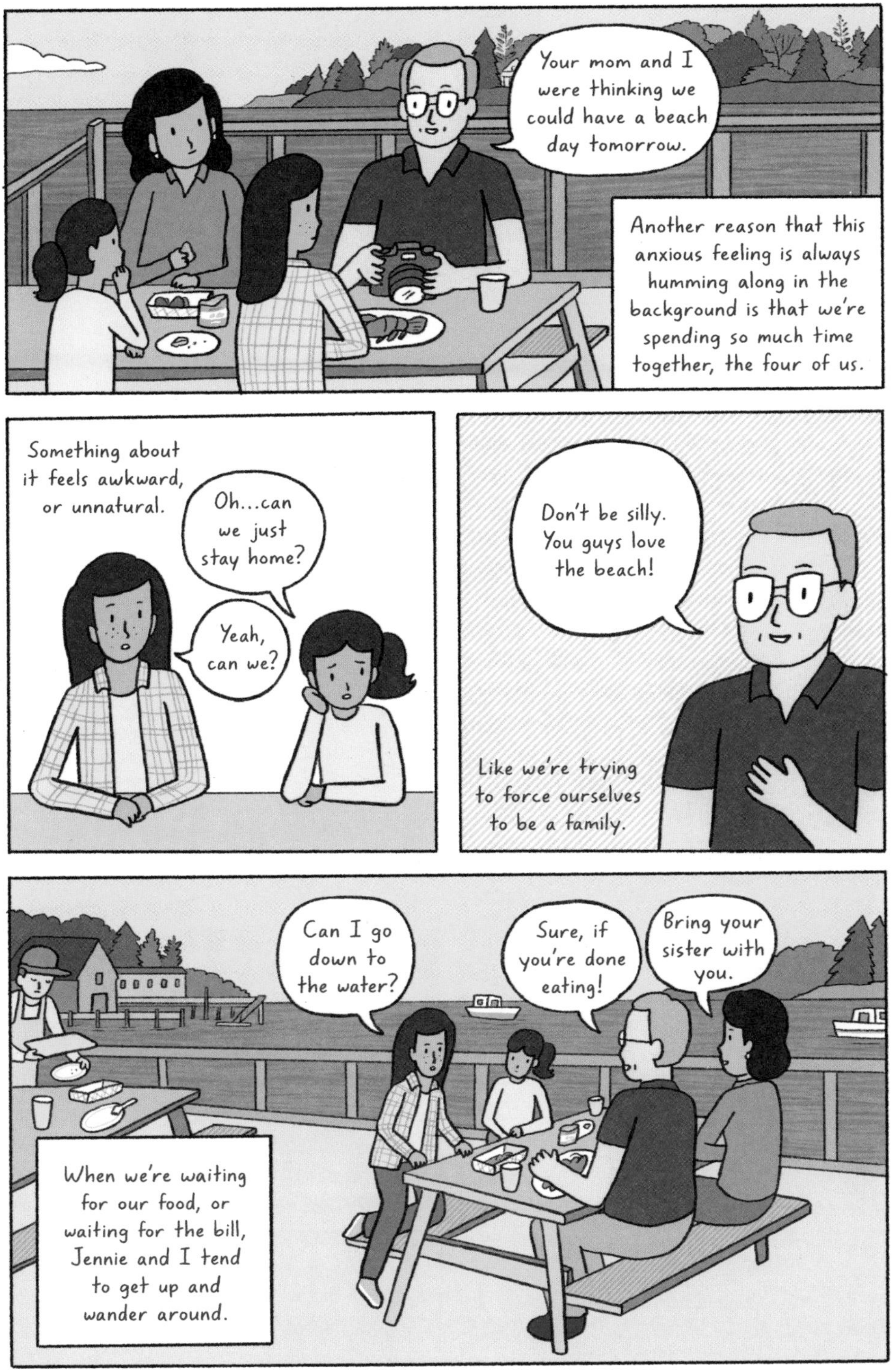
Your mom and I were thinking we could have a beach day tomorrow.
Another reason that this anxious feeling is always humming along in the background is that we're spending so much time together, the four of us.
Something about it feels awkward, or unnatural.
Oh...can we just stay home?
Yeah, can we?
Don't be silly. You guys love the beach!
Like we're trying to force ourselves to be a family.
Can I go down to the water?
Sure, if you're done eating!
Bring your sister with you.
When we're waiting for our food, or waiting for the bill, Jennie and I tend to get up and wander around.

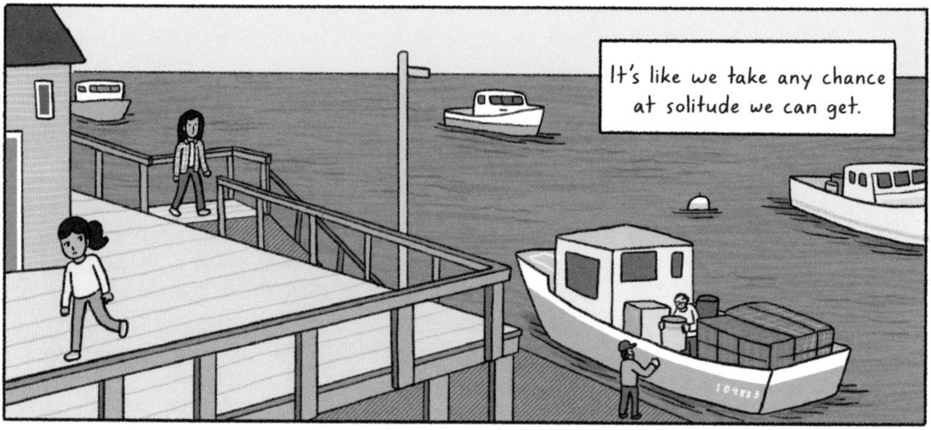
It's like we take any chance at solitude we can get.

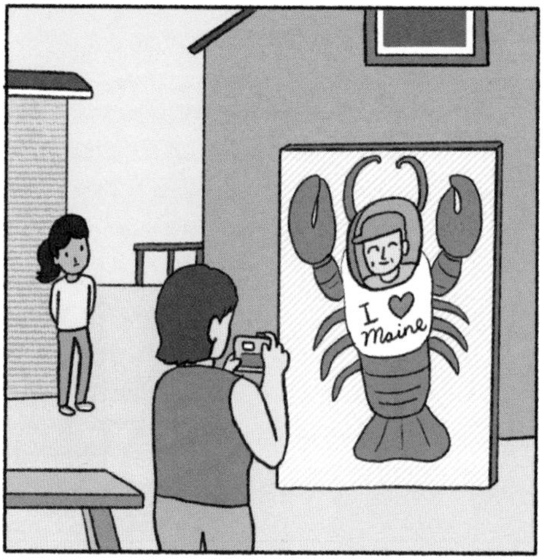
I ♥ Maine

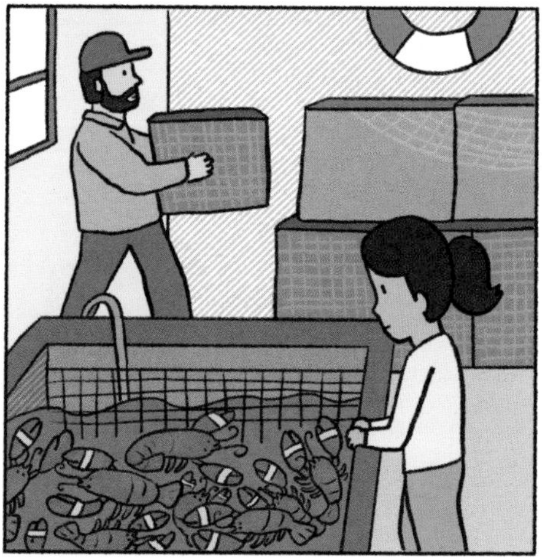

We wander to the gift shop, to the lobster tanks, down to the pier—but never together.

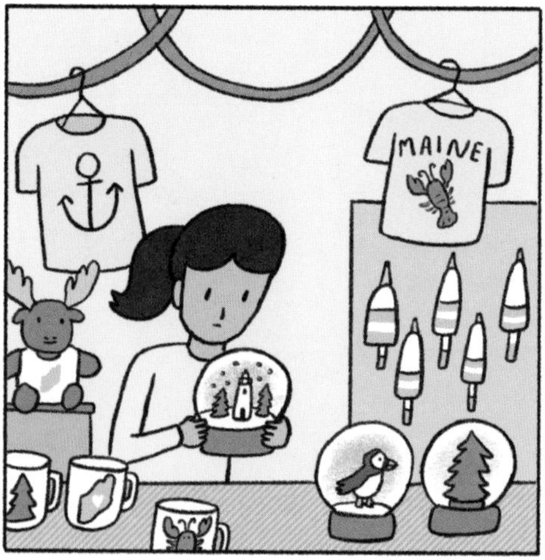
MAINE

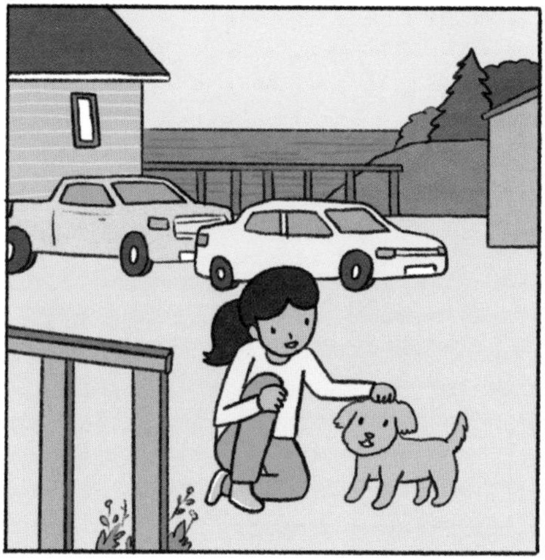

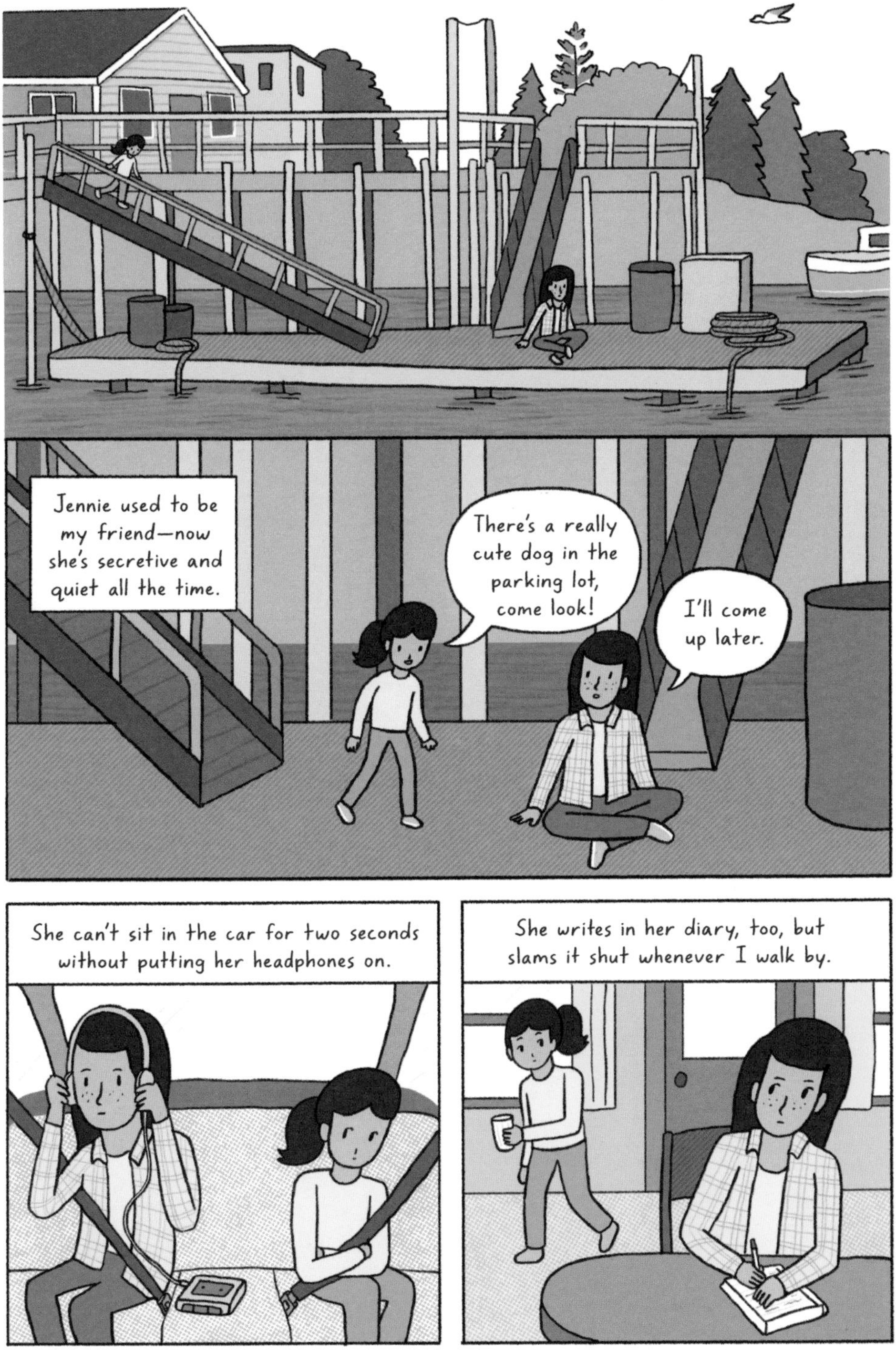
Jennie used to be my friend—now she's secretive and quiet all the time.
There's a really cute dog in the parking lot, come look!
I'll come up later.
She can't sit in the car for two seconds without putting her headphones on.
She writes in her diary, too, but slams it shut whenever I walk by.

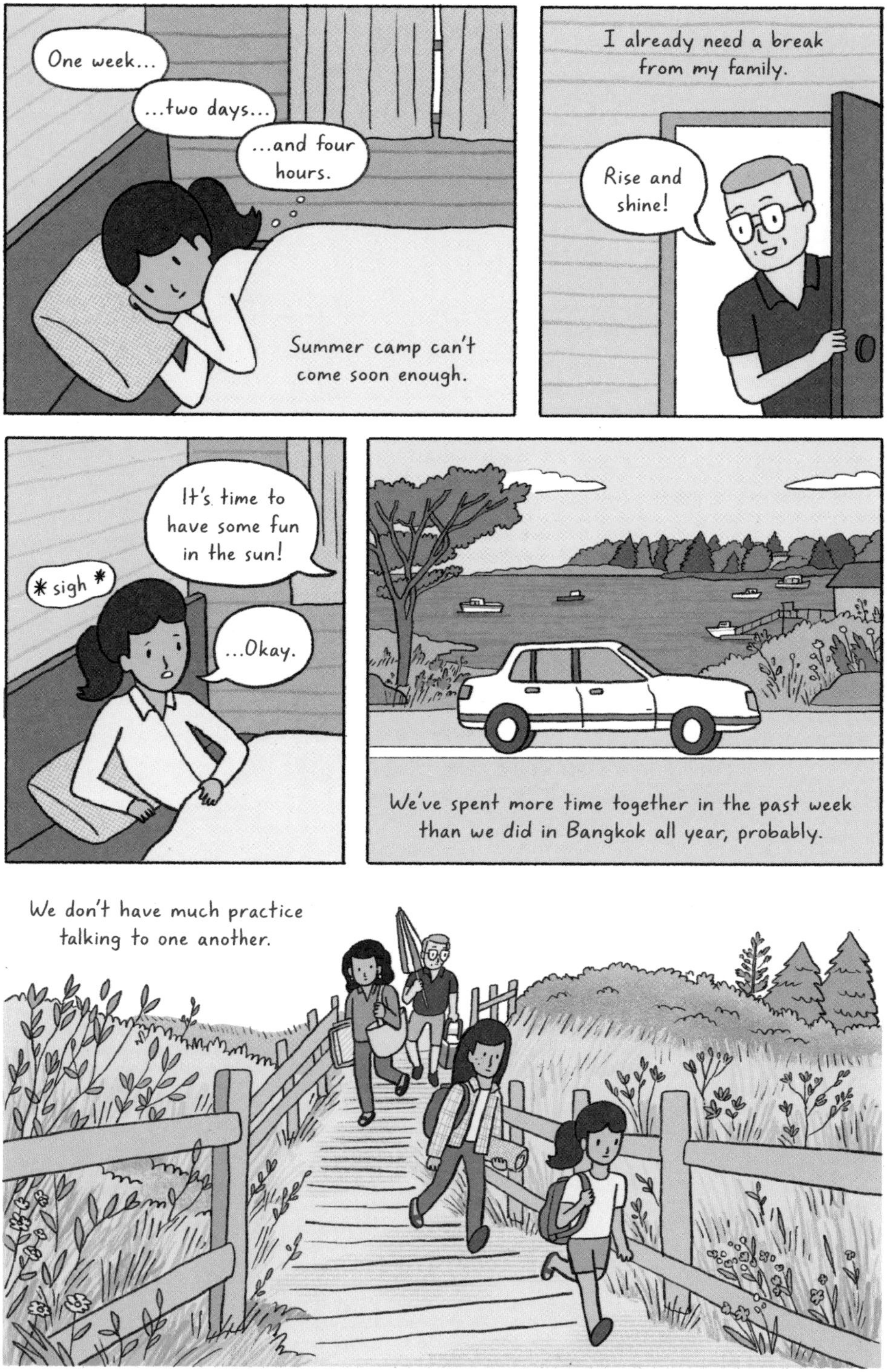
One week...
...two days...
...and four hours.
Summer camp can't come soon enough.
I already need a break from my family.
Rise and shine!
It's time to have some fun in the sun!
sigh
...Okay.
We've spent more time together in the past week than we did in Bangkok all year, probably.
We don't have much practice talking to one another.

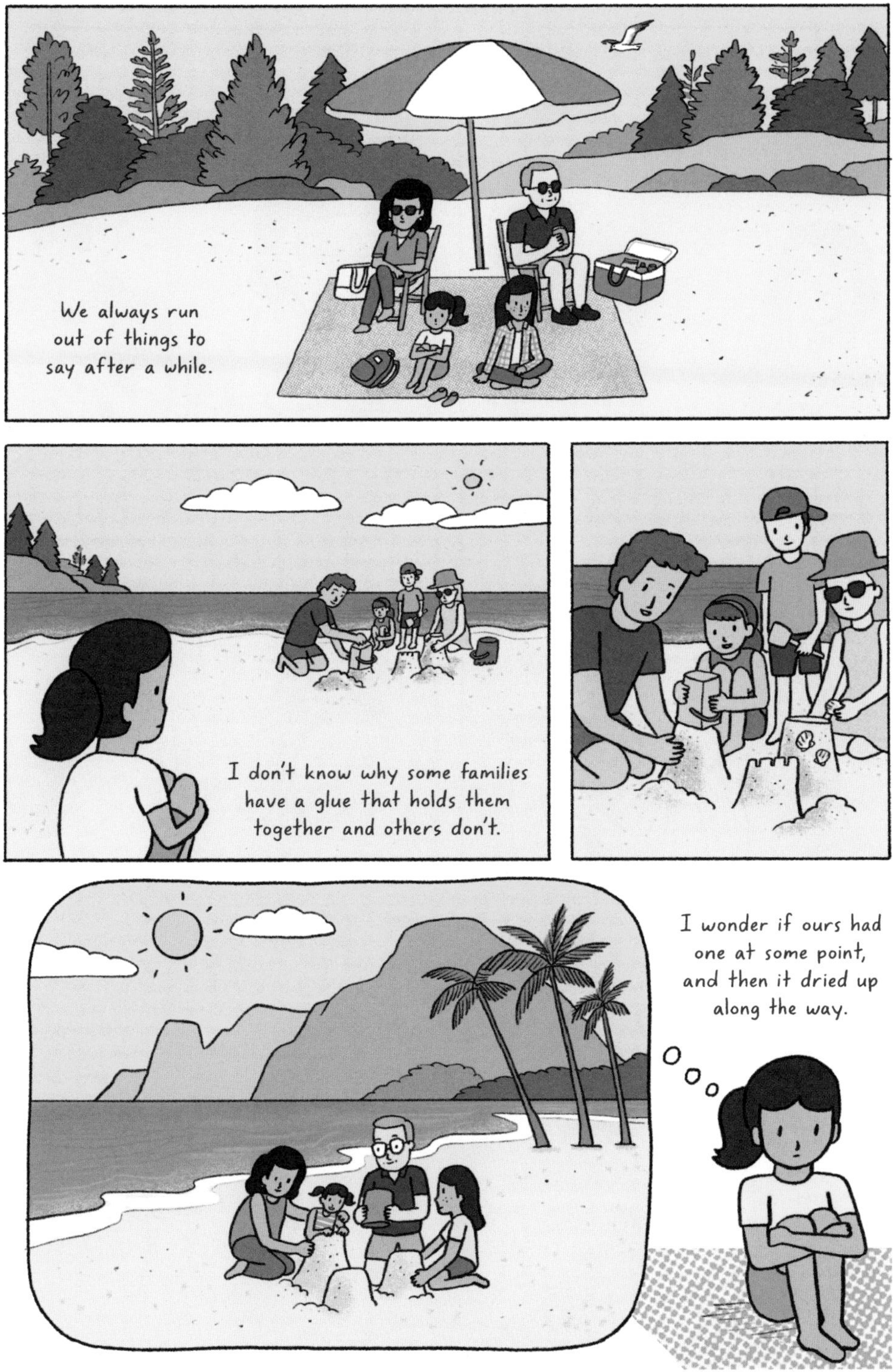
We always run out of things to say after a while.
I don't know why some families have a glue that holds them together and others don't.
I wonder if ours had one at some point, and then it dried up along the way.

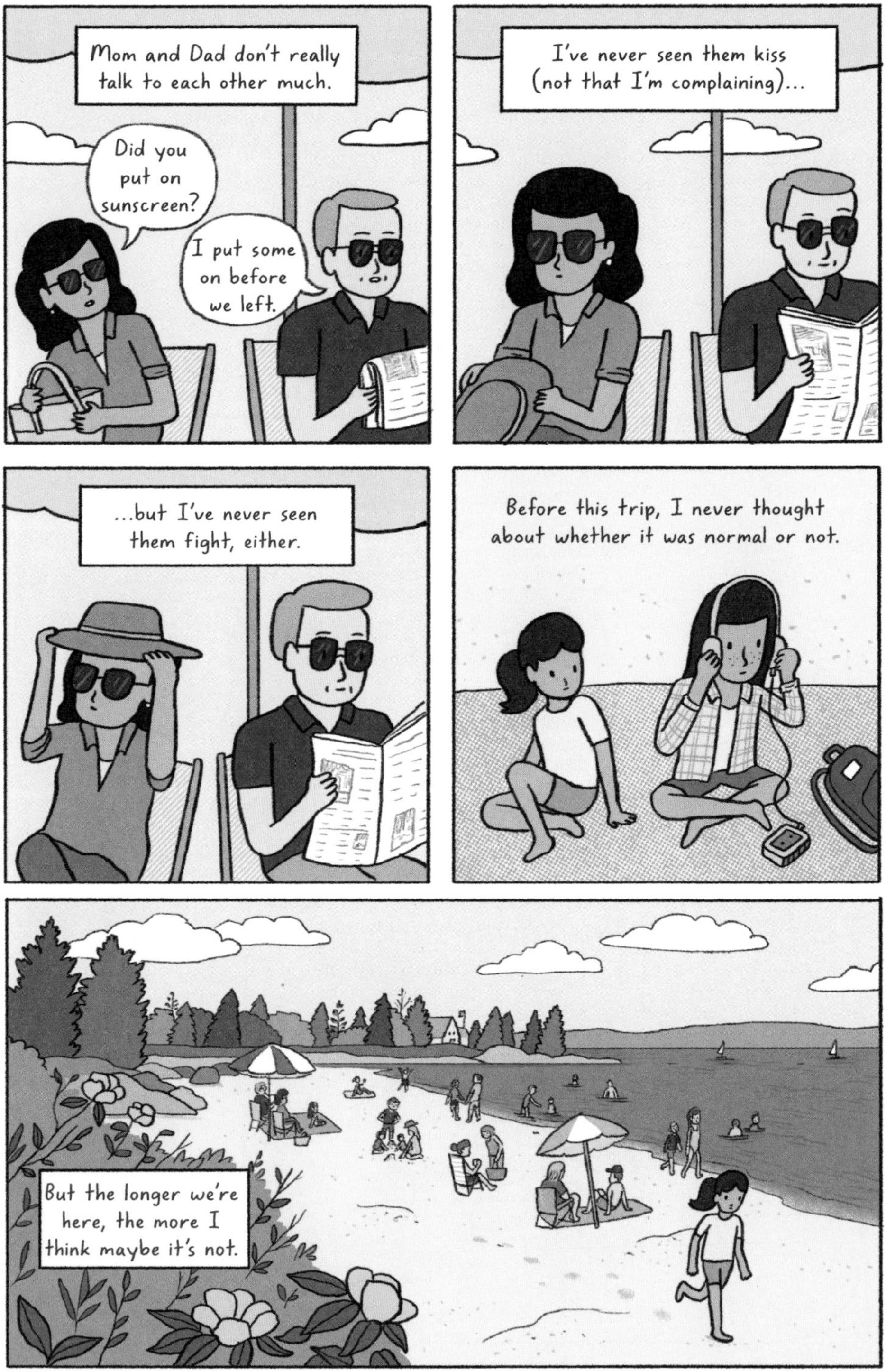
Mom and Dad don't really talk to each other much.
Did you put on sunscreen?
I put some on before we left.
I've never seen them kiss (not that I'm complaining)...
...but I've never seen them fight, either.
Before this trip, I never thought about whether it was normal or not.
But the longer we're here, the more I think maybe it's not.

Aunt Louise and Uncle Bob are always debating
and arguing, but in a playful and loving way.

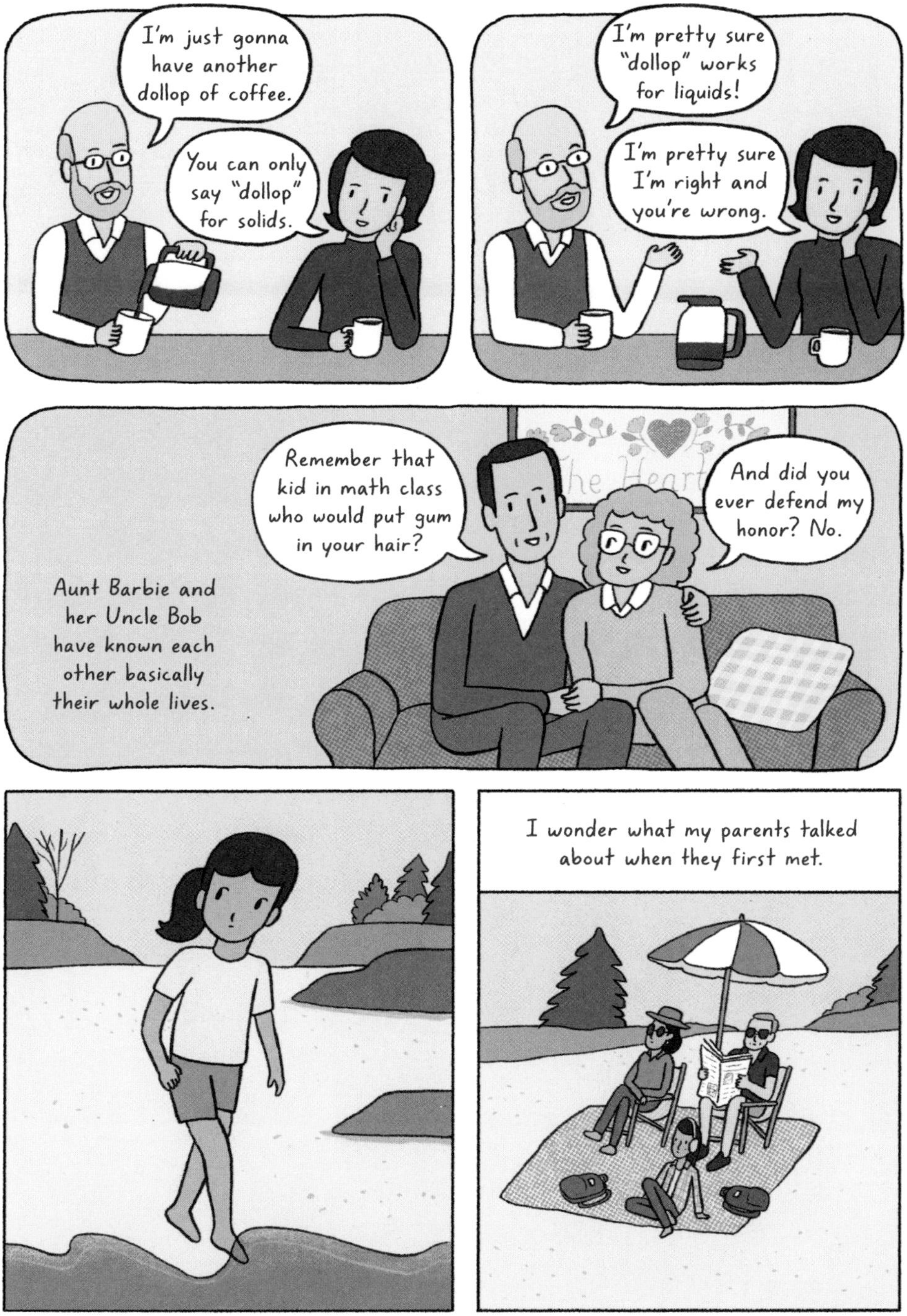
I'm just gonna have another dollop of coffee.
You can only say "dollop" for solids.
I'm pretty sure "dollop" works for liquids!
I'm pretty sure I'm right and you're wrong.
Aunt Barbie and her Uncle Bob have known each other basically their whole lives.
Remember that kid in math class who would put gum in your hair?
And did you ever defend my honor? No.
I wonder what my parents talked about when they first met.

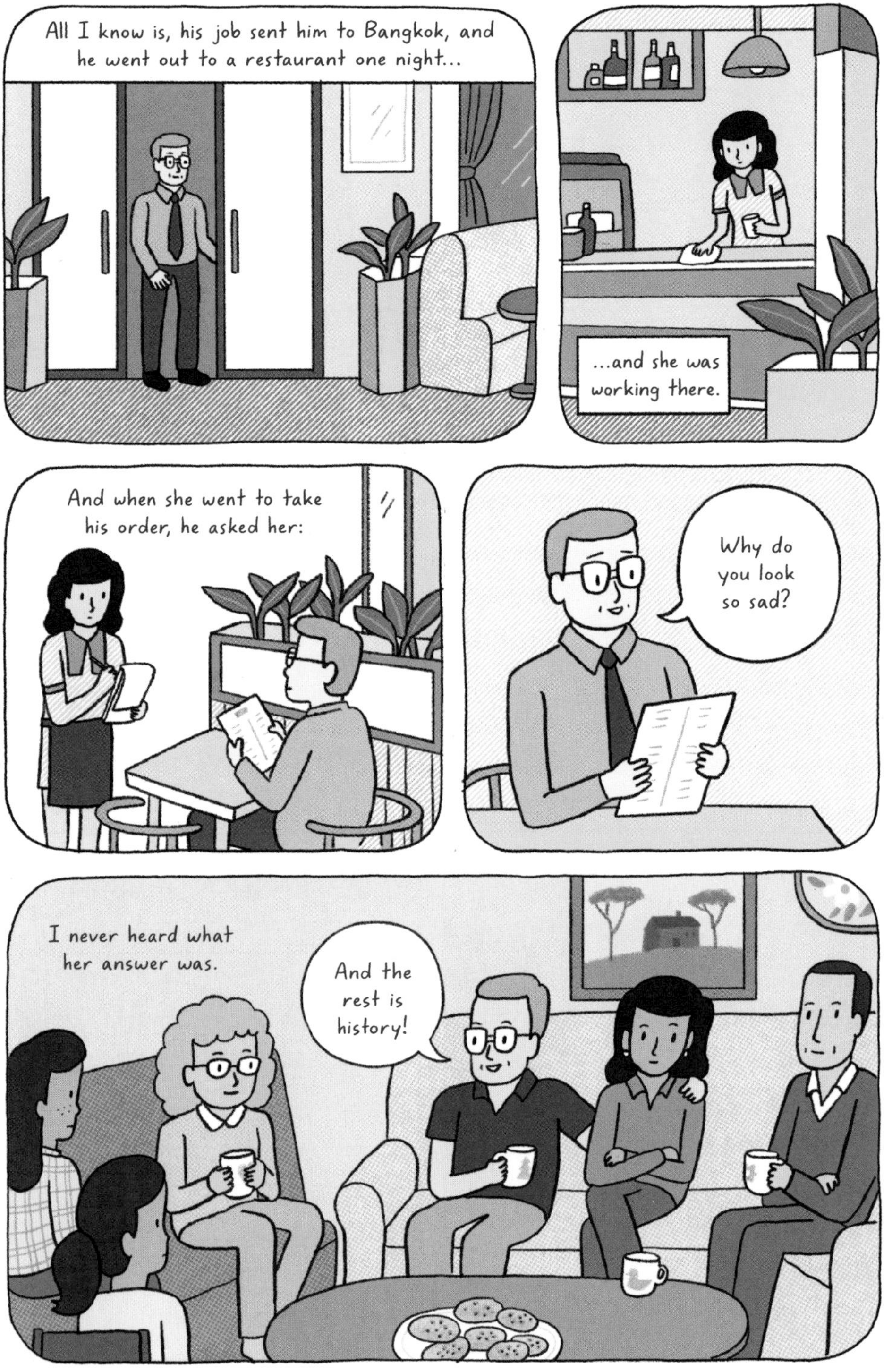

All I know is, his job sent him to Bangkok, and he went out to a restaurant one night...
...and she was working there.
And when she went to take his order, he asked her:
Why do you look so sad?
I never heard what her answer was.
And the rest is history!

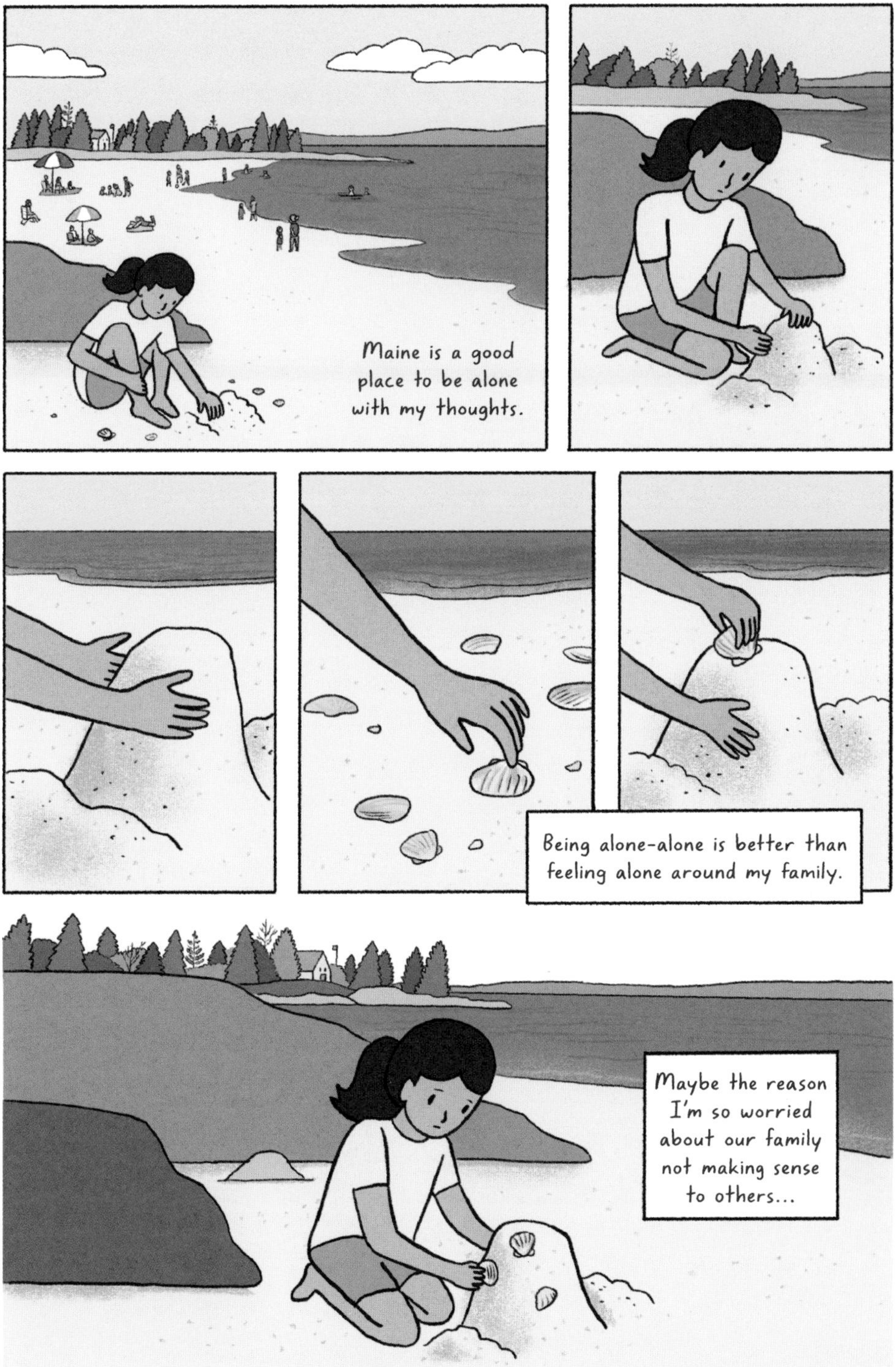
Maine is a good place to be alone with my thoughts.
Being alone-alone is better than feeling alone around my family.
Maybe the reason I'm so worried about our family not making sense to others...

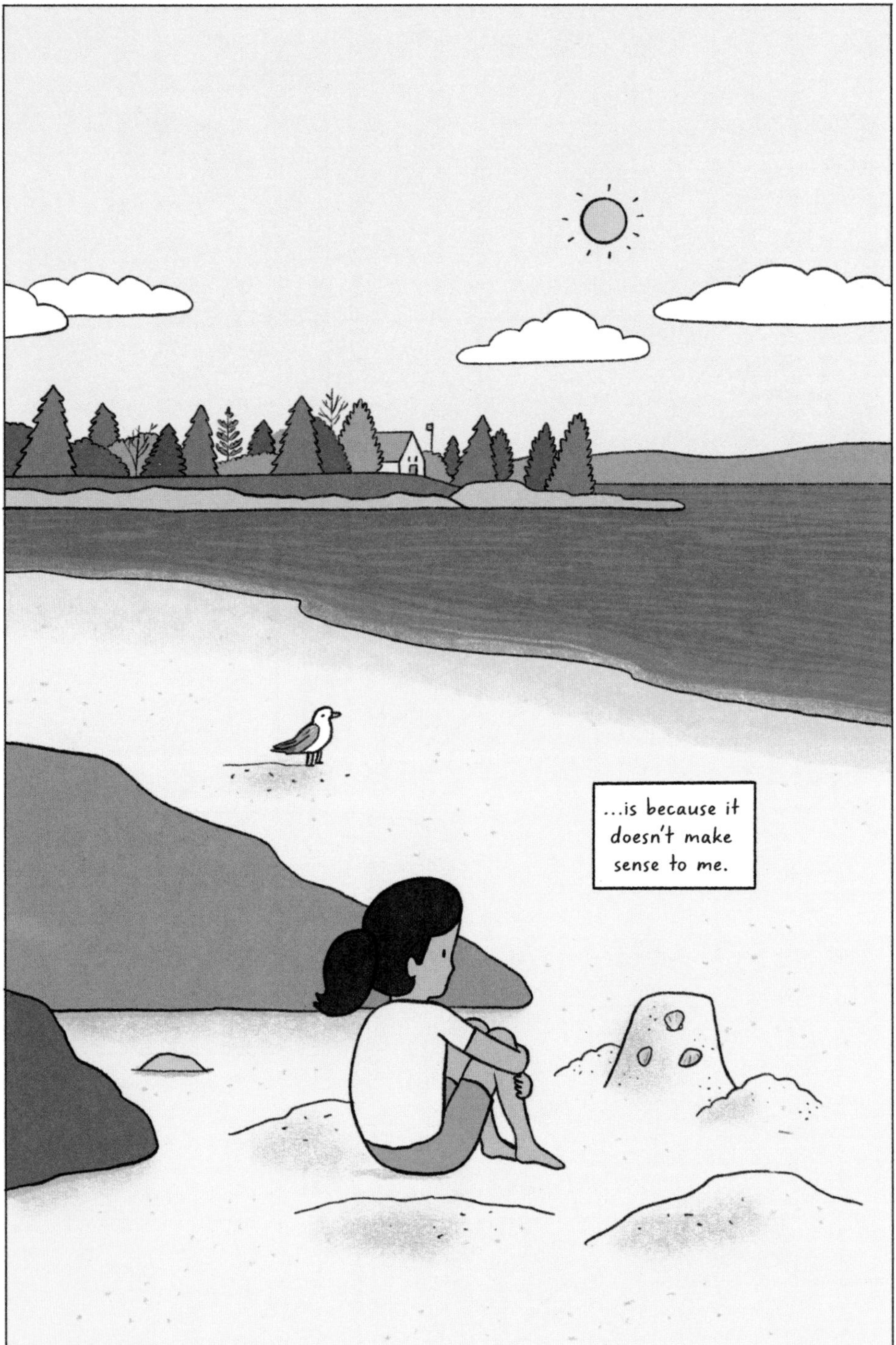
...is because it doesn't make sense to me.

6

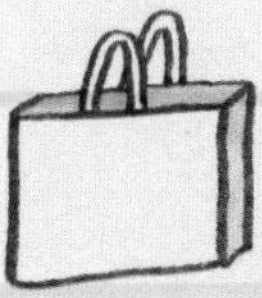

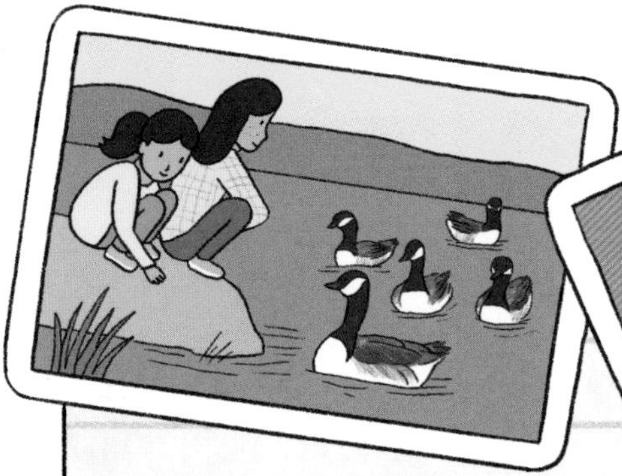

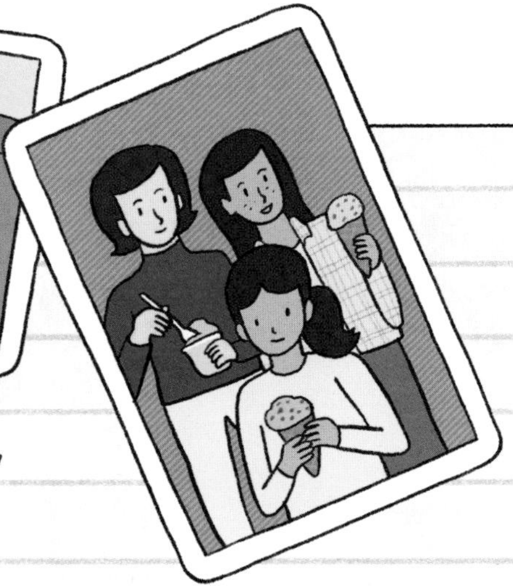

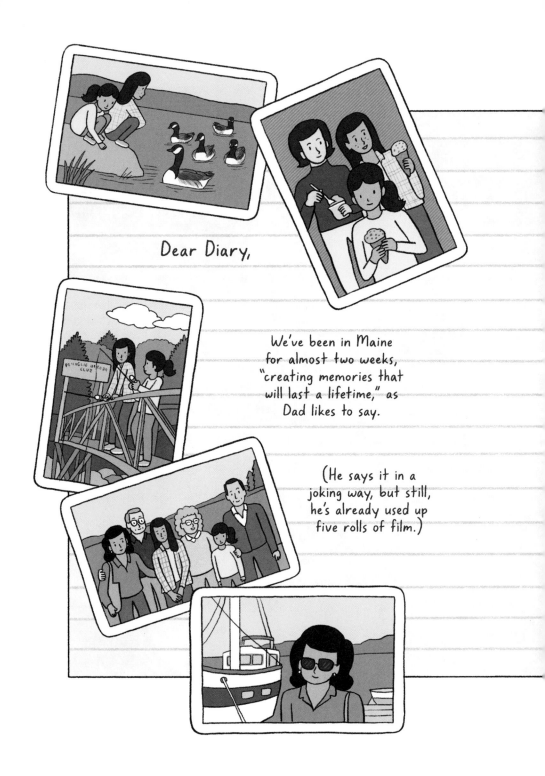

Dear Diary,

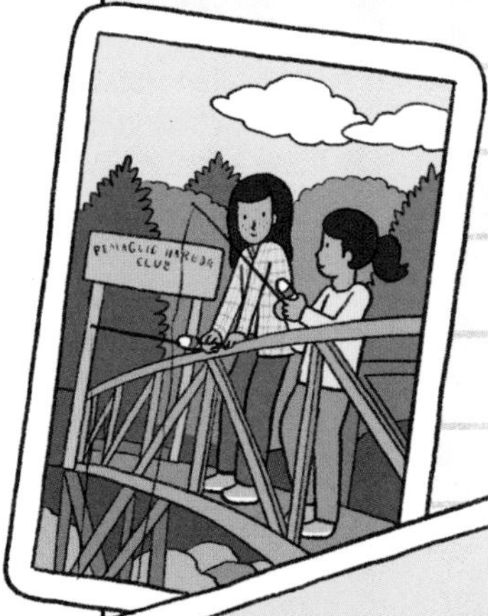

We've been in Maine
for almost two weeks,
"creating memories that
will last a lifetime," as
Dad likes to say.

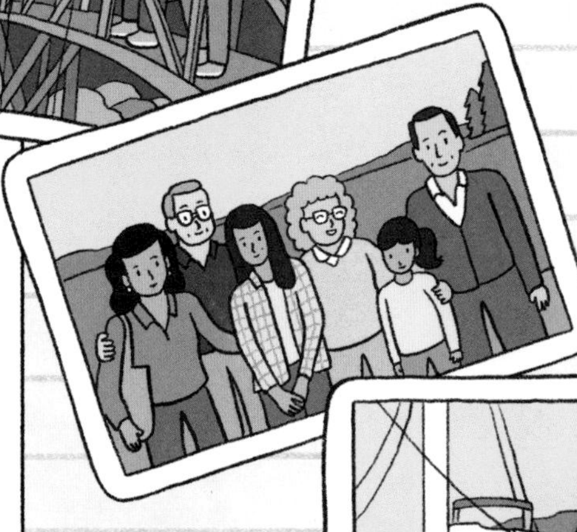

(He says it in a
joking way, but still,
he's already used up
five rolls of film.)

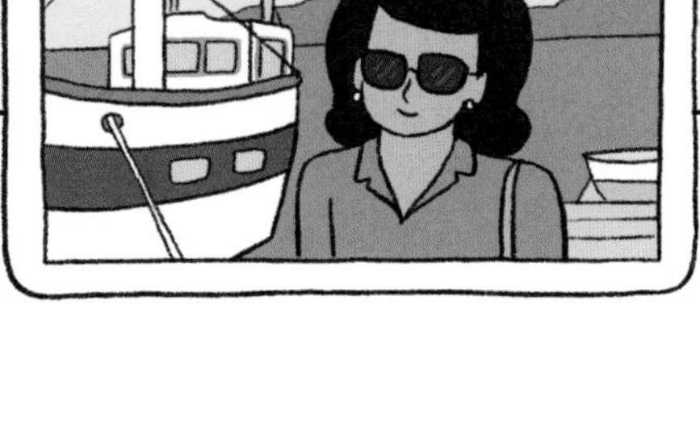

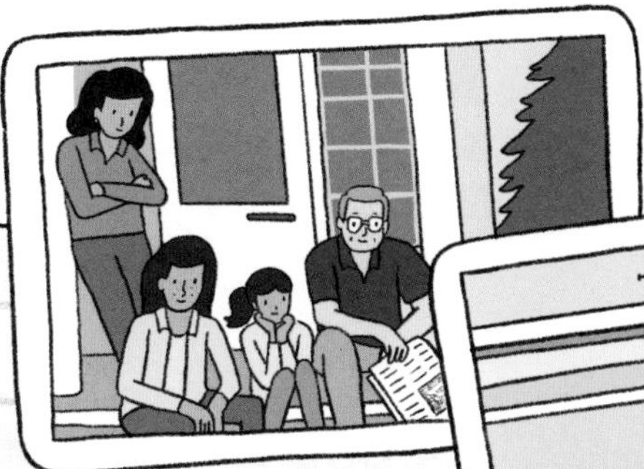

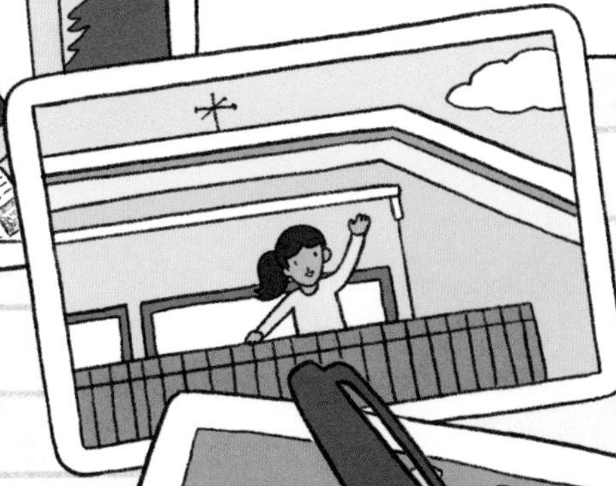

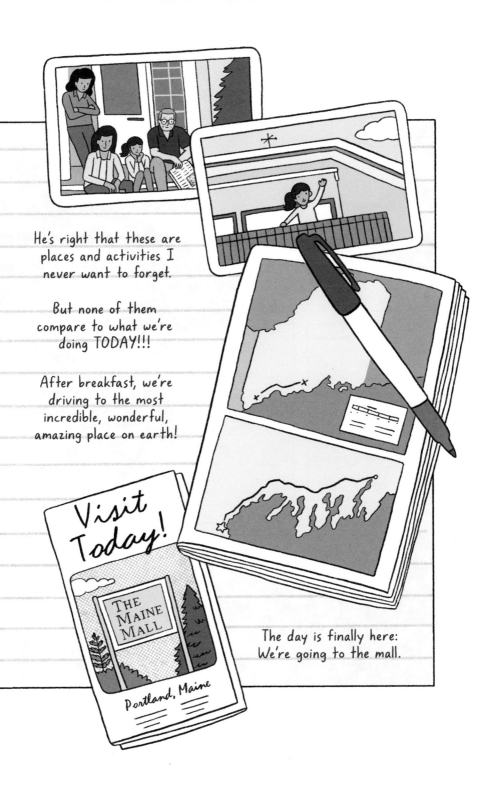

He's right that these are
places and activities I
never want to forget.

But none of them
compare to what we're
doing TODAY!!!

After breakfast, we're
driving to the most
incredible, wonderful,
amazing place on earth!

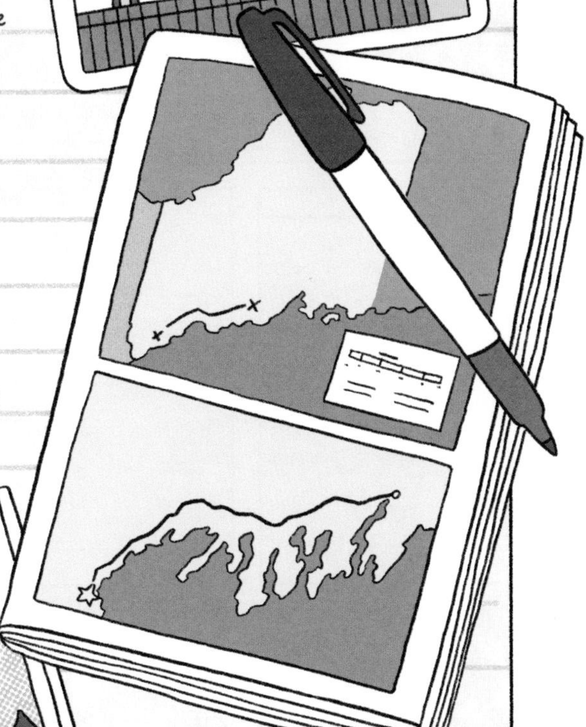

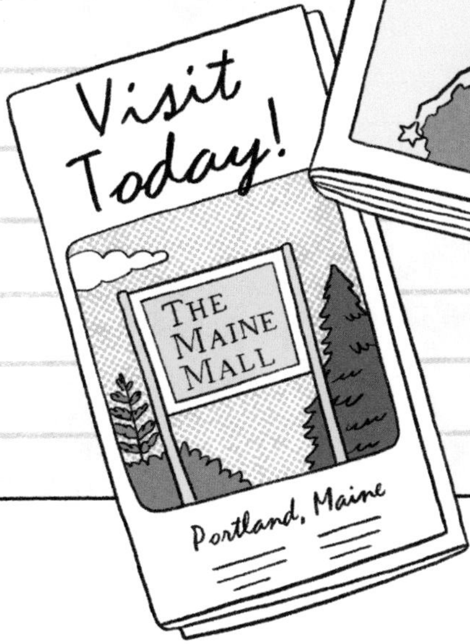
Visit Today!
THE MAINE MALL
Portland, Maine

The day is finally here:
We're going to the mall.

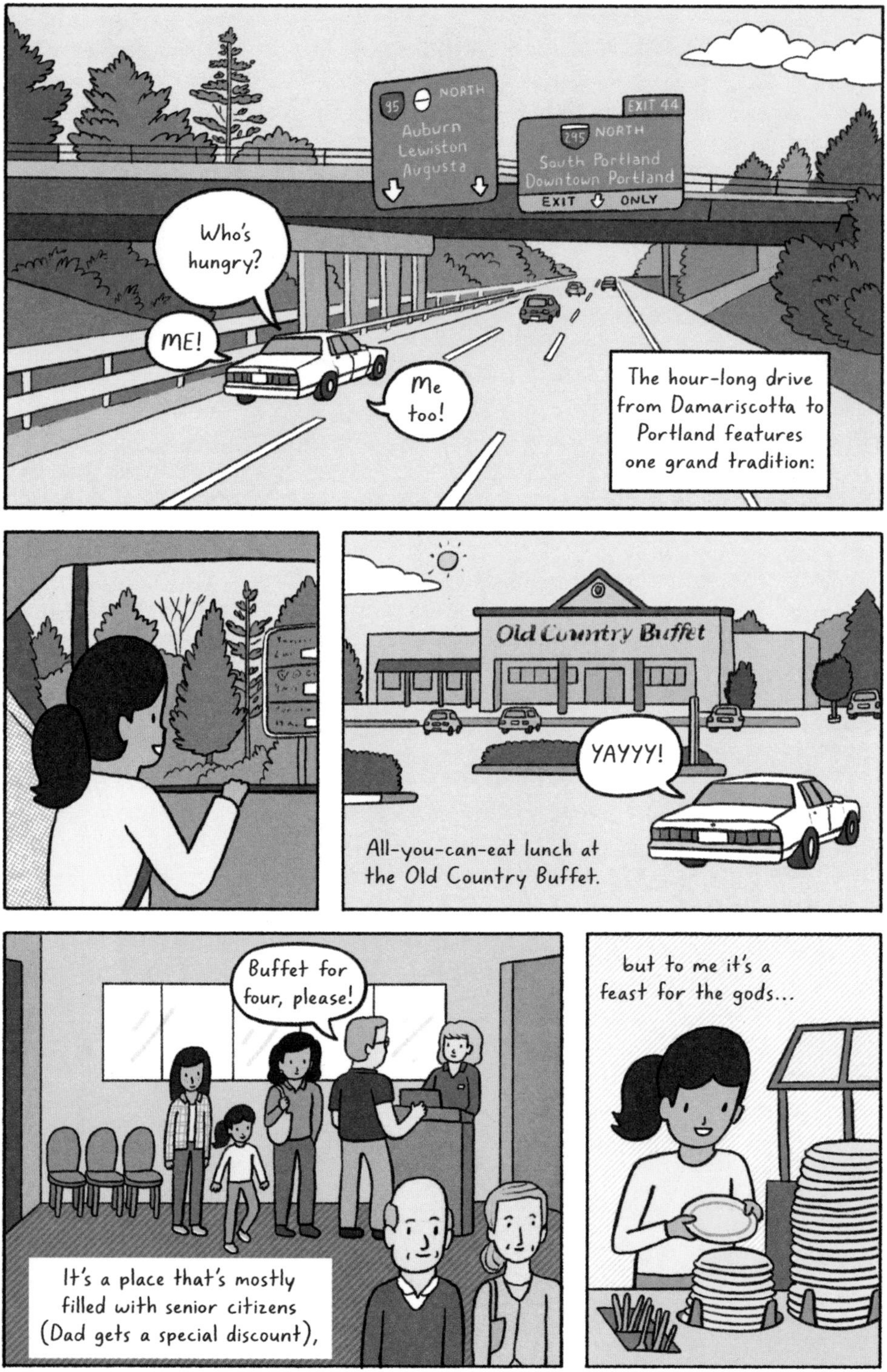
95 NORTH
Auburn
Lewiston
Augusta
EXIT 44
295 NORTH
South Portland
Downtown Portland
EXIT ONLY
Who's hungry?
ME!
Me too!
The hour-long drive from Damariscotta to Portland features one grand tradition:
Old Country Buffet
YAYYY!
All-you-can-eat lunch at the Old Country Buffet.
Buffet for four, please!
It's a place that's mostly filled with senior citizens (Dad gets a special discount),
but to me it's a feast for the gods...

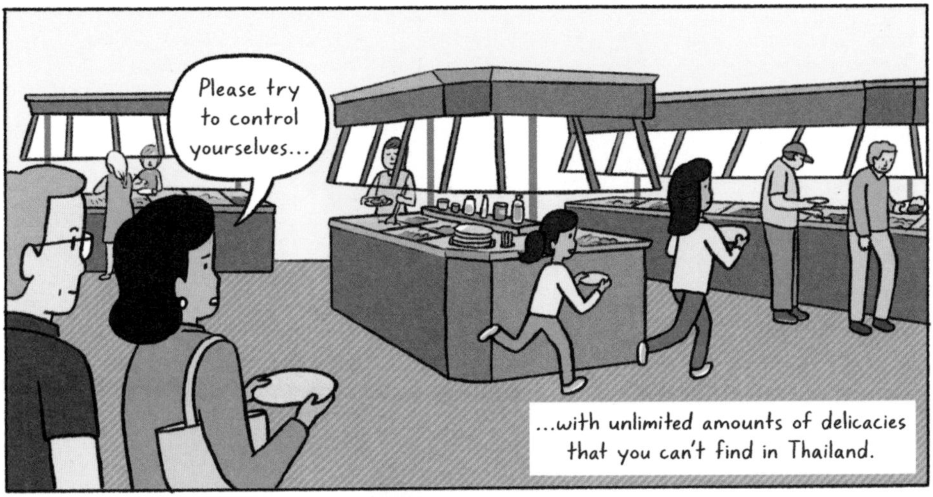
Please try to control yourselves...
...with unlimited amounts of delicacies that you can't find in Thailand.

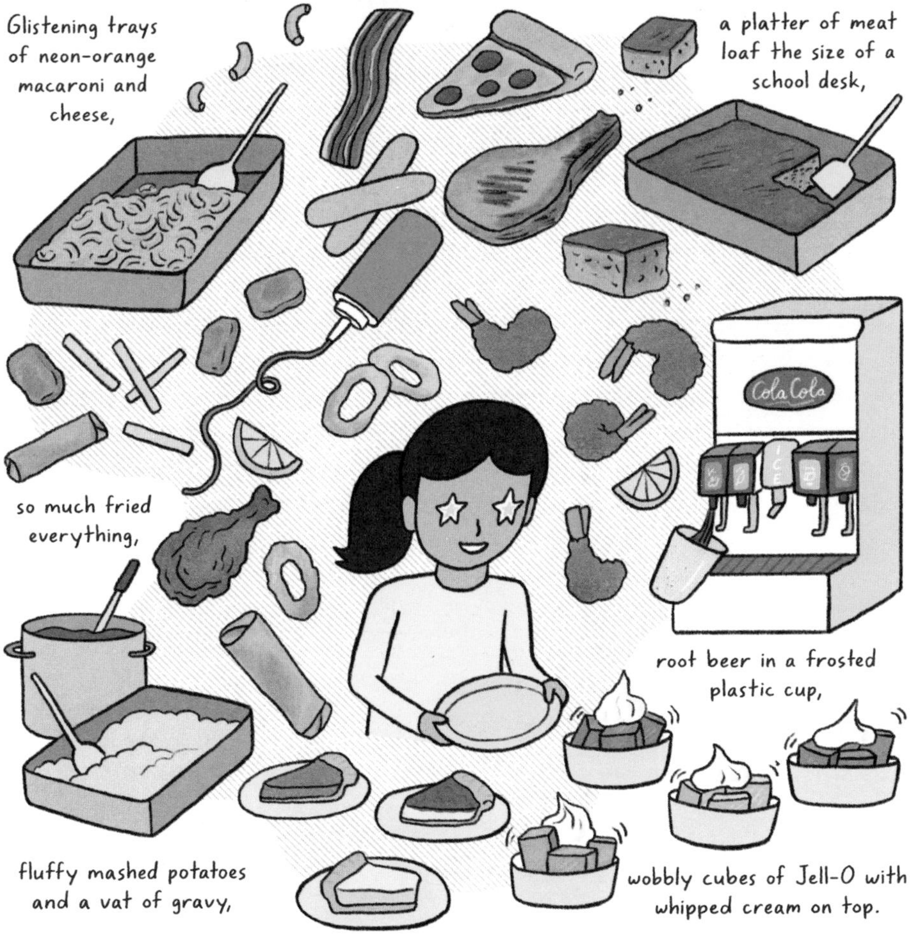
Glistening trays of neon-orange macaroni and cheese,
a platter of meat loaf the size of a school desk,
Cola Cola
so much fried everything,
root beer in a frosted plastic cup,
fluffy mashed potatoes and a vat of gravy,
wobbly cubes of Jell-O with whipped cream on top.

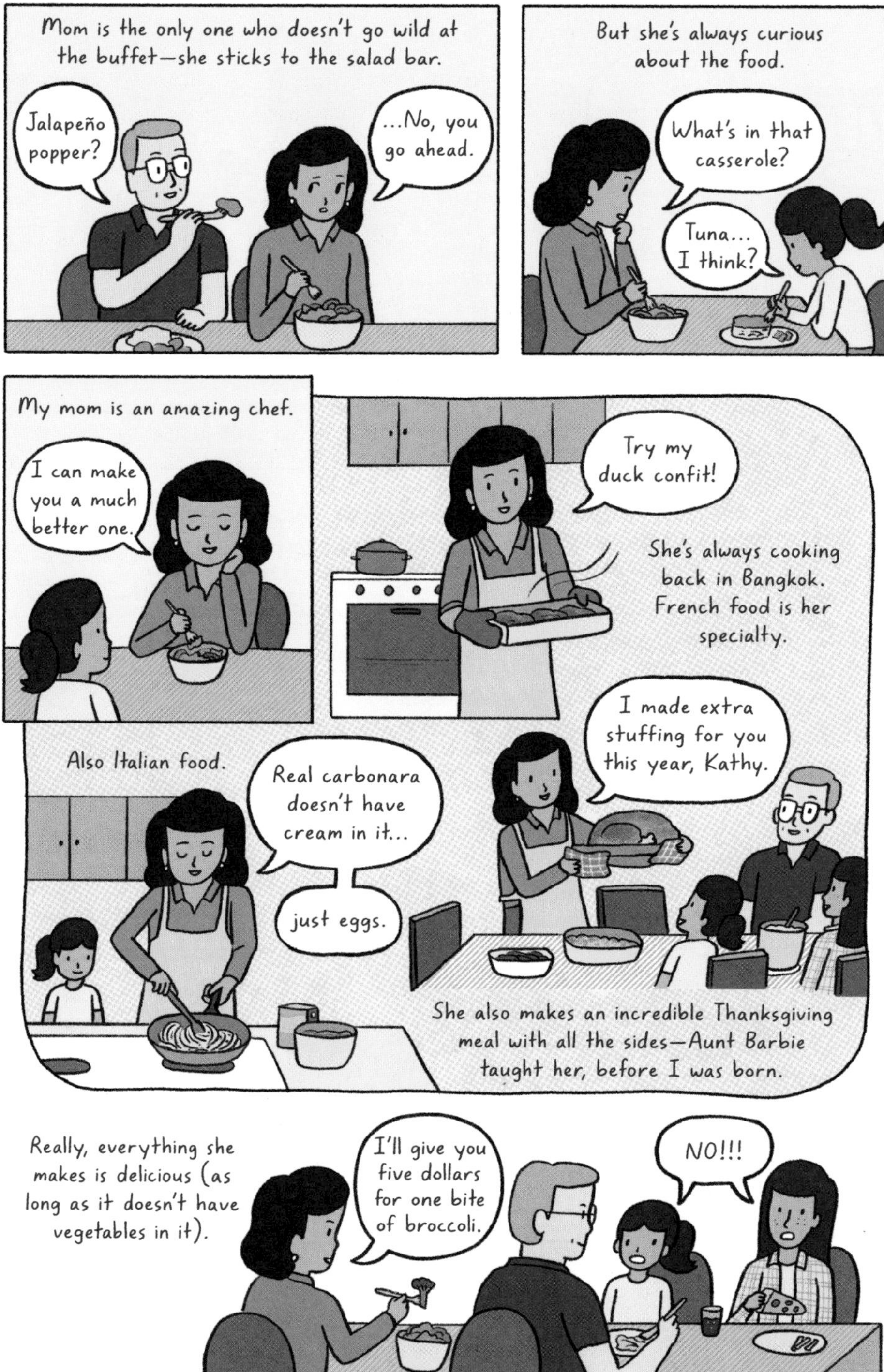
Mom is the only one who doesn't go wild at the buffet—she sticks to the salad bar.
Jalapeño popper?
...No, you go ahead.
But she's always curious about the food.
What's in that casserole?
Tuna... I think?
My mom is an amazing chef.
I can make you a much better one.
Try my duck confit!
She's always cooking back in Bangkok. French food is her specialty.
Also Italian food.
Real carbonara doesn't have cream in it...
just eggs.
I made extra stuffing for you this year, Kathy.
She also makes an incredible Thanksgiving meal with all the sides—Aunt Barbie taught her, before I was born.
Really, everything she makes is delicious (as long as it doesn't have vegetables in it).
I'll give you five dollars for one bite of broccoli.
NO!!!

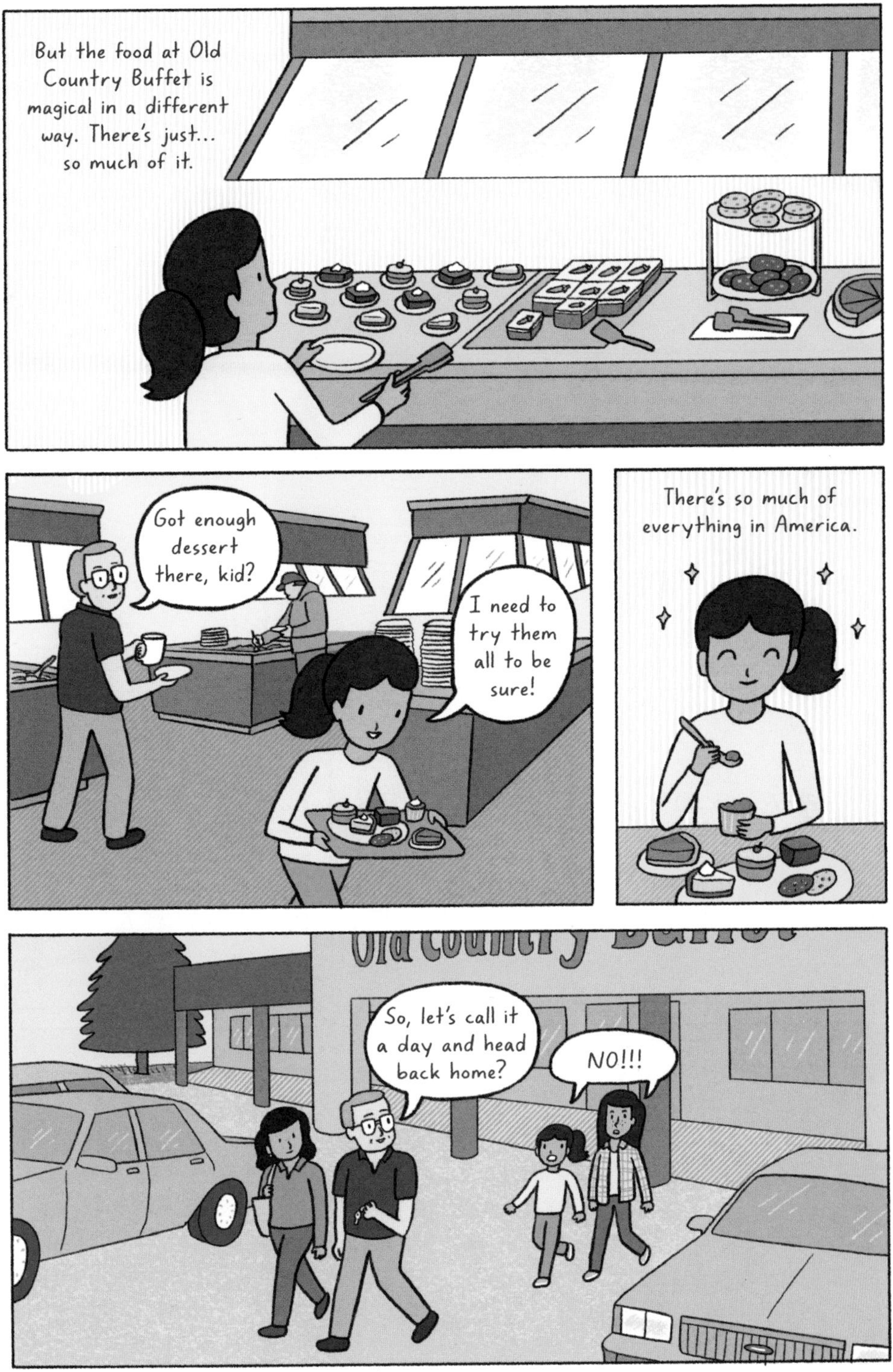
But the food at Old Country Buffet is magical in a different way. There's just... so much of it.
Got enough dessert there, kid?
I need to try them all to be sure!
There's so much of everything in America.
So, let's call it a day and head back home?
NO!!!

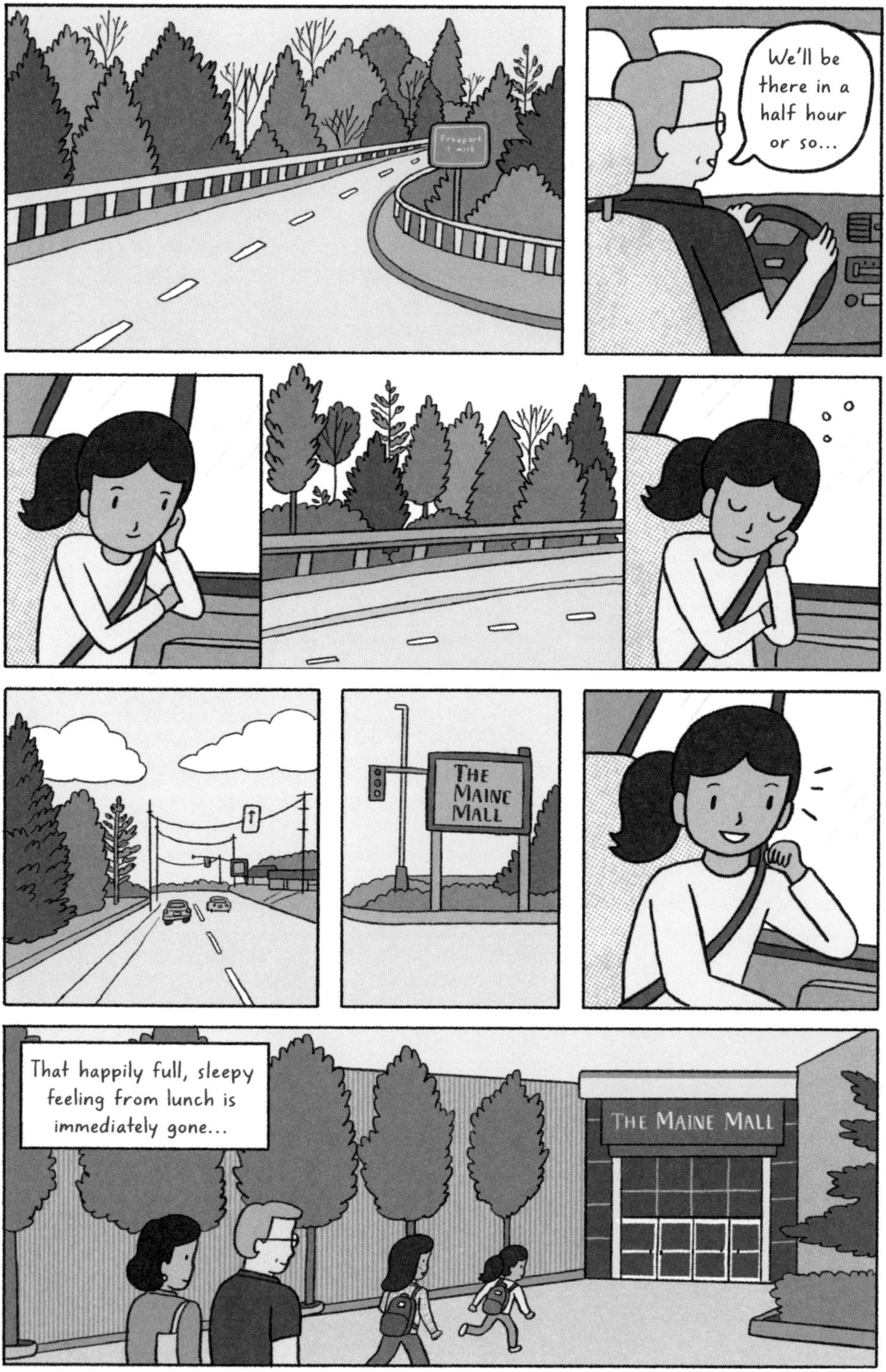
We'll be there in a half hour or so...
THE MAINE MALL
That happily full, sleepy feeling from lunch is immediately gone...
THE MAINE MALL

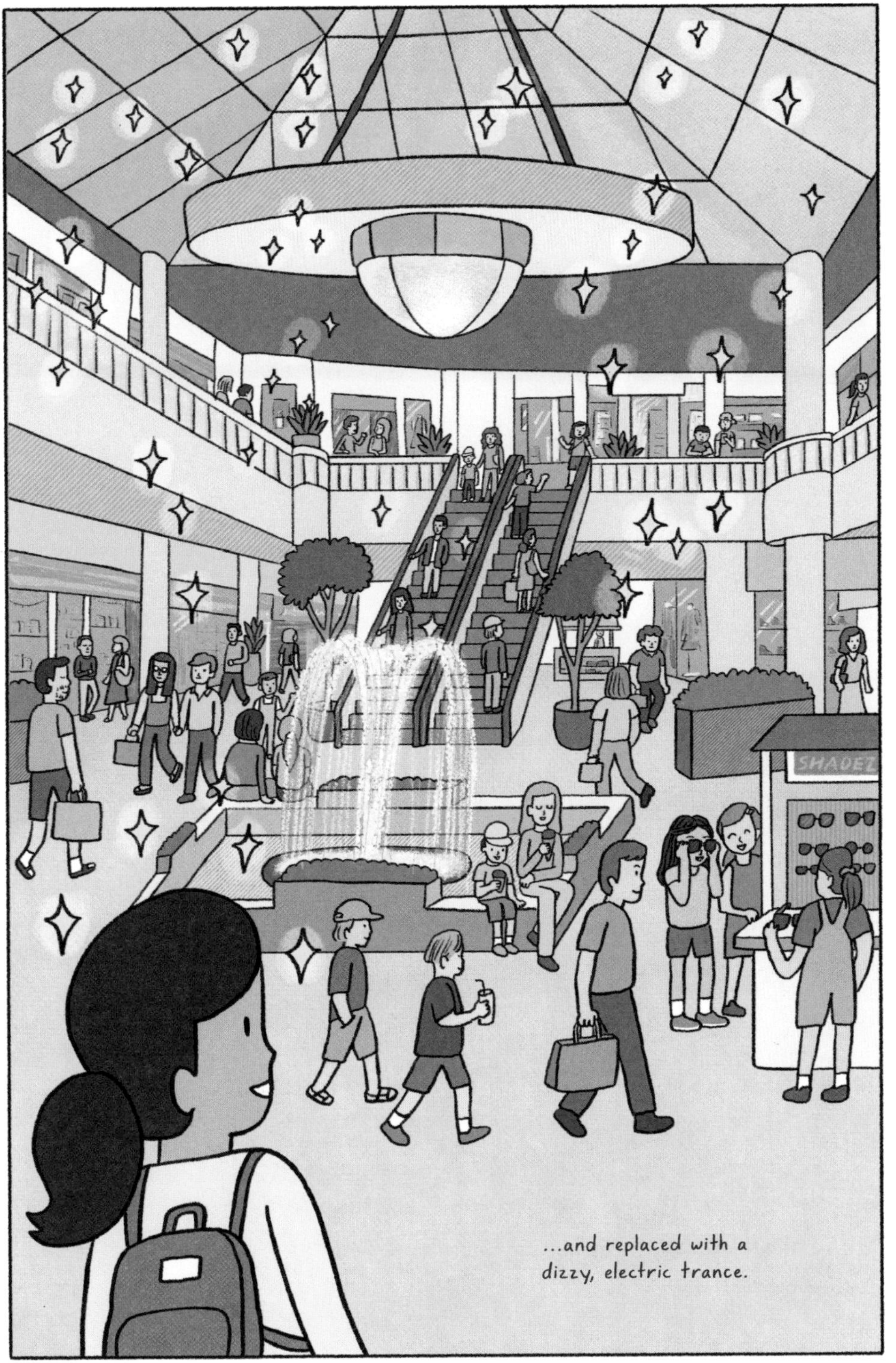
SHADEZ
...and replaced with a
dizzy, electric trance.

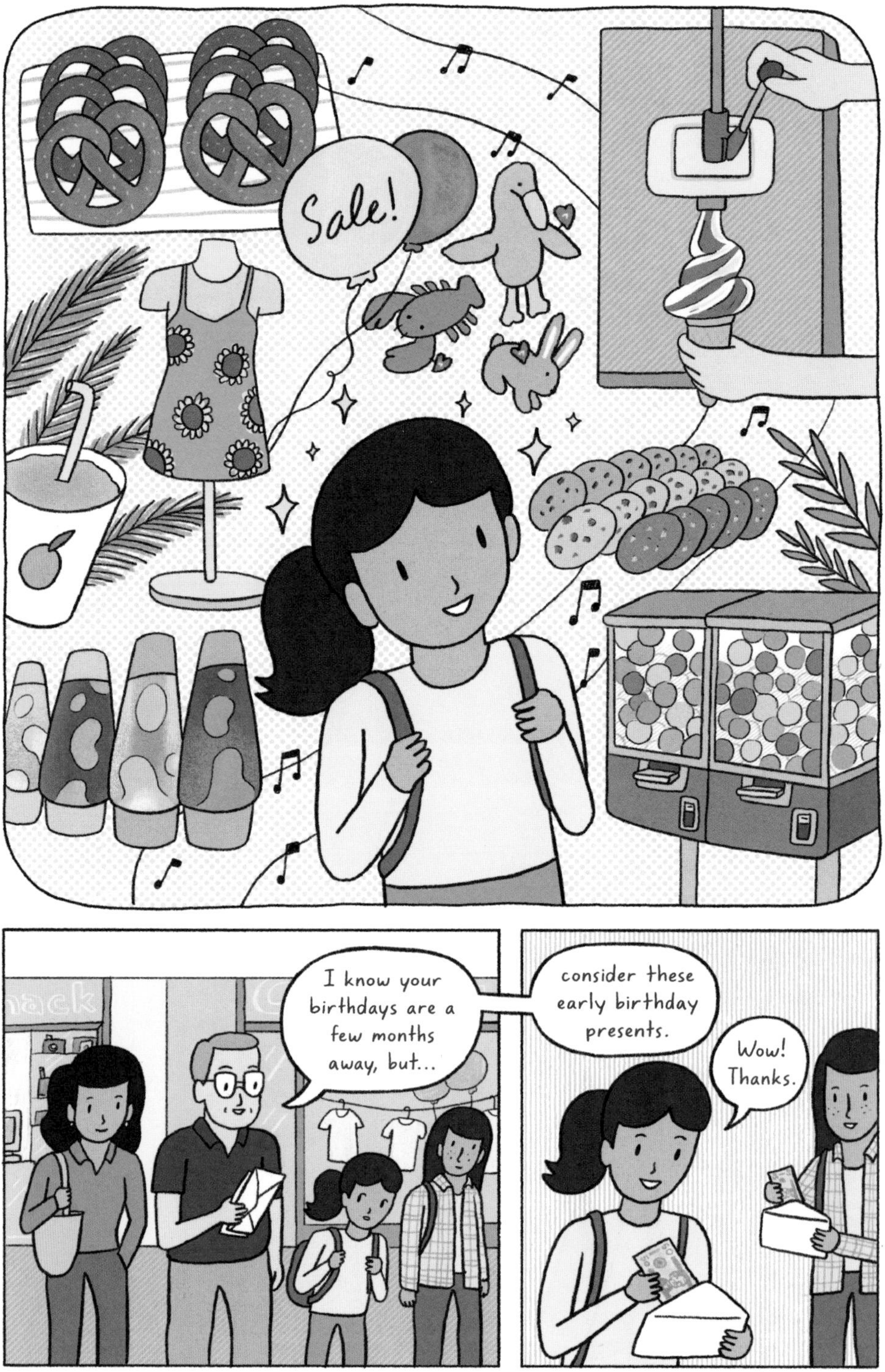
Sale!
I know your birthdays are a few months away, but...
consider these early birthday presents.
Wow! Thanks.

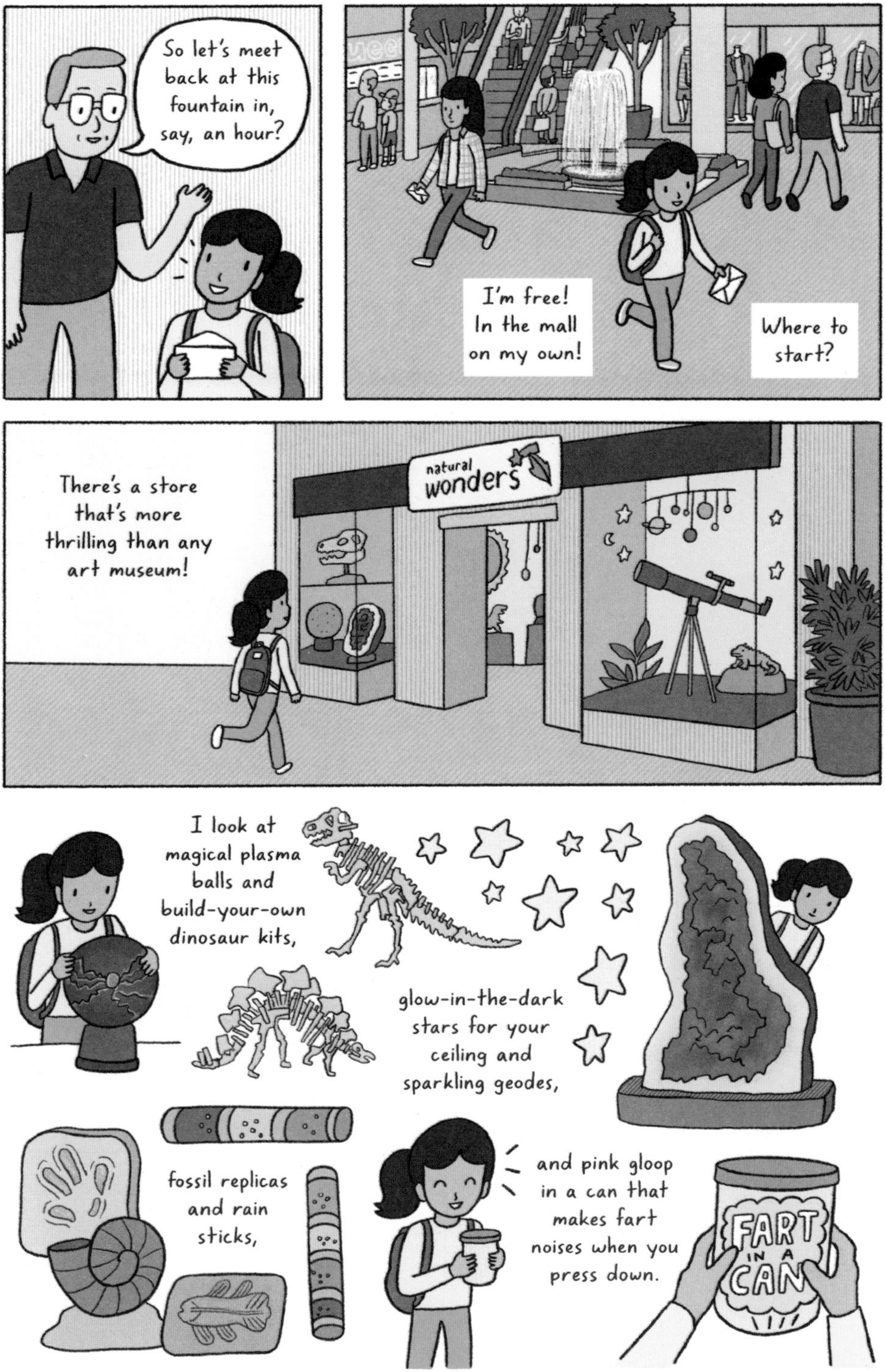

So let's meet back at this fountain in, say, an hour?
I'm free! In the mall on my own!
Where to start?
There's a store that's more thrilling than any art museum!
natural wonders
I look at magical plasma balls and build-your-own dinosaur kits,
glow-in-the-dark stars for your ceiling and sparkling geodes,
fossil replicas and rain sticks,
and pink gloop in a can that makes fart noises when you press down.
FART IN A CAN

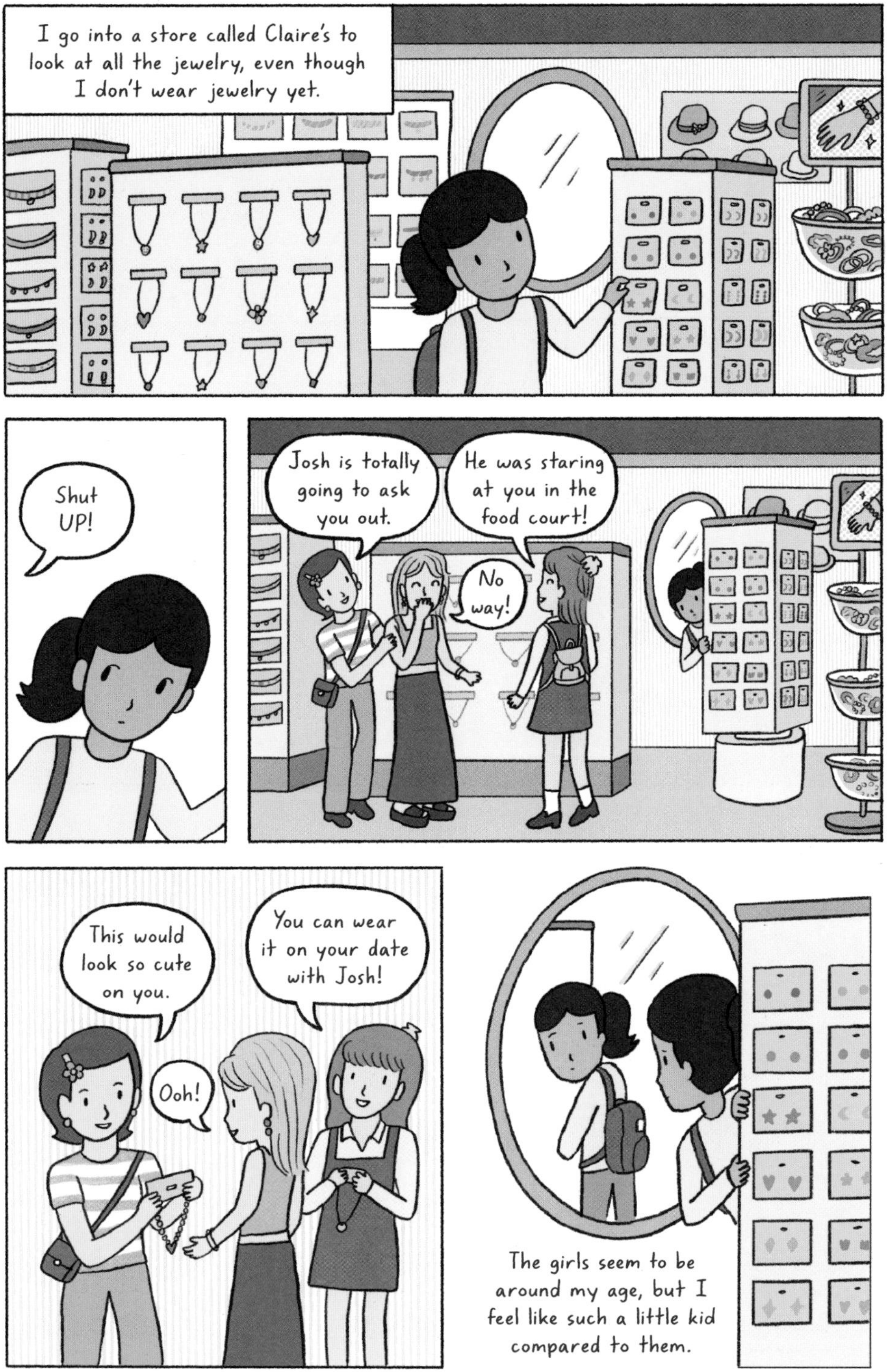
I go into a store called Claire's to look at all the jewelry, even though I don't wear jewelry yet.
Shut UP!
Josh is totally going to ask you out.
He was staring at you in the food court!
No way!
This would look so cute on you.
You can wear it on your date with Josh!
Ooh!
The girls seem to be around my age, but I feel like such a little kid compared to them.

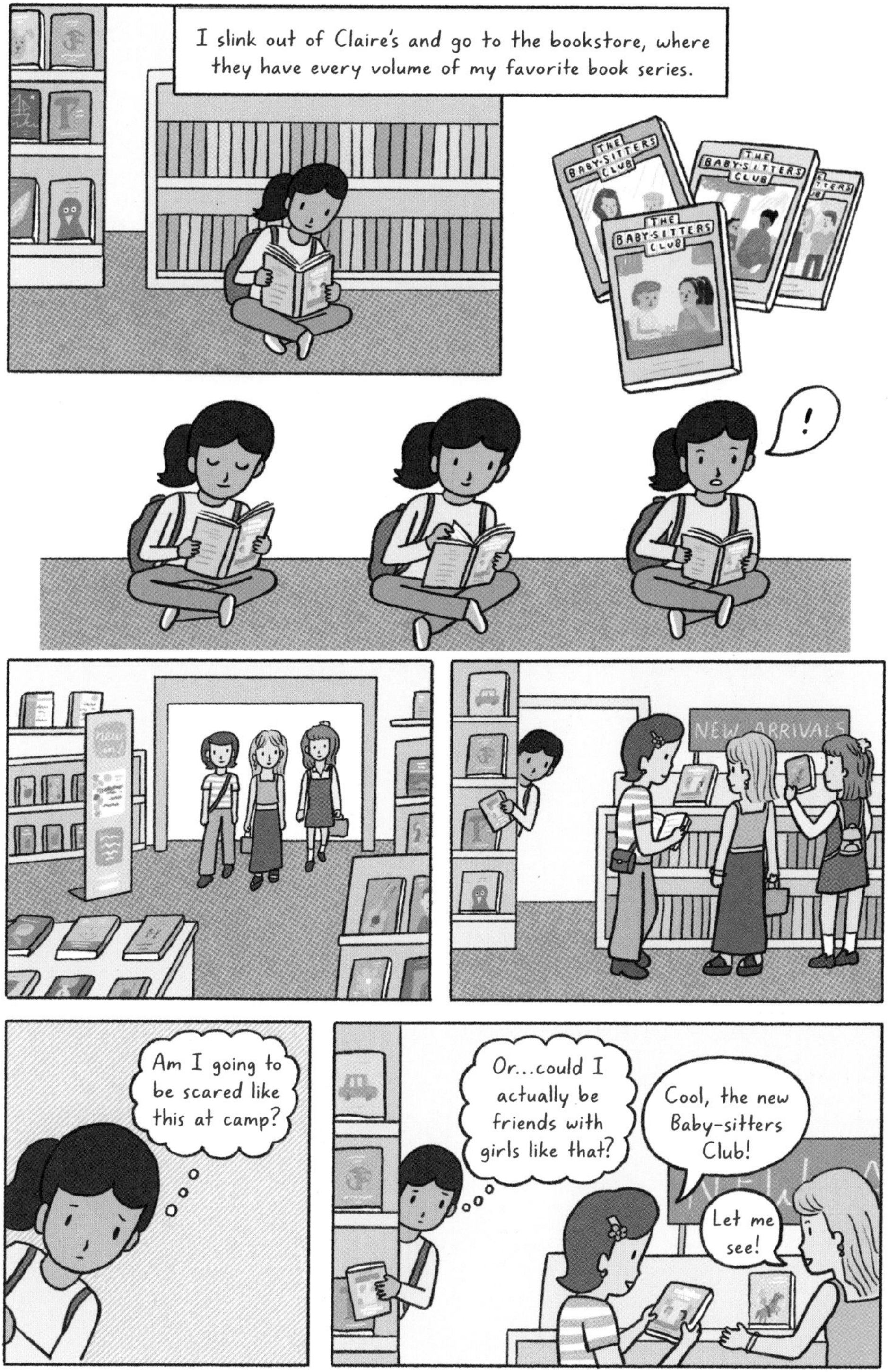

I slink out of Claire's and go to the bookstore, where they have every volume of my favorite book series.
THE BABY-SITTERS CLUB
THE BABY-SITTERS CLUB
THE BABY-SITTERS CLUB
!
NEW ARRIVALS
Am I going to be scared like this at camp?
Or...could I actually be friends with girls like that?
Cool, the new Baby-sitters Club!
Let me see!

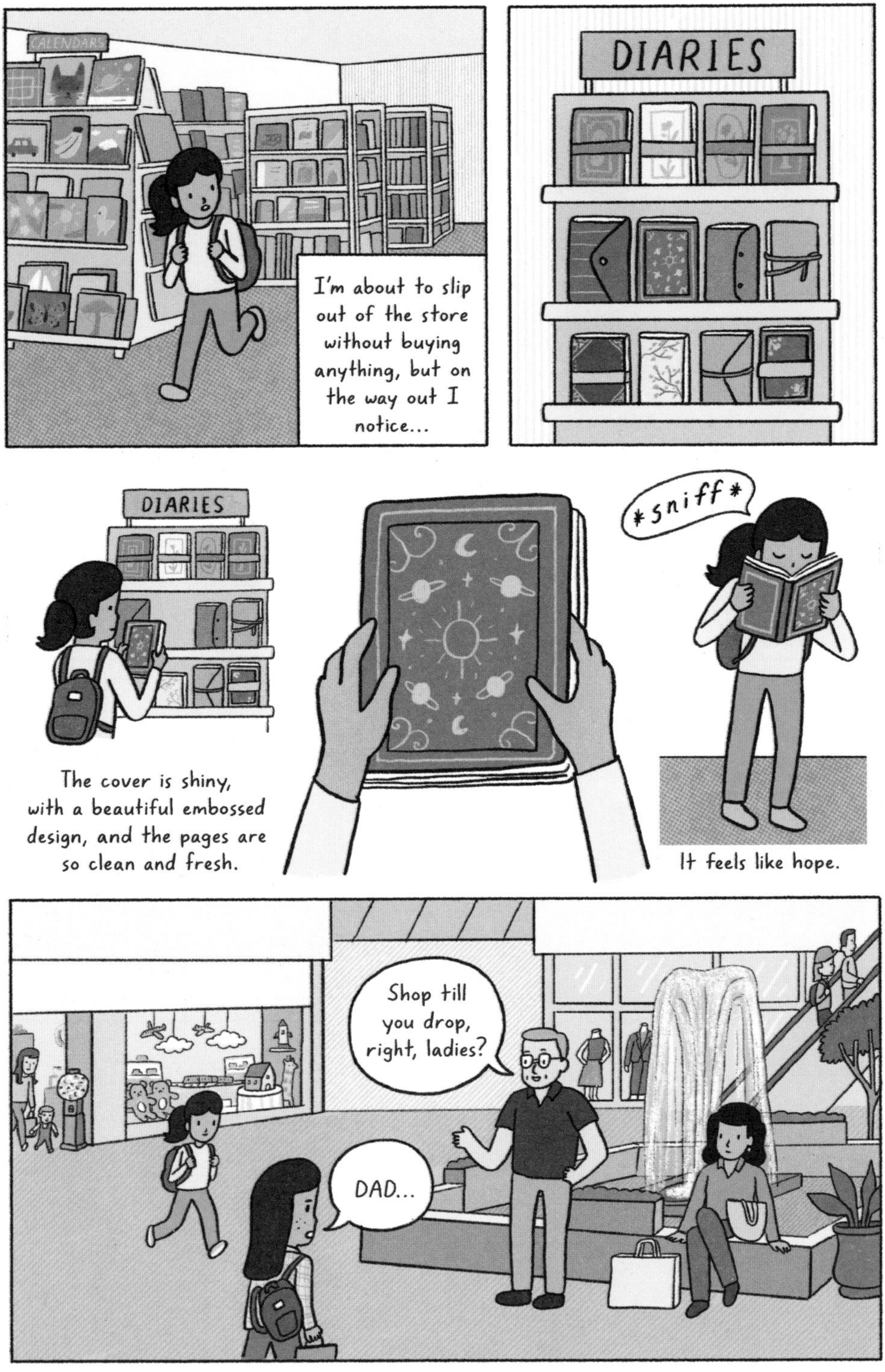
CALENDARS
I'm about to slip out of the store without buying anything, but on the way out I notice...
DIARIES
DIARIES
The cover is shiny, with a beautiful embossed design, and the pages are so clean and fresh.
sniff
It feels like hope.
Shop till you drop, right, ladies?
DAD...

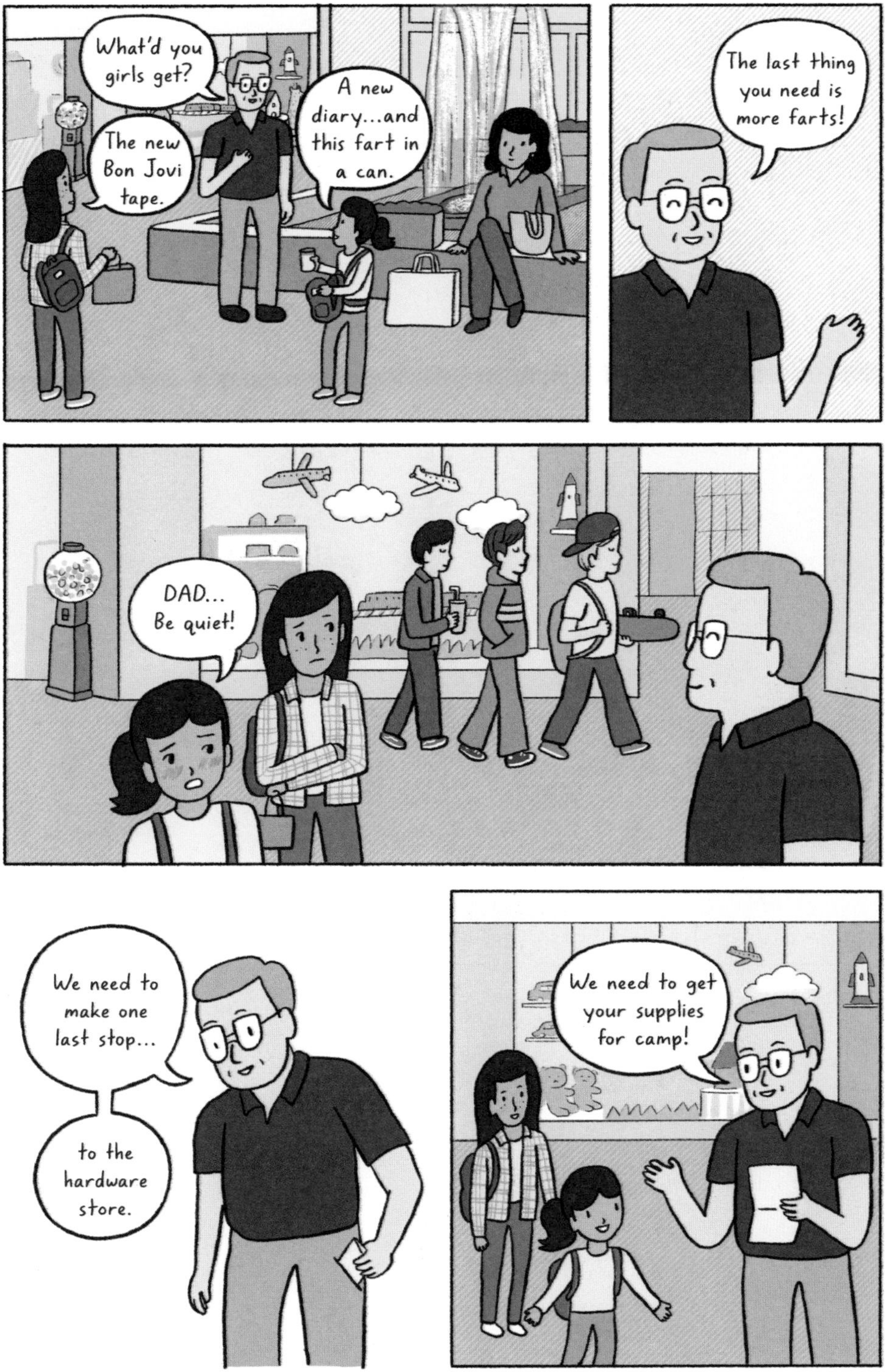
What'd you girls get?
The new Bon Jovi tape.
A new diary...and this fart in a can.
The last thing you need is more farts!
DAD... Be quiet!
We need to make one last stop...
to the hardware store.
We need to get your supplies for camp!

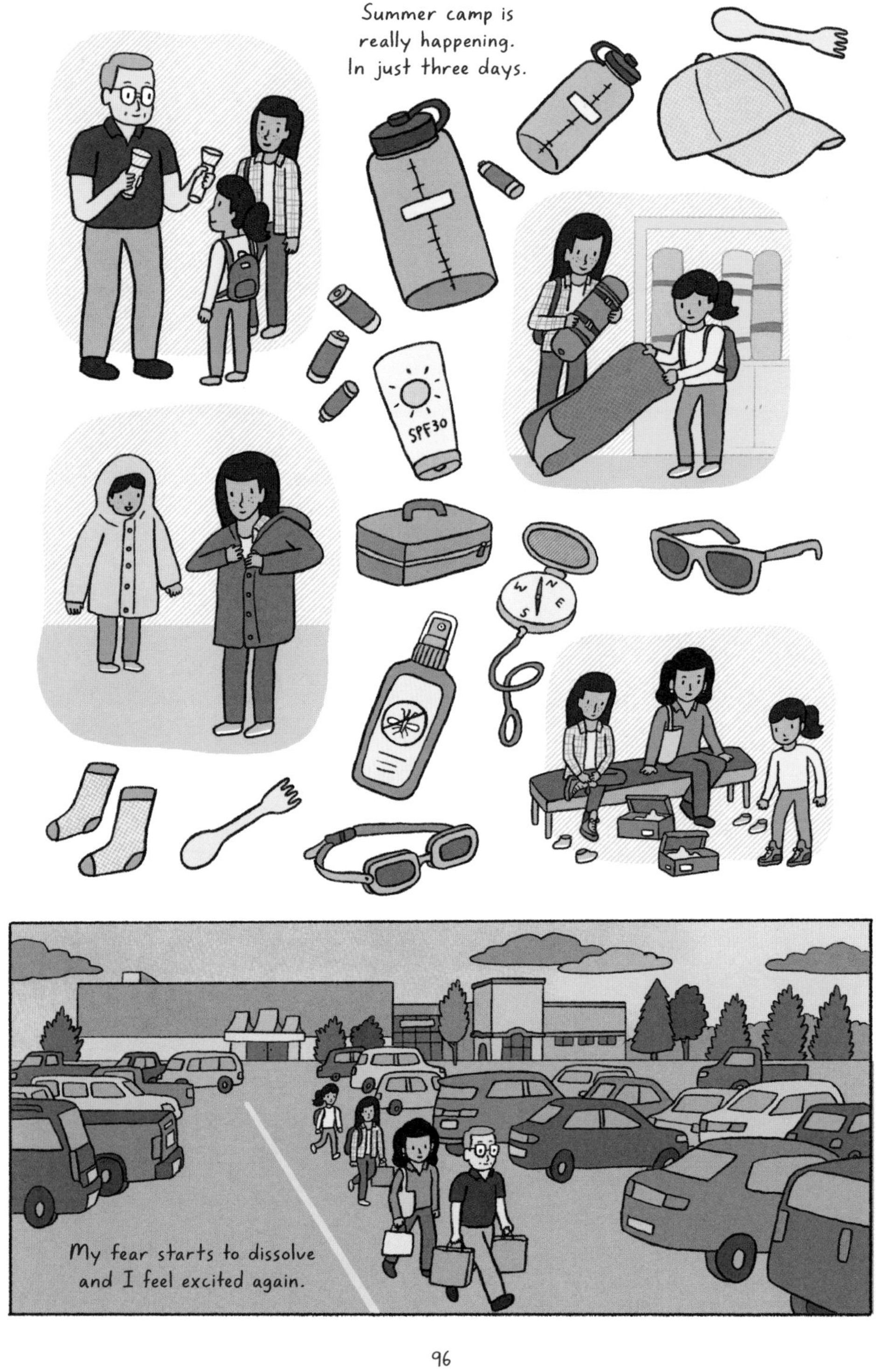
Summer camp is really happening. In just three days.
SPF30
My fear starts to dissolve and I feel excited again.

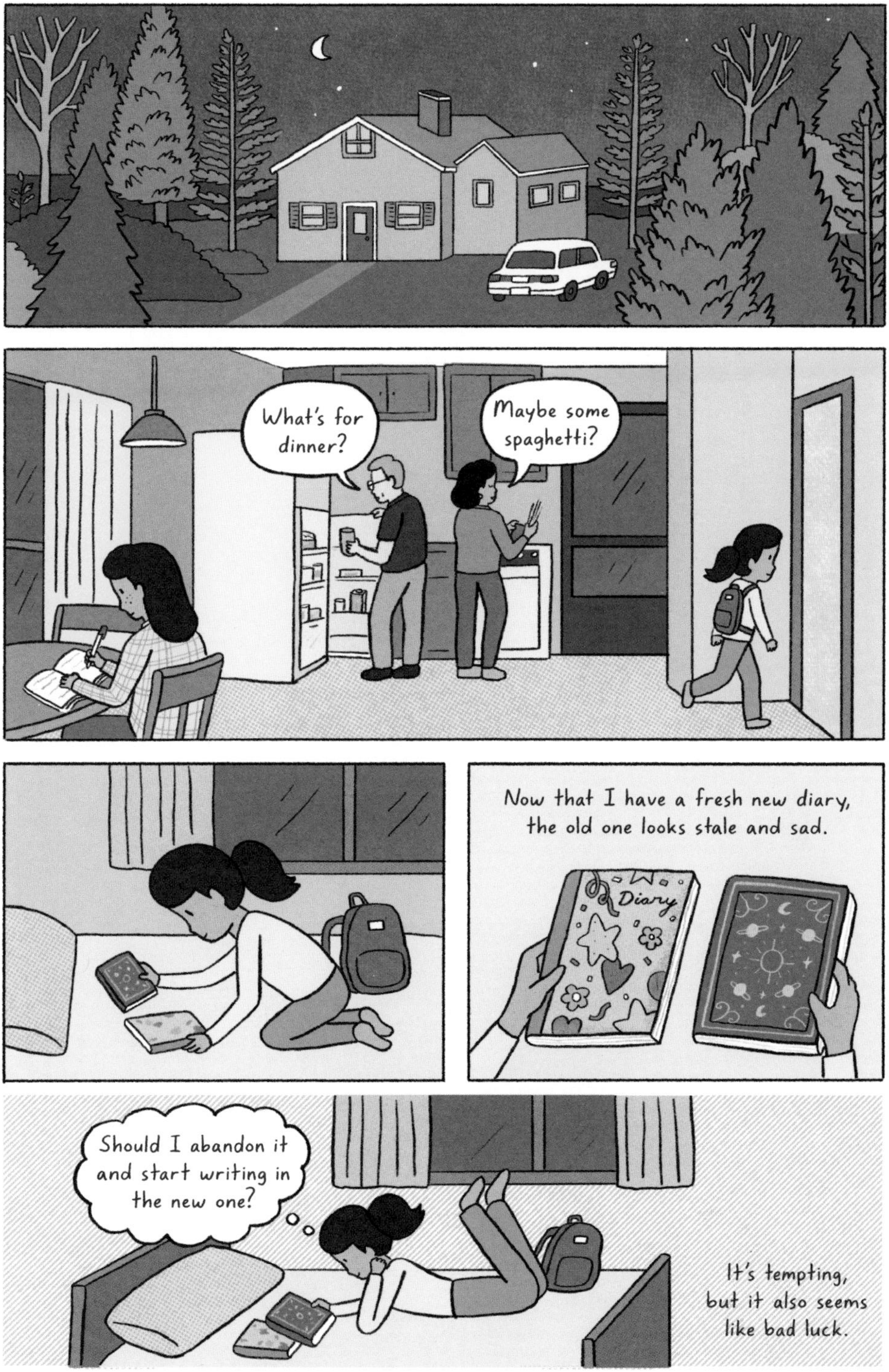
What's for dinner?
Maybe some spaghetti?
Now that I have a fresh new diary, the old one looks stale and sad.
Diary
Should I abandon it and start writing in the new one?
It's tempting, but it also seems like bad luck.

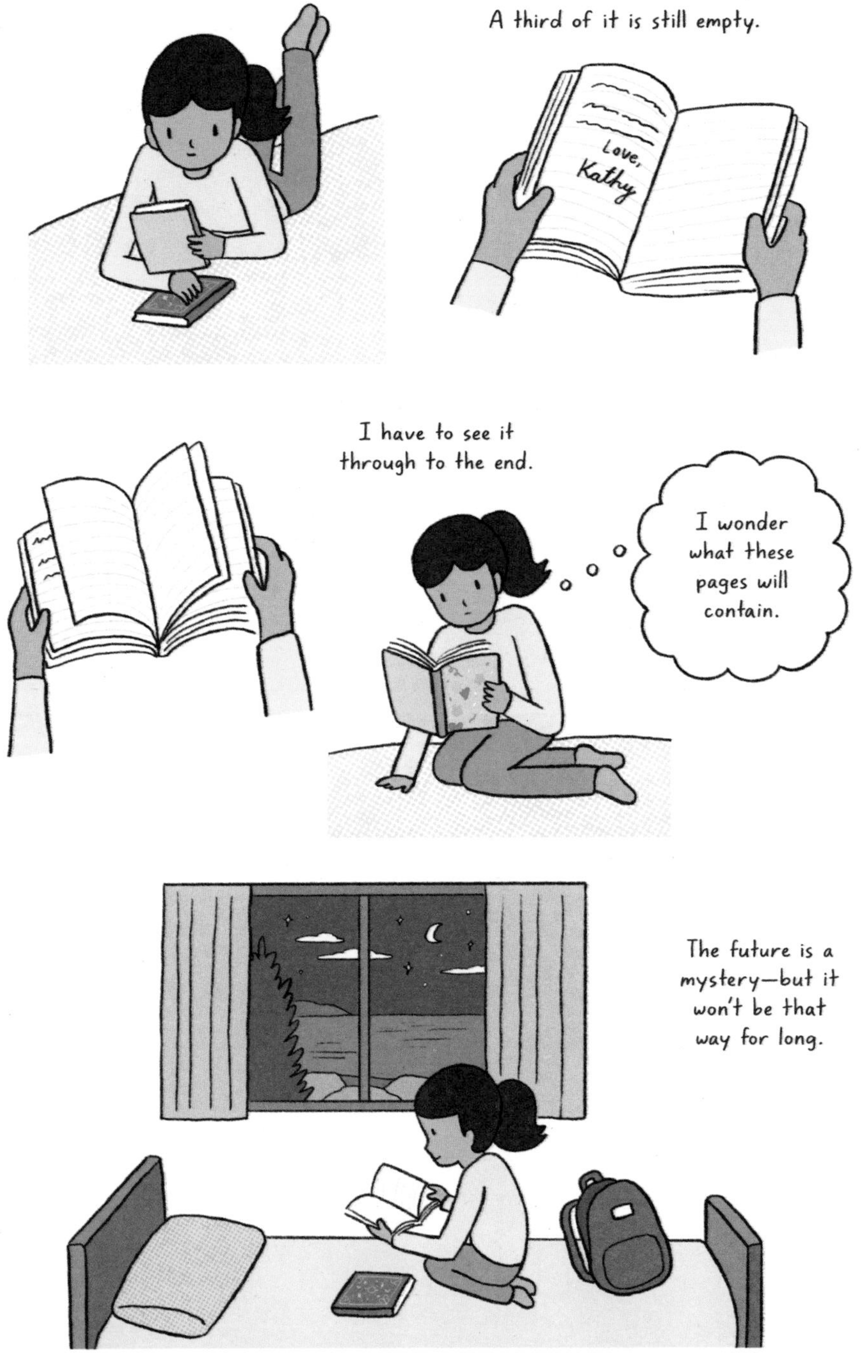
A third of it is still empty.
Love,
Kathy
I have to see it through to the end.
I wonder what these pages will contain.
The future is a mystery—but it won't be that way for long.

7

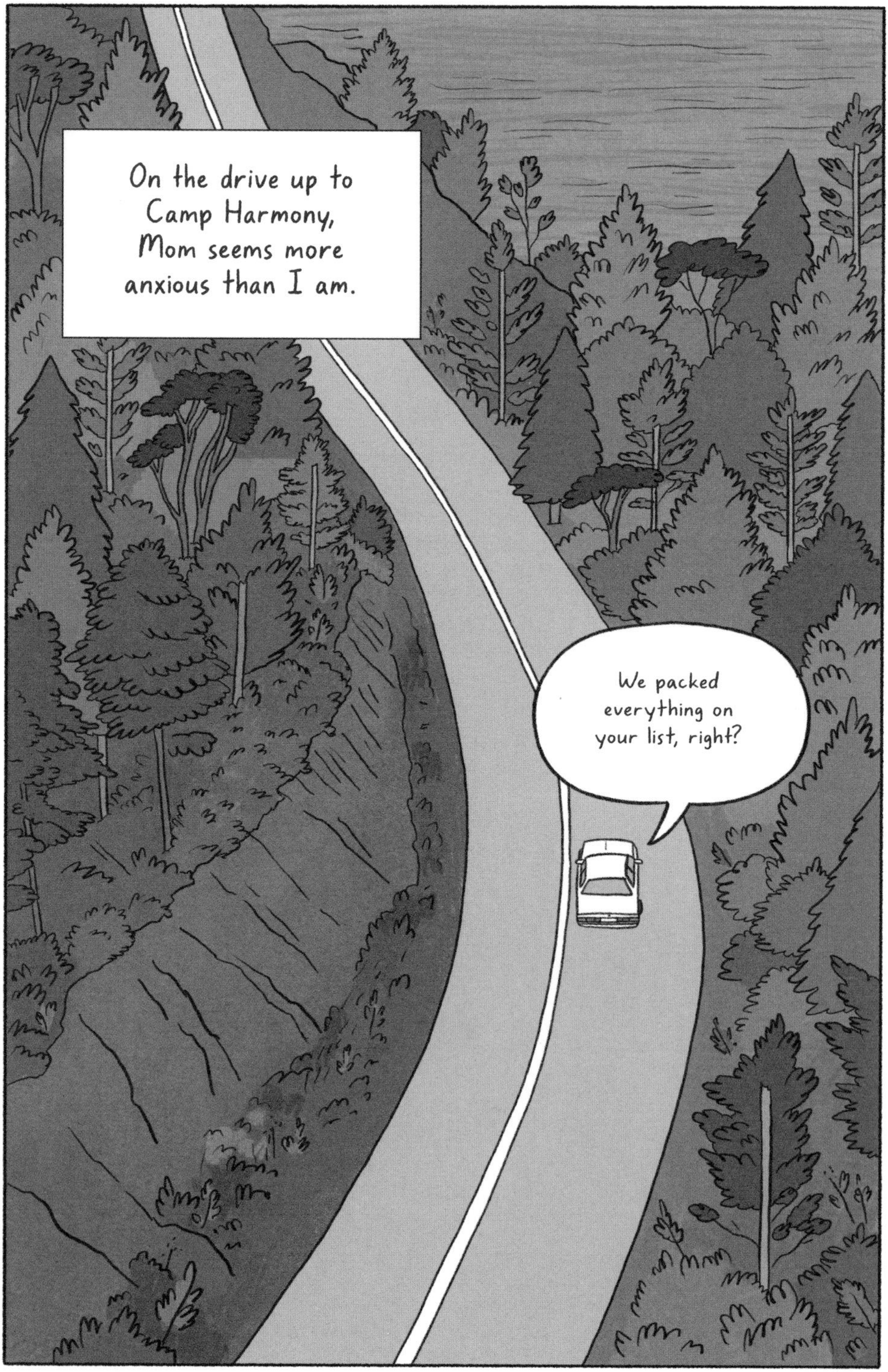
On the drive up to Camp Harmony, Mom seems more anxious than I am.
We packed everything on your list, right?

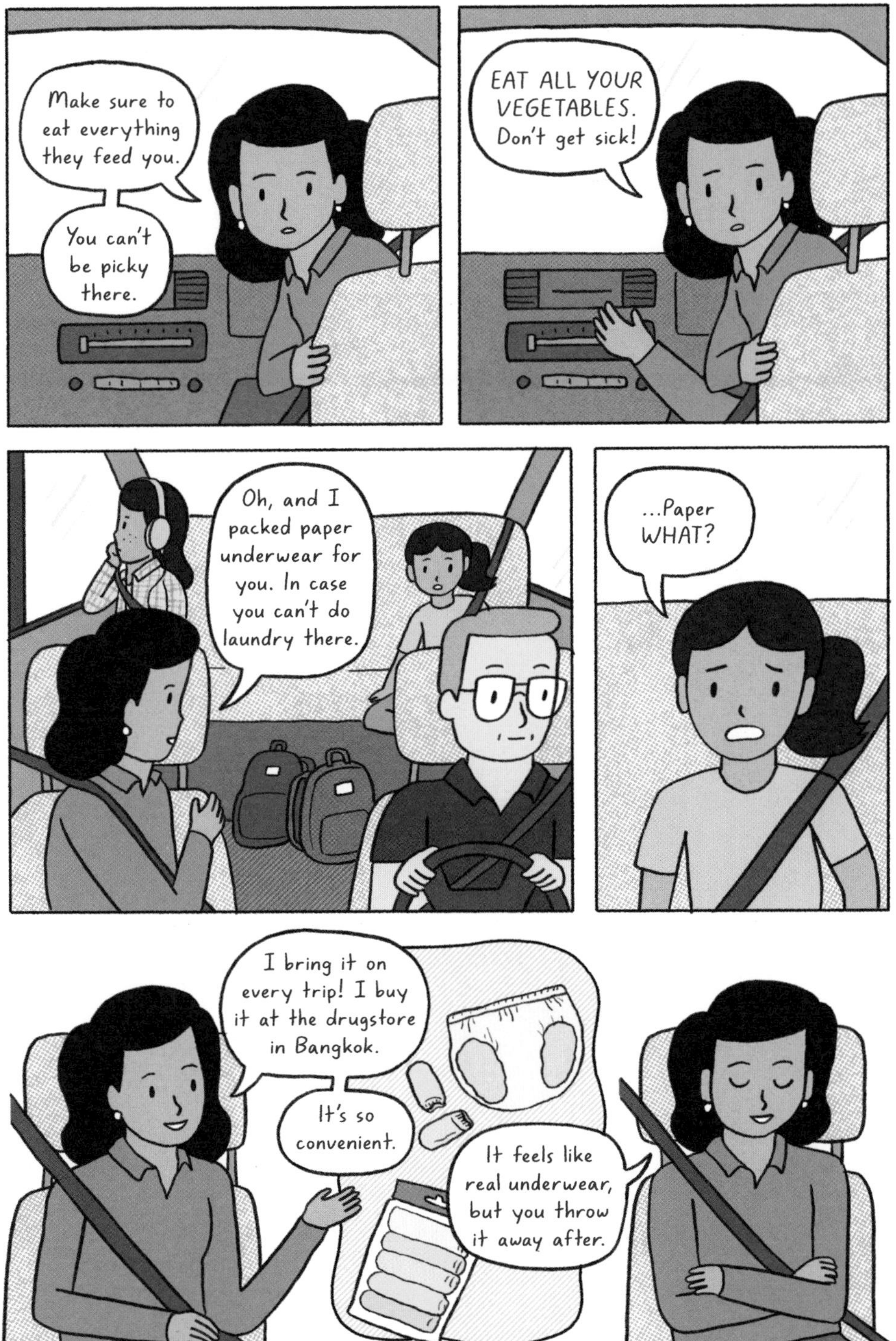

Make sure to eat everything they feed you.
You can't be picky there.
EAT ALL YOUR VEGETABLES. Don't get sick!
Oh, and I packed paper underwear for you. In case you can't do laundry there.
...Paper WHAT?
I bring it on every trip! I buy it at the drugstore in Bangkok.
It's so convenient.
It feels like real underwear, but you throw it away after.

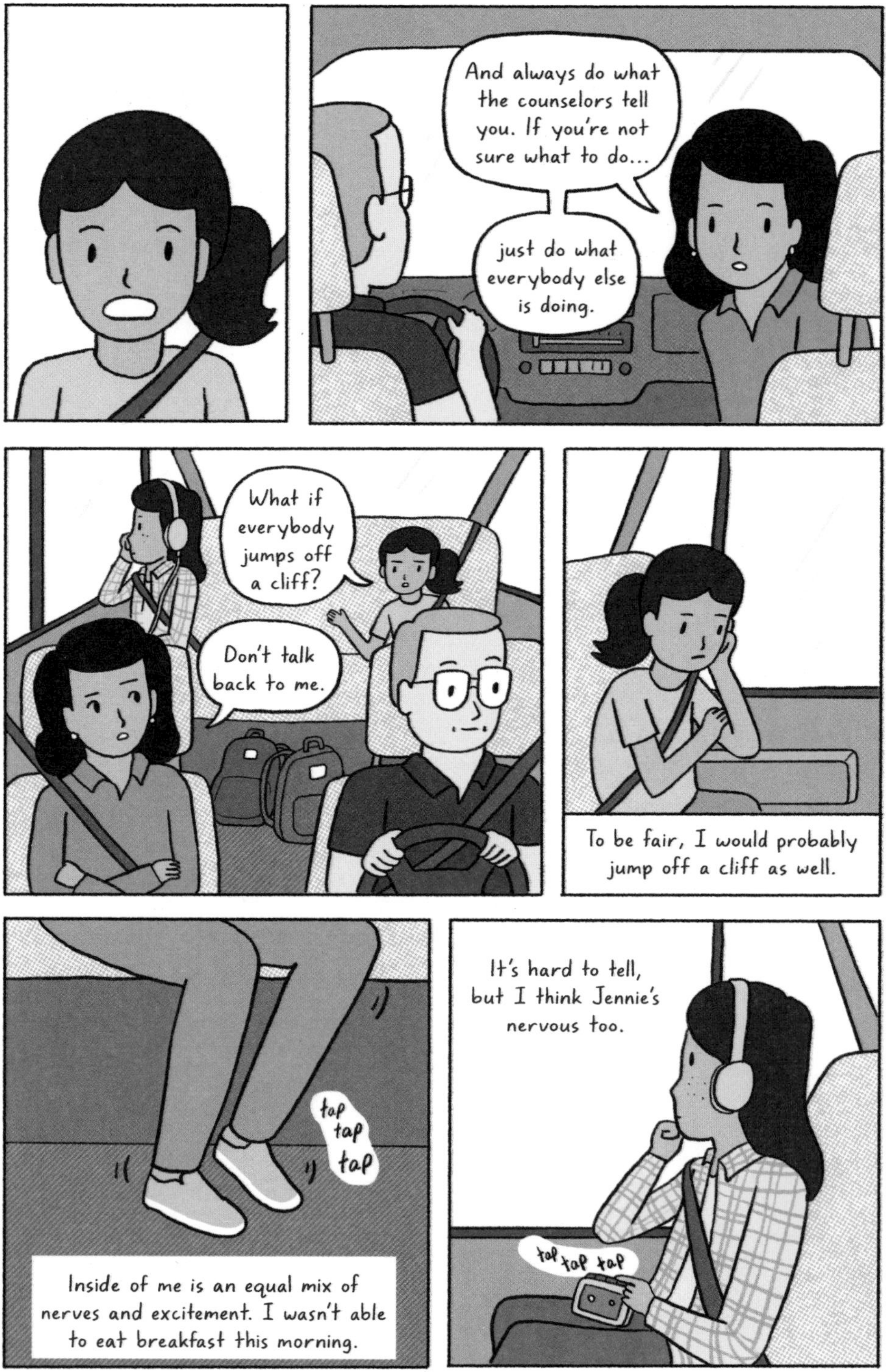
And always do what the counselors tell you. If you're not sure what to do...
just do what everybody else is doing.
What if everybody jumps off a cliff?
Don't talk back to me.
To be fair, I would probably jump off a cliff as well.
tap tap tap
Inside of me is an equal mix of nerves and excitement. I wasn't able to eat breakfast this morning.
It's hard to tell, but I think Jennie's nervous too.
tap tap tap

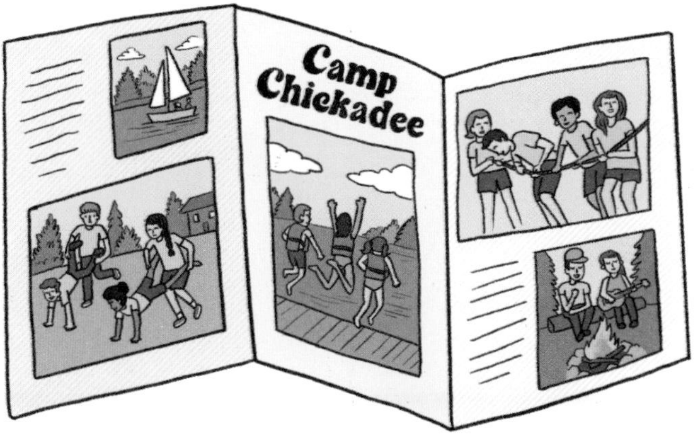
Camp Chickadee

To my relief, my parents are sending her to a different camp, for older kids.

A coed camp! With BOYS!

I would be nervous if I were her.

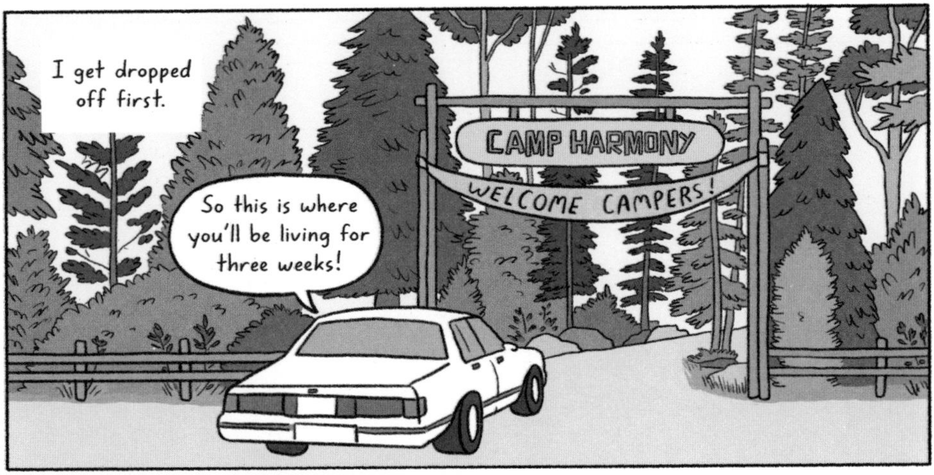
I get dropped off first.
CAMP HARMONY
WELCOME CAMPERS!
So this is where you'll be living for three weeks!

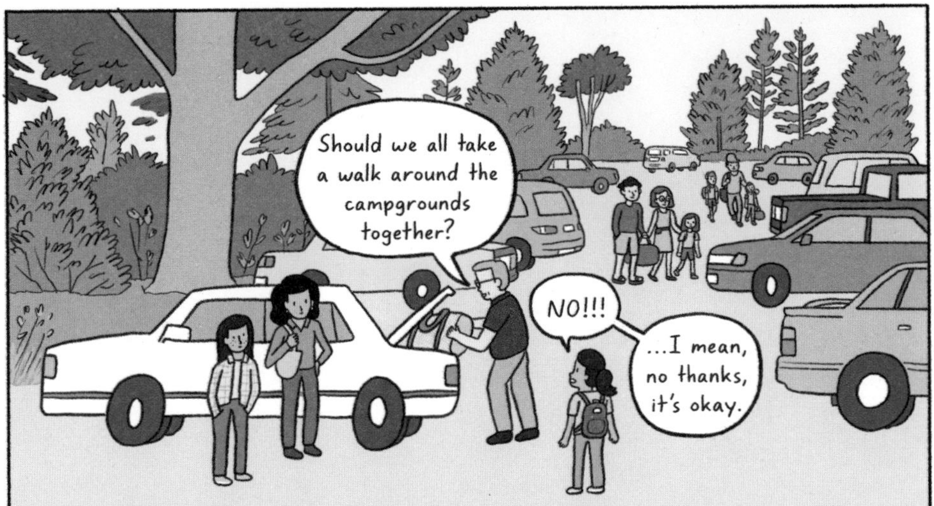
Should we all take a walk around the campgrounds together?
NO!!!
...I mean, no thanks, it's okay.

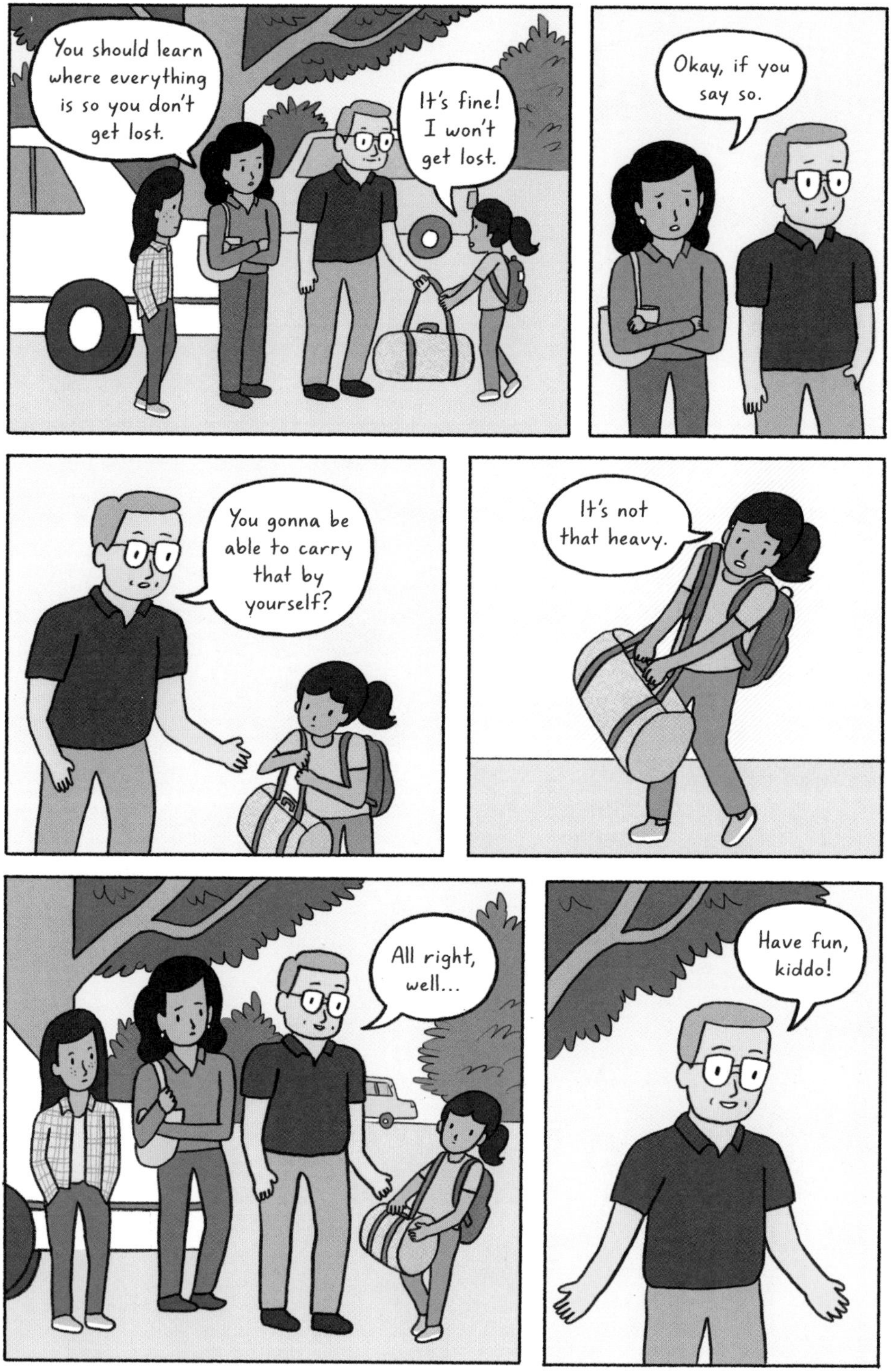
You should learn where everything is so you don't get lost.
It's fine! I won't get lost.
Okay, if you say so.
You gonna be able to carry that by yourself?
It's not that heavy.
All right, well...
Have fun, kiddo!

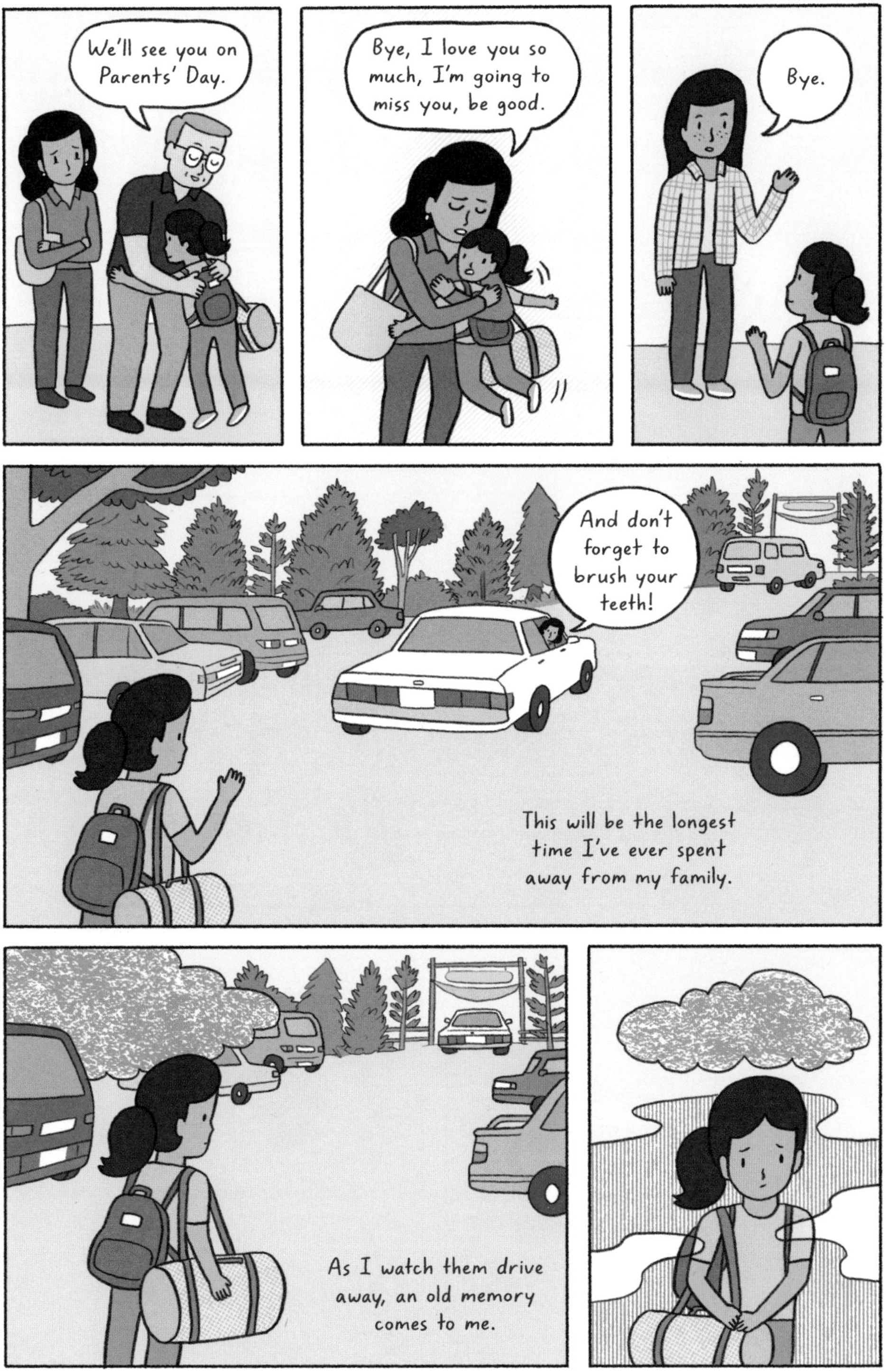
We'll see you on Parents' Day.
Bye, I love you so much, I'm going to miss you, be good.
Bye.
And don't forget to brush your teeth!
This will be the longest time I've ever spent away from my family.
As I watch them drive away, an old memory comes to me.

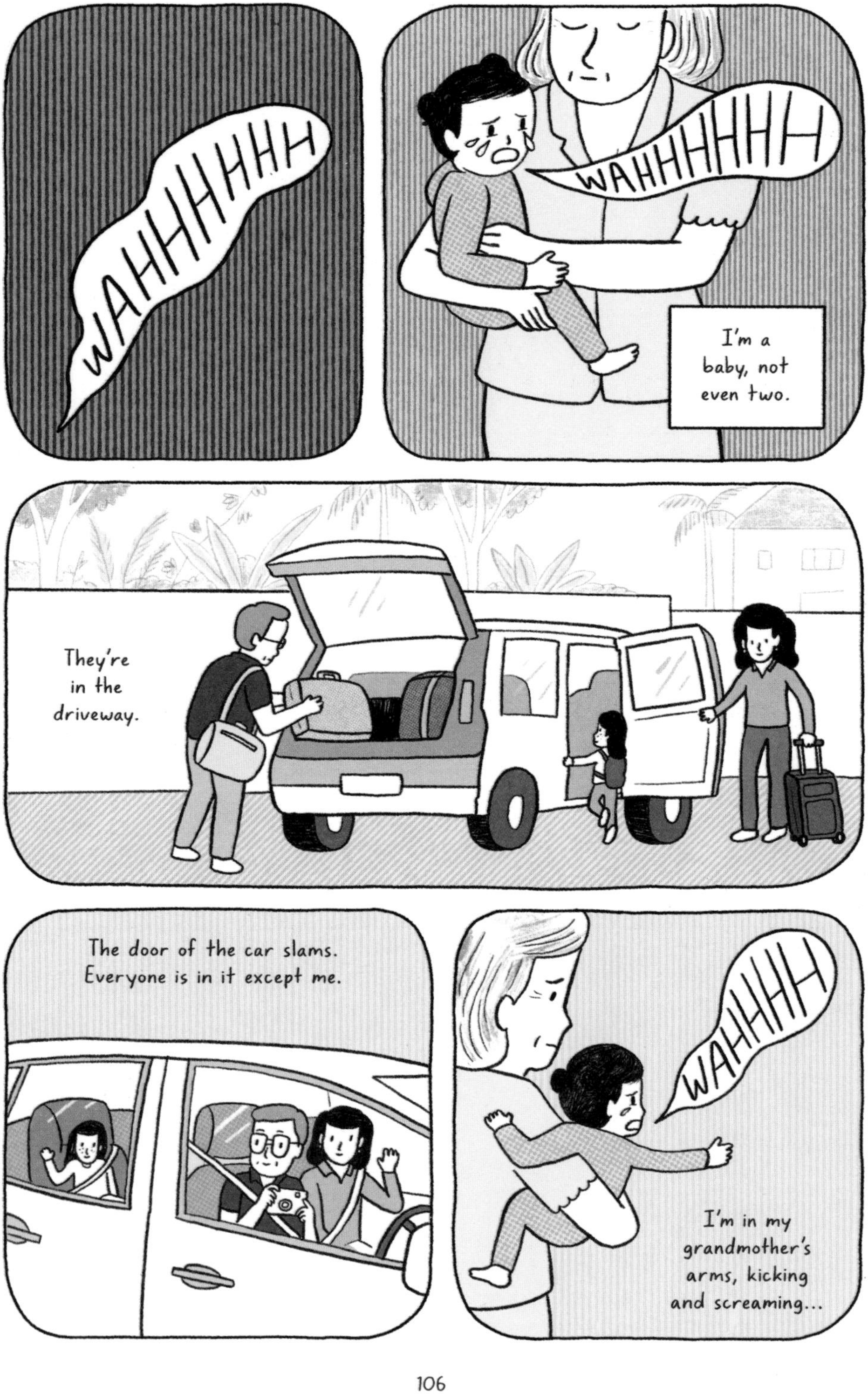
WAHHHHHH
WAHHHHHHH
I'm a baby, not even two.
They're in the driveway.
The door of the car slams. Everyone is in it except me.
WAHHHH
I'm in my grandmother's arms, kicking and screaming...

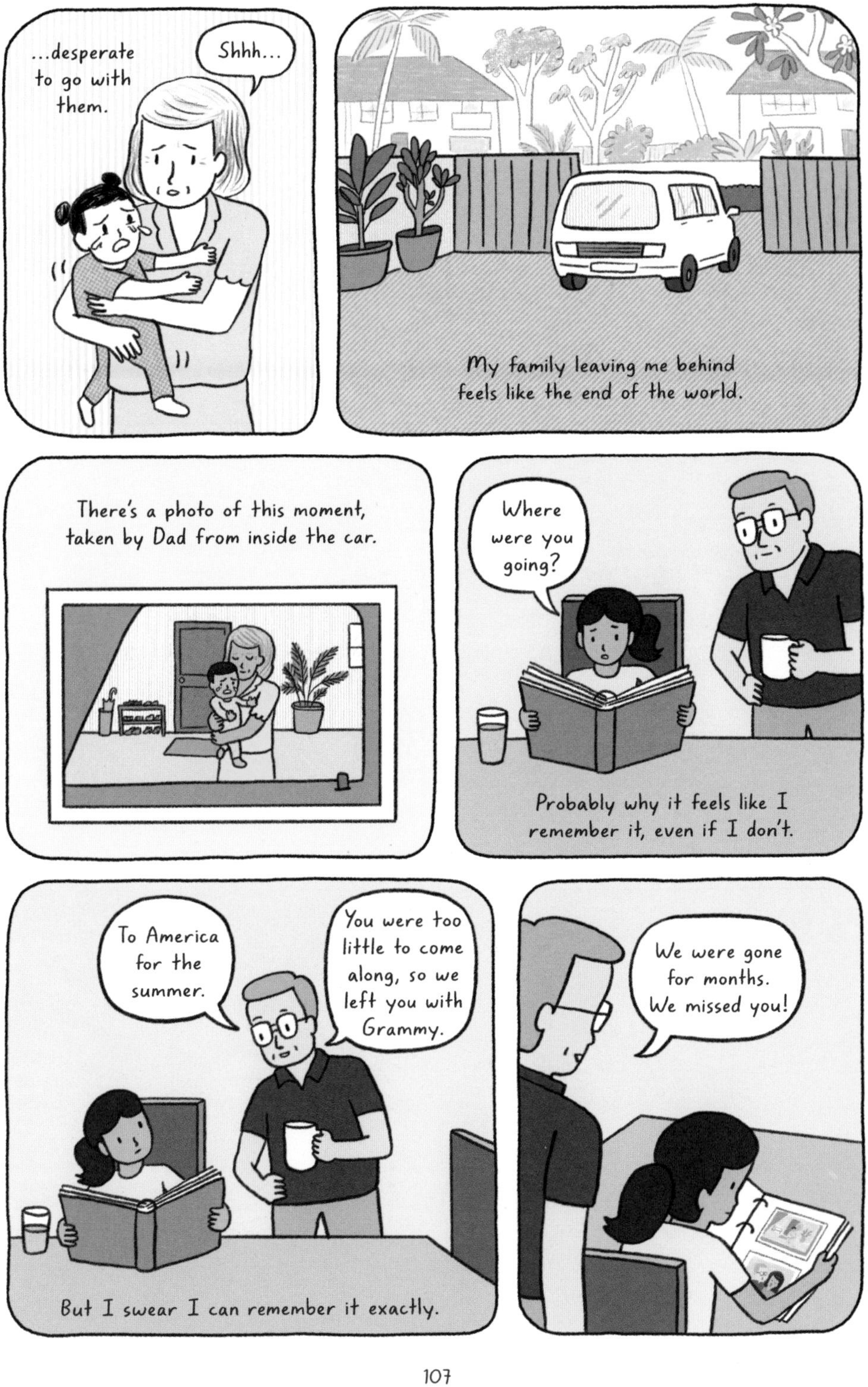
...desperate to go with them.
Shhh...
My family leaving me behind feels like the end of the world.
There's a photo of this moment, taken by Dad from inside the car.
Where were you going?
Probably why it feels like I remember it, even if I don't.
To America for the summer.
You were too little to come along, so we left you with Grammy.
But I swear I can remember it exactly.
We were gone for months. We missed you!

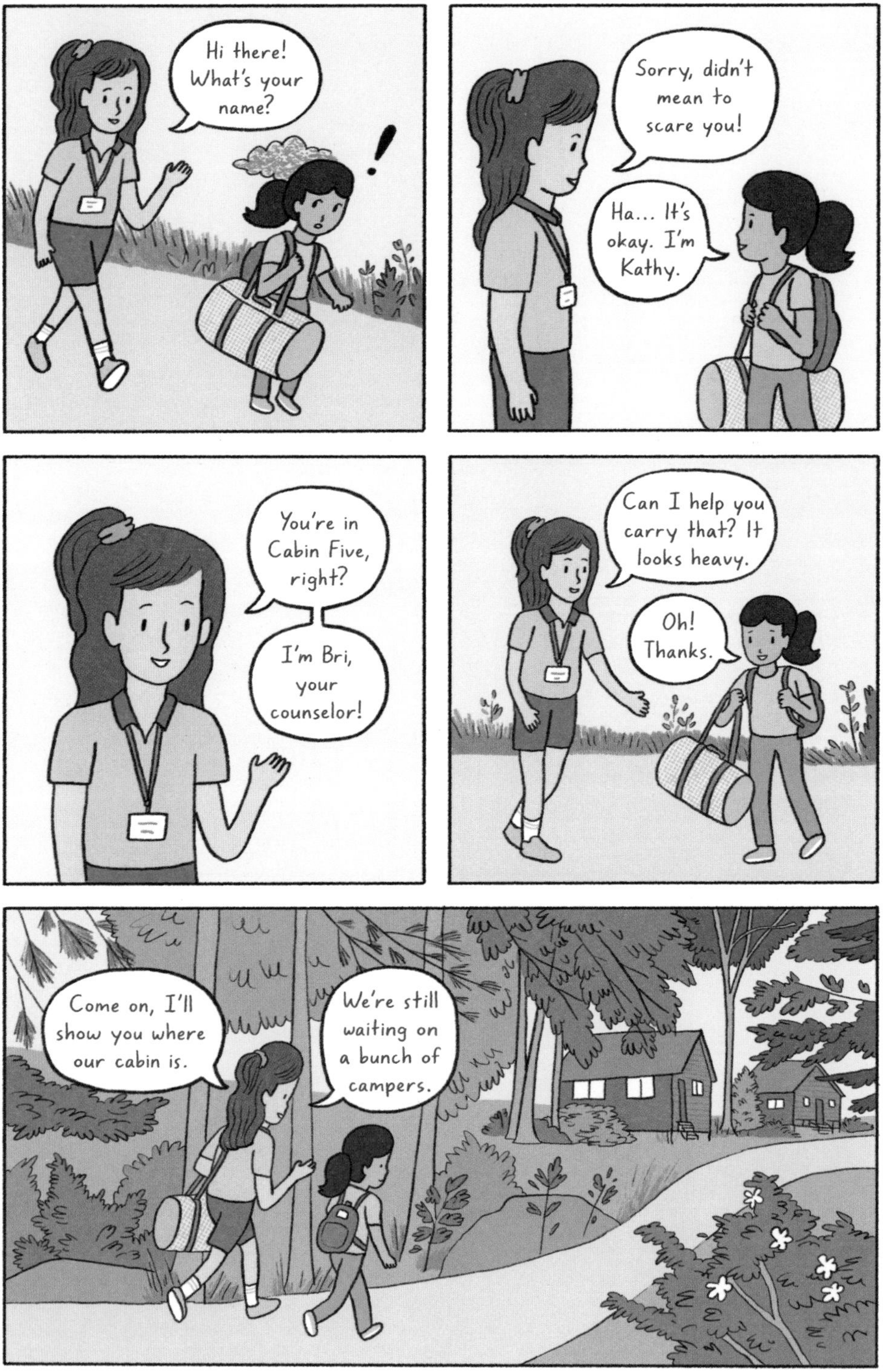
Hi there! What's your name?
!
Sorry, didn't mean to scare you!
Ha... It's okay. I'm Kathy.
You're in Cabin Five, right?
I'm Bri, your counselor!
Can I help you carry that? It looks heavy.
Oh! Thanks.
Come on, I'll show you where our cabin is.
We're still waiting on a bunch of campers.

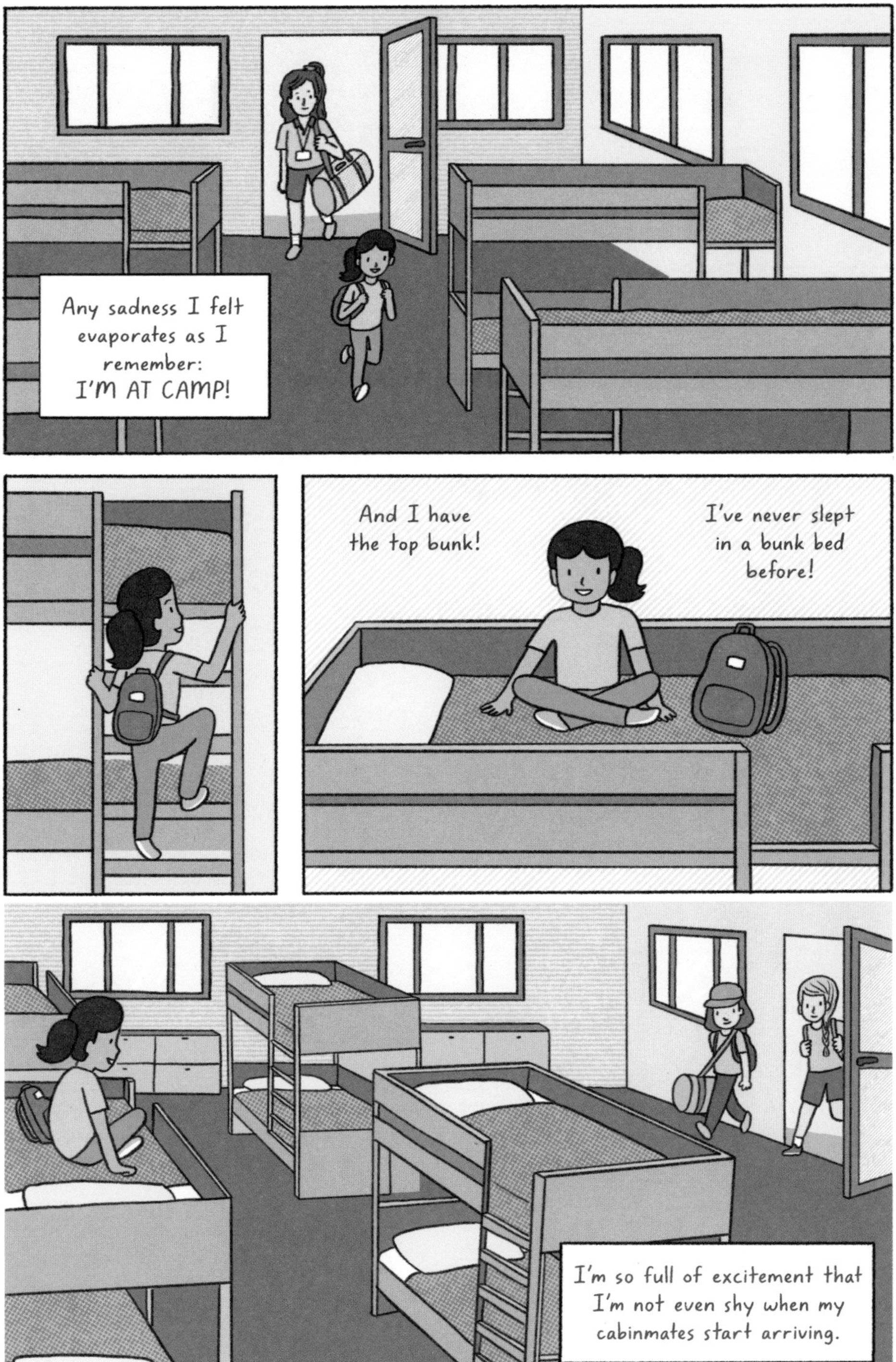
Any sadness I felt evaporates as I remember: I'M AT CAMP!
And I have the top bunk!
I've never slept in a bunk bed before!
I'm so full of excitement that I'm not even shy when my cabinmates start arriving.

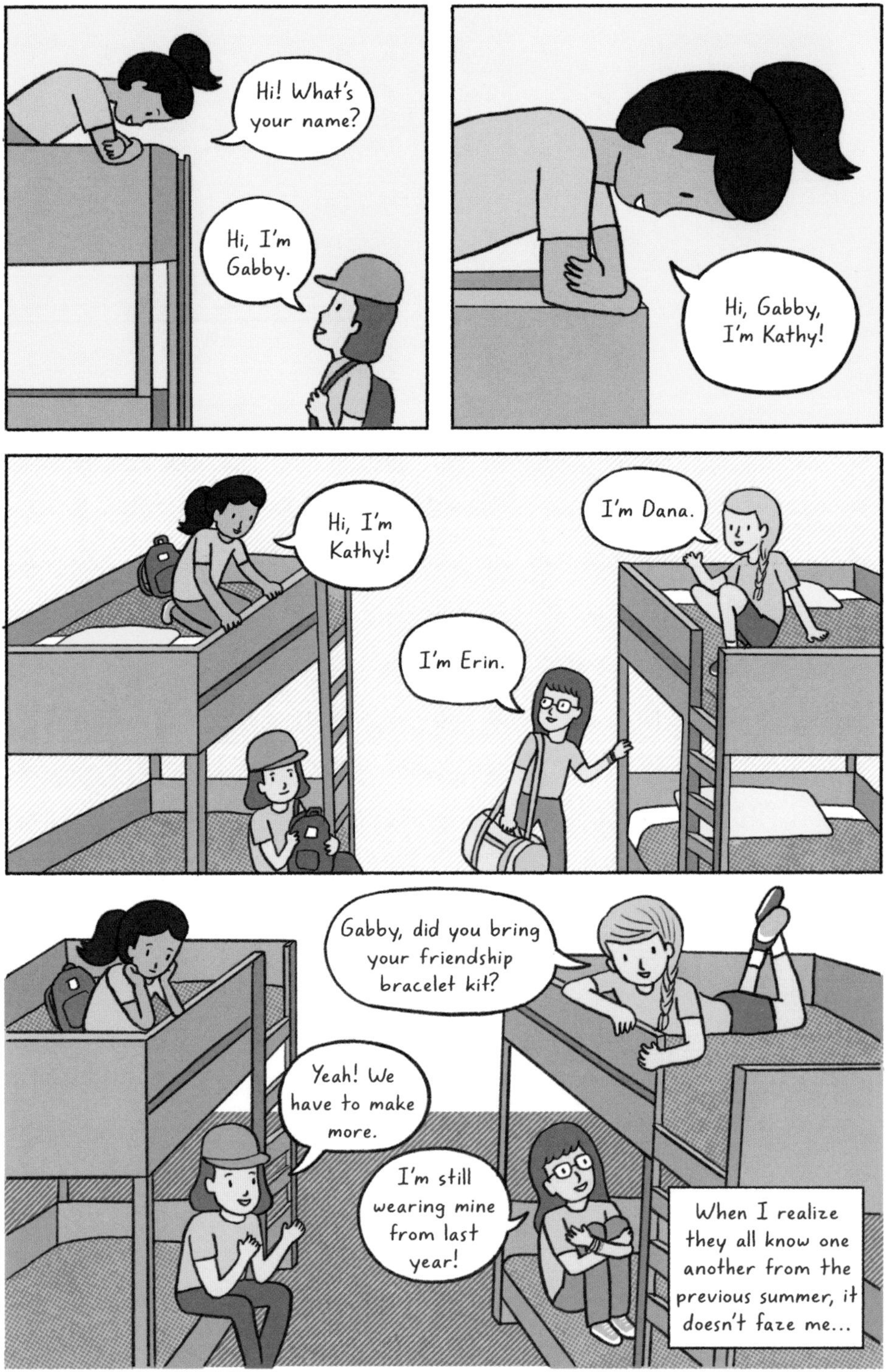
Hi! What's your name?
Hi, I'm Gabby.
Hi, Gabby, I'm Kathy!
Hi, I'm Kathy!
I'm Dana.
I'm Erin.
Gabby, did you bring your friendship bracelet kit?
Yeah! We have to make more.
I'm still wearing mine from last year!
When I realize they all know one another from the previous summer, it doesn't faze me...

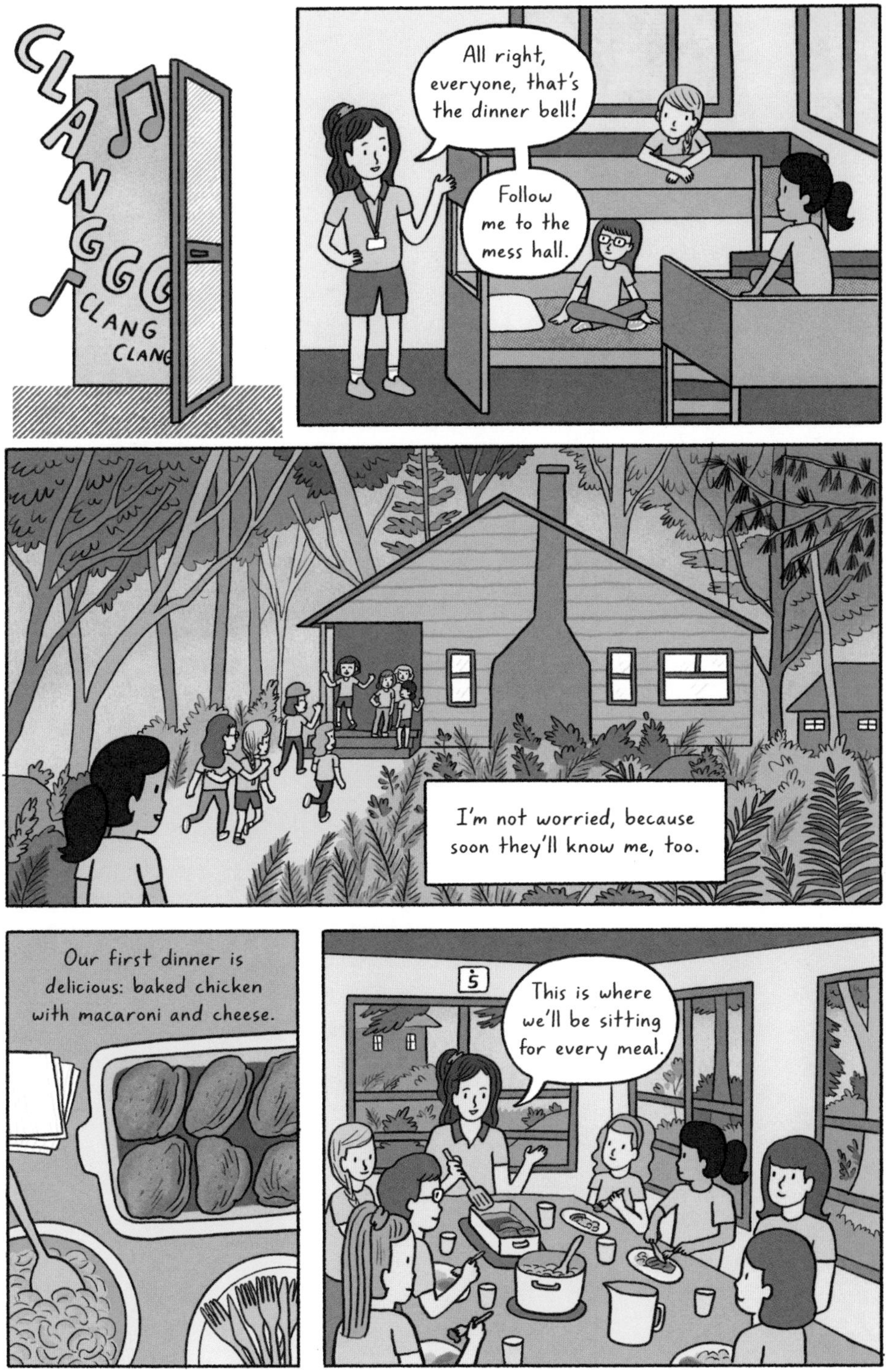
CLANGG
CLANG
CLANG
All right, everyone, that's the dinner bell!
Follow me to the mess hall.
I'm not worried, because soon they'll know me, too.
Our first dinner is delicious: baked chicken with macaroni and cheese.
5
This is where we'll be sitting for every meal.

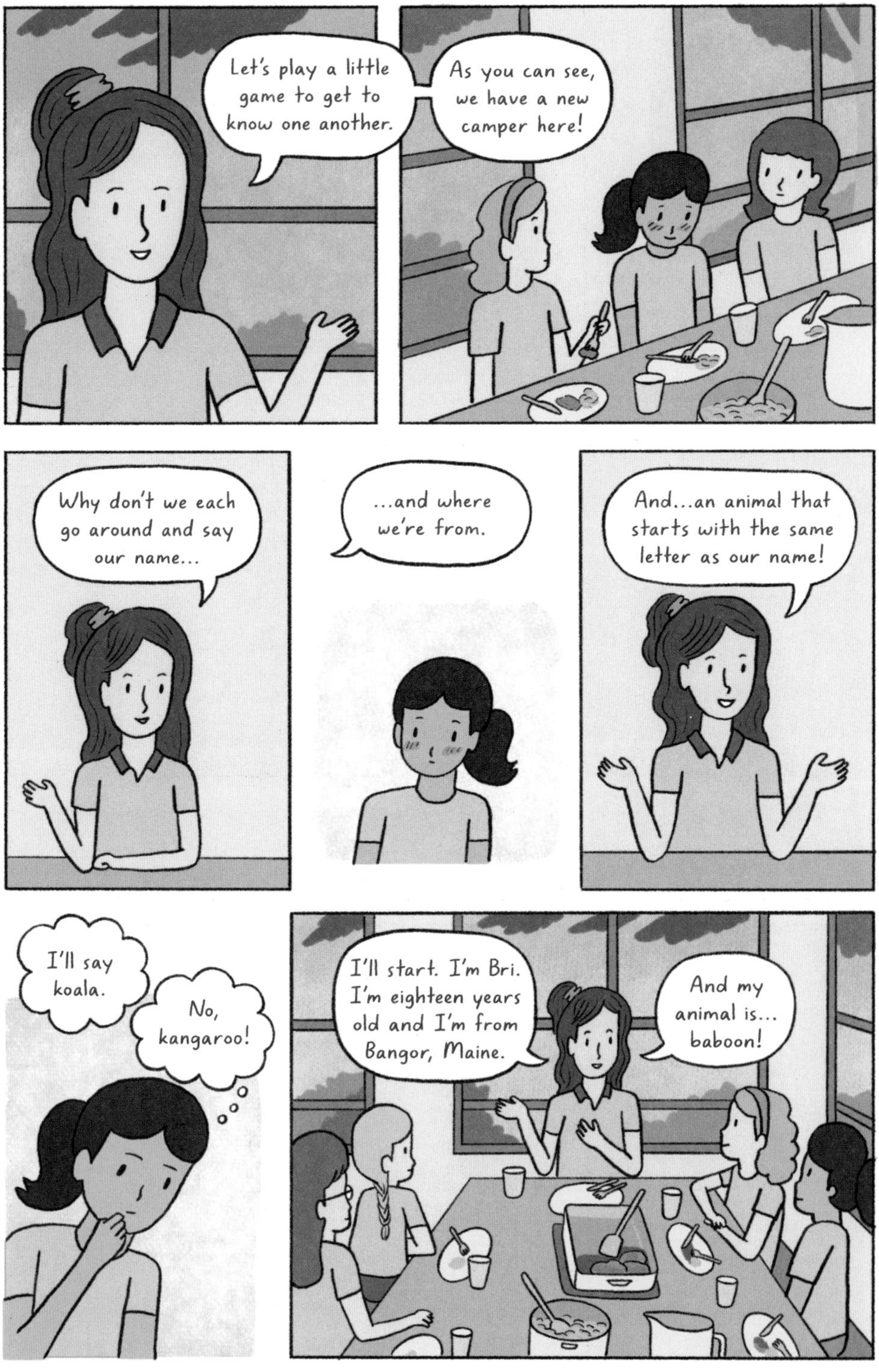
Let's play a little game to get to know one another.
As you can see, we have a new camper here!
Why don't we each go around and say our name...
...and where we're from.
And...an animal that starts with the same letter as our name!
I'll say koala.
No, kangaroo!
I'll start. I'm Bri. I'm eighteen years old and I'm from Bangor, Maine.
And my animal is... baboon!

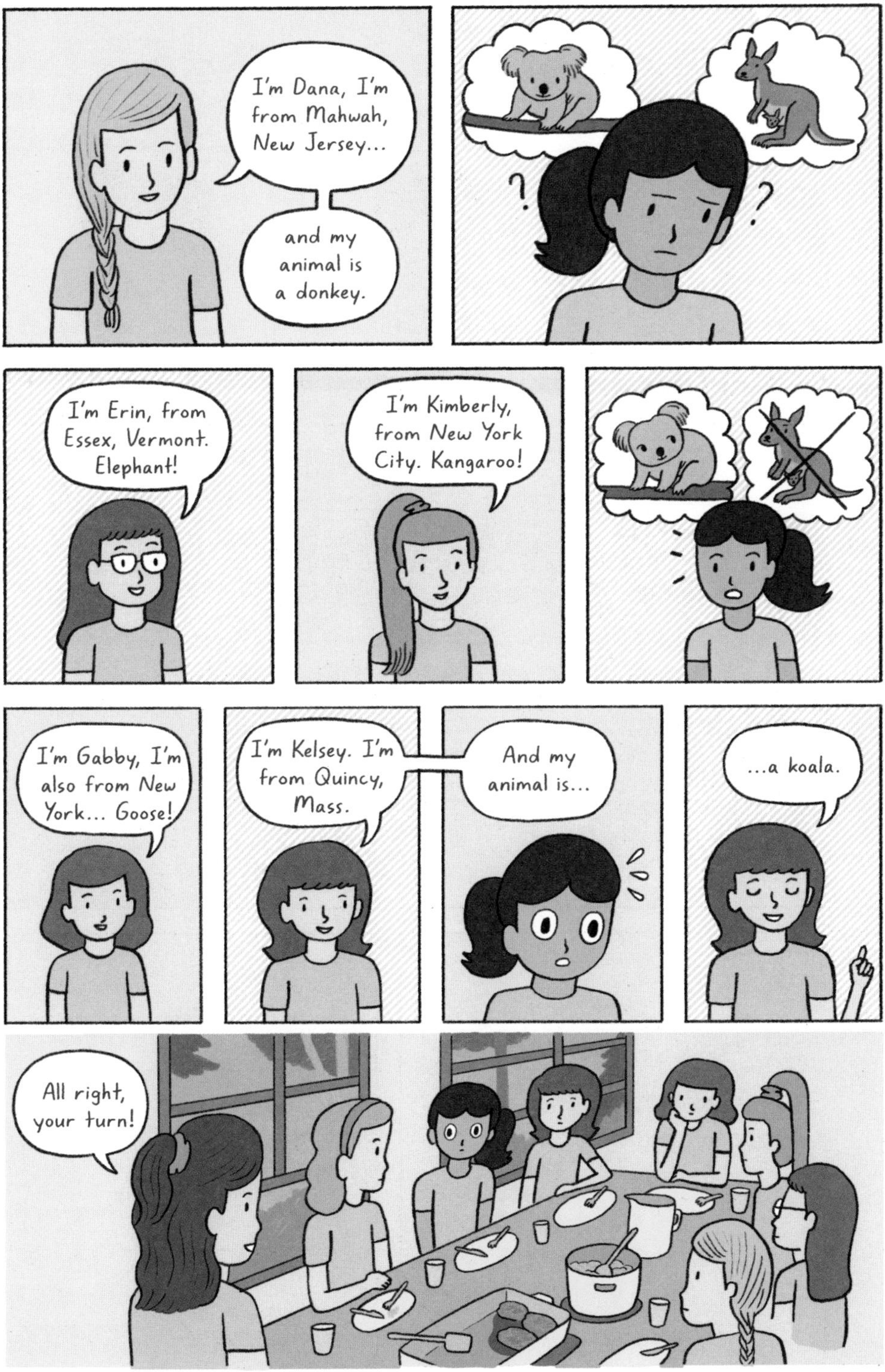
I'm Dana, I'm from Mahwah, New Jersey...
and my animal is a donkey.
?
?
I'm Erin, from Essex, Vermont. Elephant!
I'm Kimberly, from New York City. Kangaroo!
I'm Gabby, I'm also from New York... Goose!
I'm Kelsey. I'm from Quincy, Mass.
And my animal is...
...a koala.
All right, your turn!

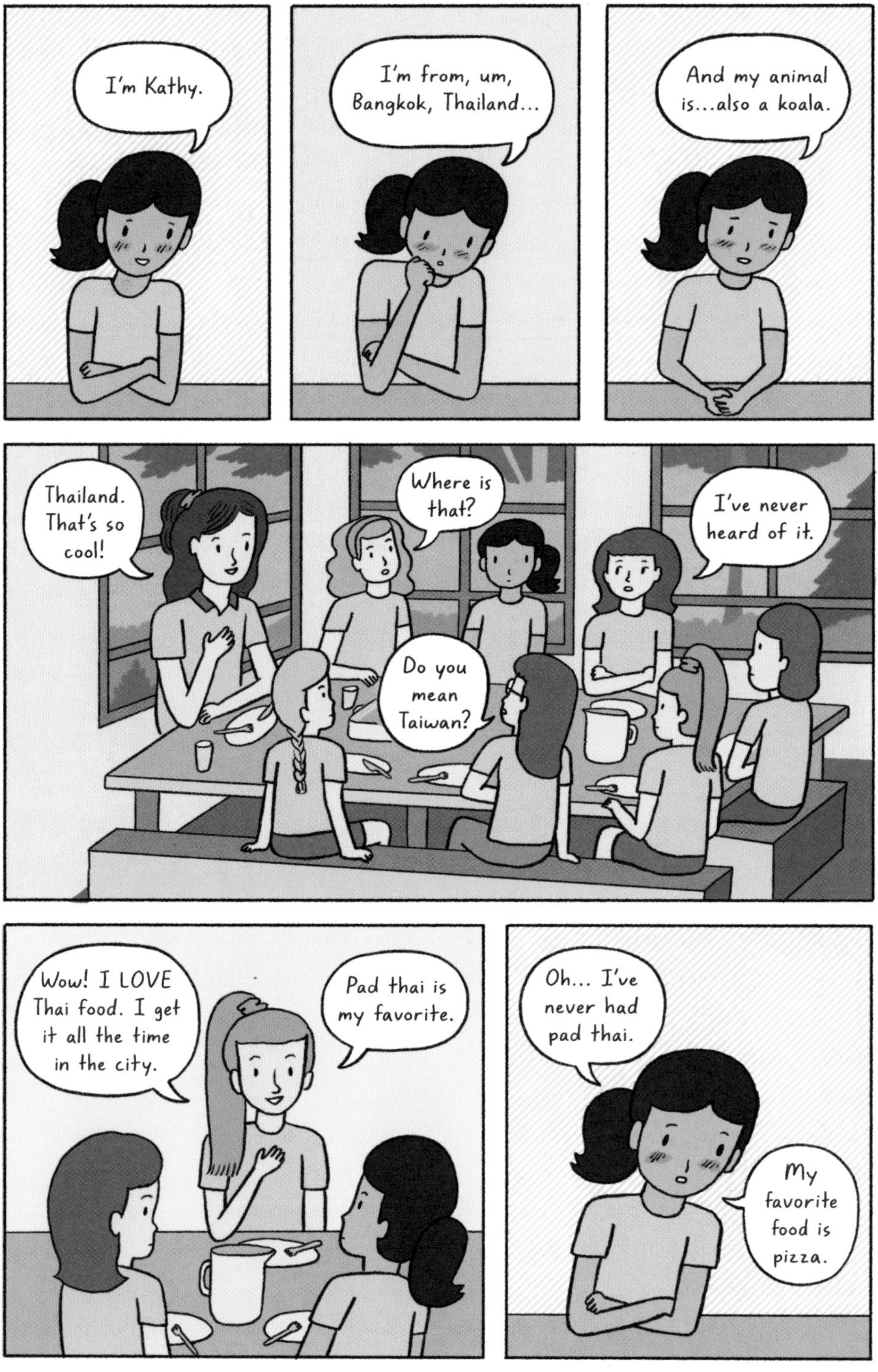
I'm Kathy.
I'm from, um, Bangkok, Thailand...
And my animal is...also a koala.
Thailand. That's so cool!
Where is that?
I've never heard of it.
Do you mean Taiwan?
Wow! I LOVE Thai food. I get it all the time in the city.
Pad thai is my favorite.
Oh... I've never had pad thai.
My favorite food is pizza.

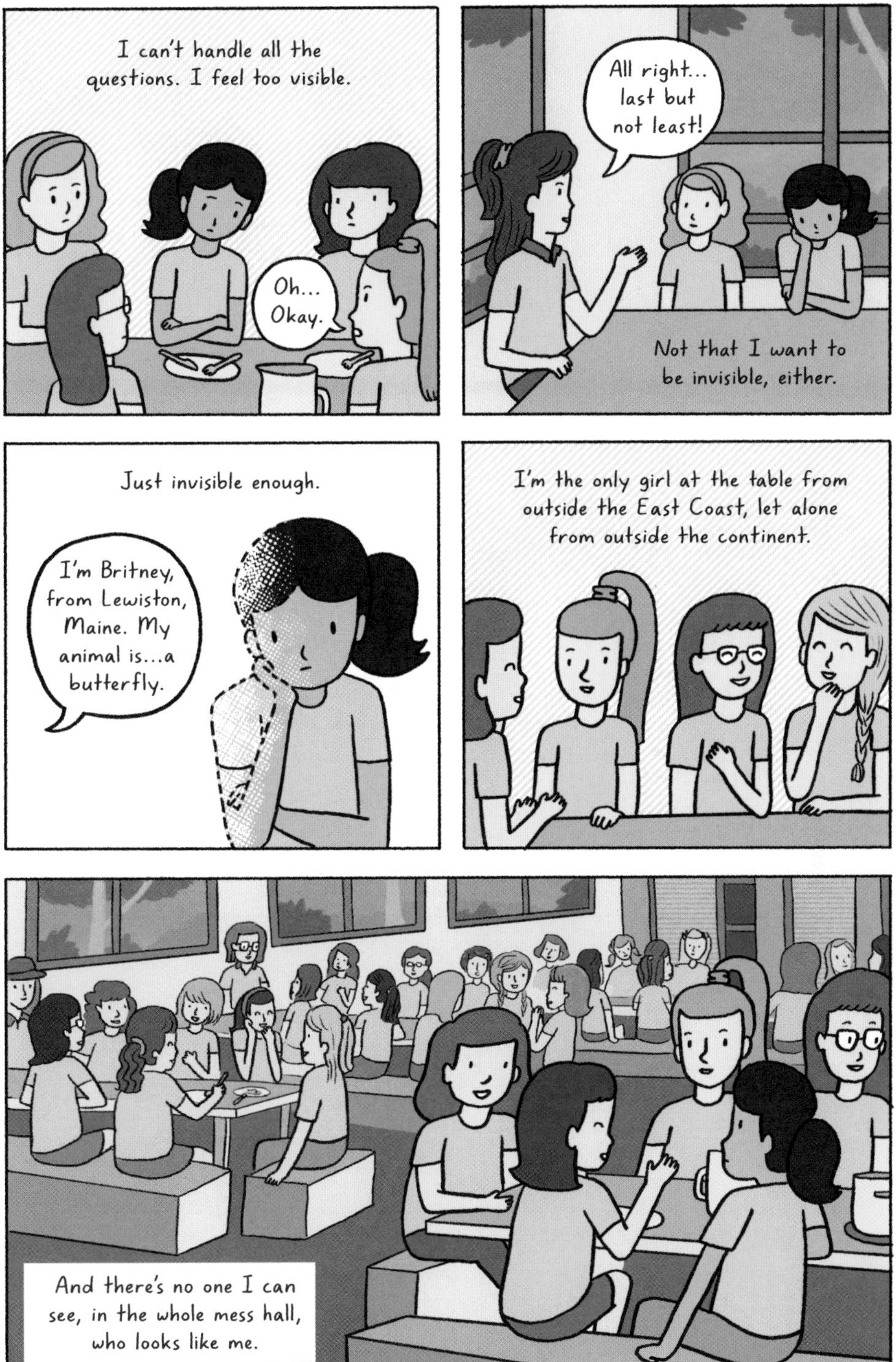
I can't handle all the questions. I feel too visible.
Oh... Okay.
All right... last but not least!
Not that I want to be invisible, either.
Just invisible enough.
I'm Britney, from Lewiston, Maine. My animal is...a butterfly.
I'm the only girl at the table from outside the East Coast, let alone from outside the continent.
And there's no one I can see, in the whole mess hall, who looks like me.

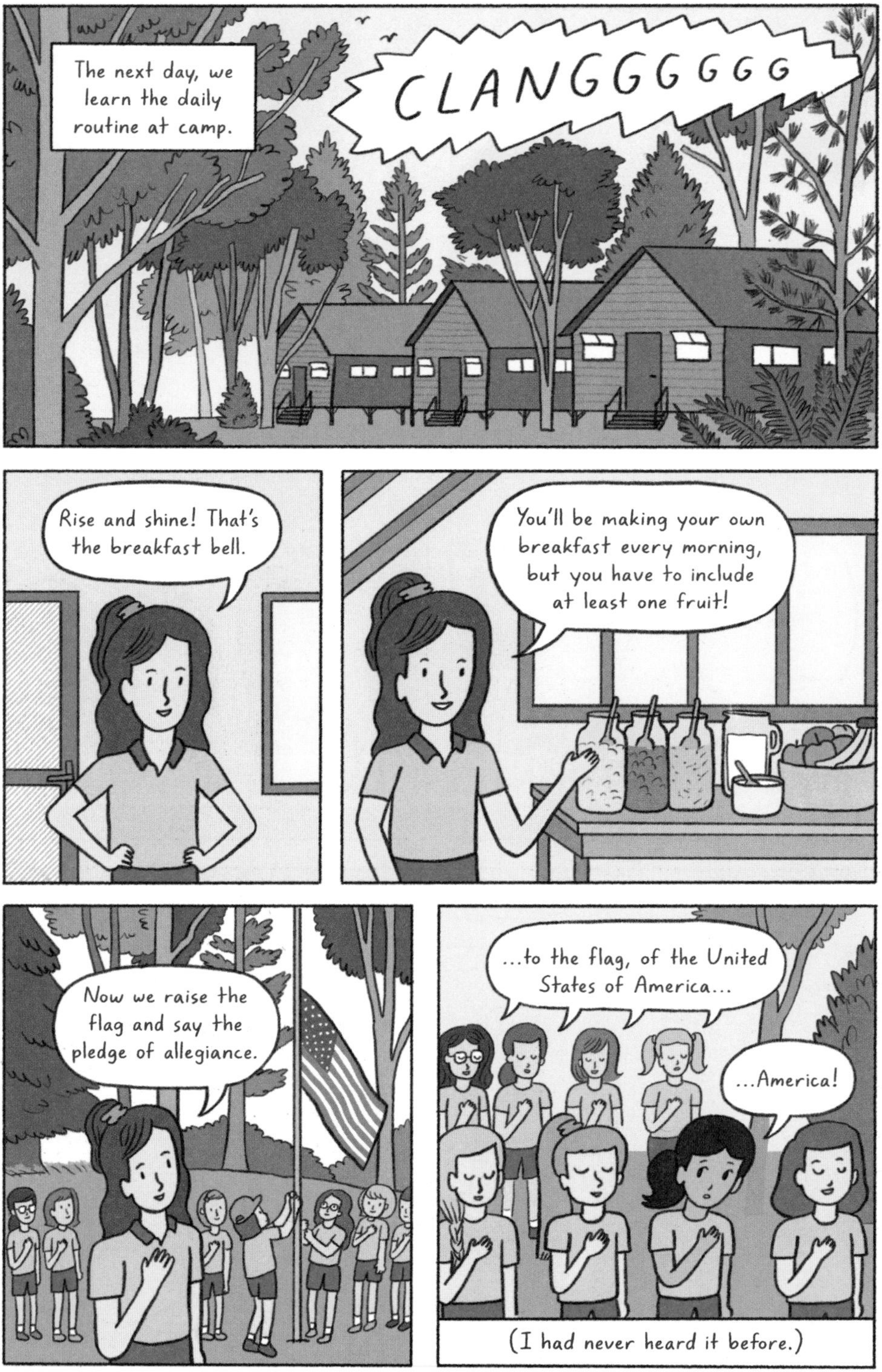
The next day, we learn the daily routine at camp.
CLANGGGGGG
Rise and shine! That's the breakfast bell.
You'll be making your own breakfast every morning, but you have to include at least one fruit!
Now we raise the flag and say the pledge of allegiance.
...to the flag, of the United States of America...
...America!
(I had never heard it before.)

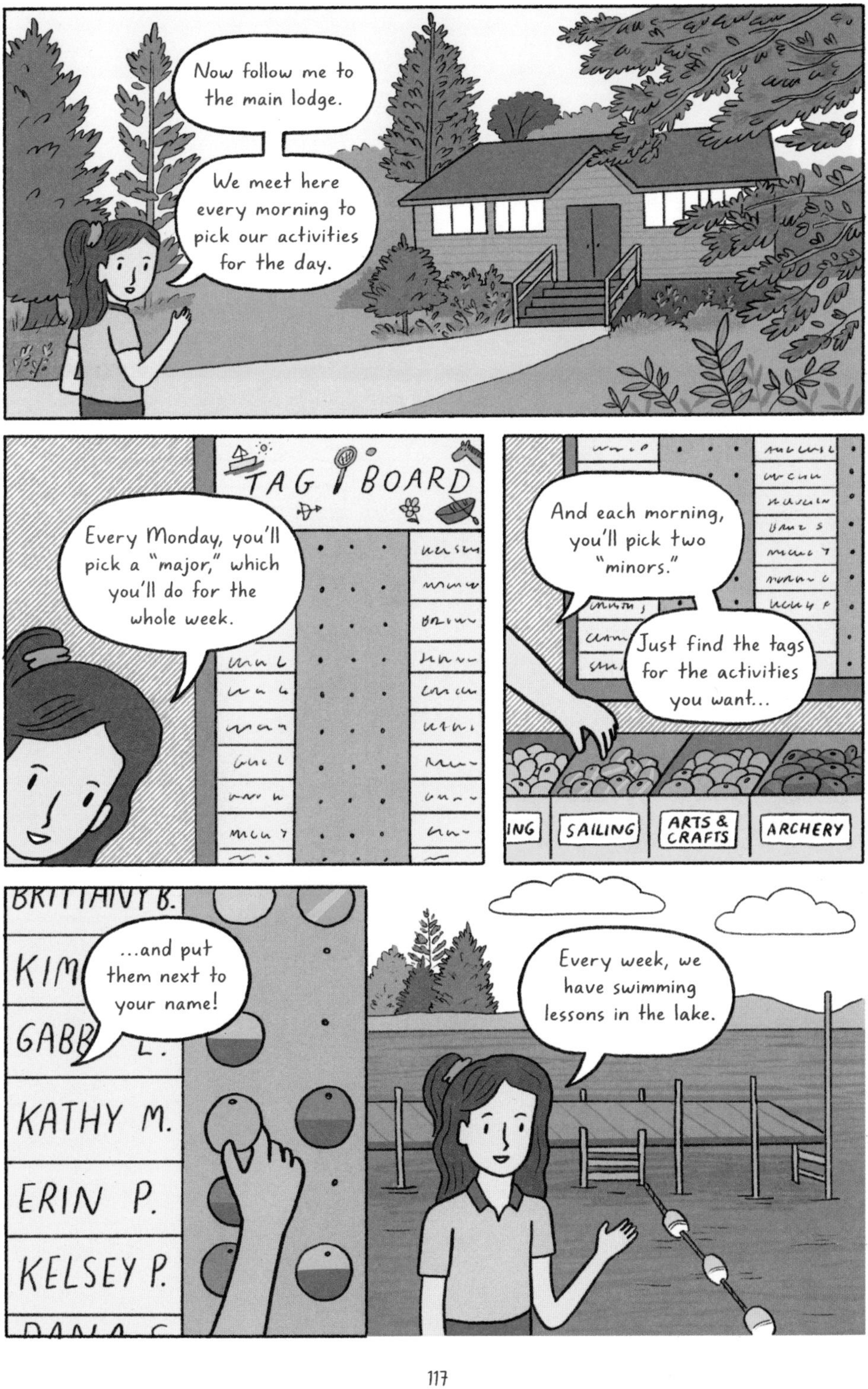
Now follow me to the main lodge.
We meet here every morning to pick our activities for the day.
TAG BOARD
Every Monday, you'll pick a "major," which you'll do for the whole week.
And each morning, you'll pick two "minors."
Just find the tags for the activities you want...
ING
SAILING
ARTS & CRAFTS
ARCHERY
BRITTANY B.
KIM
GABB
KATHY M.
ERIN P.
KELSEY P.
...and put them next to your name!
Every week, we have swimming lessons in the lake.

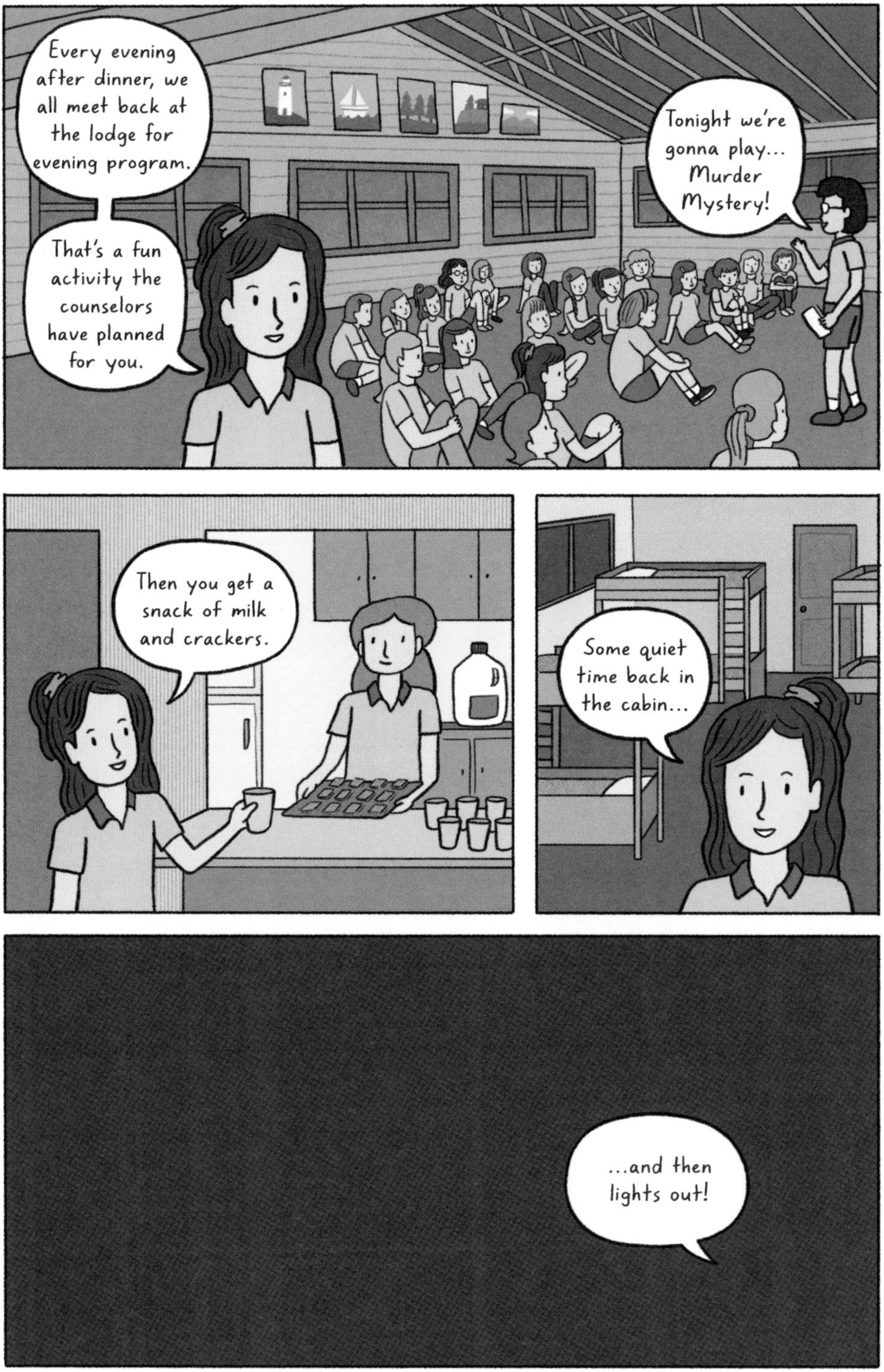
Every evening after dinner, we all meet back at the lodge for evening program.
That's a fun activity the counselors have planned for you.
Tonight we're gonna play... Murder Mystery!
Then you get a snack of milk and crackers.
Some quiet time back in the cabin...
...and then lights out!

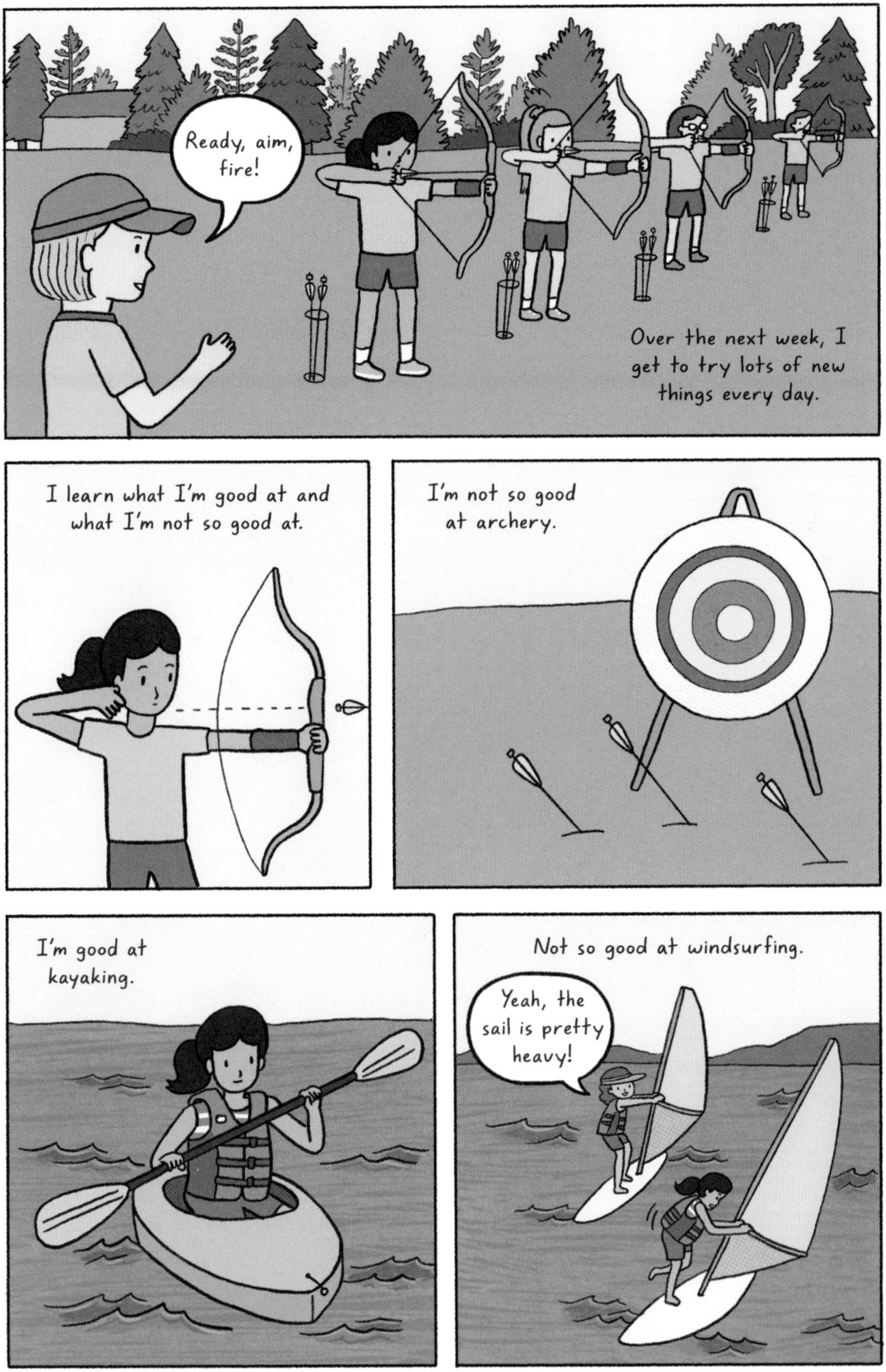
Ready, aim, fire!
Over the next week, I get to try lots of new things every day.
I learn what I'm good at and what I'm not so good at.
I'm not so good at archery.
I'm good at kayaking.
Not so good at windsurfing.
Yeah, the sail is pretty heavy!

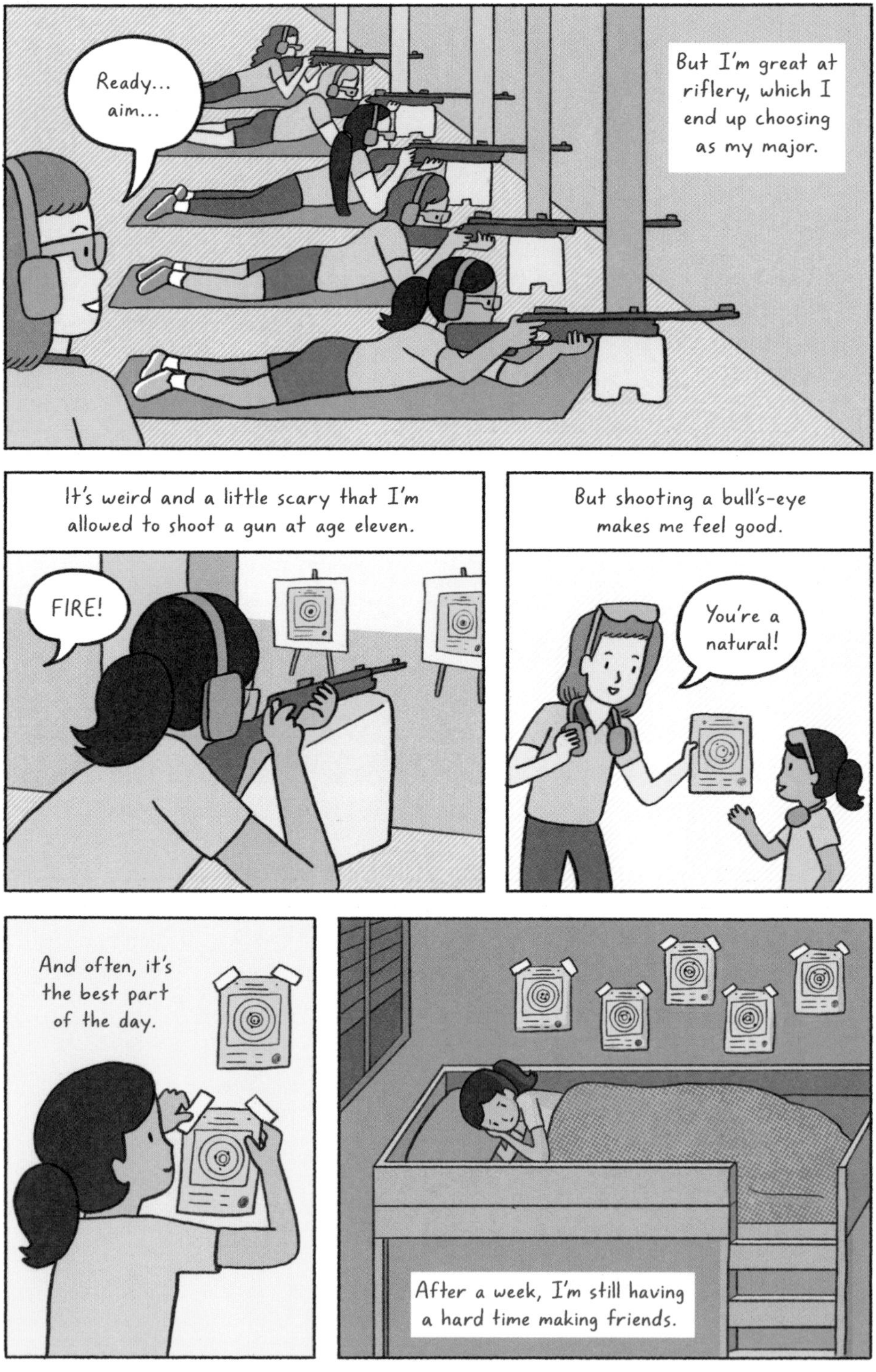
Ready... aim...
But I'm great at riflery, which I end up choosing as my major.
It's weird and a little scary that I'm allowed to shoot a gun at age eleven.
FIRE!
But shooting a bull's-eye makes me feel good.
You're a natural!
And often, it's the best part of the day.
After a week, I'm still having a hard time making friends.

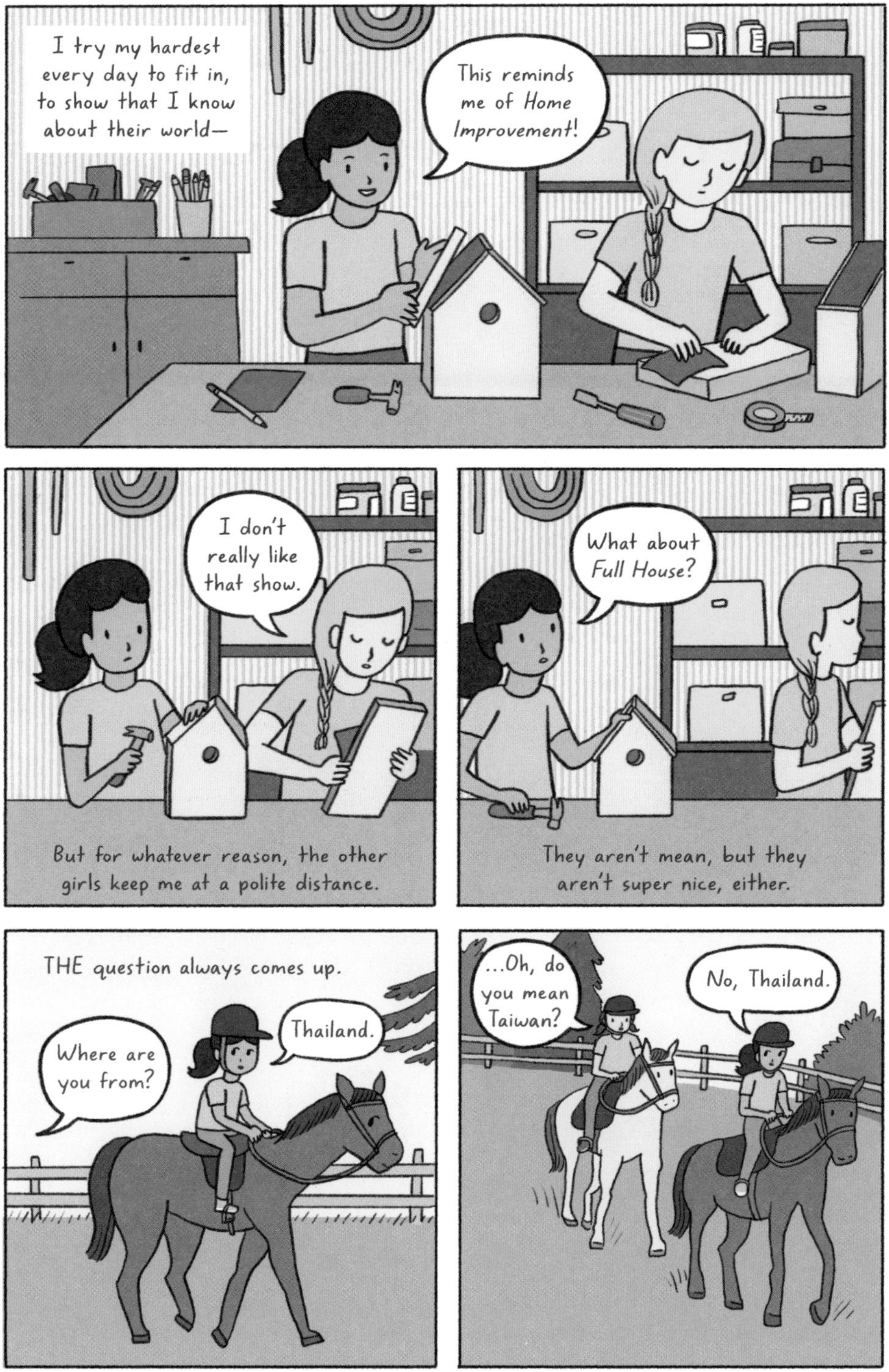
I try my hardest every day to fit in, to show that I know about their world—
This reminds me of *Home Improvement*!
I don't really like that show.
But for whatever reason, the other girls keep me at a polite distance.
What about *Full House*?
They aren't mean, but they aren't super nice, either.
THE question always comes up.
Where are you from?
Thailand.
...Oh, do you mean Taiwan?
No, Thailand.

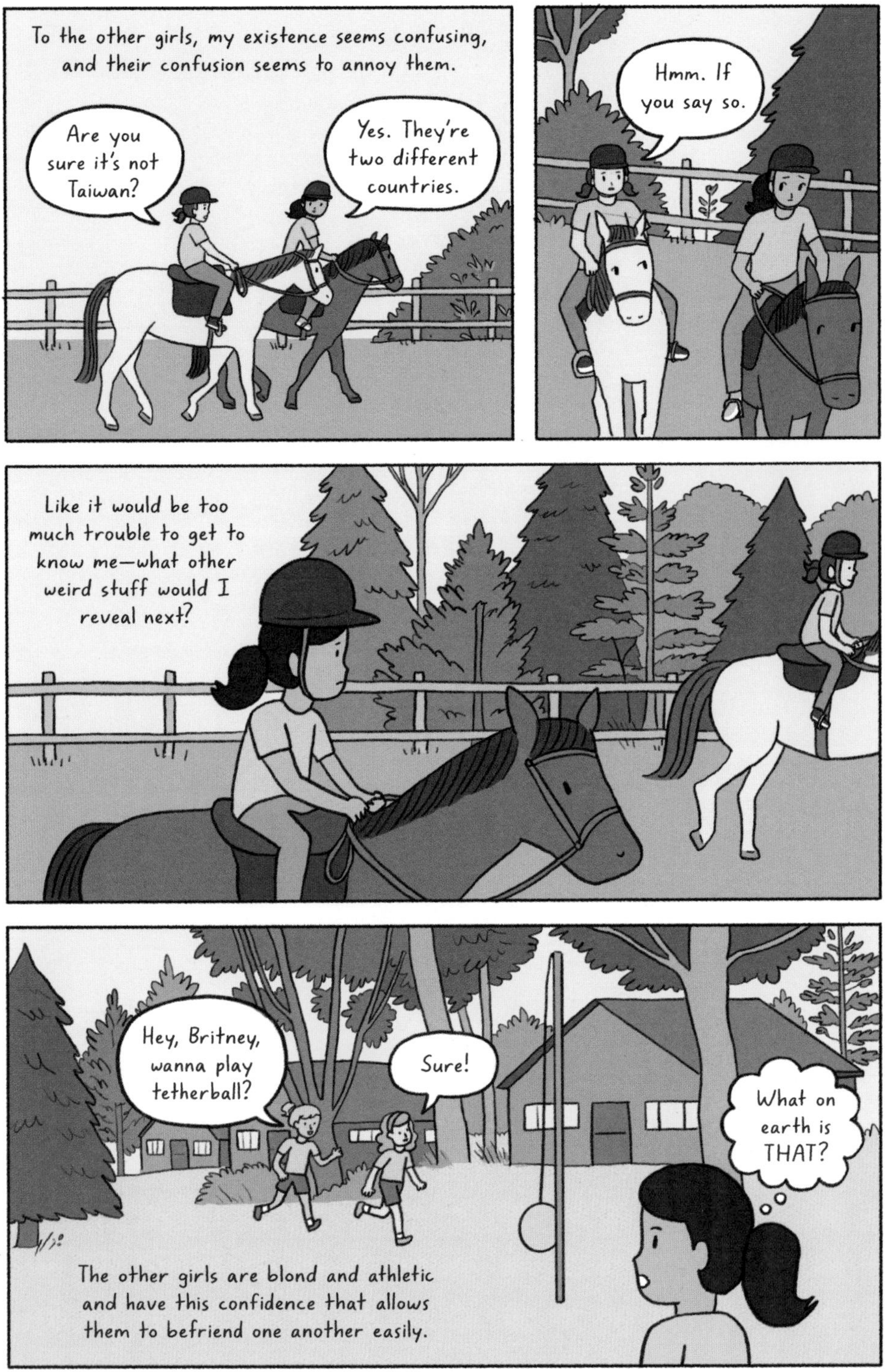

To the other girls, my existence seems confusing, and their confusion seems to annoy them.
Are you sure it's not Taiwan?
Yes. They're two different countries.
Hmm. If you say so.
Like it would be too much trouble to get to know me—what other weird stuff would I reveal next?
Hey, Britney, wanna play tetherball?
Sure!
What on earth is THAT?
The other girls are blond and athletic and have this confidence that allows them to befriend one another easily.

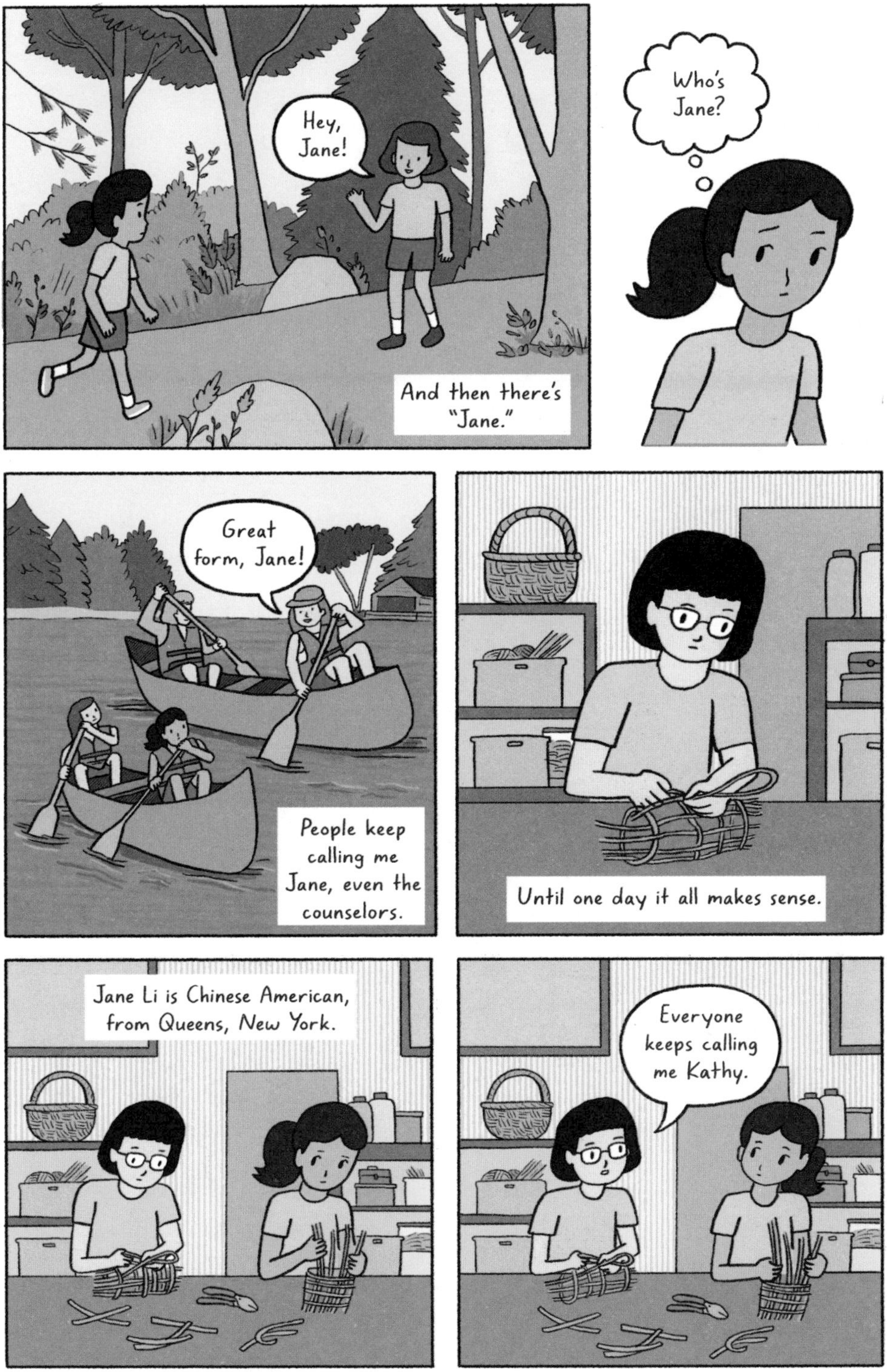
Hey, Jane!
And then there's "Jane."
Who's Jane?
Great form, Jane!
People keep calling me Jane, even the counselors.
Until one day it all makes sense.
Jane Li is Chinese American, from Queens, New York.
Everyone keeps calling me Kathy.

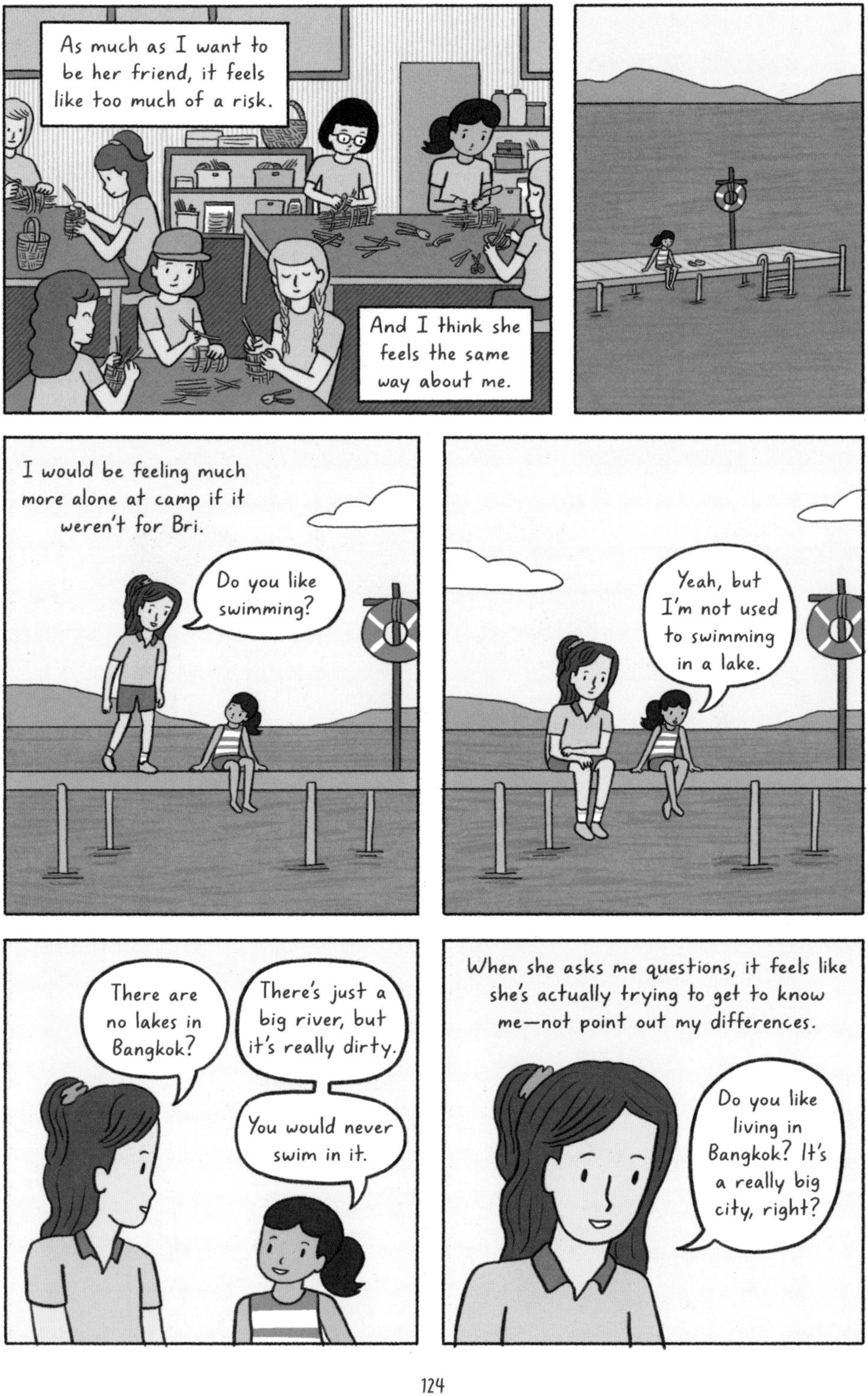
As much as I want to be her friend, it feels like too much of a risk.
And I think she feels the same way about me.
I would be feeling much more alone at camp if it weren't for Bri.
Do you like swimming?
Yeah, but I'm not used to swimming in a lake.
There are no lakes in Bangkok?
There's just a big river, but it's really dirty.
You would never swim in it.
When she asks me questions, it feels like she's actually trying to get to know me—not point out my differences.
Do you like living in Bangkok? It's a really big city, right?

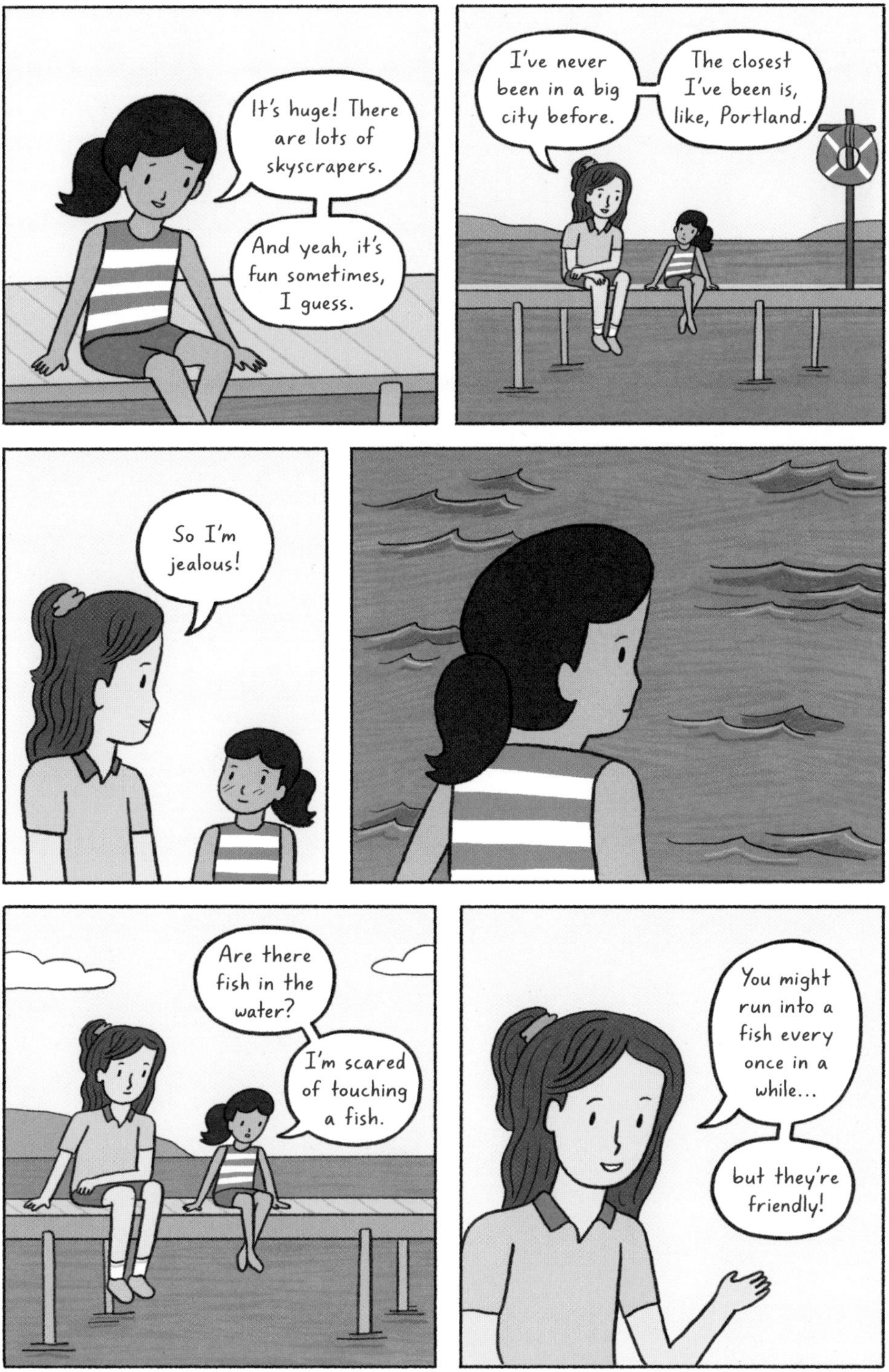
It's huge! There are lots of skyscrapers.
And yeah, it's fun sometimes, I guess.
I've never been in a big city before.
The closest I've been is, like, Portland.
So I'm jealous!
Are there fish in the water?
I'm scared of touching a fish.
You might run into a fish every once in a while...
but they're friendly!

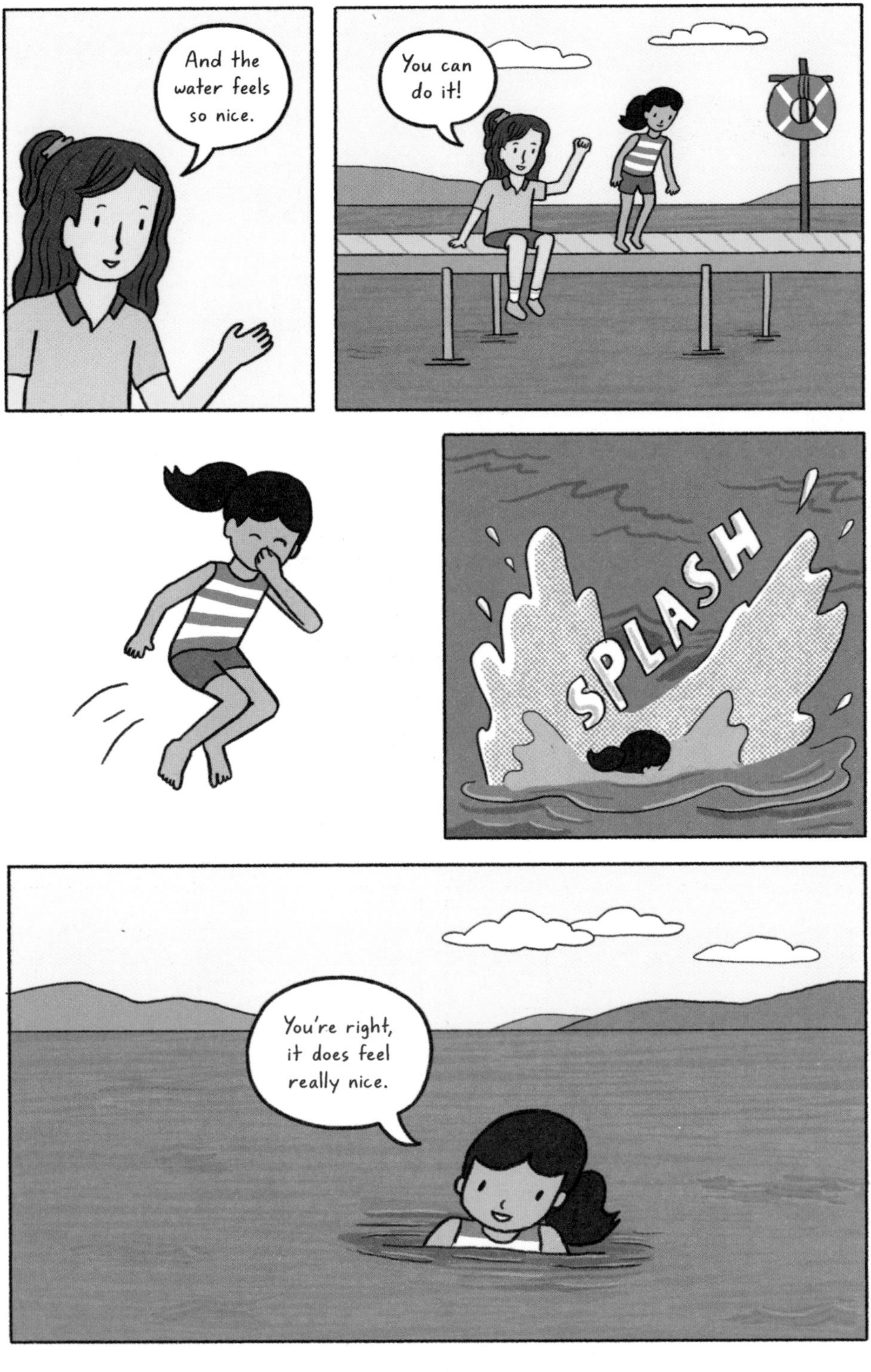
And the water feels so nice.
You can do it!
SPLASH
You're right, it does feel really nice.

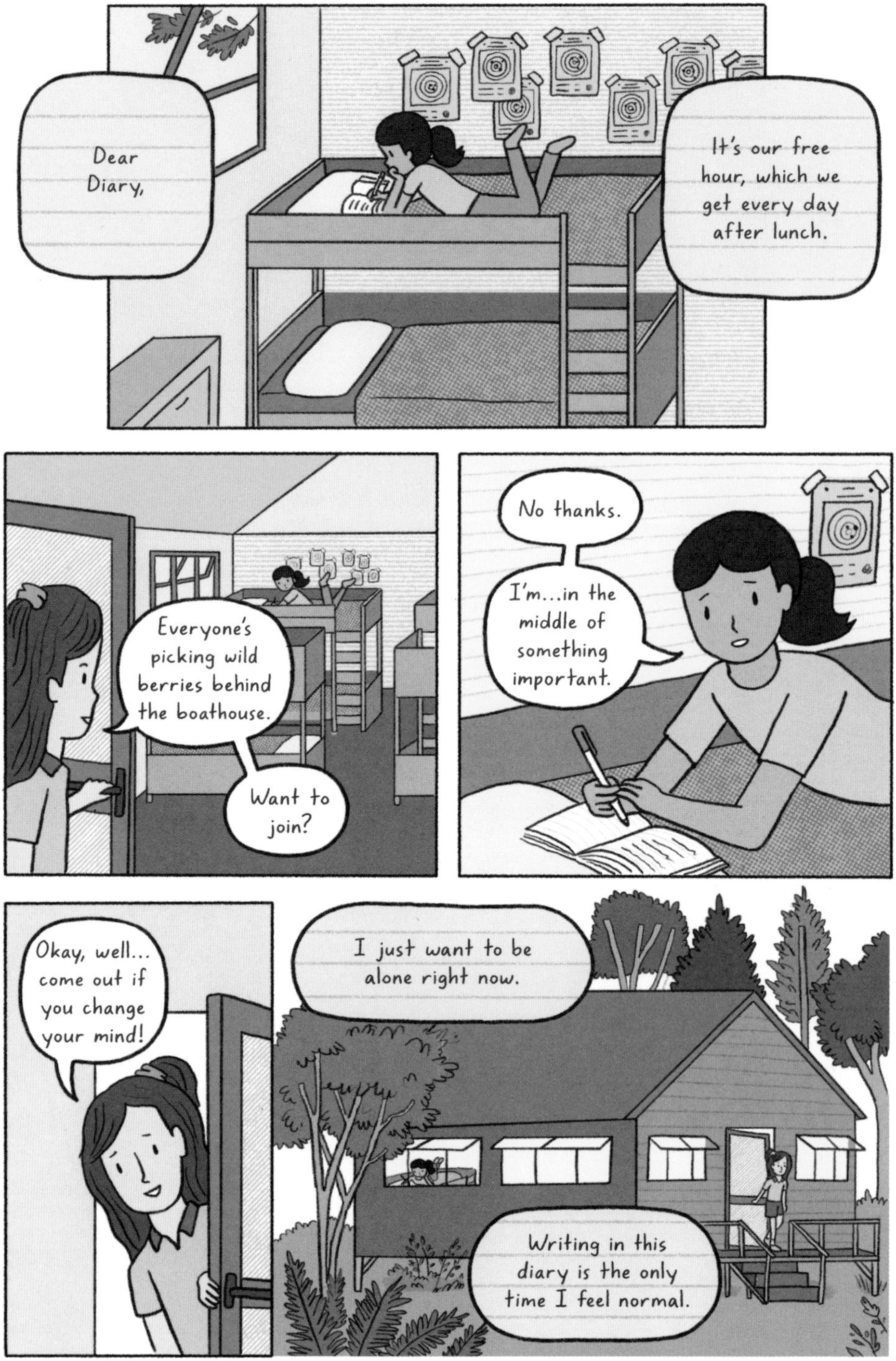
Dear Diary,
It's our free hour, which we get every day after lunch.
Everyone's picking wild berries behind the boathouse.
Want to join?
No thanks.
I'm...in the middle of something important.
Okay, well... come out if you change your mind!
I just want to be alone right now.
Writing in this diary is the only time I feel normal.

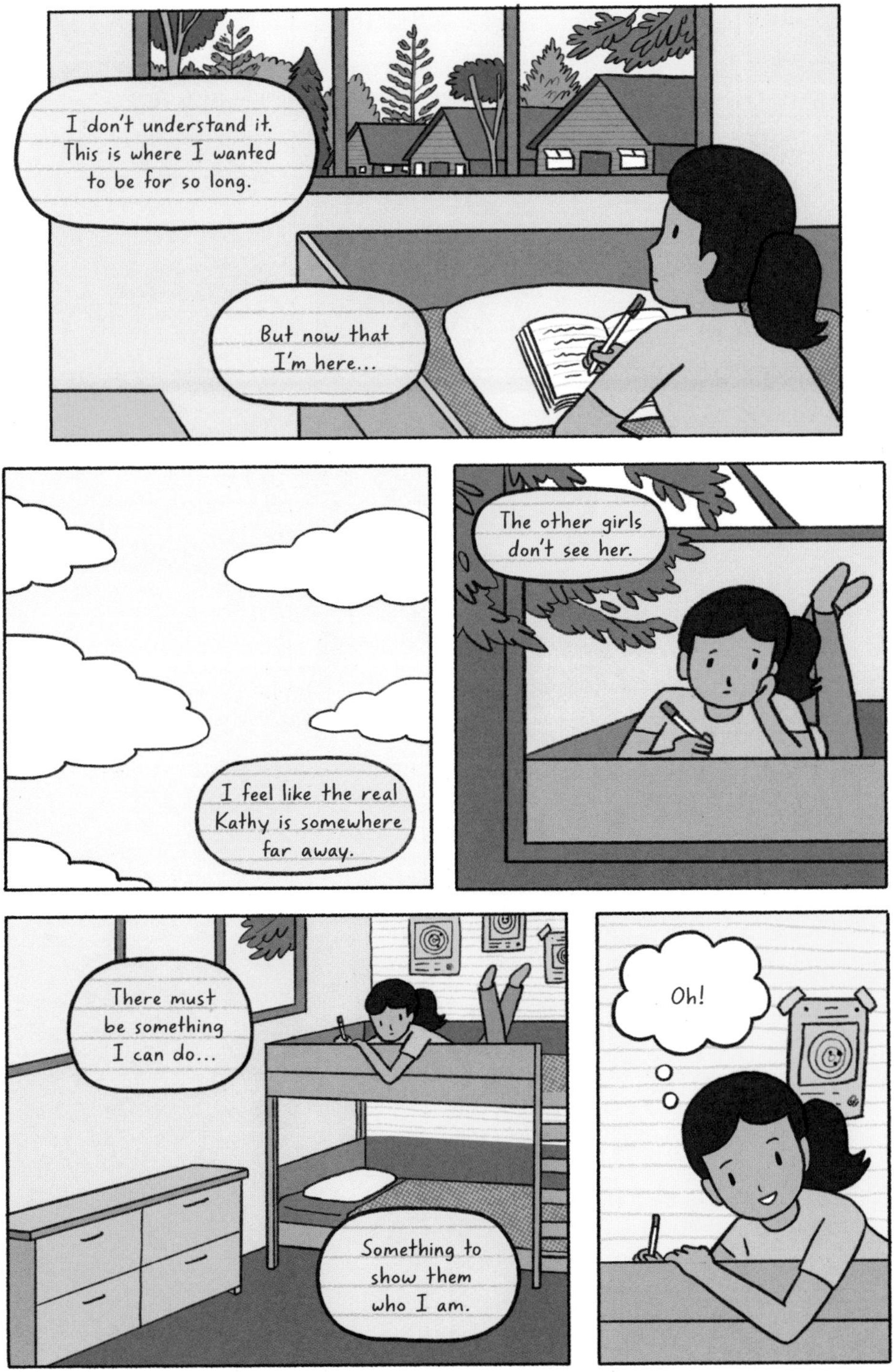
I don't understand it. This is where I wanted to be for so long.
But now that I'm here...
I feel like the real Kathy is somewhere far away.
The other girls don't see her.
There must be something I can do...
Something to show them who I am.
Oh!

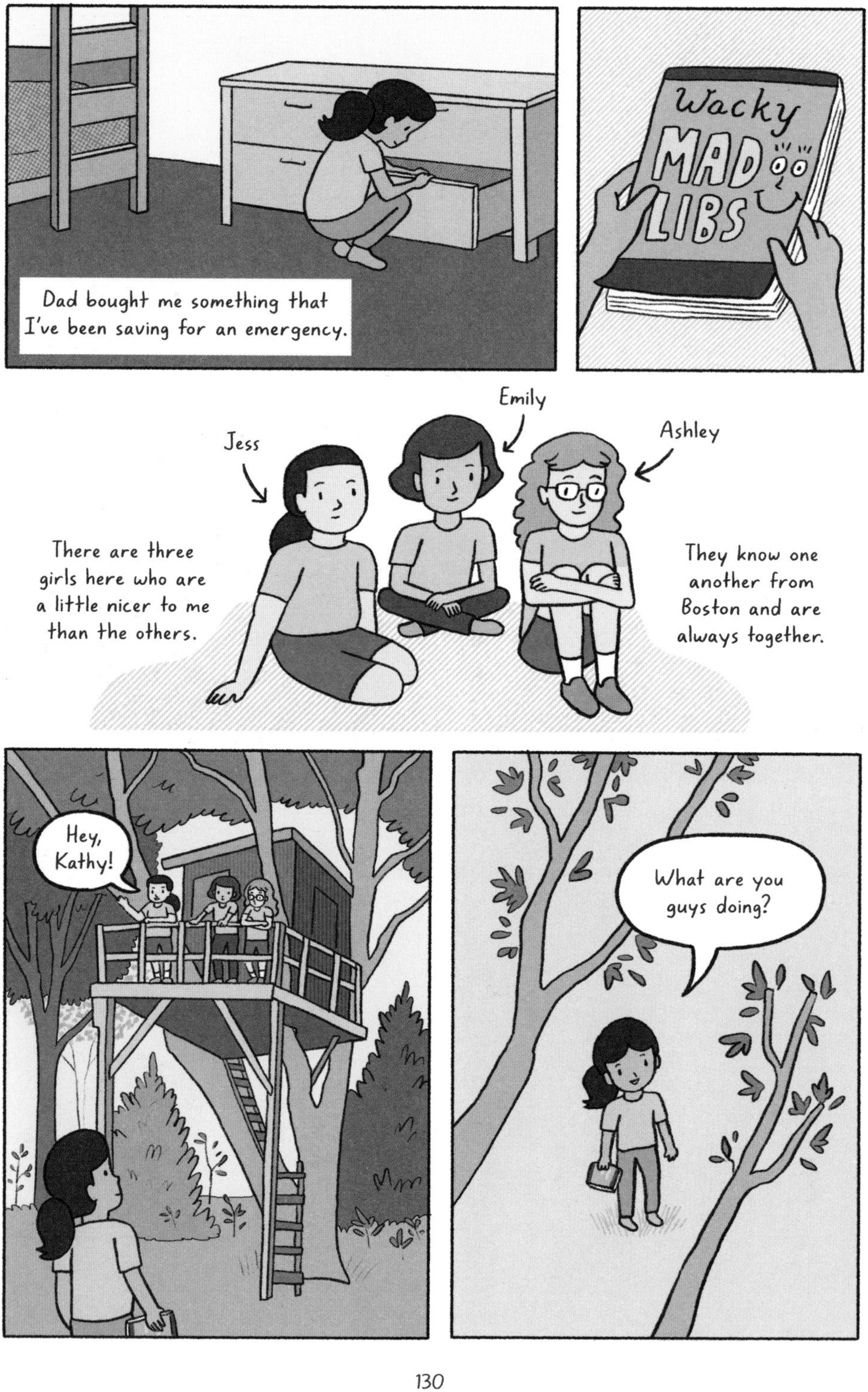

Dad bought me something that I've been saving for an emergency.
Wacky MAD LIBS
Jess
Emily
Ashley
There are three girls here who are a little nicer to me than the others.
They know one another from Boston and are always together.
Hey, Kathy!
What are you guys doing?

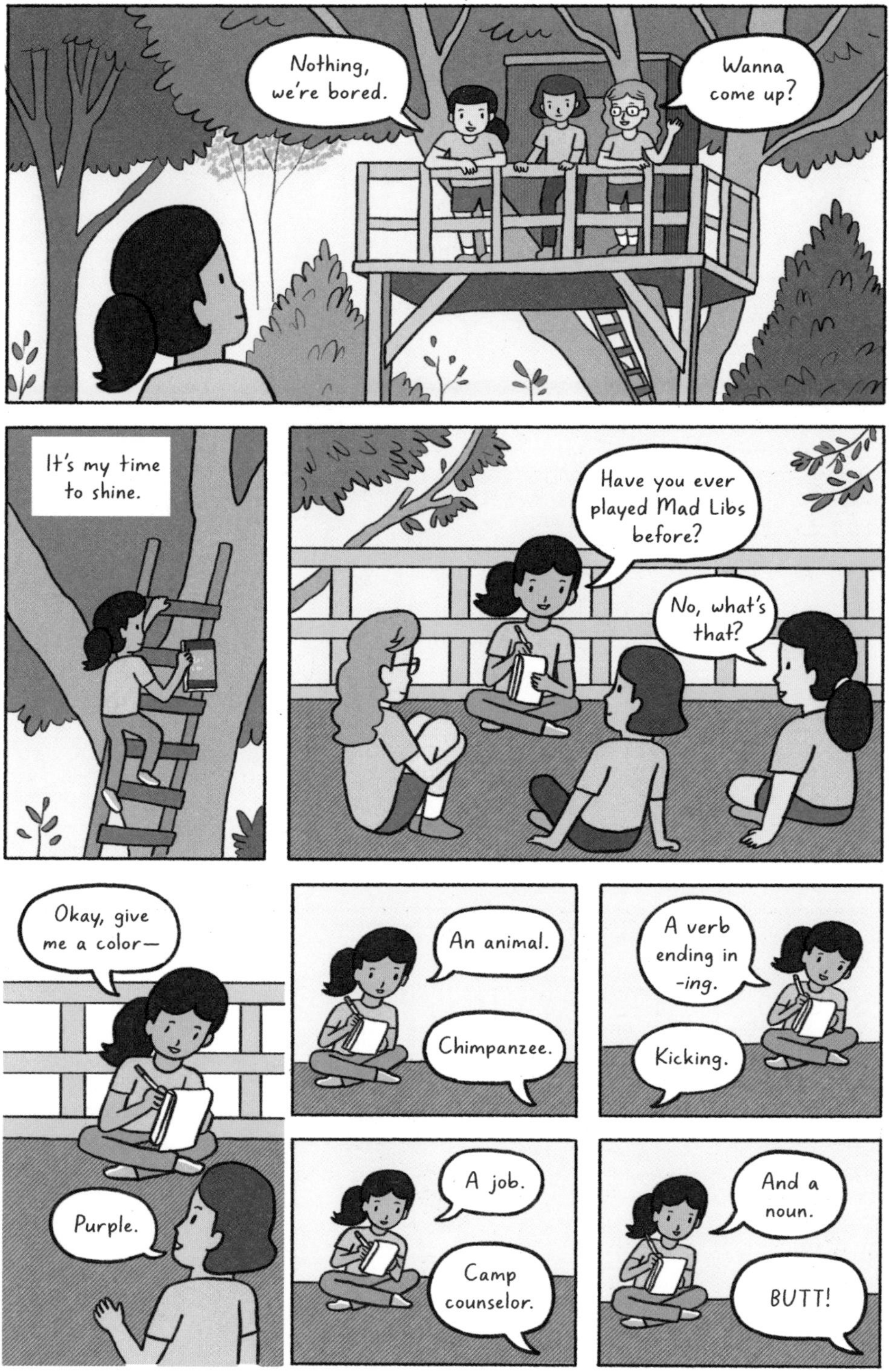

Nothing, we're bored.
Wanna come up?
It's my time to shine.
Have you ever played Mad Libs before?
No, what's that?
Okay, give me a color—
Purple.
An animal.
Chimpanzee.
A verb ending in -ing.
Kicking.
A job.
Camp counselor.
And a noun.
BUTT!

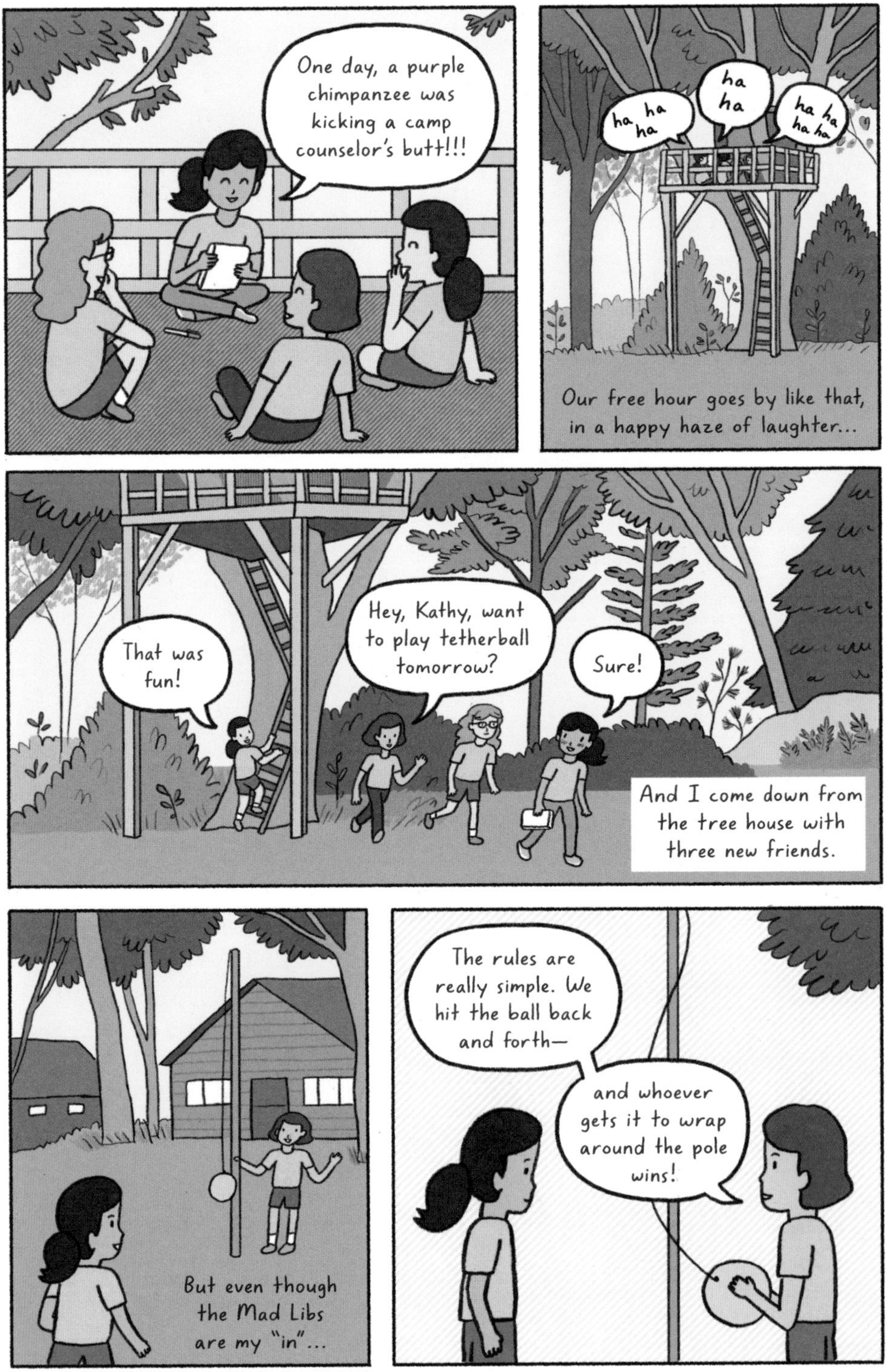
One day, a purple chimpanzee was kicking a camp counselor's butt!!!
ha ha ha
ha ha
ha ha ha ha
Our free hour goes by like that, in a happy haze of laughter...
That was fun!
Hey, Kathy, want to play tetherball tomorrow?
Sure!
And I come down from the tree house with three new friends.
But even though the Mad Libs are my "in"...
The rules are really simple. We hit the ball back and forth—
and whoever gets it to wrap around the pole wins!

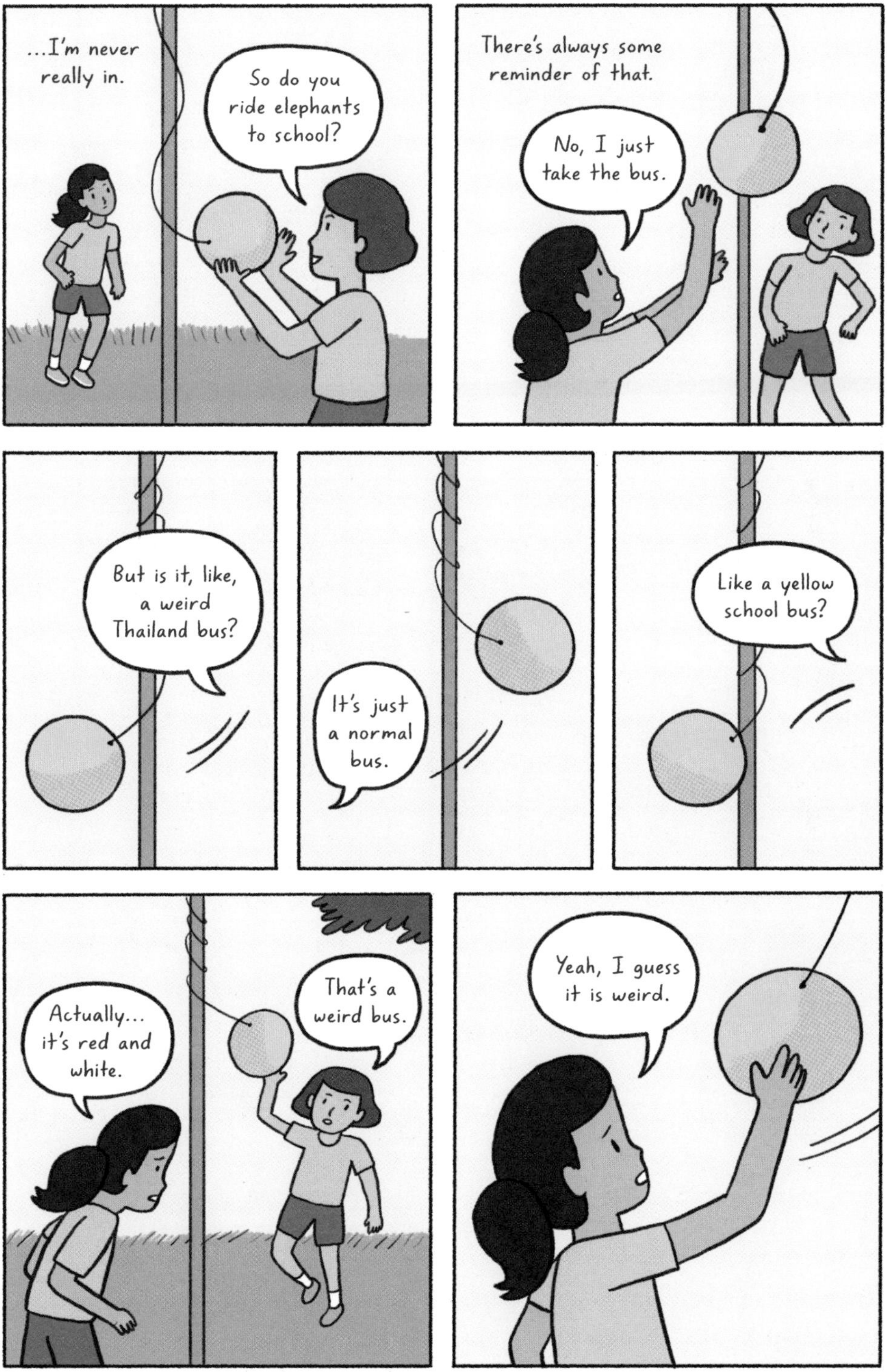
...I'm never really in.
So do you ride elephants to school?
There's always some reminder of that.
No, I just take the bus.
But is it, like, a weird Thailand bus?
It's just a normal bus.
Like a yellow school bus?
Actually... it's red and white.
That's a weird bus.
Yeah, I guess it is weird.

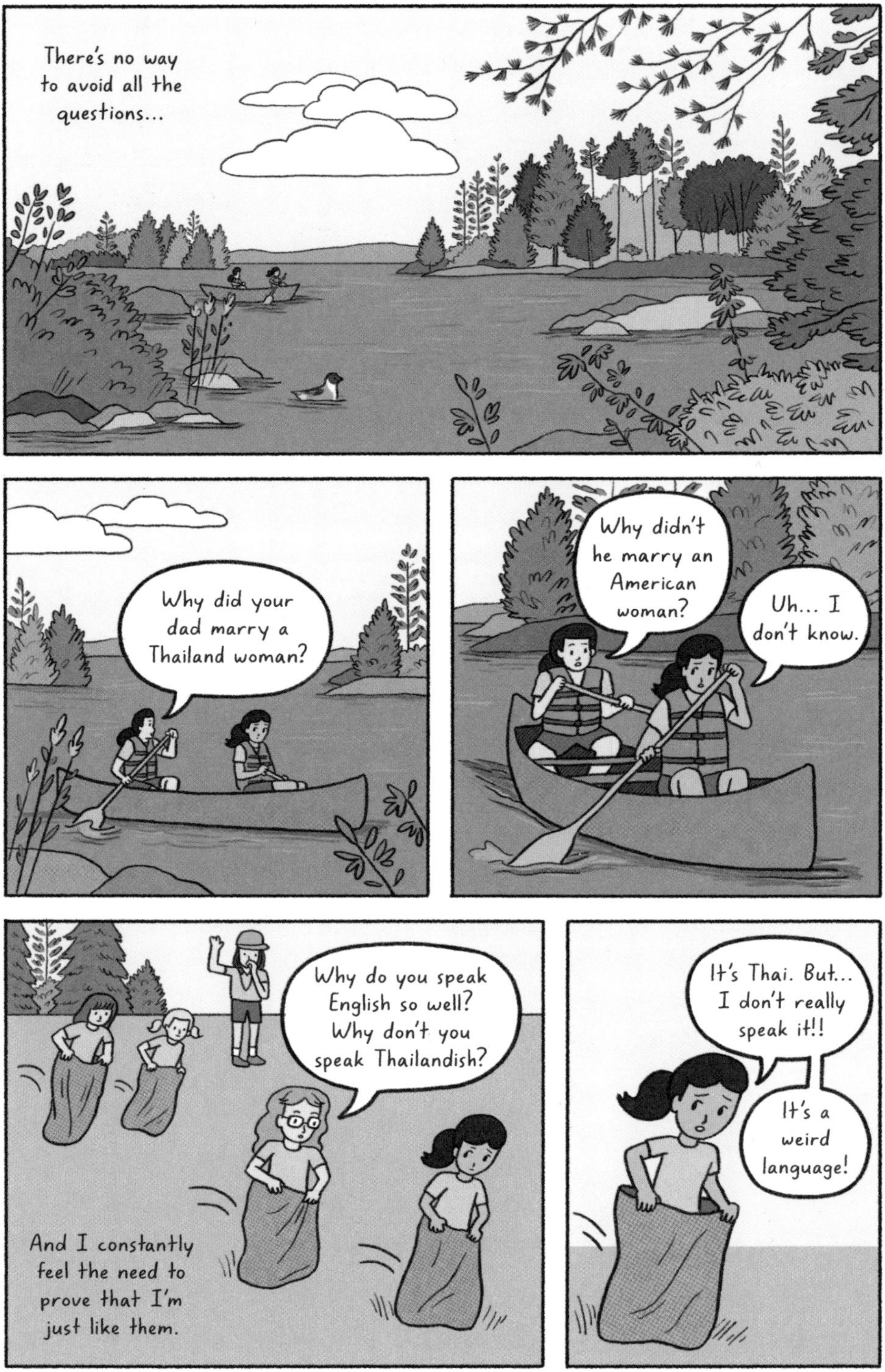
There's no way to avoid all the questions...
Why did your dad marry a Thailand woman?
Why didn't he marry an American woman?
Uh... I don't know.
Why do you speak English so well? Why don't you speak Thailandish?
And I constantly feel the need to prove that I'm just like them.
It's Thai. But... I don't really speak it!!
It's a weird language!

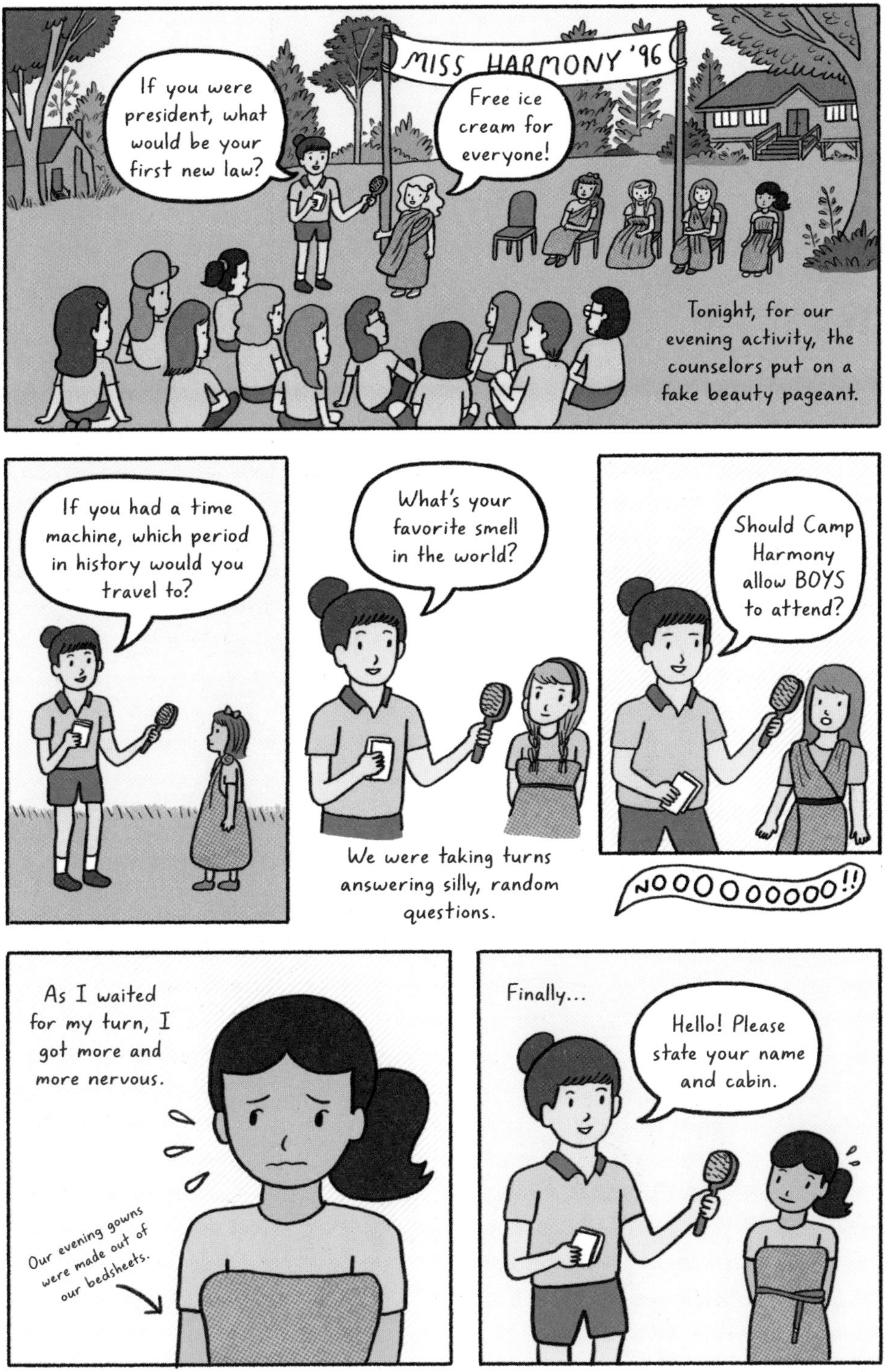
MISS HARMONY '96
If you were president, what would be your first new law?
Free ice cream for everyone!
Tonight, for our evening activity, the counselors put on a fake beauty pageant.
If you had a time machine, which period in history would you travel to?
What's your favorite smell in the world?
We were taking turns answering silly, random questions.
Should Camp Harmony allow BOYS to attend?
NOOOOOOOOO!!
As I waited for my turn, I got more and more nervous.
Our evening gowns were made out of our bedsheets.
Finally...
Hello! Please state your name and cabin.

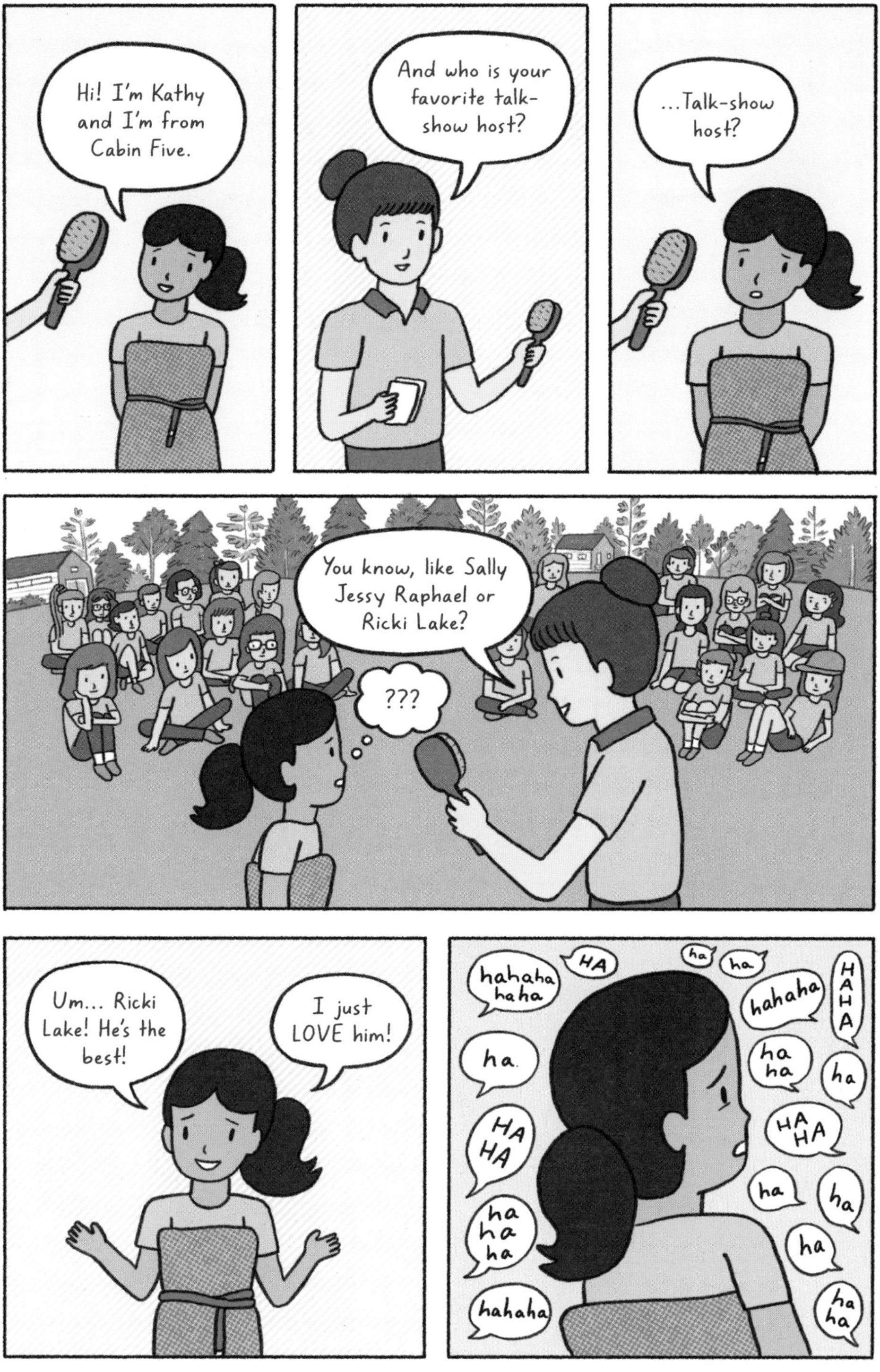

Hi! I'm Kathy and I'm from Cabin Five.
And who is your favorite talk-show host?
...Talk-show host?
You know, like Sally Jessy Raphael or Ricki Lake?
???
Um... Ricki Lake! He's the best!
I just LOVE him!
hahaha haha
HA
ha
ha
hahaha
HAHA
ha.
ha ha
ha
HA HA
HA HA
ha ha ha
ha
ha
ha
hahaha
ha ha

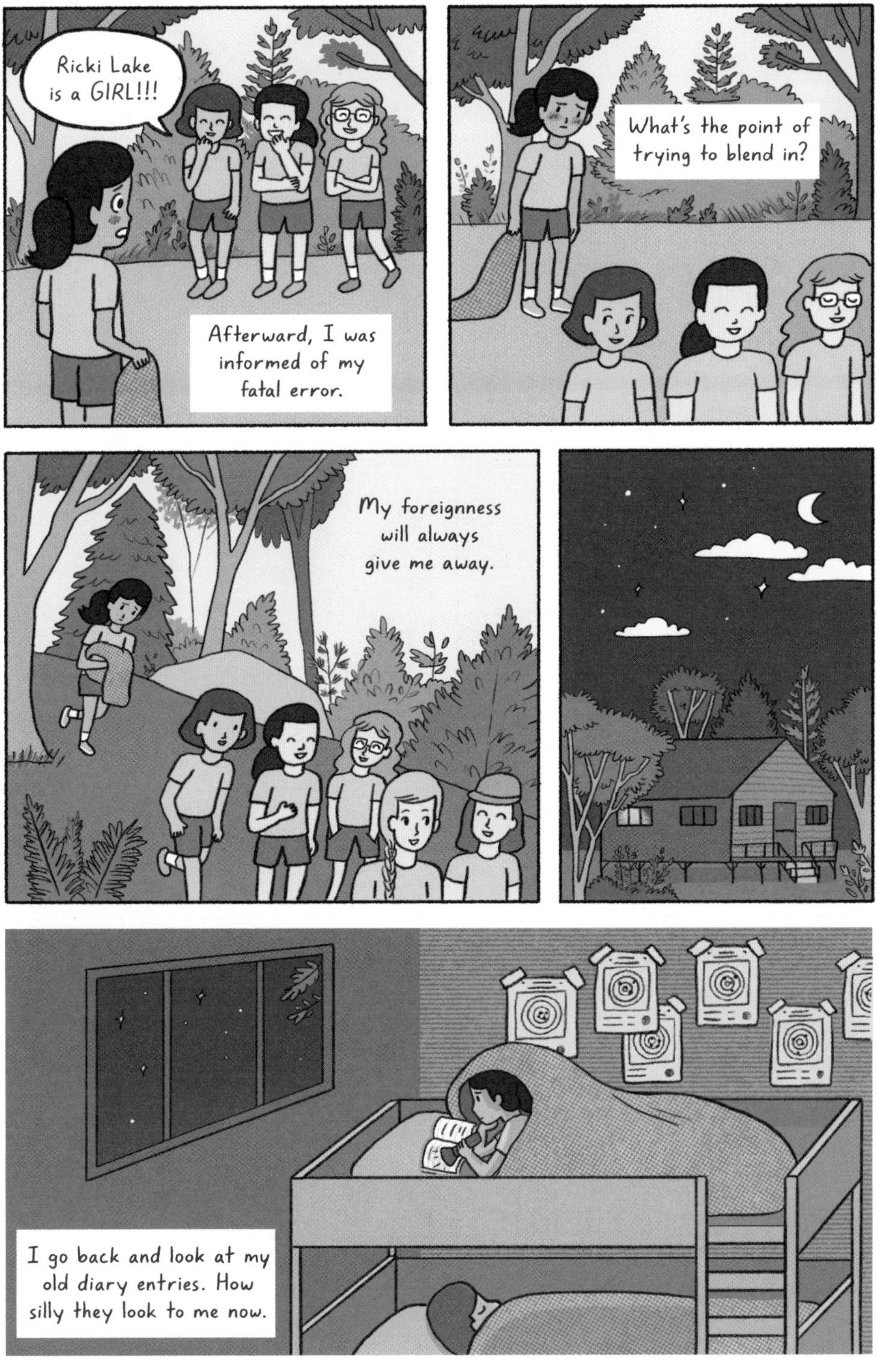
Ricki Lake is a GIRL!!!
Afterward, I was informed of my fatal error.
What's the point of trying to blend in?
My foreignness will always give me away.
I go back and look at my old diary entries. How silly they look to me now.

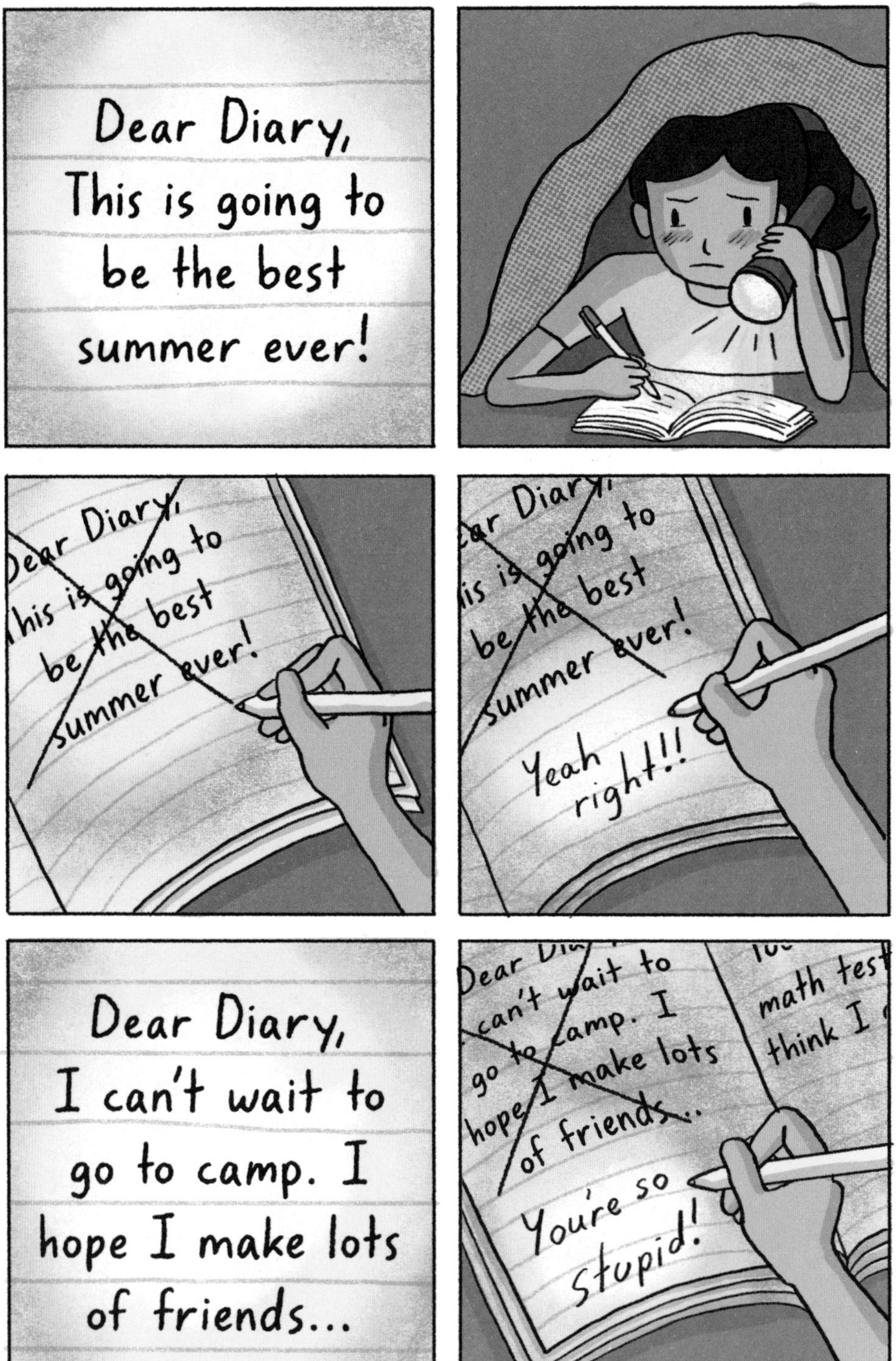
Dear Diary,
This is going to be the best summer ever!
Yeah right!!
Dear Diary,
I can't wait to go to camp. I hope I make lots of friends...
math test
You're so stupid!

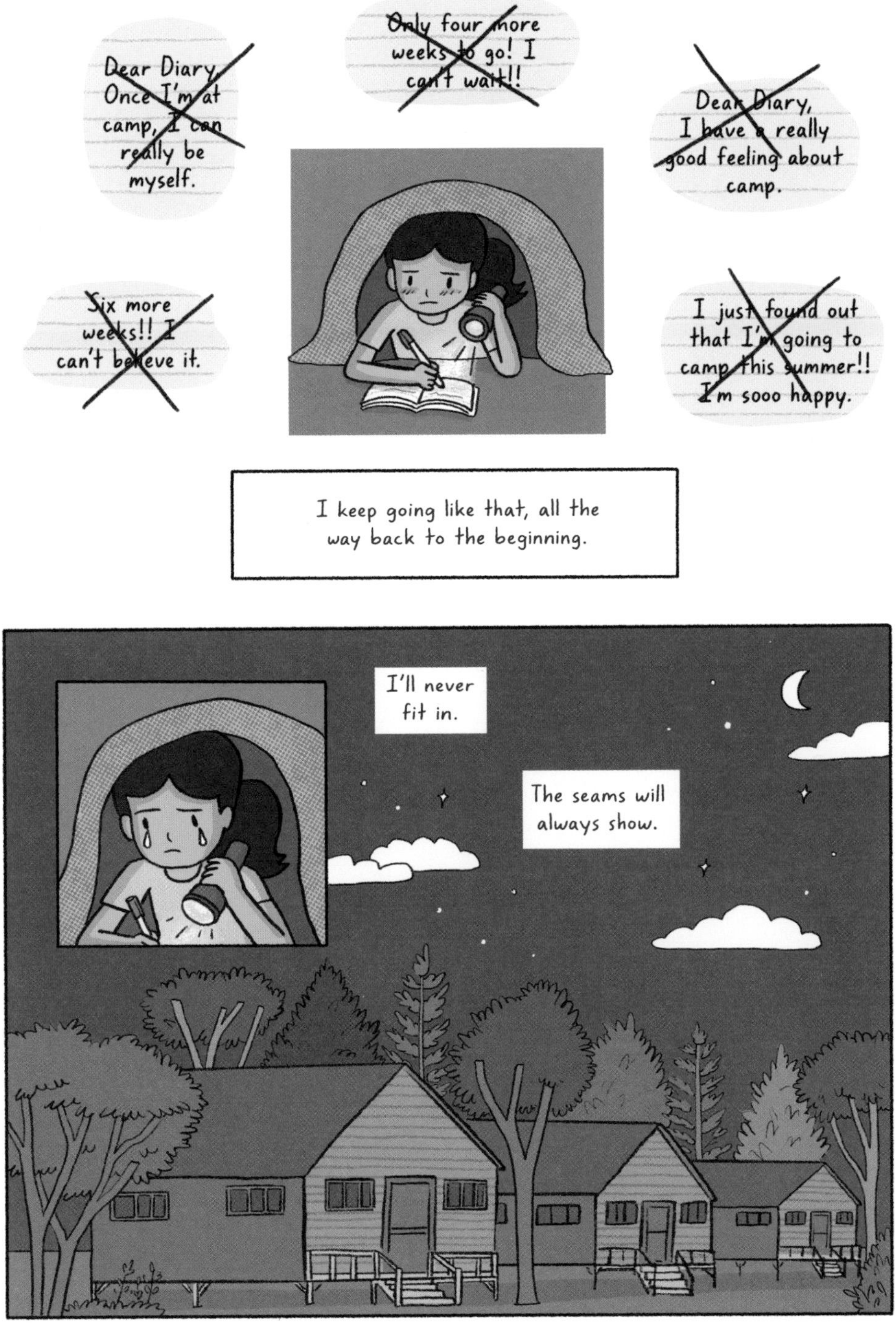
Dear Diary, Once I'm at camp, I can really be myself.
Only four more weeks to go! I can't wait!!
Dear Diary, I have a really good feeling about camp.
Six more weeks!! I can't believe it.
I just found out that I'm going to camp this summer!! I'm sooo happy.
I keep going like that, all the way back to the beginning.
I'll never fit in.
The seams will always show.

9

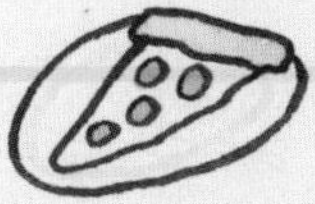

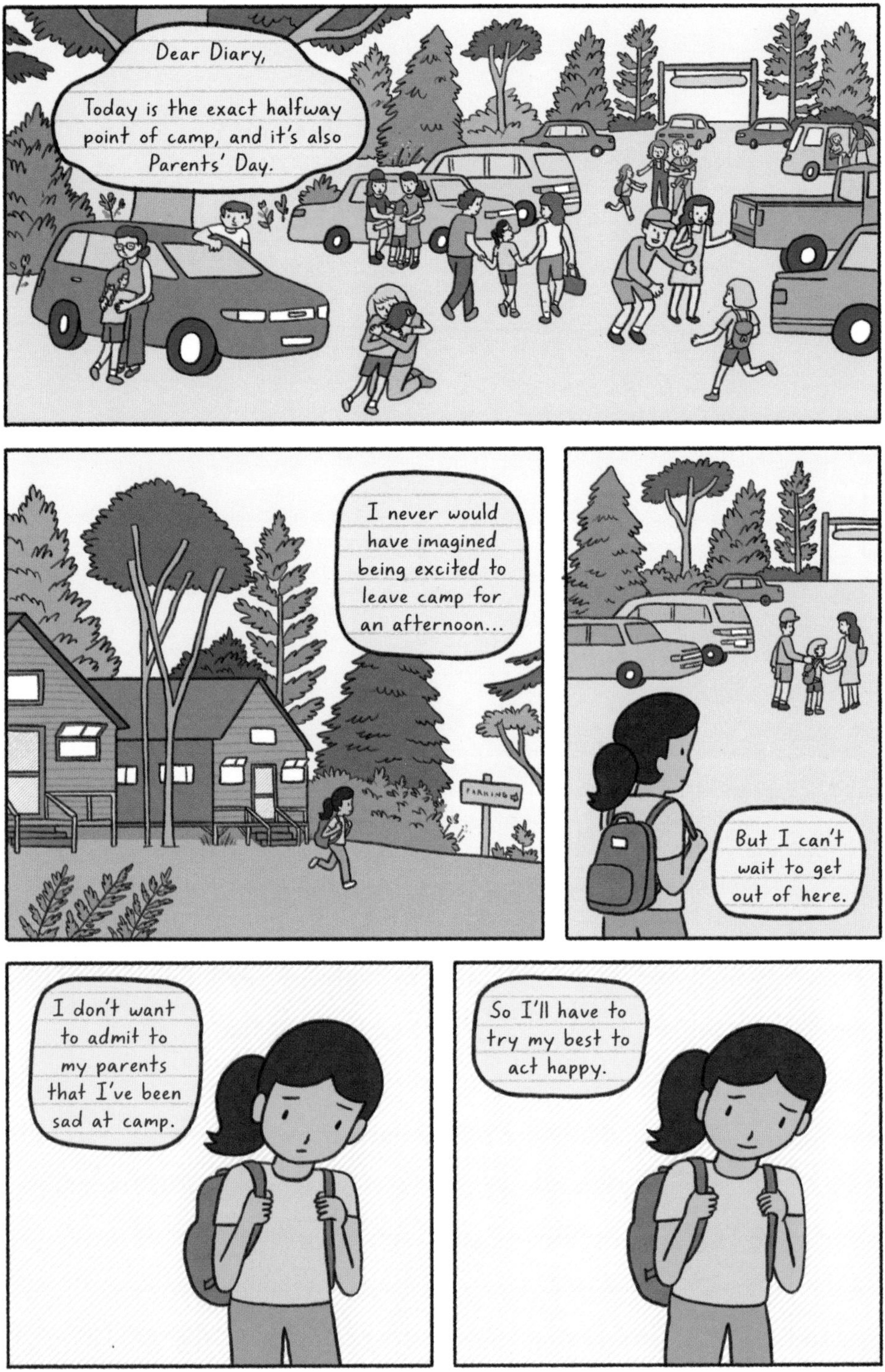
Dear Diary,
Today is the exact halfway point of camp, and it's also Parents' Day.
I never would have imagined being excited to leave camp for an afternoon...
PARKING
But I can't wait to get out of here.
I don't want to admit to my parents that I've been sad at camp.
So I'll have to try my best to act happy.

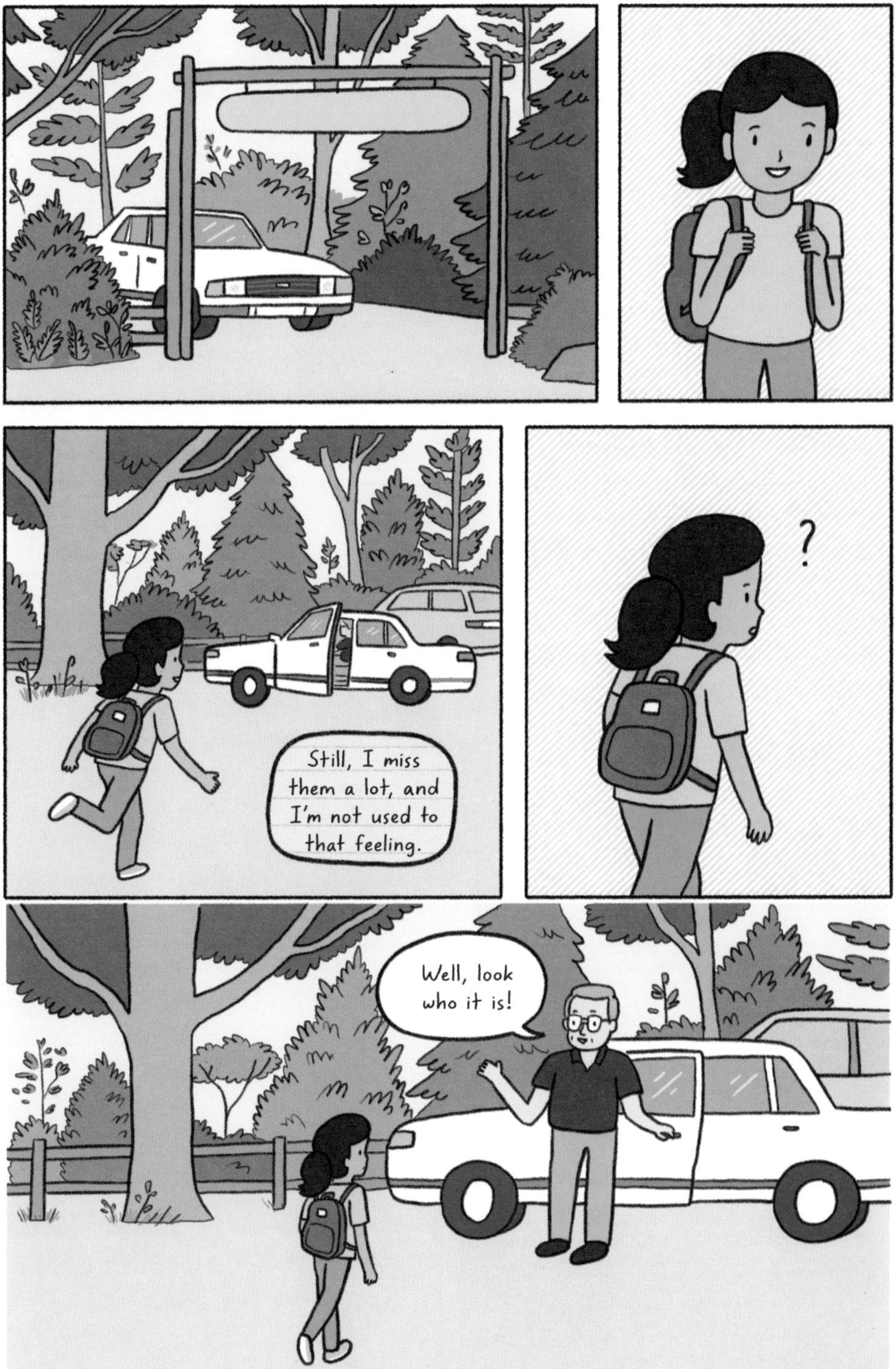
?
Still, I miss them a lot, and I'm not used to that feeling.
Well, look who it is!

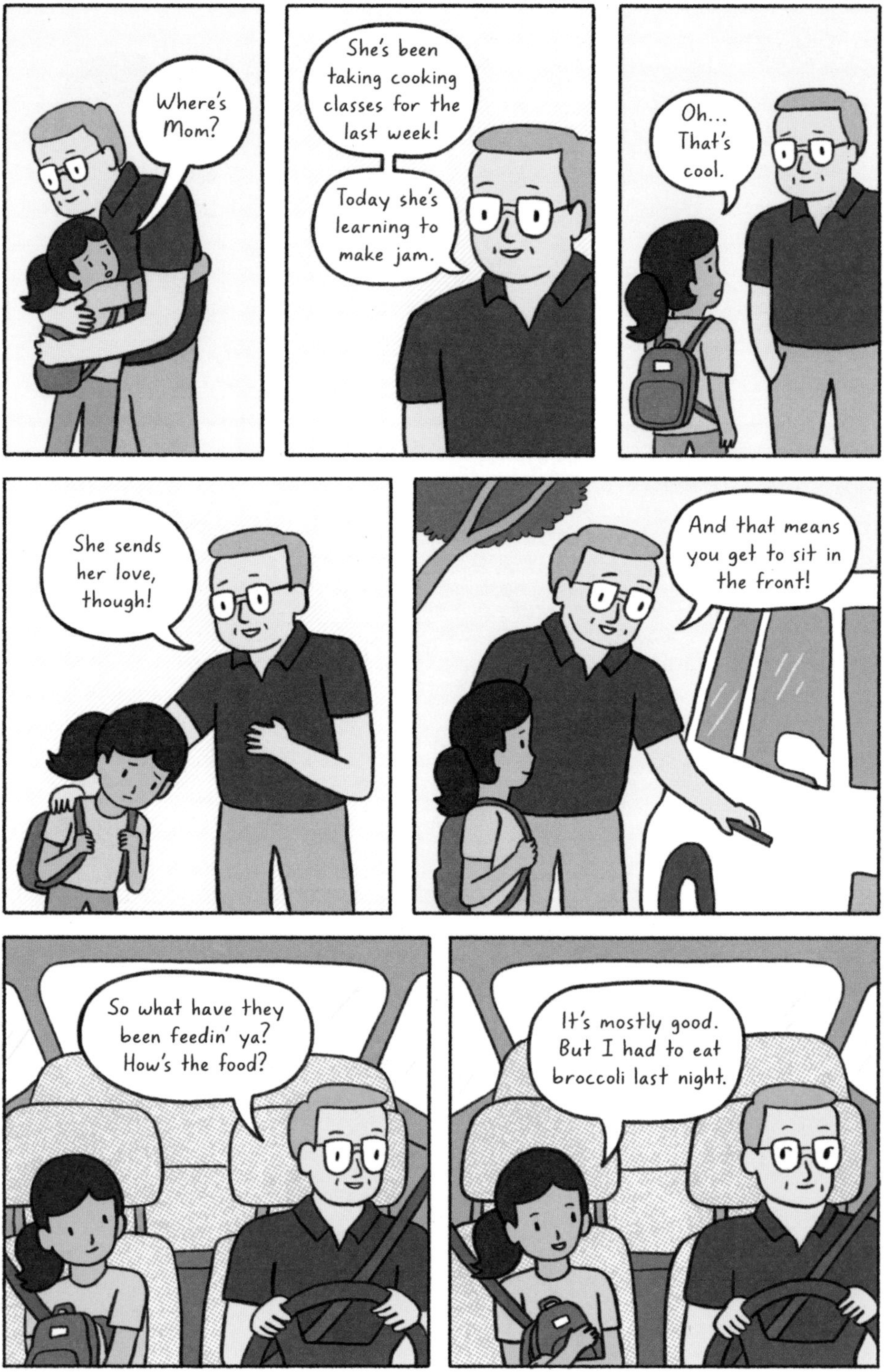
Where's Mom?
She's been taking cooking classes for the last week!
Today she's learning to make jam.
Oh... That's cool.
She sends her love, though!
And that means you get to sit in the front!
So what have they been feedin' ya? How's the food?
It's mostly good. But I had to eat broccoli last night.

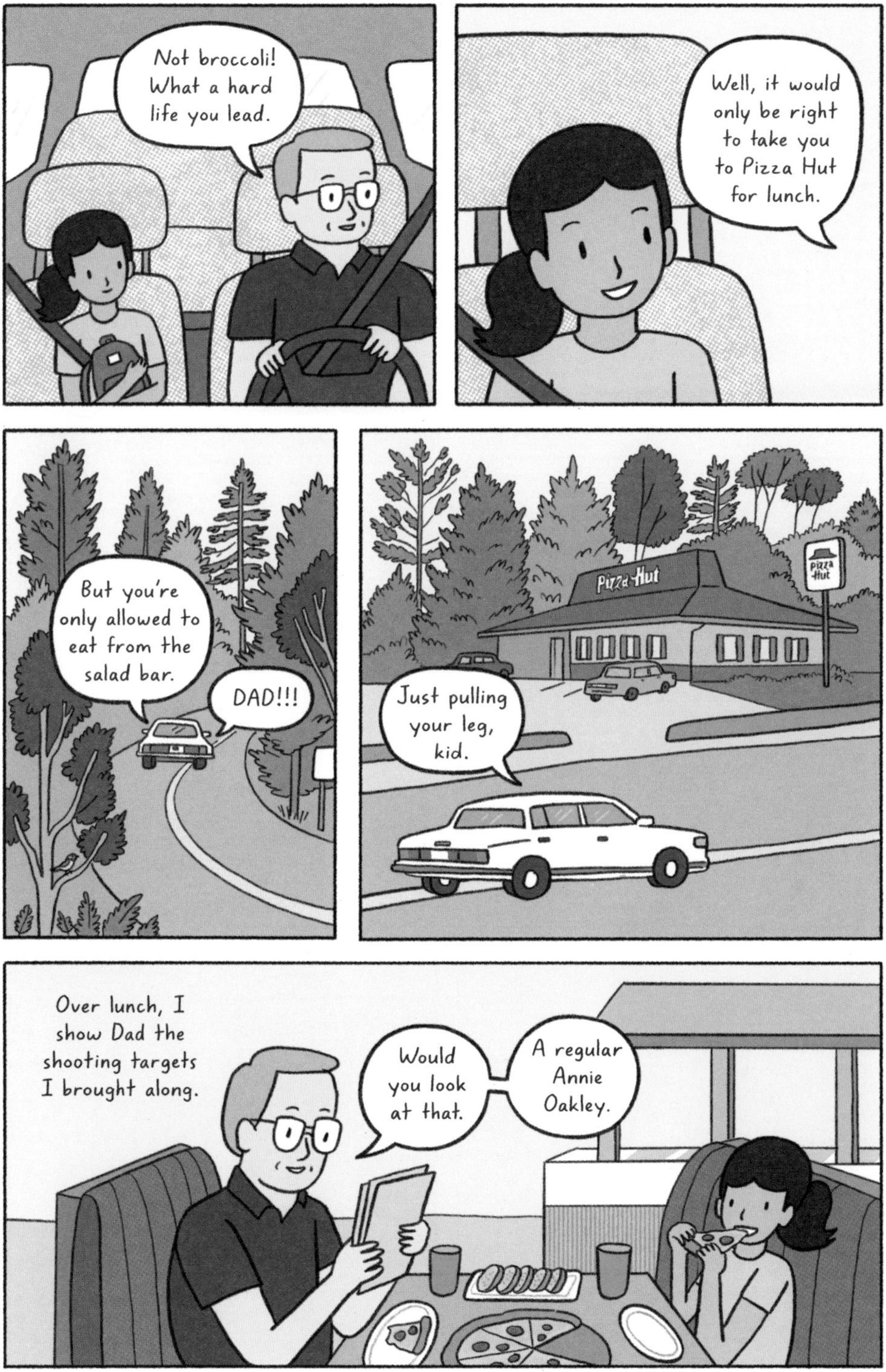
Not broccoli! What a hard life you lead.
Well, it would only be right to take you to Pizza Hut for lunch.
But you're only allowed to eat from the salad bar.
DAD!!!
Pizza Hut
Pizza Hut
Just pulling your leg, kid.
Over lunch, I show Dad the shooting targets I brought along.
Would you look at that.
A regular Annie Oakley.

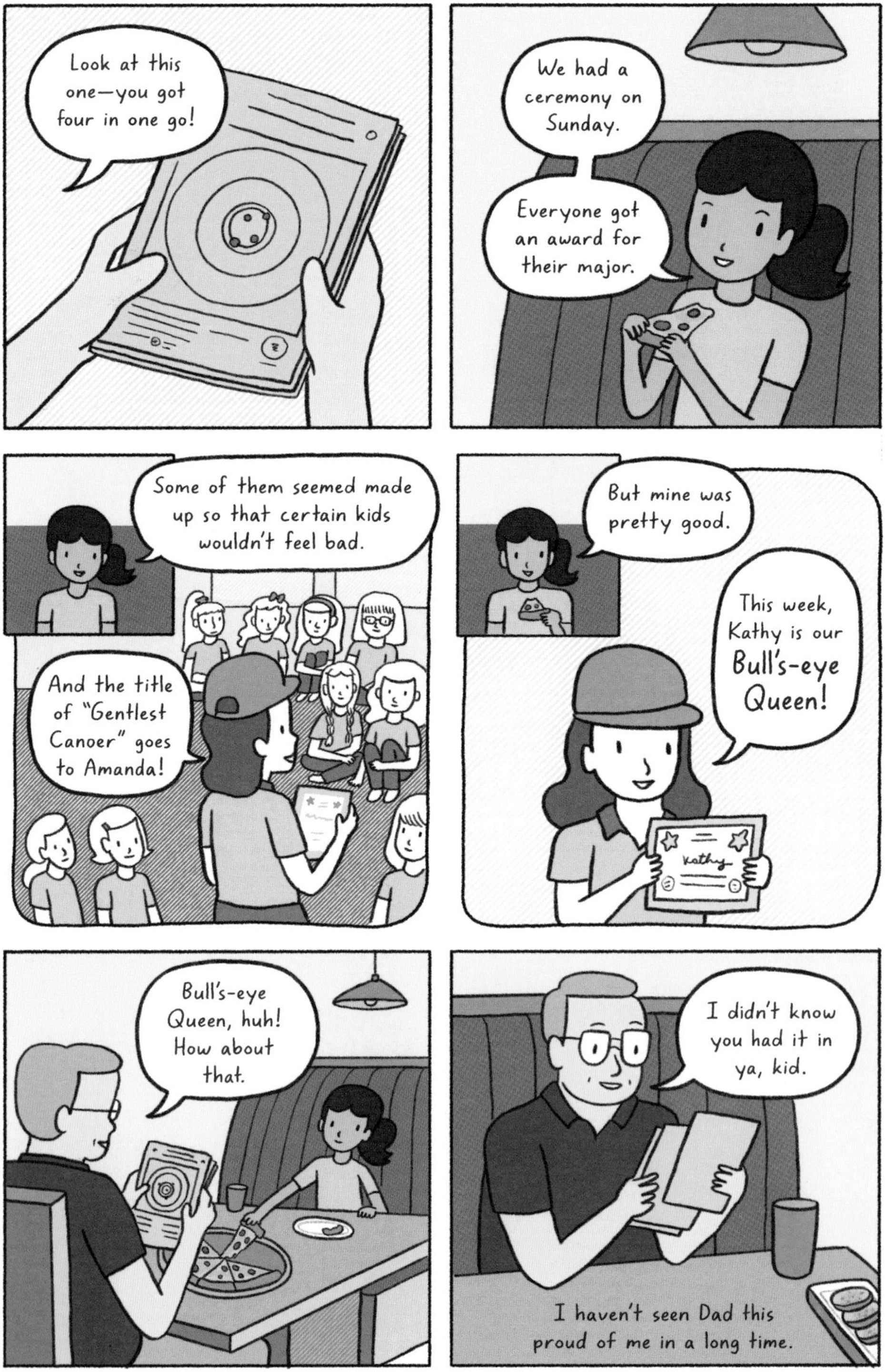

Look at this one—you got four in one go!
We had a ceremony on Sunday.
Everyone got an award for their major.
Some of them seemed made up so that certain kids wouldn't feel bad.
And the title of "Gentlest Canoer" goes to Amanda!
But mine was pretty good.
This week, Kathy is our Bull's-eye Queen!
Kathy
Bull's-eye Queen, huh! How about that.
I didn't know you had it in ya, kid.
I haven't seen Dad this proud of me in a long time.

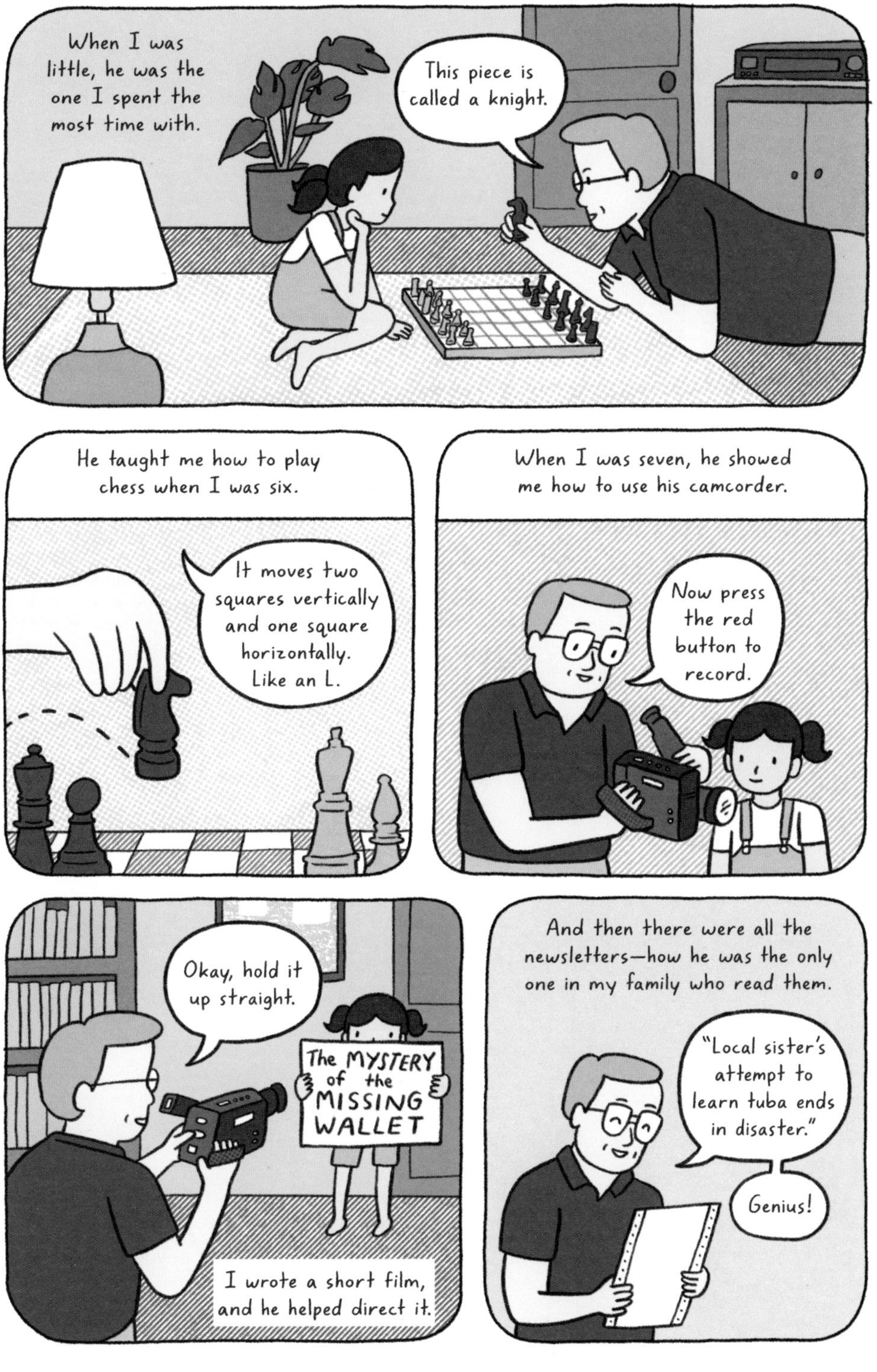
When I was little, he was the one I spent the most time with.
This piece is called a knight.
He taught me how to play chess when I was six.
It moves two squares vertically and one square horizontally. Like an L.
When I was seven, he showed me how to use his camcorder.
Now press the red button to record.
Okay, hold it up straight.
The MYSTERY of the MISSING WALLET
I wrote a short film, and he helped direct it.
And then there were all the newsletters—how he was the only one in my family who read them.
"Local sister's attempt to learn tuba ends in disaster."
Genius!

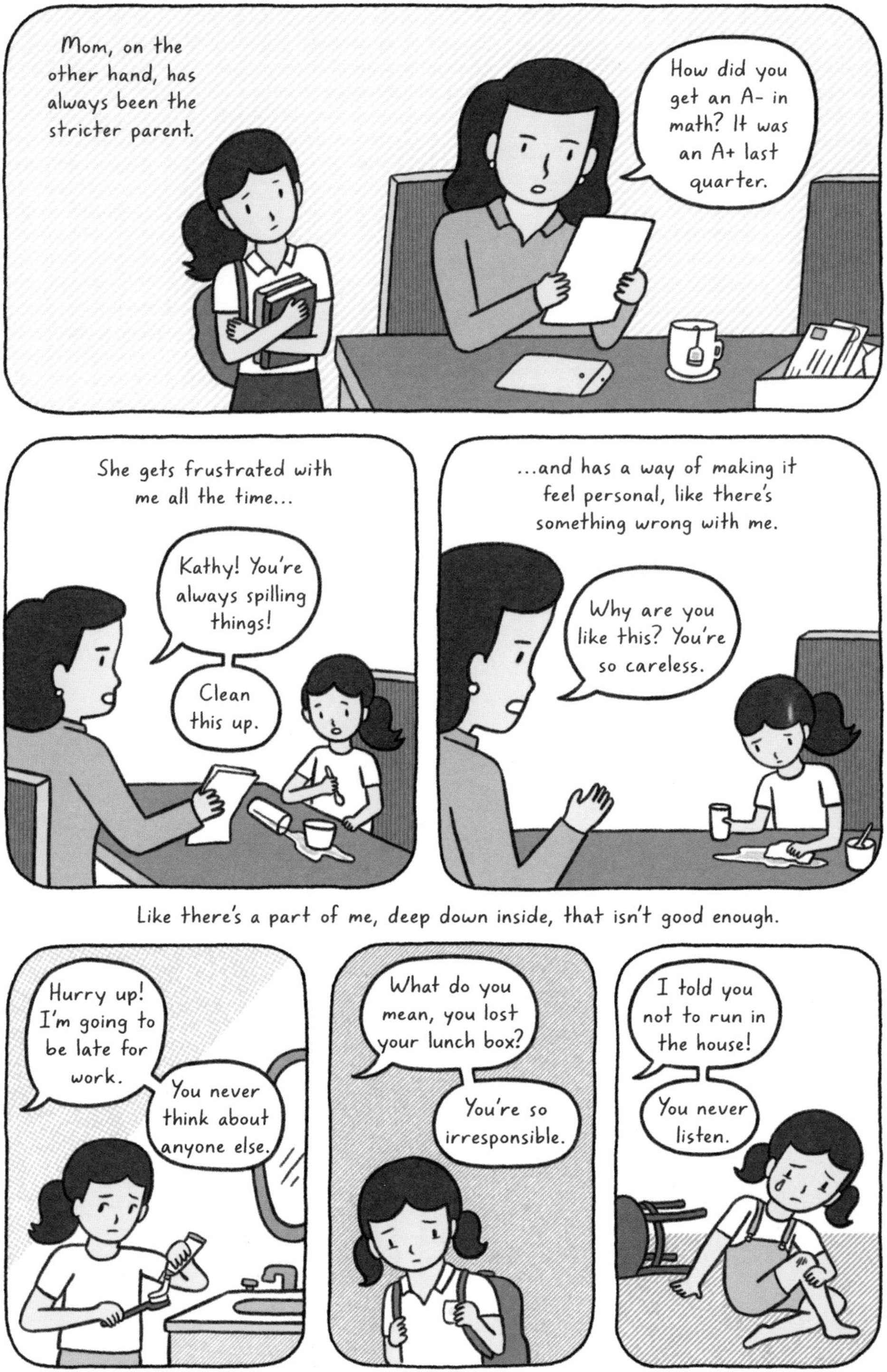
Mom, on the other hand, has always been the stricter parent.
How did you get an A- in math? It was an A+ last quarter.
She gets frustrated with me all the time...
Kathy! You're always spilling things!
Clean this up.
...and has a way of making it feel personal, like there's something wrong with me.
Why are you like this? You're so careless.
Like there's a part of me, deep down inside, that isn't good enough.
Hurry up! I'm going to be late for work.
You never think about anyone else.
What do you mean, you lost your lunch box?
You're so irresponsible.
I told you not to run in the house!
You never listen.

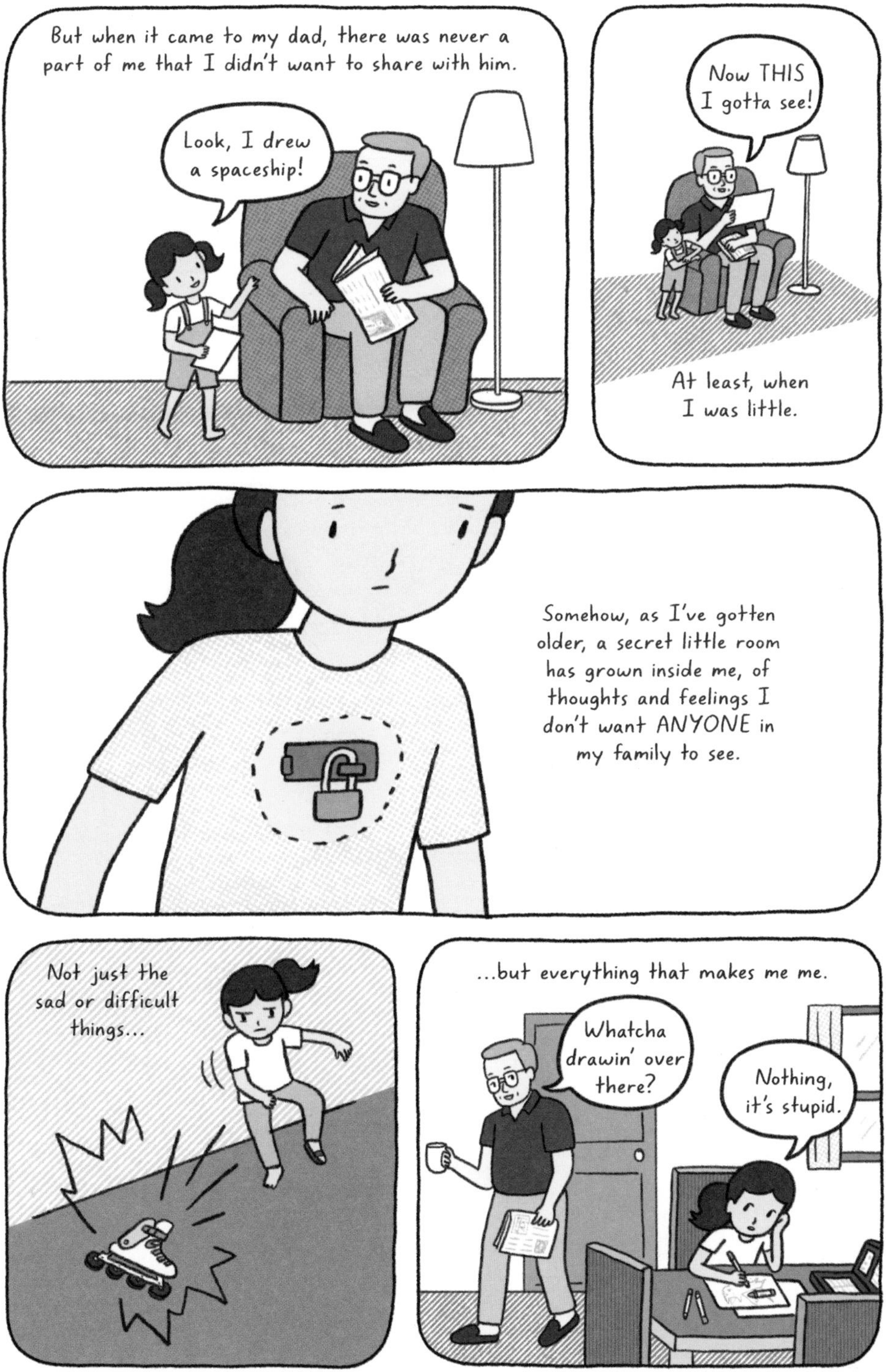
But when it came to my dad, there was never a part of me that I didn't want to share with him.
Look, I drew a spaceship!
Now THIS I gotta see!
At least, when I was little.
Somehow, as I've gotten older, a secret little room has grown inside me, of thoughts and feelings I don't want ANYONE in my family to see.
Not just the sad or difficult things...
...but everything that makes me me.
Whatcha drawin' over there?
Nothing, it's stupid.

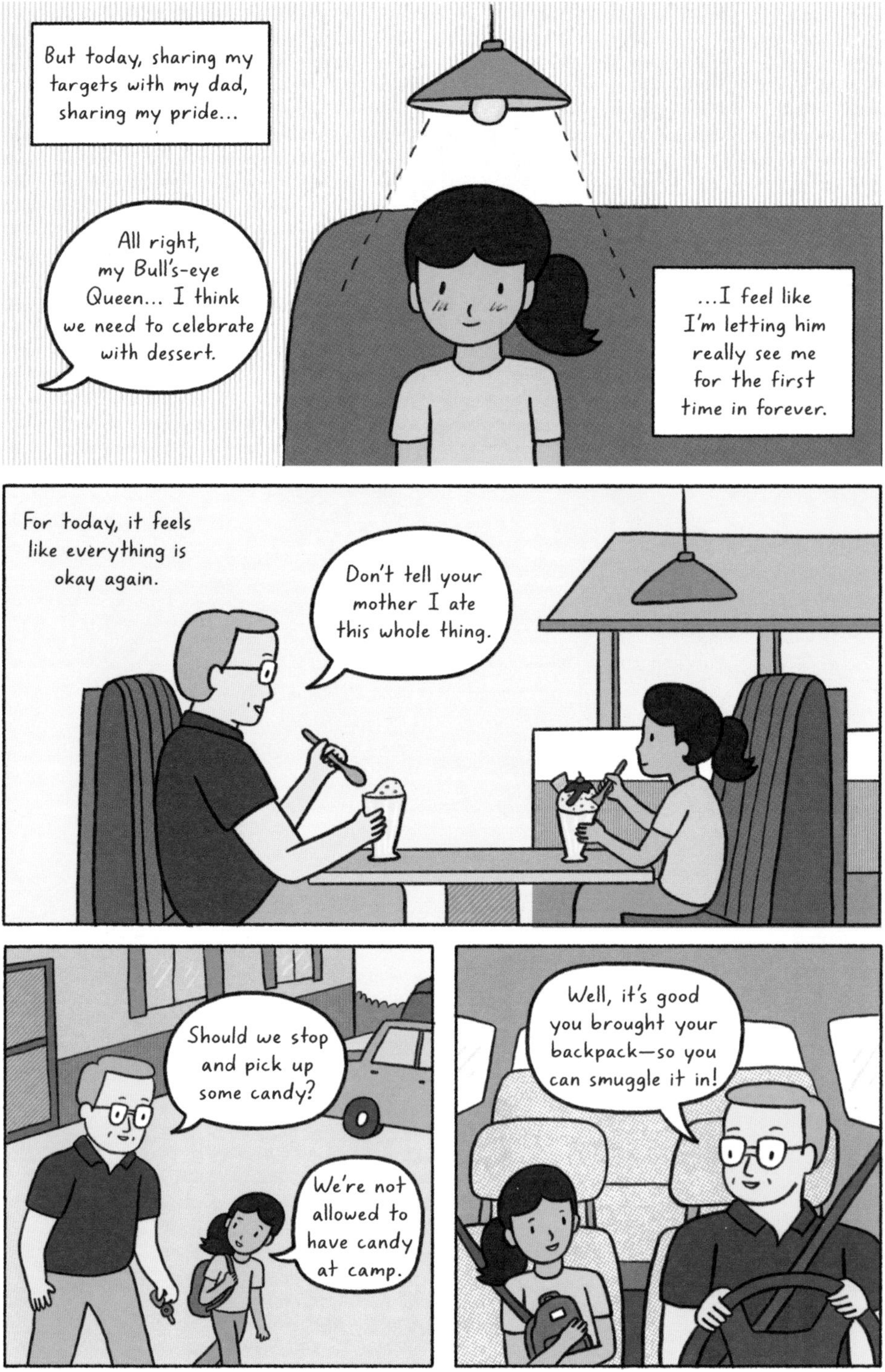
But today, sharing my targets with my dad, sharing my pride...
All right, my Bull's-eye Queen... I think we need to celebrate with dessert.
...I feel like I'm letting him really see me for the first time in forever.
For today, it feels like everything is okay again.
Don't tell your mother I ate this whole thing.
Should we stop and pick up some candy?
We're not allowed to have candy at camp.
Well, it's good you brought your backpack—so you can smuggle it in!

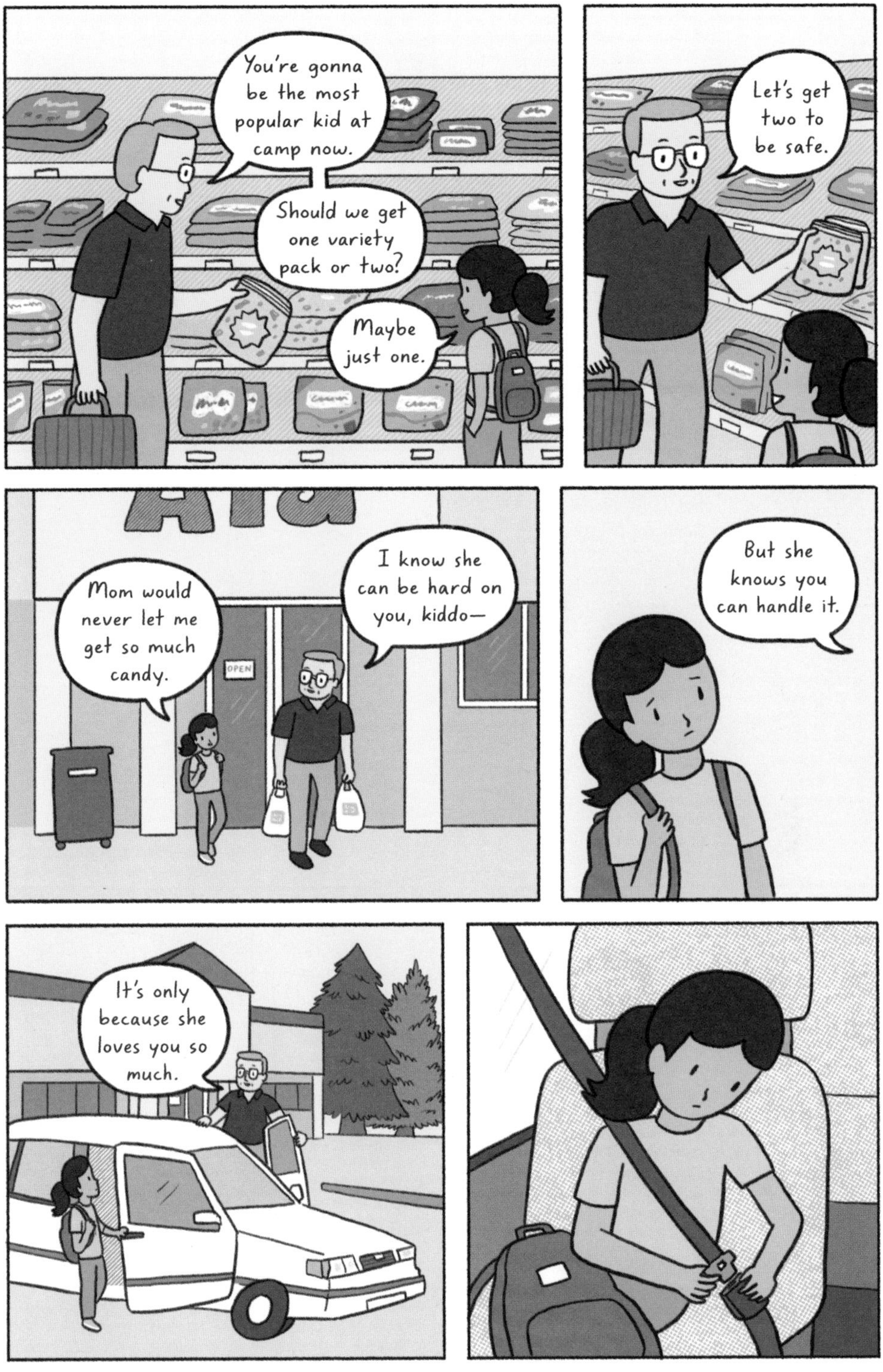
You're gonna be the most popular kid at camp now.
Should we get one variety pack or two?
Maybe just one.
Let's get two to be safe.
Mom would never let me get so much candy.
OPEN
I know she can be hard on you, kiddo—
But she knows you can handle it.
It's only because she loves you so much.

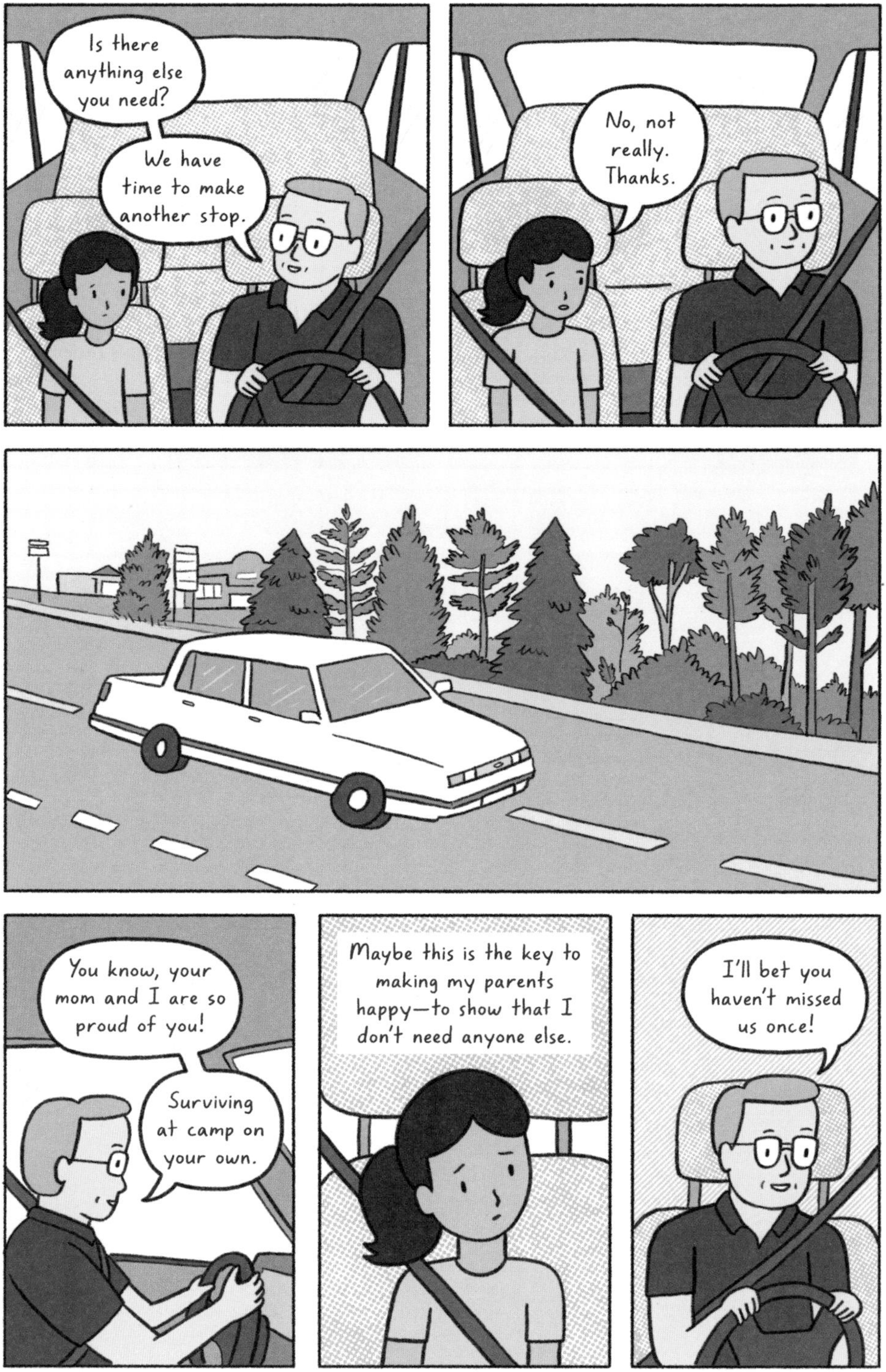
Is there anything else you need?
We have time to make another stop.
No, not really. Thanks.
You know, your mom and I are so proud of you!
Surviving at camp on your own.
Maybe this is the key to making my parents happy—to show that I don't need anyone else.
I'll bet you haven't missed us once!

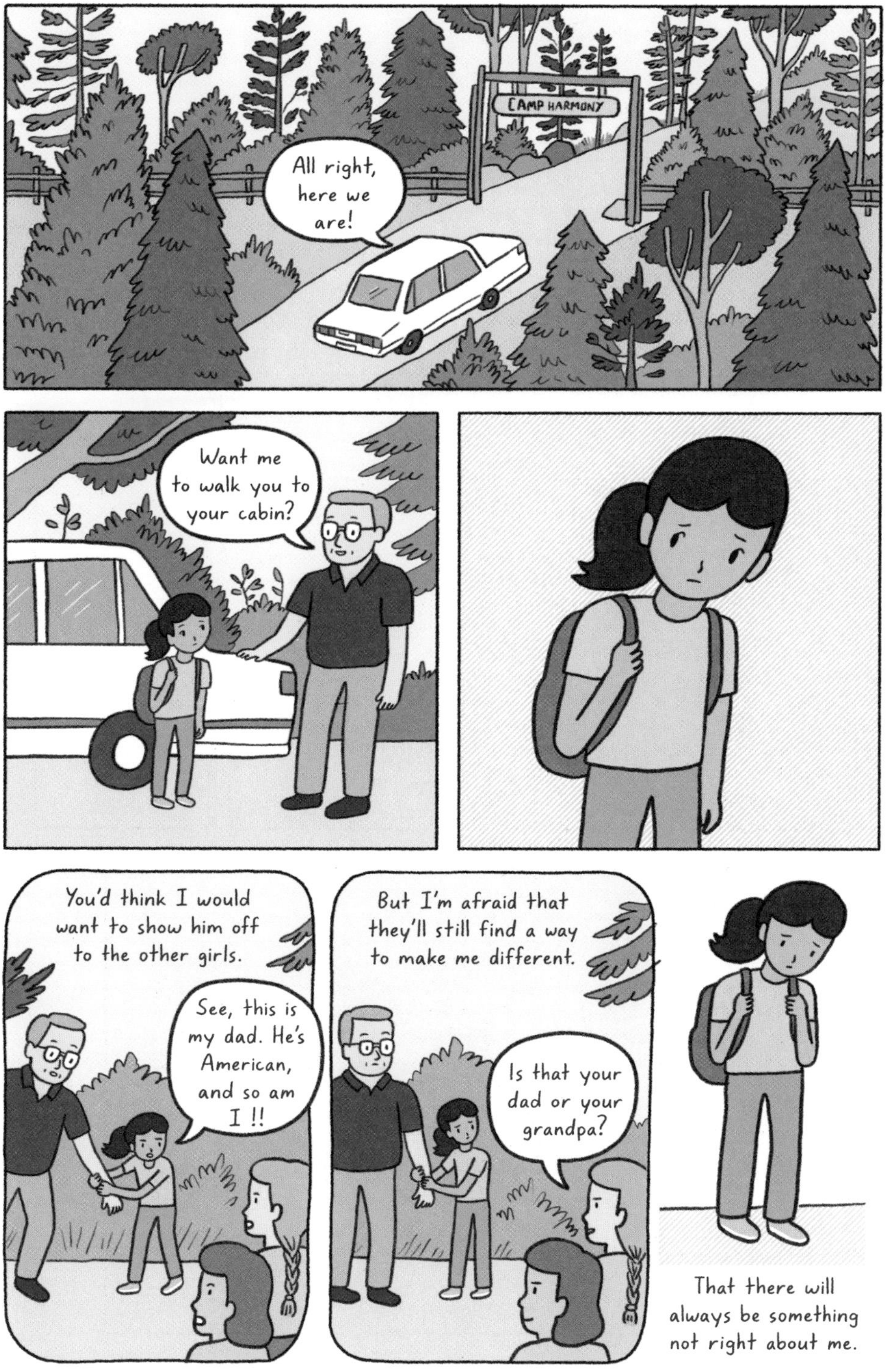
CAMP HARMONY
All right, here we are!
Want me to walk you to your cabin?
You'd think I would want to show him off to the other girls.
See, this is my dad. He's American, and so am I !!
But I'm afraid that they'll still find a way to make me different.
Is that your dad or your grandpa?
That there will always be something not right about me.

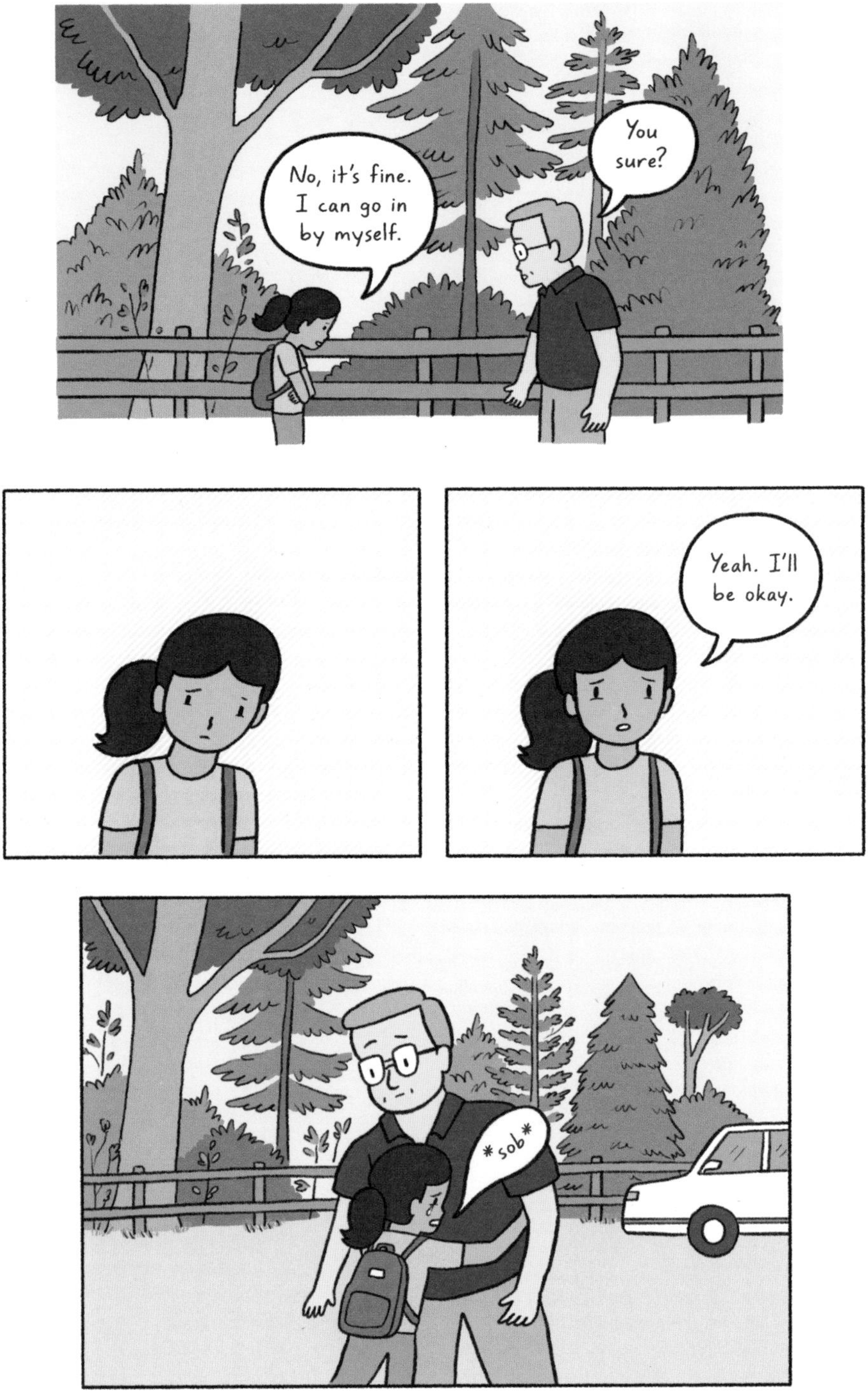
No, it's fine. I can go in by myself.
You sure?
Yeah. I'll be okay.
sob

10

My Mad Libs are almost out of pages.

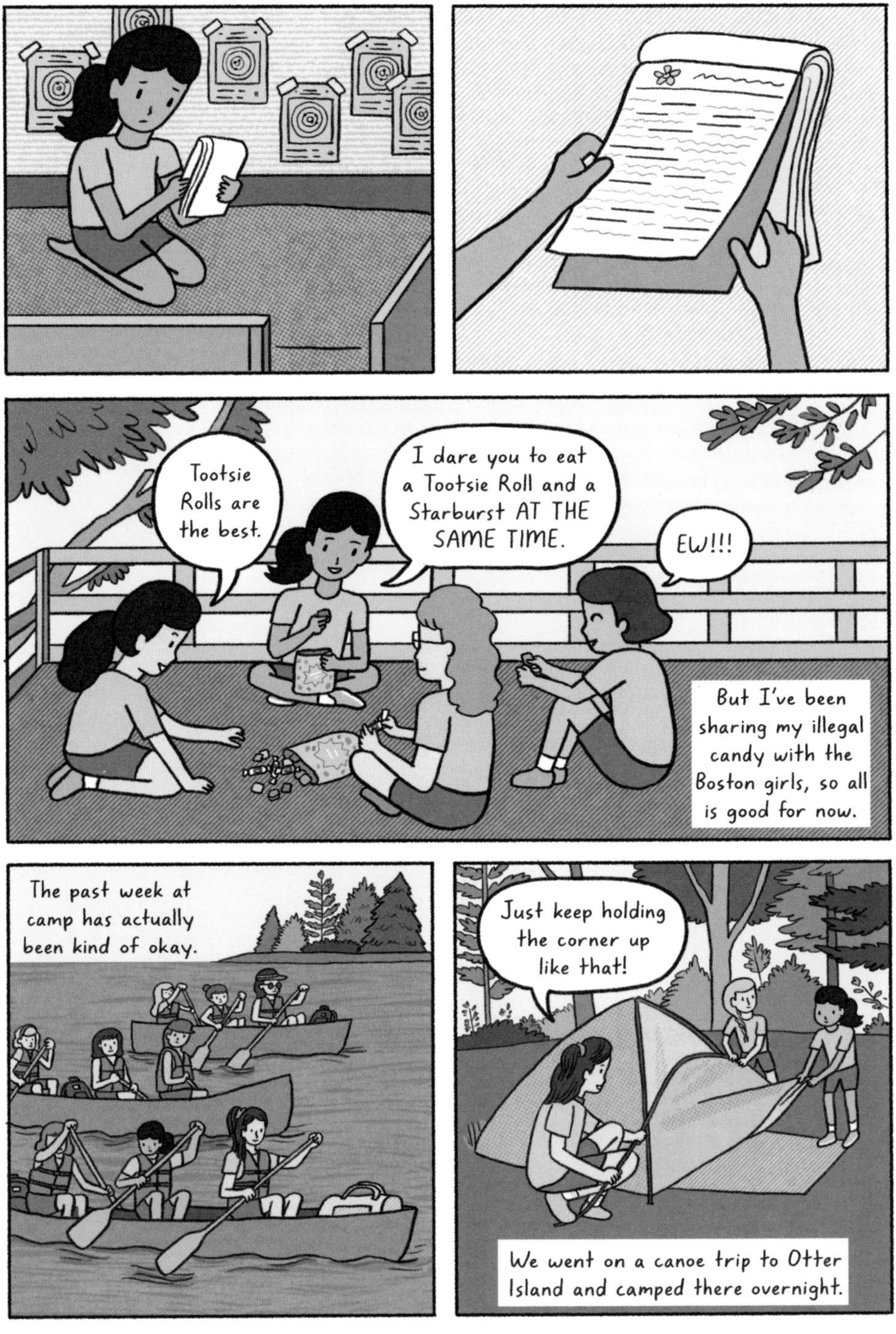

Tootsie Rolls are the best.
I dare you to eat a Tootsie Roll and a Starburst AT THE SAME TIME.
EW!!!
But I've been sharing my illegal candy with the Boston girls, so all is good for now.
The past week at camp has actually been kind of okay.
Just keep holding the corner up like that!
We went on a canoe trip to Otter Island and camped there overnight.

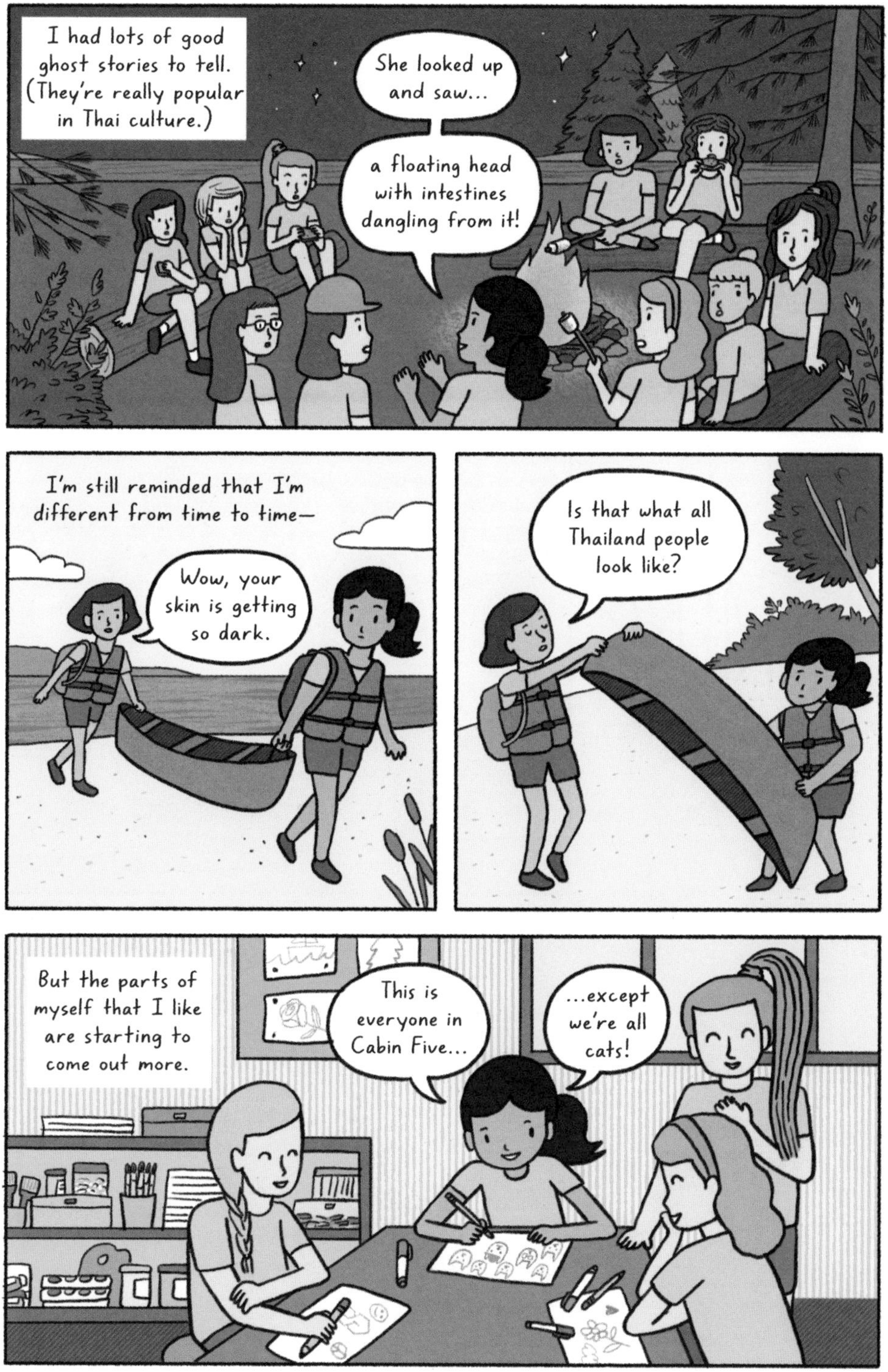
I had lots of good ghost stories to tell. (They're really popular in Thai culture.)
She looked up and saw...
a floating head with intestines dangling from it!
I'm still reminded that I'm different from time to time—
Wow, your skin is getting so dark.
Is that what all Thailand people look like?
But the parts of myself that I like are starting to come out more.
This is everyone in Cabin Five...
...except we're all cats!

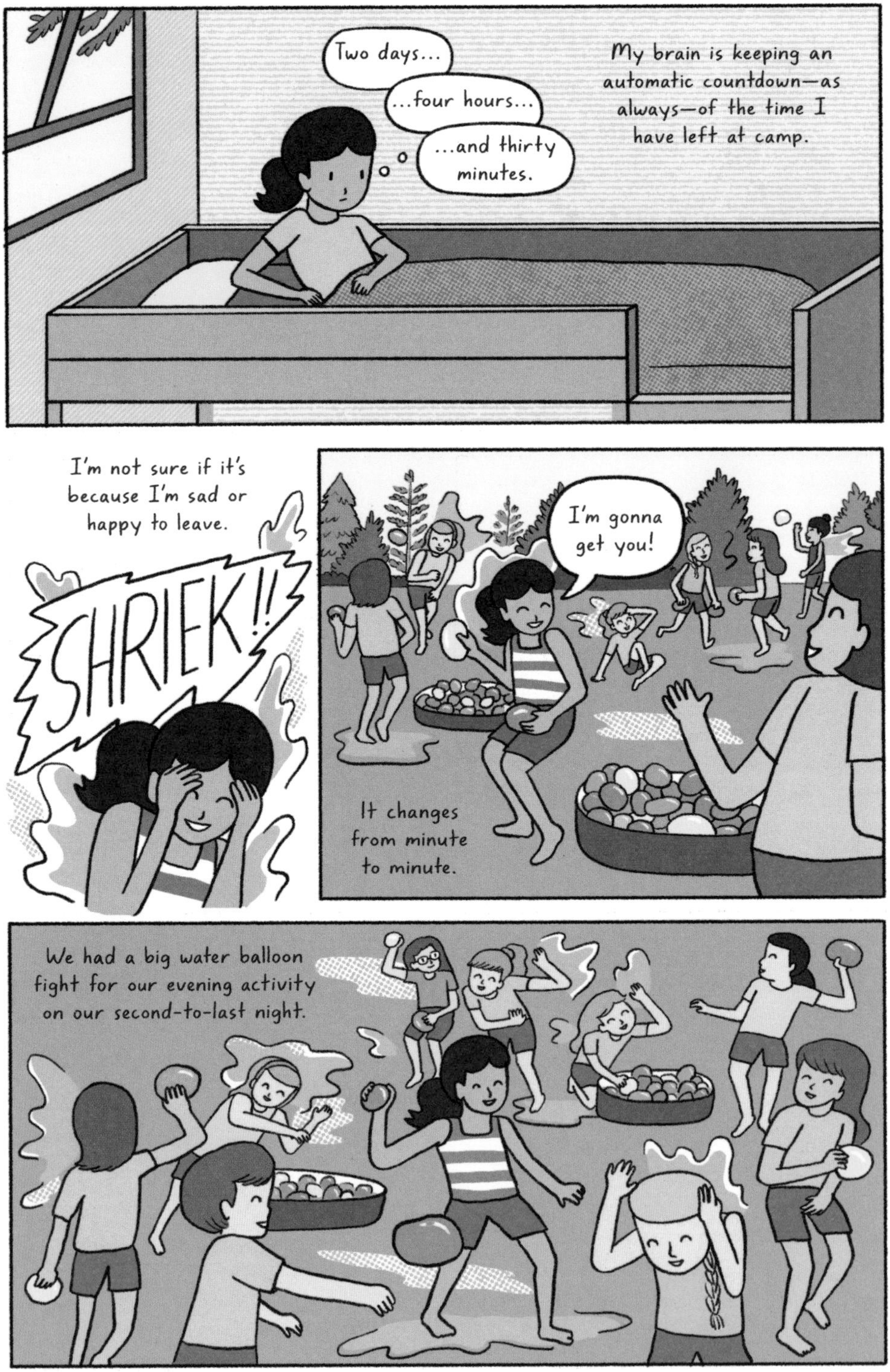
Two days...
...four hours...
...and thirty minutes.
My brain is keeping an automatic countdown—as always—of the time I have left at camp.
I'm not sure if it's because I'm sad or happy to leave.
SHRIEK!!
I'm gonna get you!
It changes from minute to minute.
We had a big water balloon fight for our evening activity on our second-to-last night.

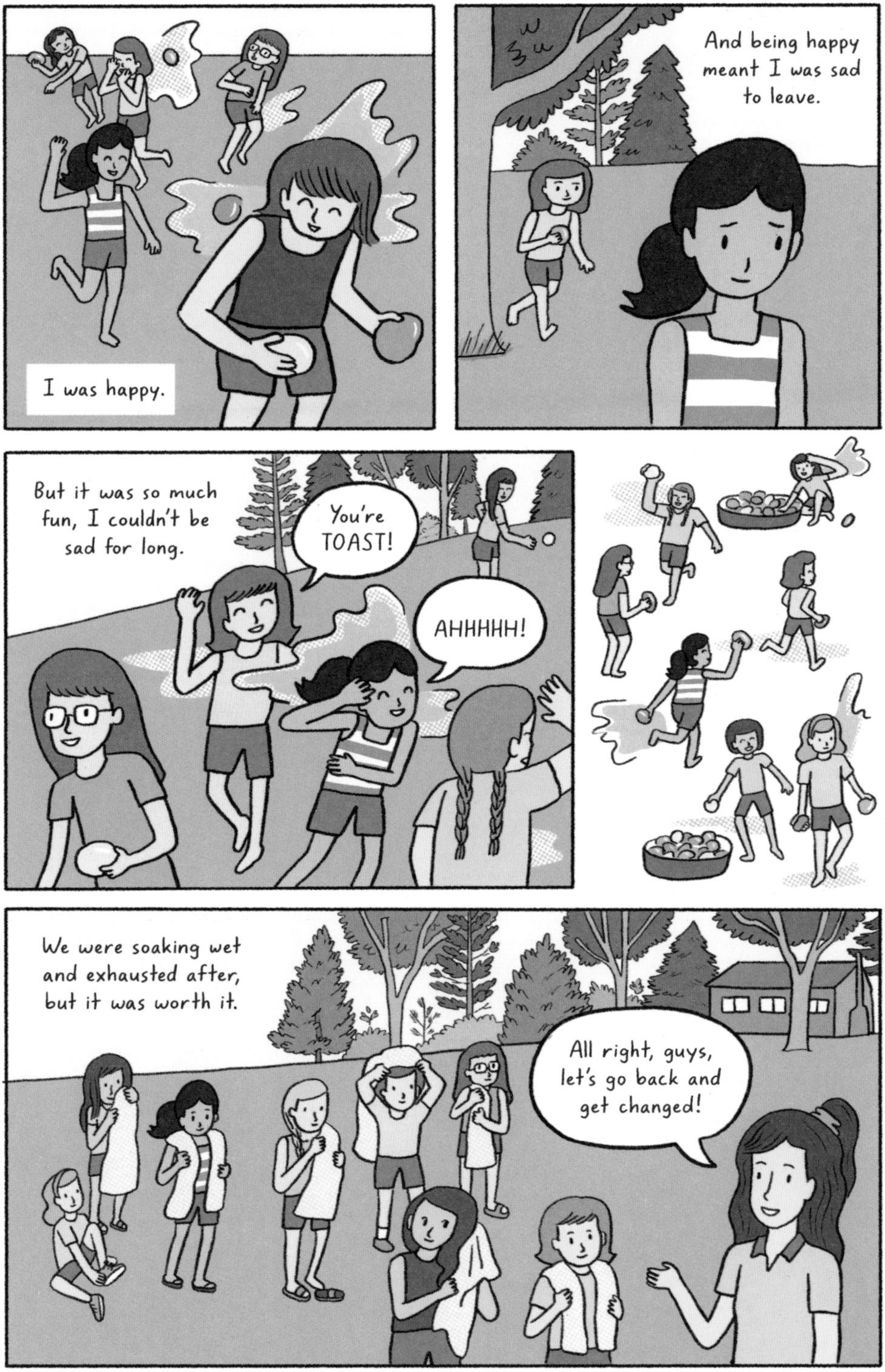
I was happy.
And being happy meant I was sad to leave.
But it was so much fun, I couldn't be sad for long.
You're TOAST!
AHHHHH!
We were soaking wet and exhausted after, but it was worth it.
All right, guys, let's go back and get changed!

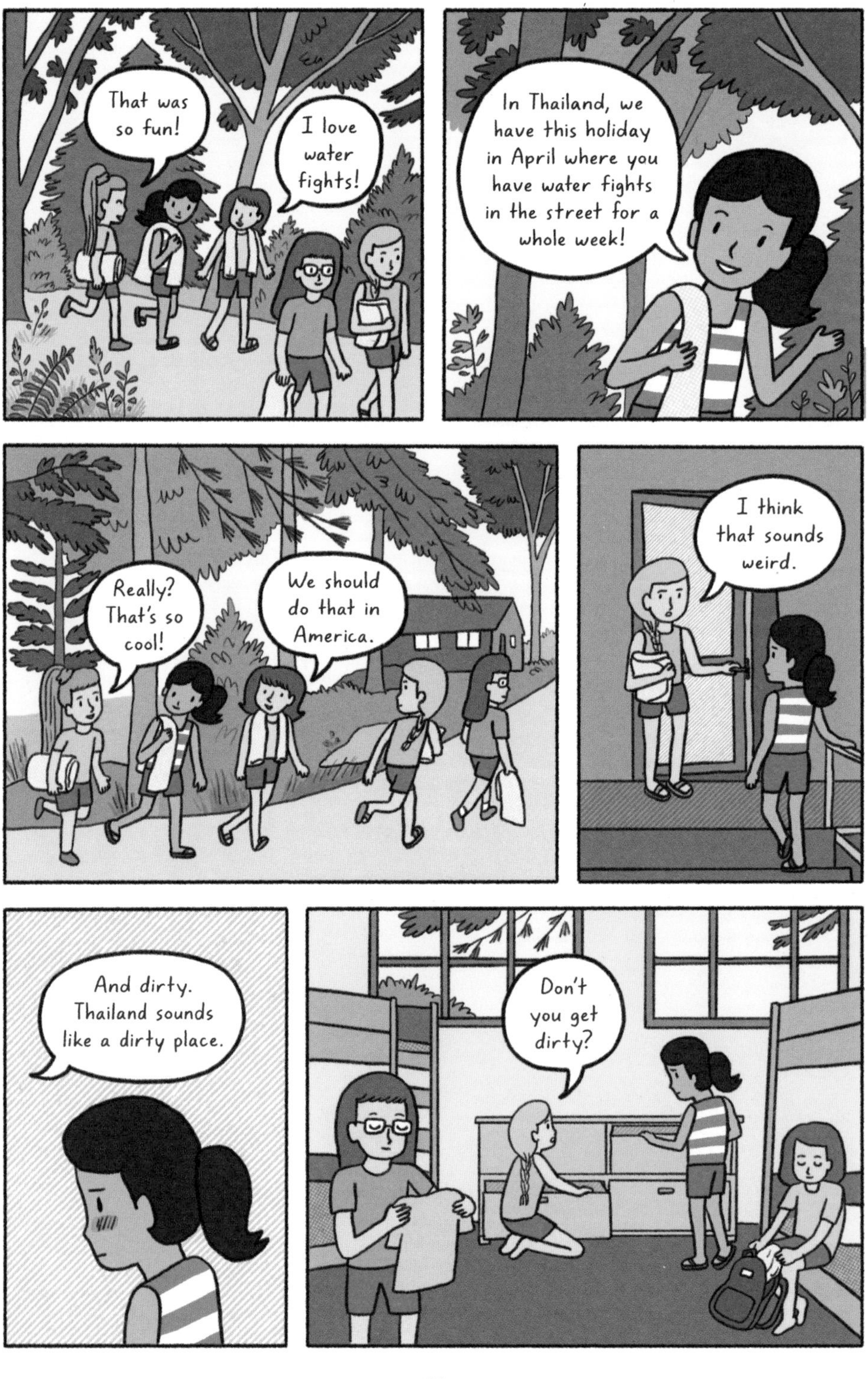
That was so fun!
I love water fights!
In Thailand, we have this holiday in April where you have water fights in the street for a whole week!
Really? That's so cool!
We should do that in America.
I think that sounds weird.
And dirty. Thailand sounds like a dirty place.
Don't you get dirty?

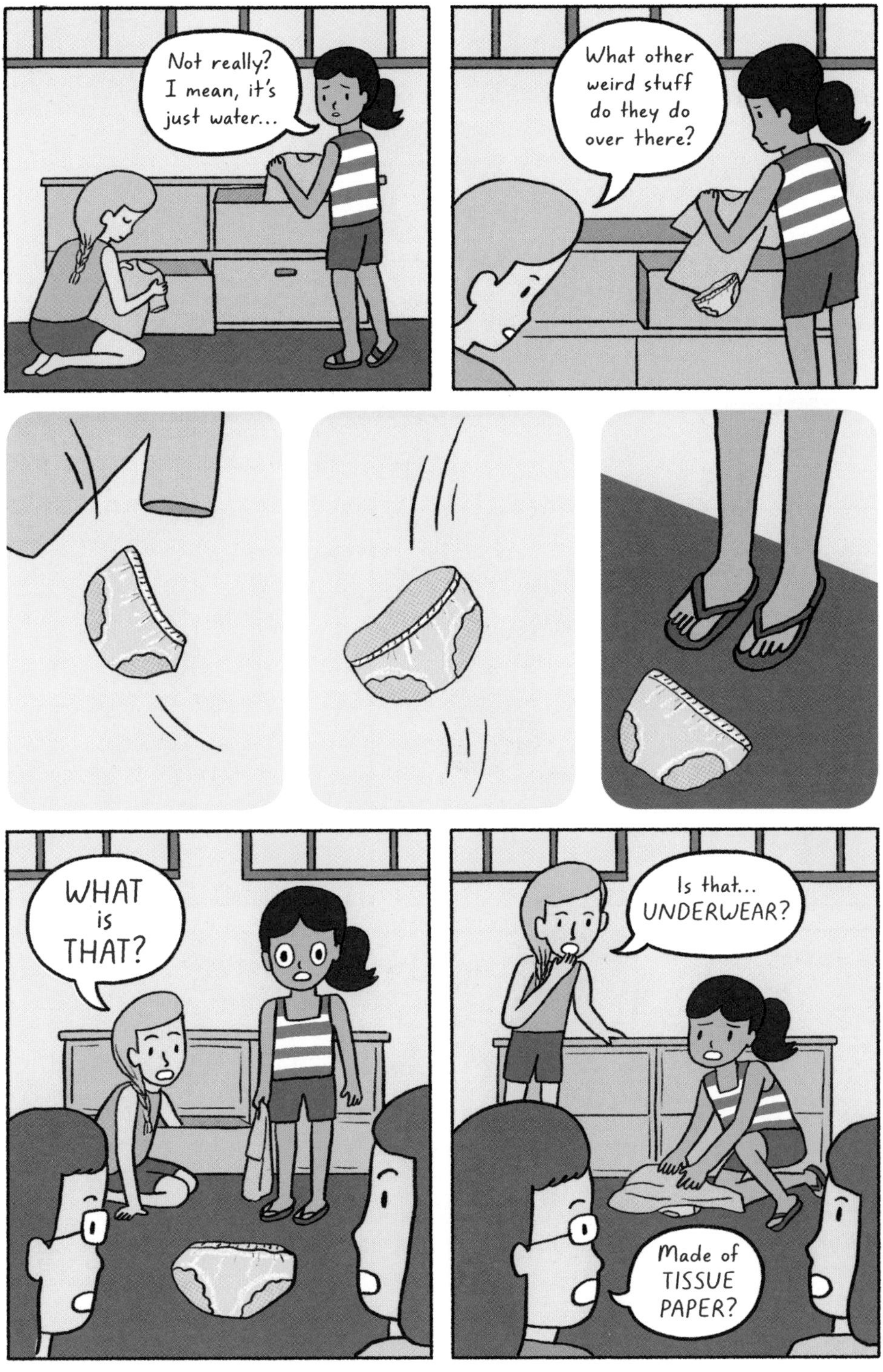
Not really? I mean, it's just water...
What other weird stuff do they do over there?
WHAT is THAT?
Is that... UNDERWEAR?
Made of TISSUE PAPER?

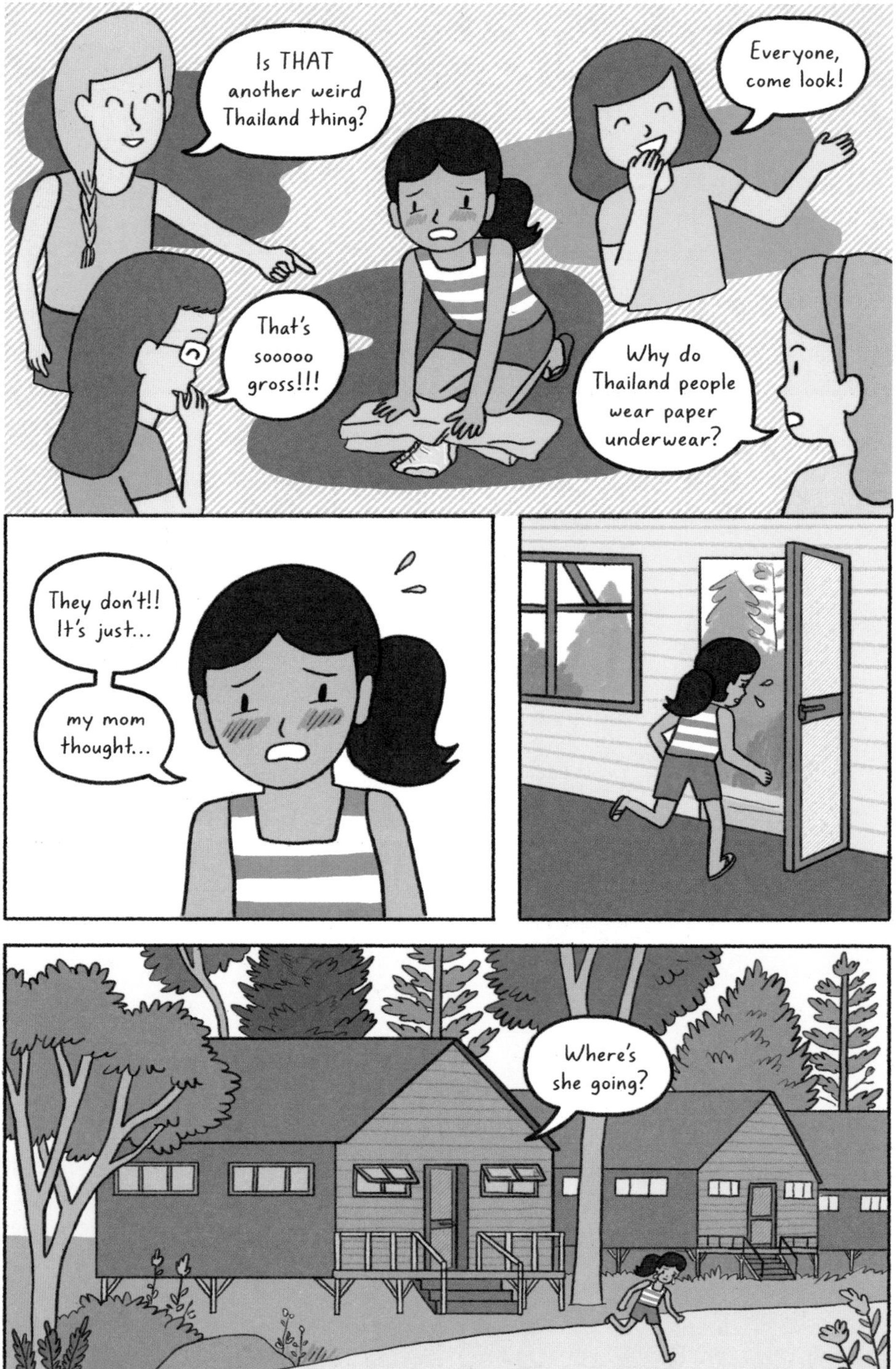
Is THAT another weird Thailand thing?
Everyone, come look!
That's sooooo gross!!!
Why do Thailand people wear paper underwear?
They don't!! It's just...
my mom thought...
Where's she going?

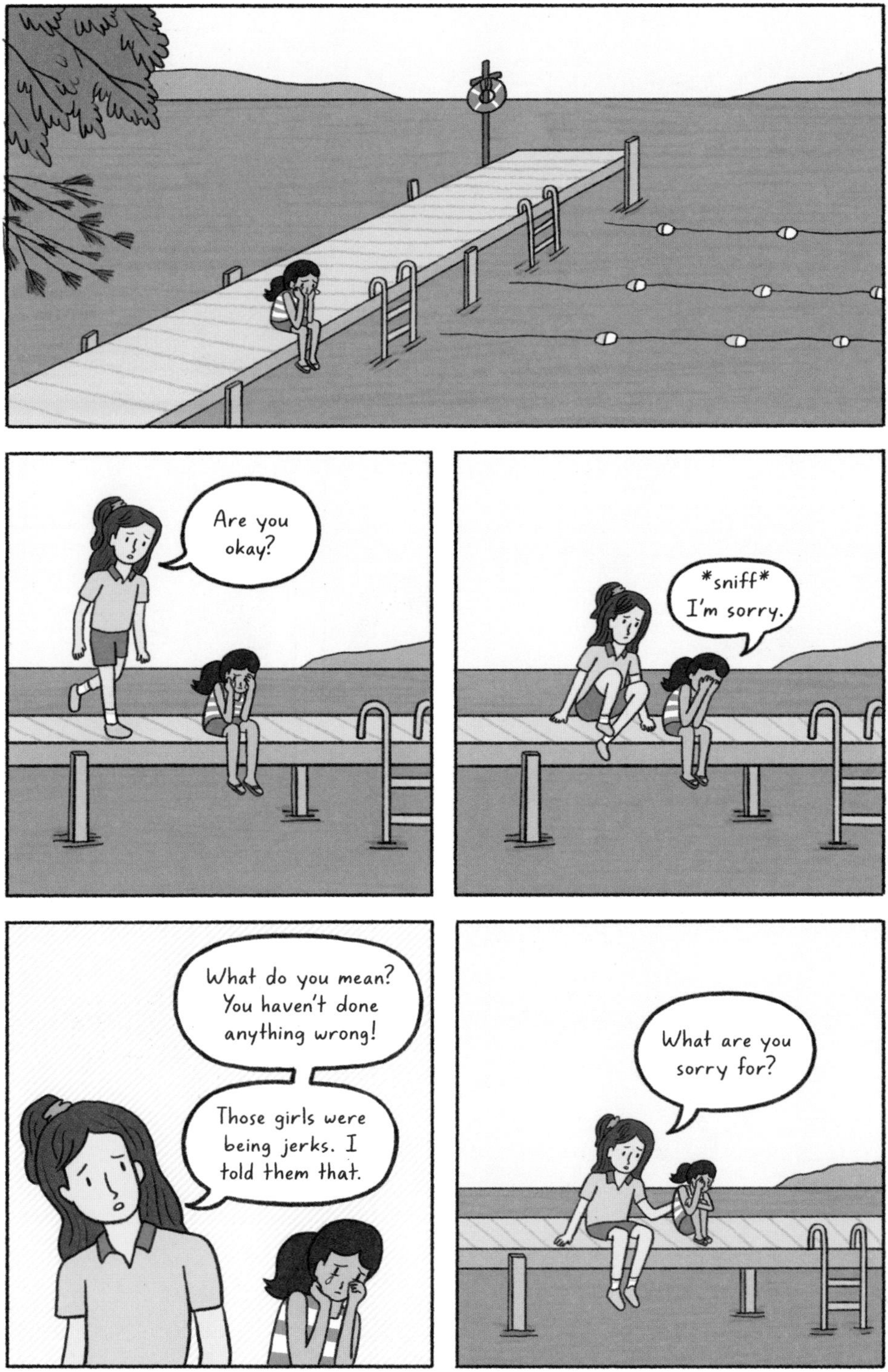
Are you okay?
sniff I'm sorry.
What do you mean? You haven't done anything wrong!
Those girls were being jerks. I told them that.
What are you sorry for?

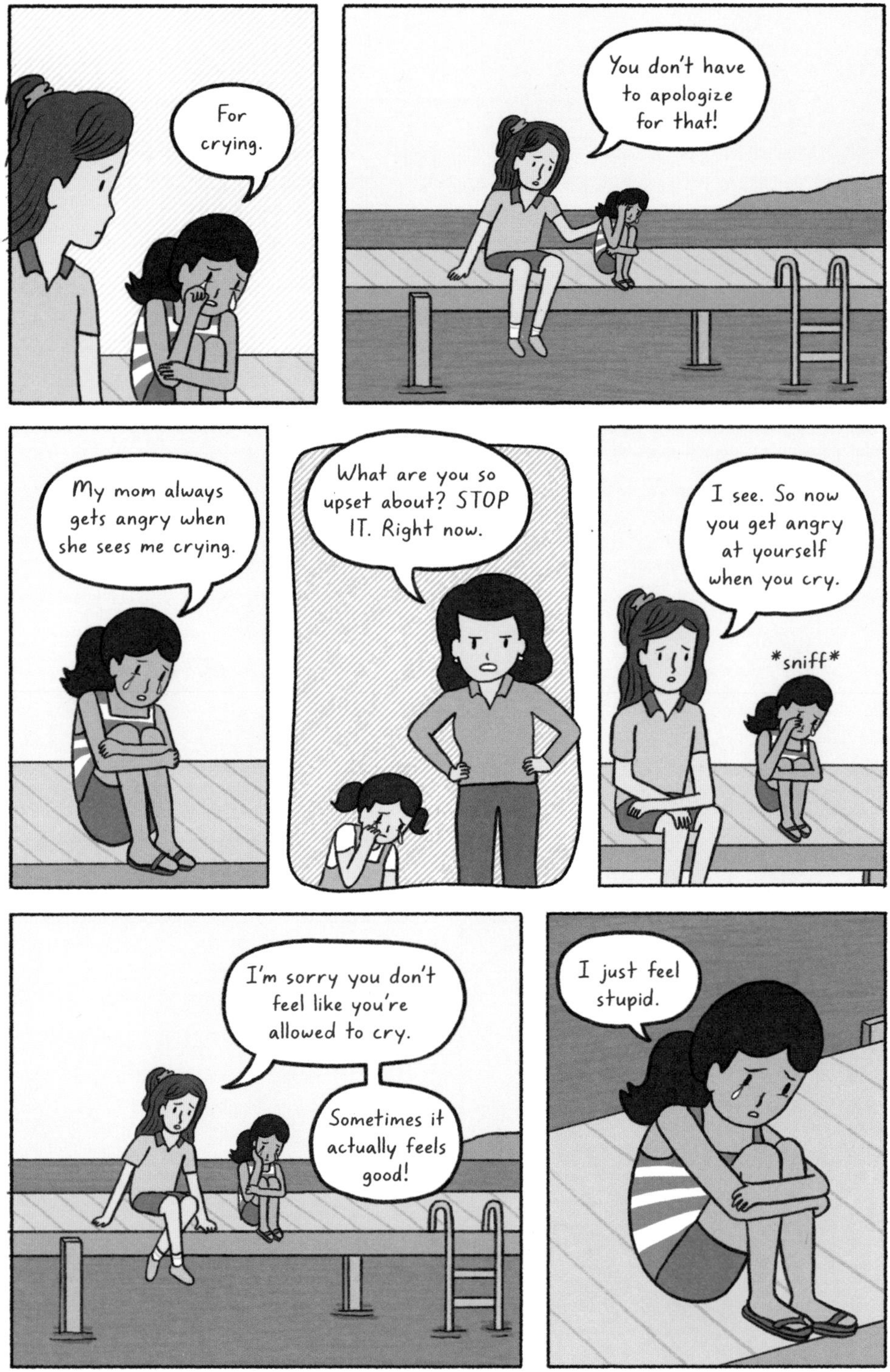
For crying.
You don't have to apologize for that!
My mom always gets angry when she sees me crying.
What are you so upset about? STOP IT. Right now.
I see. So now you get angry at yourself when you cry.
sniff
I'm sorry you don't feel like you're allowed to cry.
Sometimes it actually feels good!
I just feel stupid.

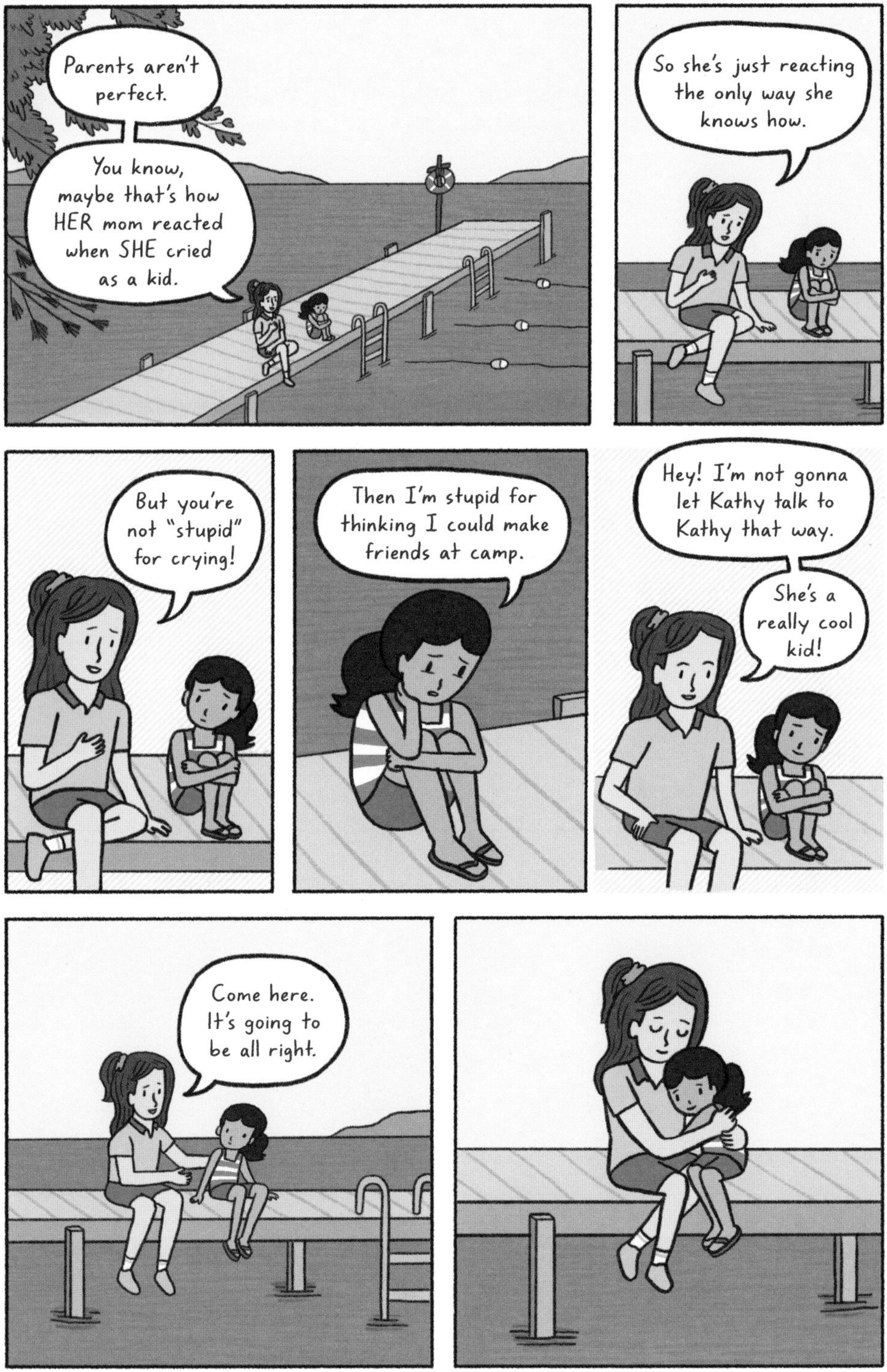

Parents aren't perfect.
You know, maybe that's how HER mom reacted when SHE cried as a kid.
So she's just reacting the only way she knows how.
But you're not "stupid" for crying!
Then I'm stupid for thinking I could make friends at camp.
Hey! I'm not gonna let Kathy talk to Kathy that way.
She's a really cool kid!
Come here. It's going to be all right.

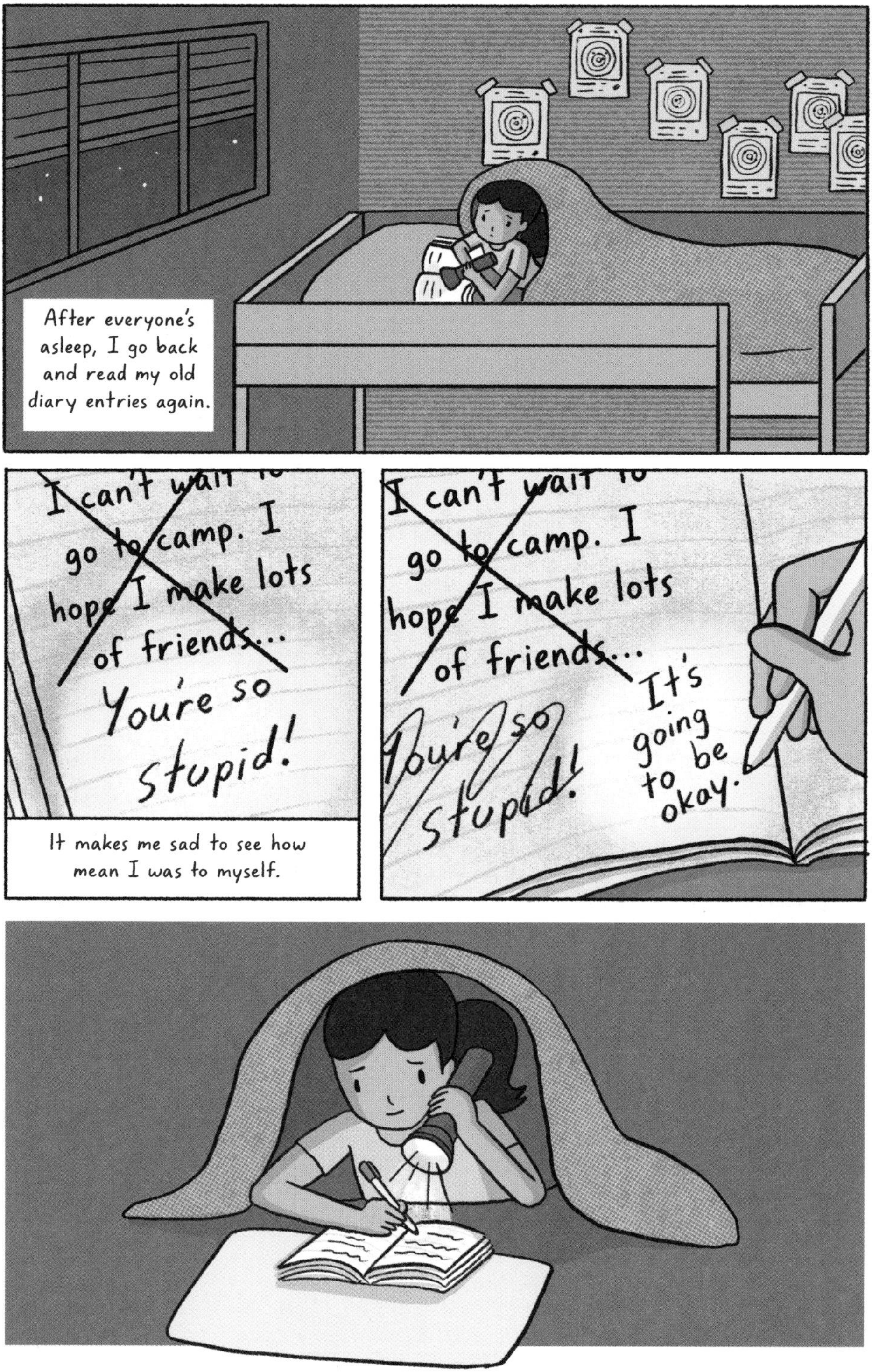
After everyone's asleep, I go back and read my old diary entries again.
I can't wait to go to camp. I hope I make lots of friends...
You're so stupid!
It makes me sad to see how mean I was to myself.
I can't wait to go to camp. I hope I make lots of friends...
You're so stupid!
It's going to be okay.

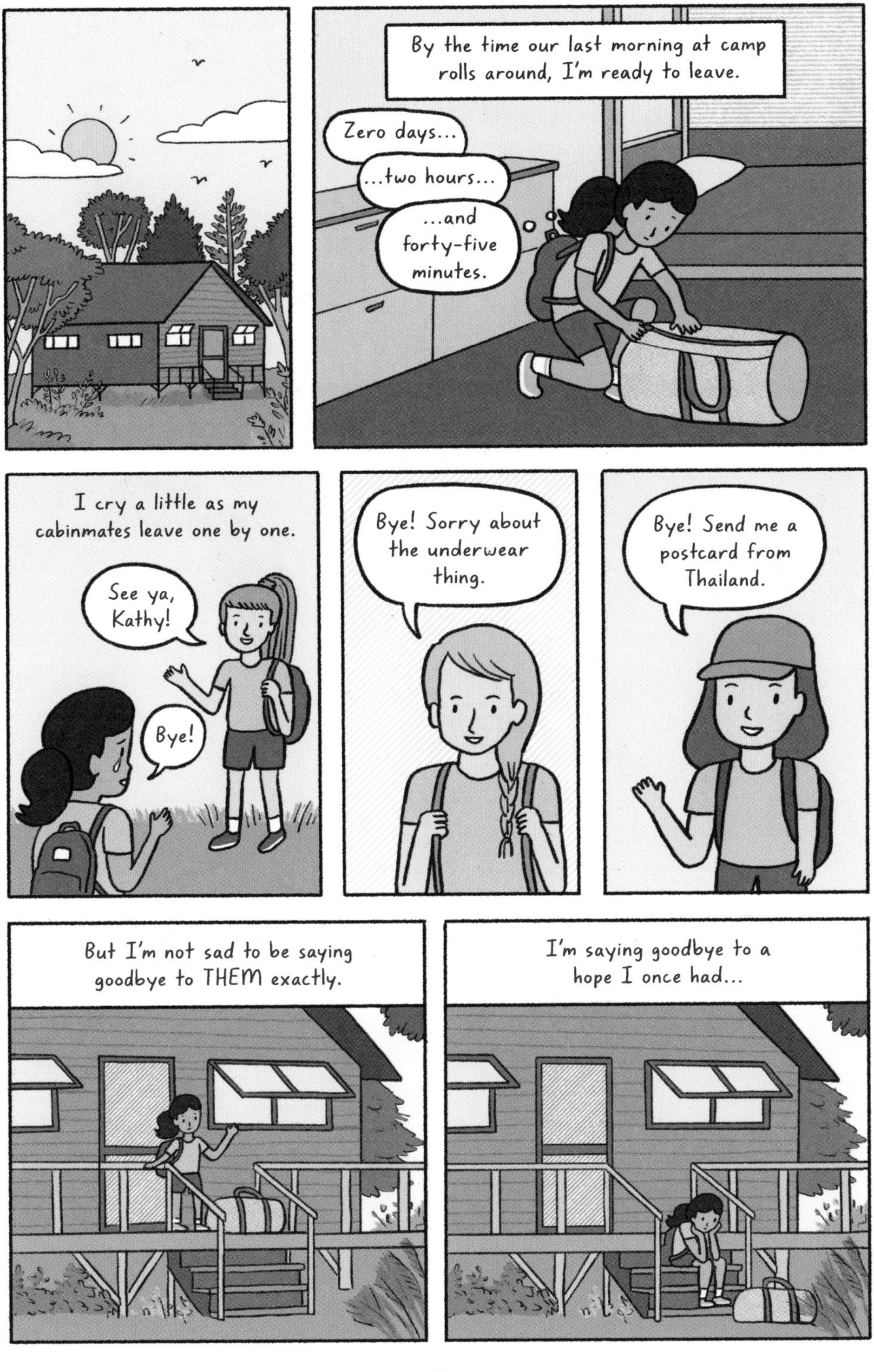
By the time our last morning at camp rolls around, I'm ready to leave.
Zero days...
...two hours...
...and forty-five minutes.
I cry a little as my cabinmates leave one by one.
See ya, Kathy!
Bye!
Bye! Sorry about the underwear thing.
Bye! Send me a postcard from Thailand.
But I'm not sad to be saying goodbye to THEM exactly.
I'm saying goodbye to a hope I once had...

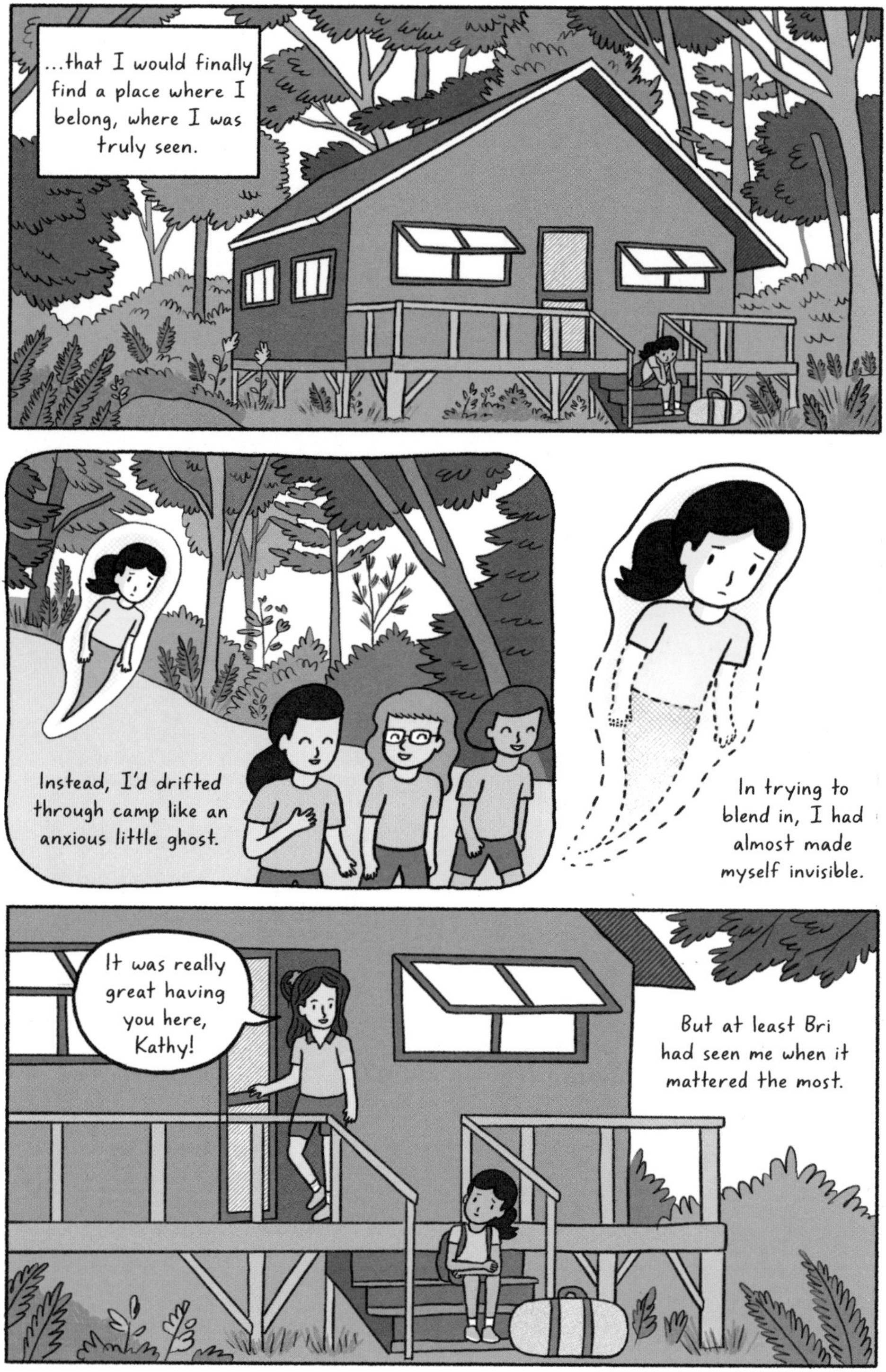
...that I would finally find a place where I belong, where I was truly seen.
Instead, I'd drifted through camp like an anxious little ghost.
In trying to blend in, I had almost made myself invisible.
It was really great having you here, Kathy!
But at least Bri had seen me when it mattered the most.

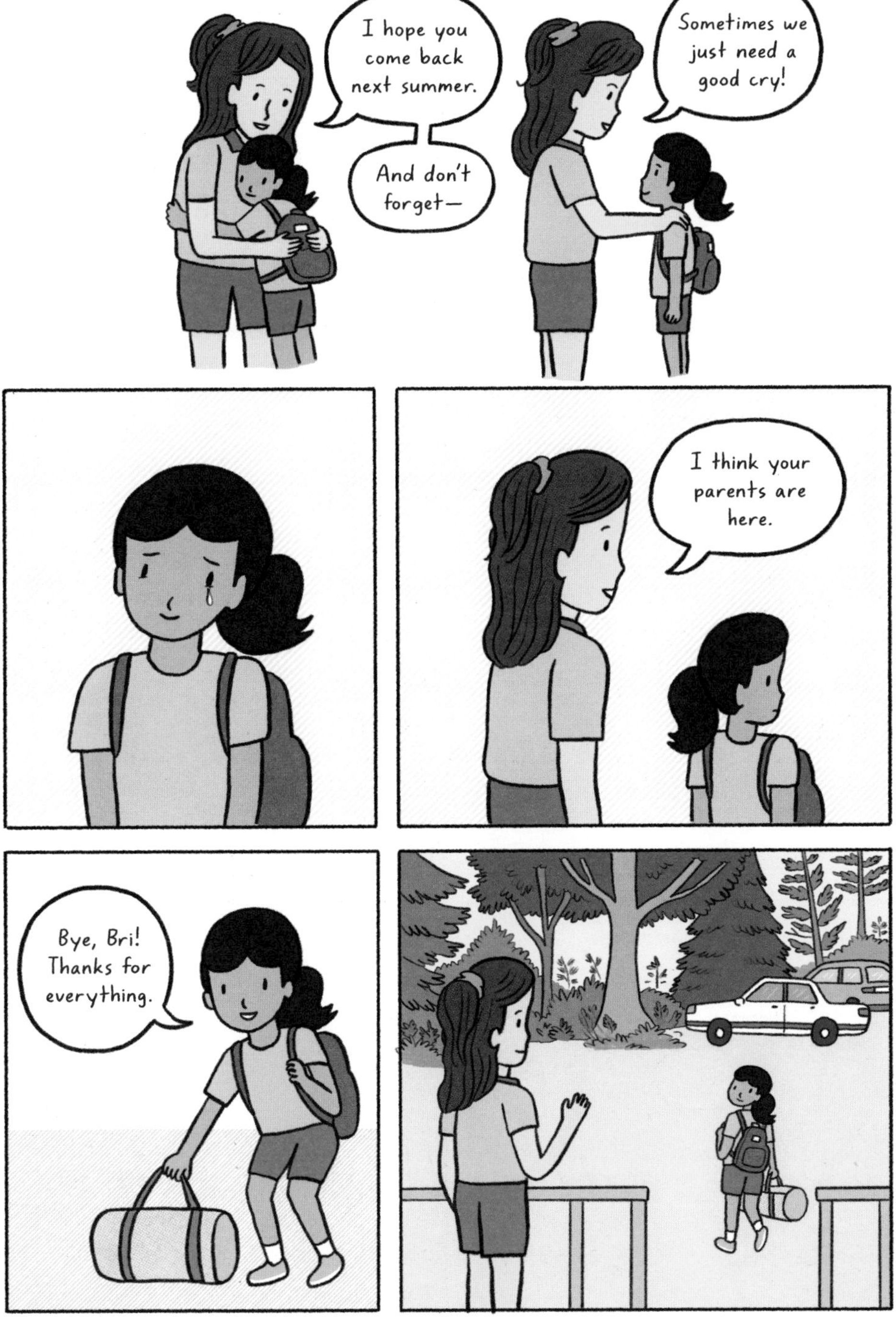
I hope you come back next summer.
And don't forget—
Sometimes we just need a good cry!
I think your parents are here.
Bye, Bri! Thanks for everything.

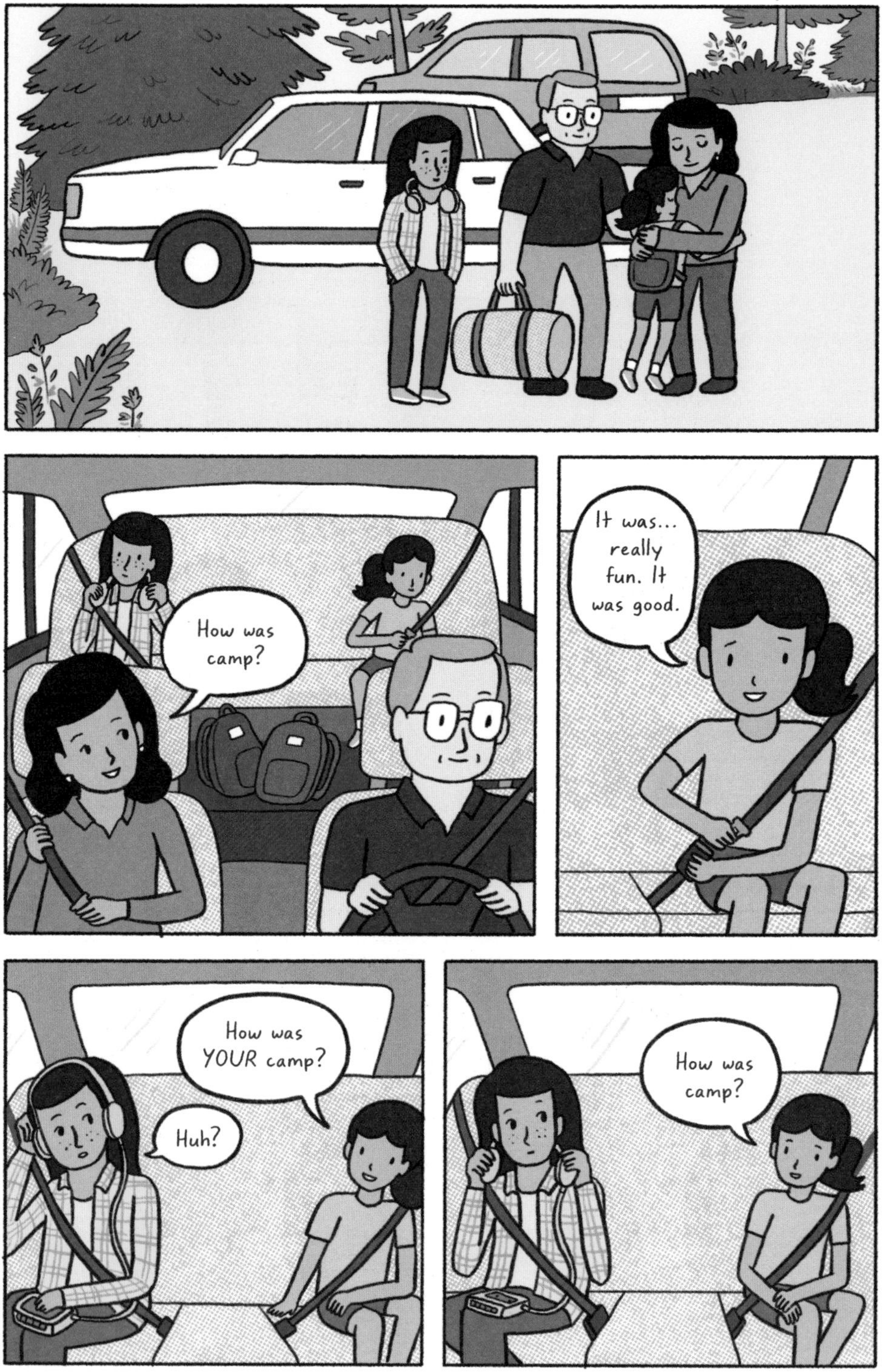
How was camp?
It was... really fun. It was good.
How was YOUR camp?
Huh?
How was camp?

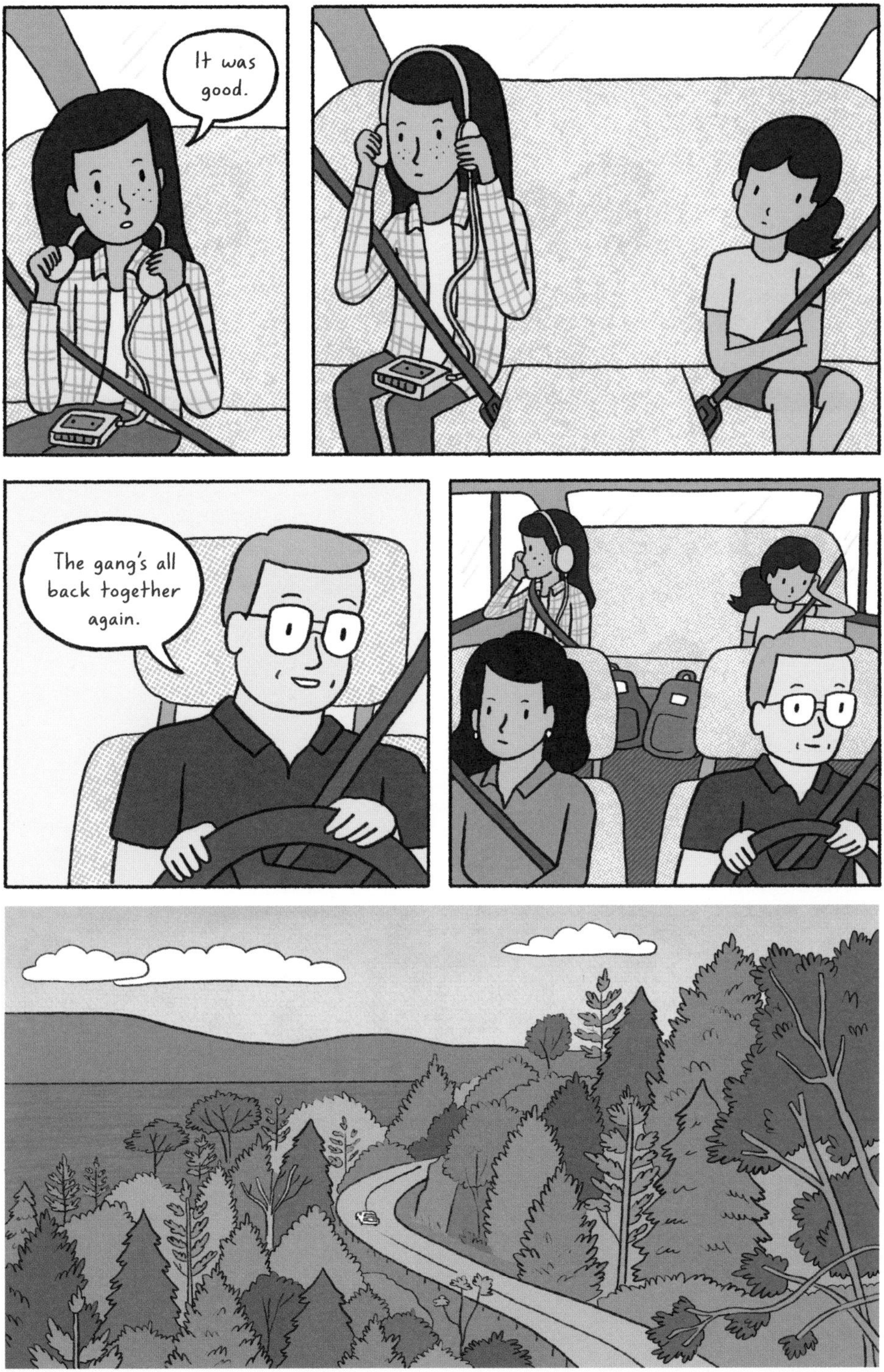
It was good.
The gang's all back together again.

11

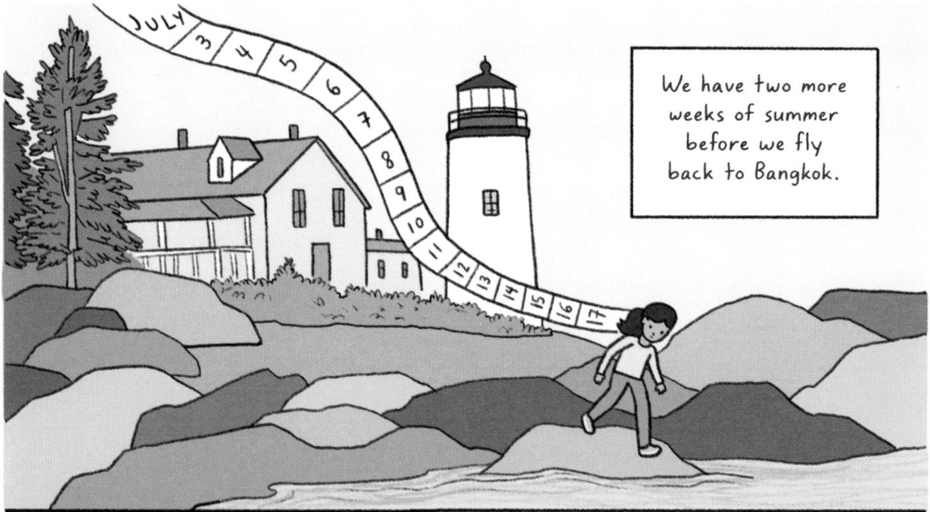
JULY 3 4 5 6 7 8 9 10 11 12 13 14 15 16 17
We have two more weeks of summer before we fly back to Bangkok.

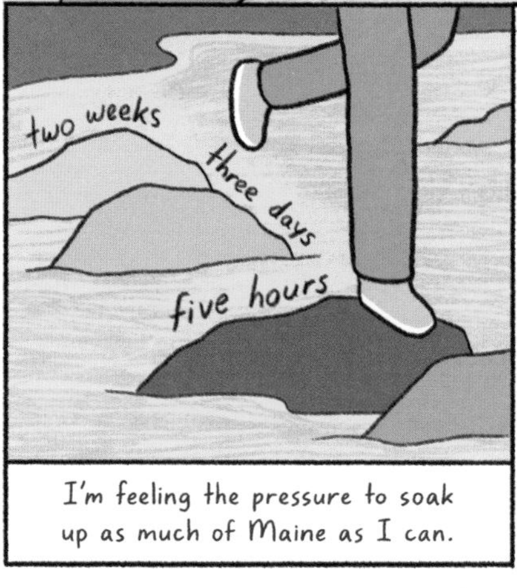
two weeks
three days
five hours
I'm feeling the pressure to soak up as much of Maine as I can.

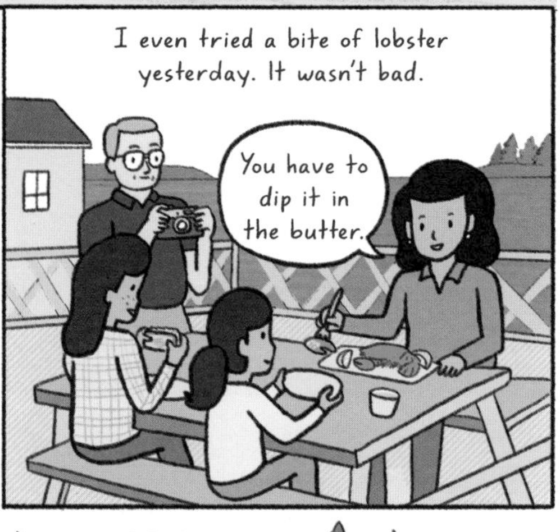
I even tried a bite of lobster yesterday. It wasn't bad.
You have to dip it in the butter.

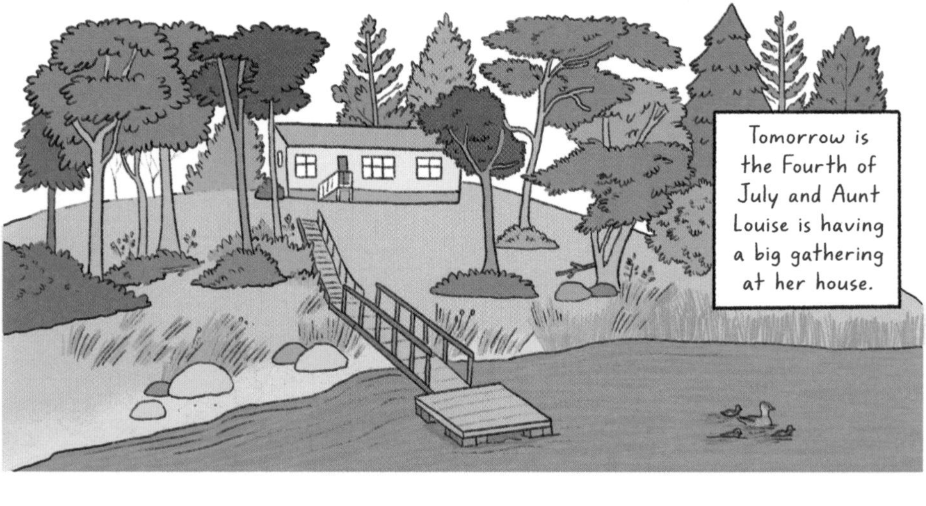
Tomorrow is the Fourth of July and Aunt Louise is having a big gathering at her house.

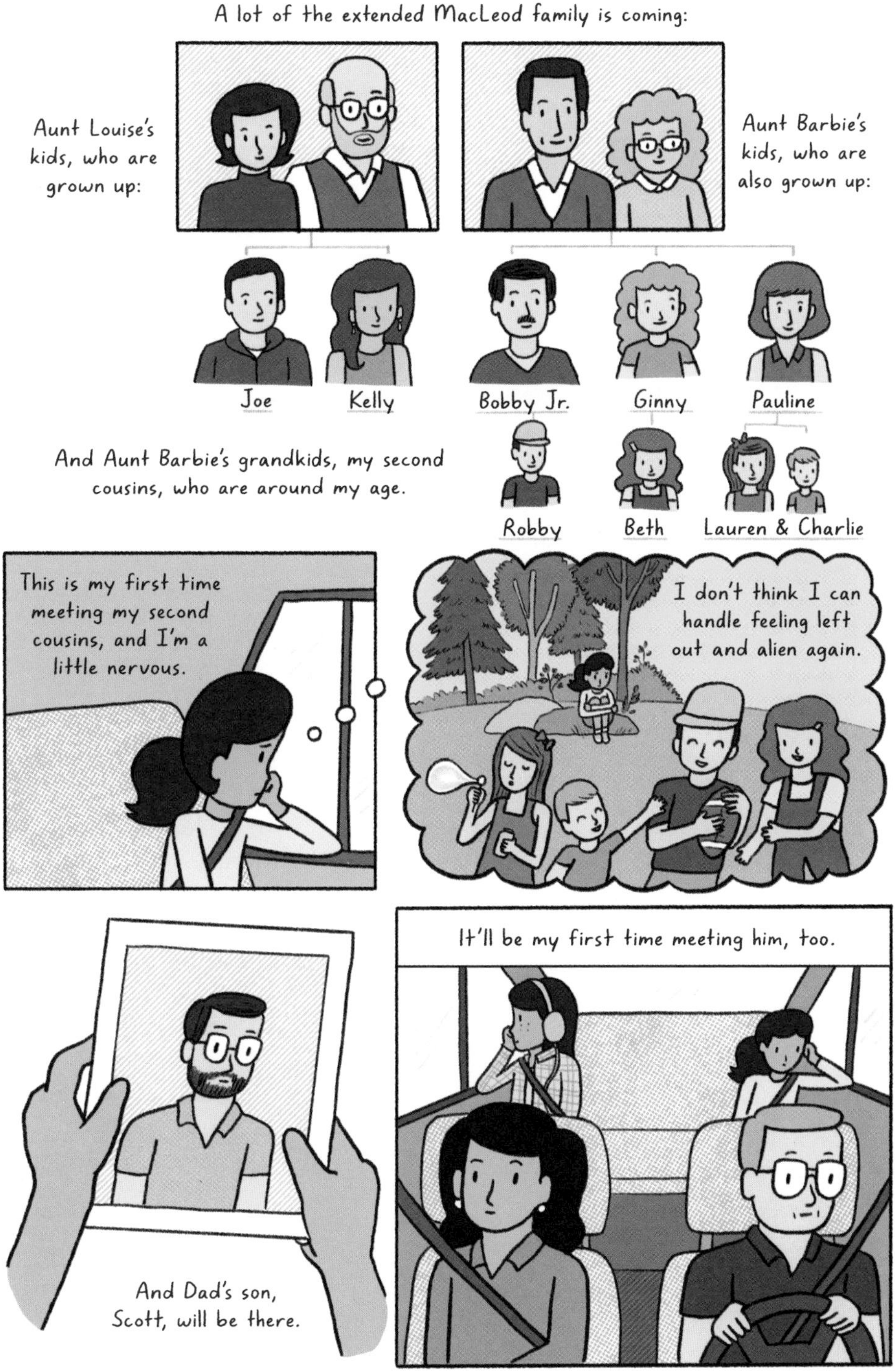
A lot of the extended MacLeod family is coming:
Aunt Louise's kids, who are grown up:
Aunt Barbie's kids, who are also grown up:
Joe
Kelly
Bobby Jr.
Ginny
Pauline
And Aunt Barbie's grandkids, my second cousins, who are around my age.
Robby
Beth
Lauren & Charlie
This is my first time meeting my second cousins, and I'm a little nervous.
I don't think I can handle feeling left out and alien again.
And Dad's son, Scott, will be there.
It'll be my first time meeting him, too.

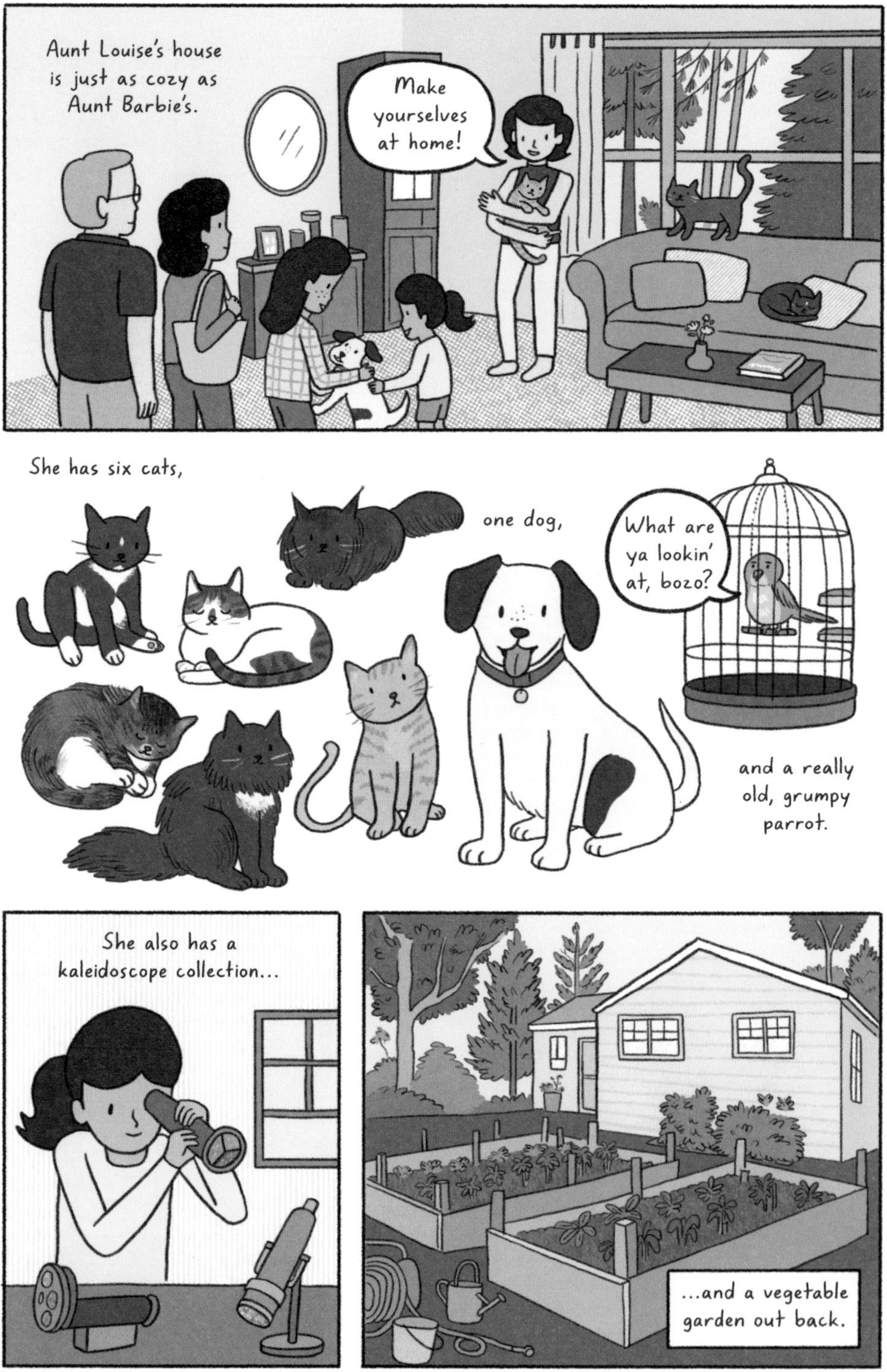
Aunt Louise's house is just as cozy as Aunt Barbie's.
Make yourselves at home!
She has six cats,
one dog,
What are ya lookin' at, bozo?
and a really old, grumpy parrot.
She also has a kaleidoscope collection...
...and a vegetable garden out back.

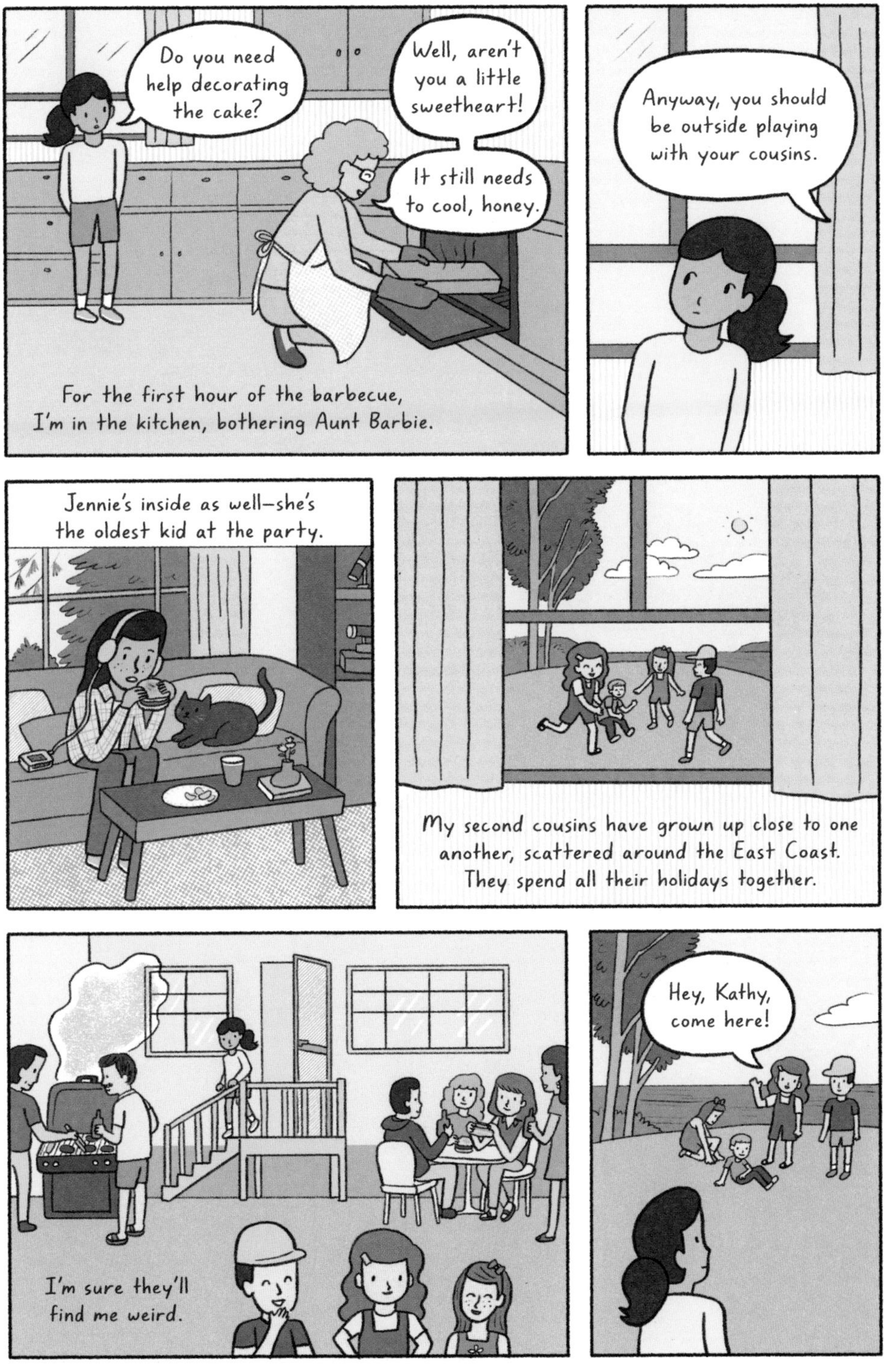
Do you need help decorating the cake?
Well, aren't you a little sweetheart!
It still needs to cool, honey.
For the first hour of the barbecue, I'm in the kitchen, bothering Aunt Barbie.
Anyway, you should be outside playing with your cousins.
Jennie's inside as well—she's the oldest kid at the party.
My second cousins have grown up close to one another, scattered around the East Coast. They spend all their holidays together.
I'm sure they'll find me weird.
Hey, Kathy, come here!

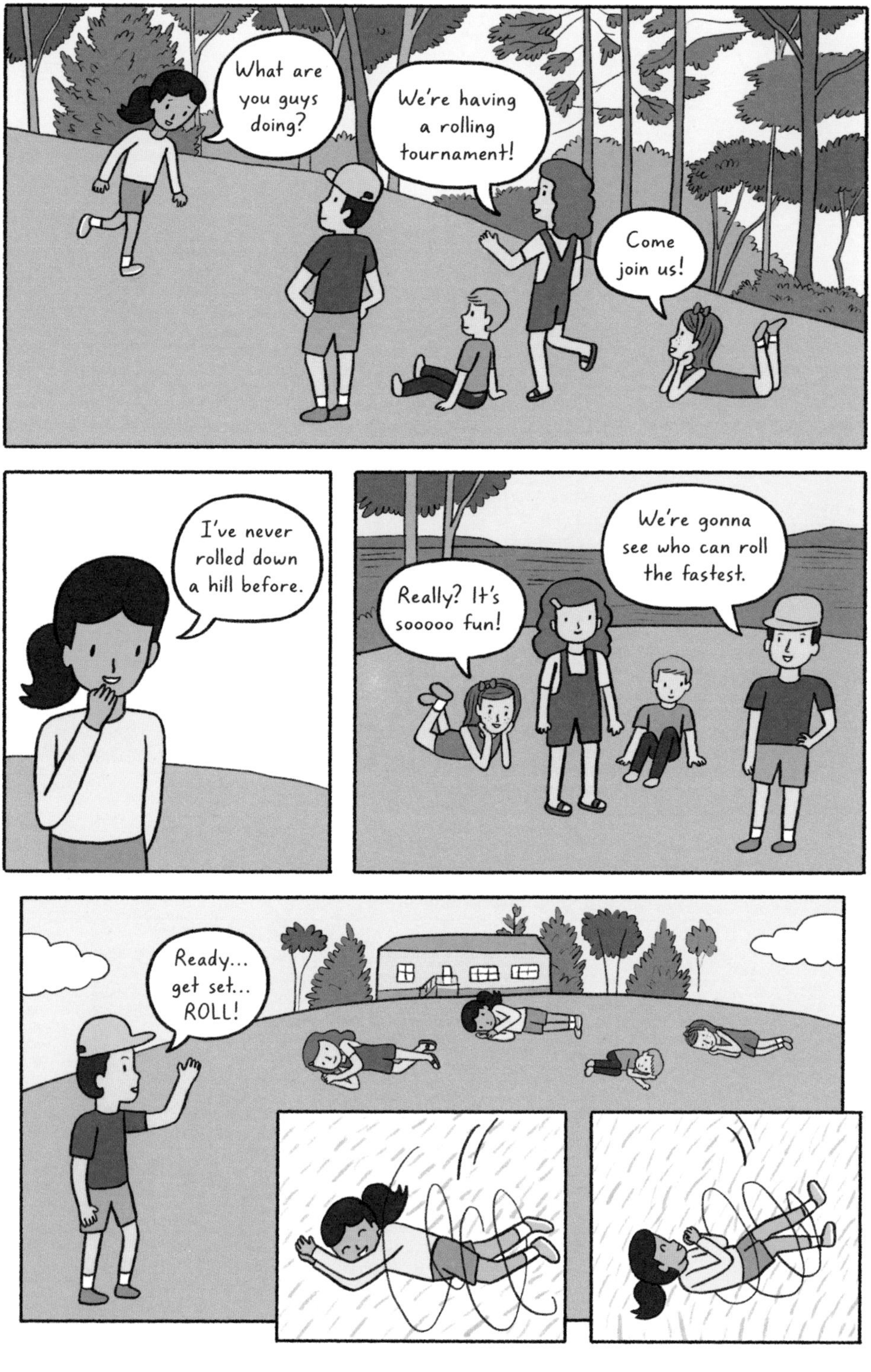
What are you guys doing?
We're having a rolling tournament!
Come join us!
I've never rolled down a hill before.
Really? It's sooooo fun!
We're gonna see who can roll the fastest.
Ready... get set... ROLL!

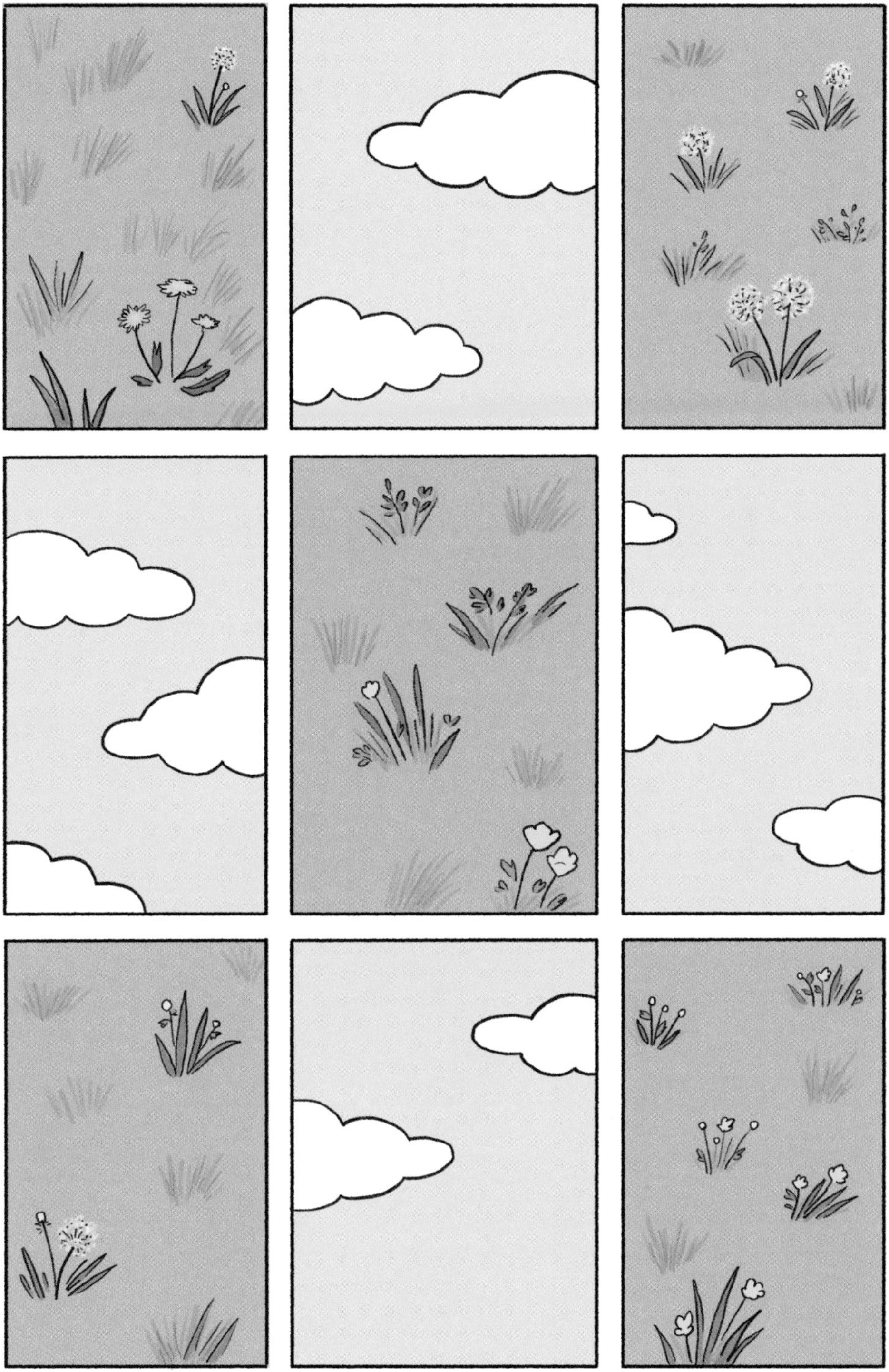

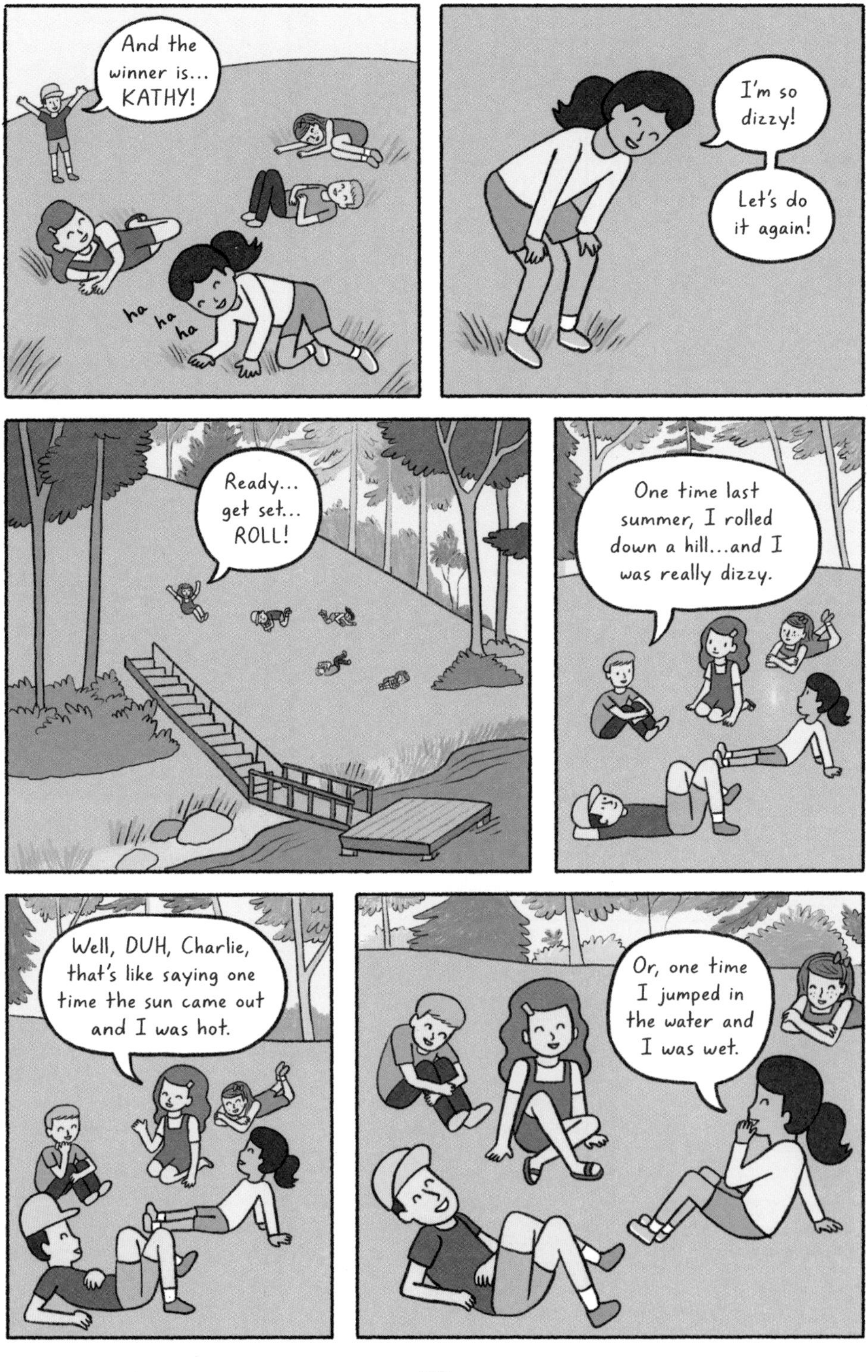
And the winner is... KATHY!
ha ha ha
I'm so dizzy!
Let's do it again!
Ready... get set... ROLL!
One time last summer, I rolled down a hill...and I was really dizzy.
Well, DUH, Charlie, that's like saying one time the sun came out and I was hot.
Or, one time I jumped in the water and I was wet.

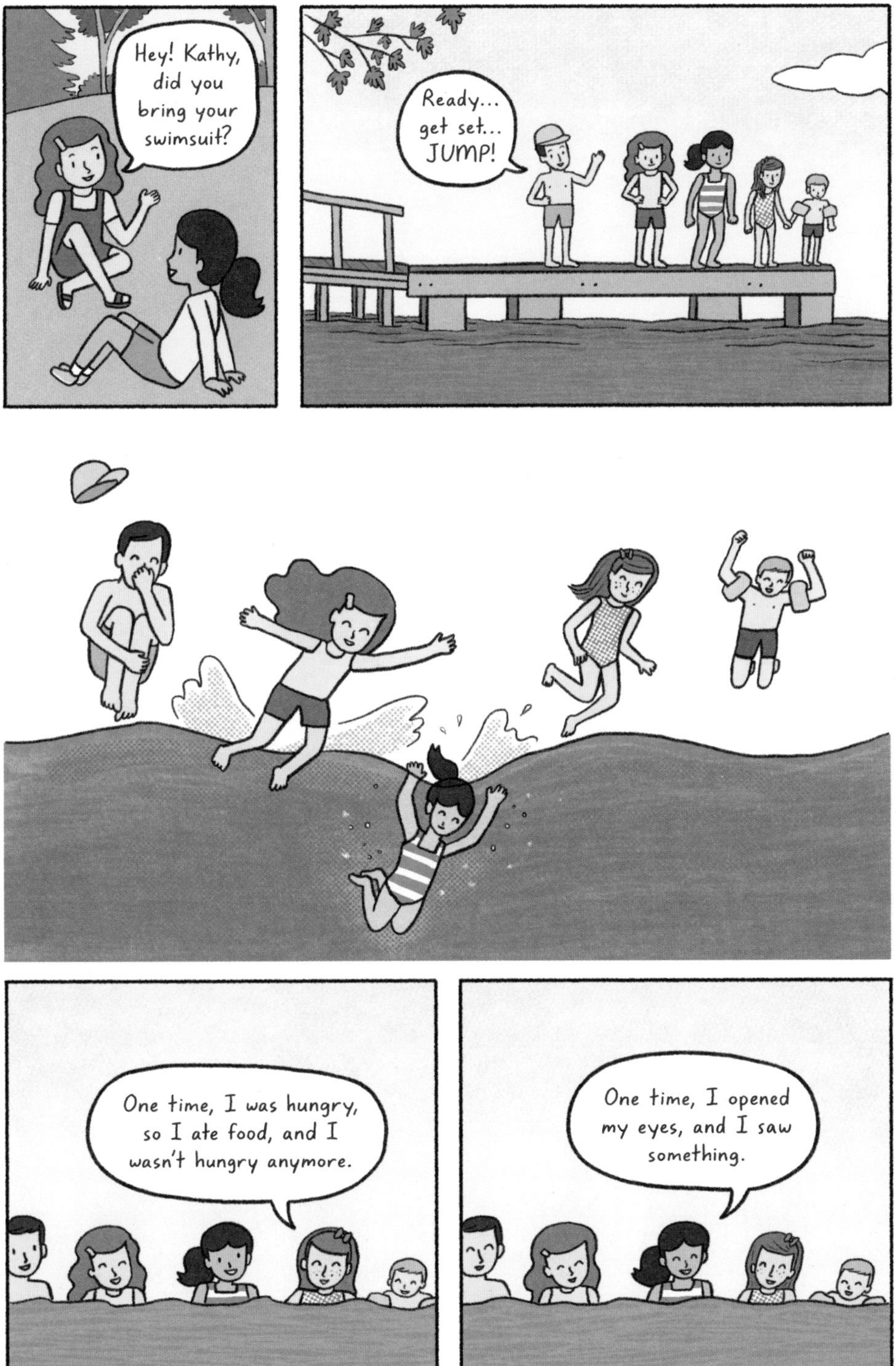
Hey! Kathy, did you bring your swimsuit?
Ready... get set... JUMP!
One time, I was hungry, so I ate food, and I wasn't hungry anymore.
One time, I opened my eyes, and I saw something.

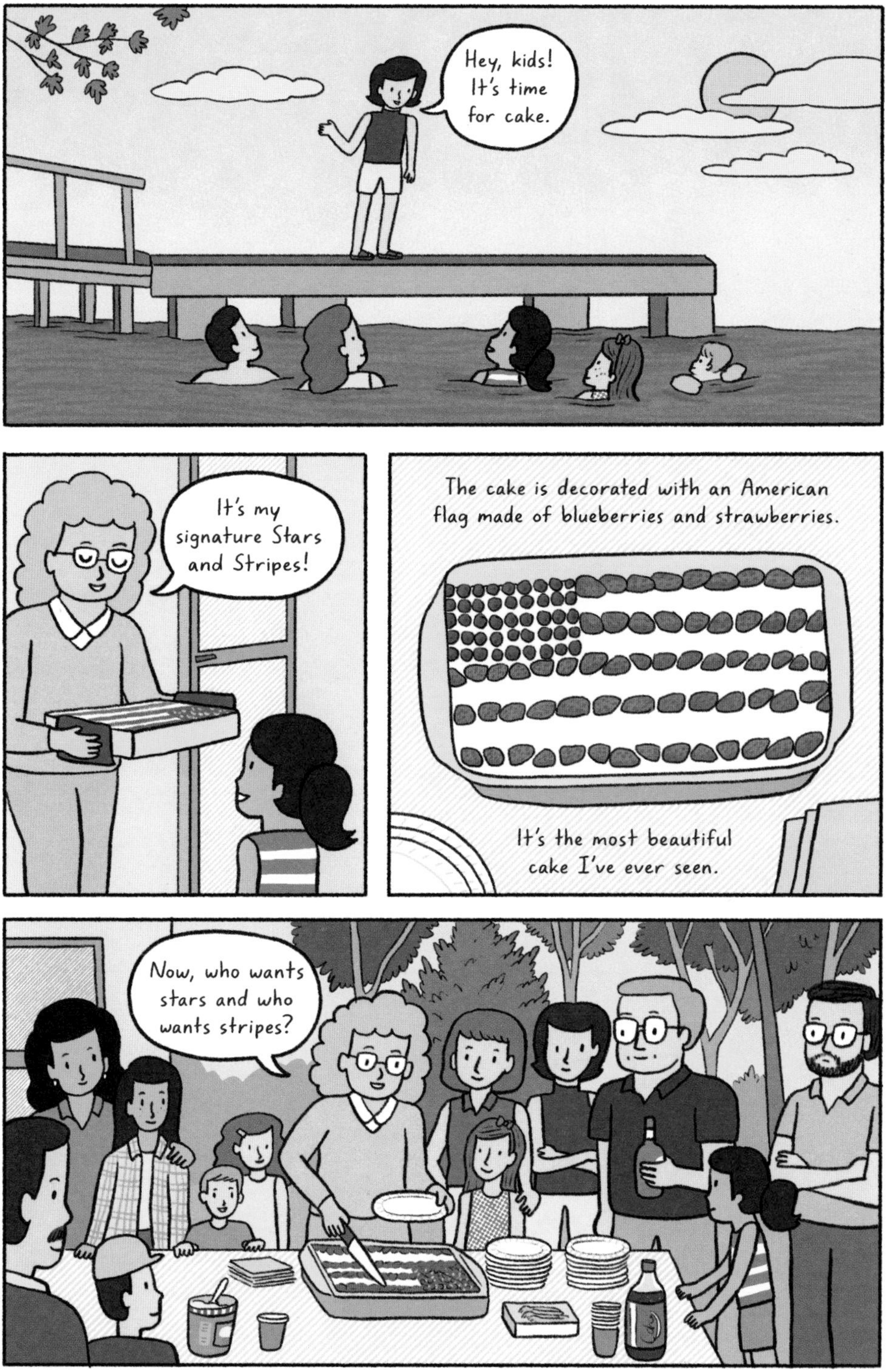
Hey, kids! It's time for cake.
It's my signature Stars and Stripes!
The cake is decorated with an American flag made of blueberries and strawberries.
It's the most beautiful cake I've ever seen.
Now, who wants stars and who wants stripes?

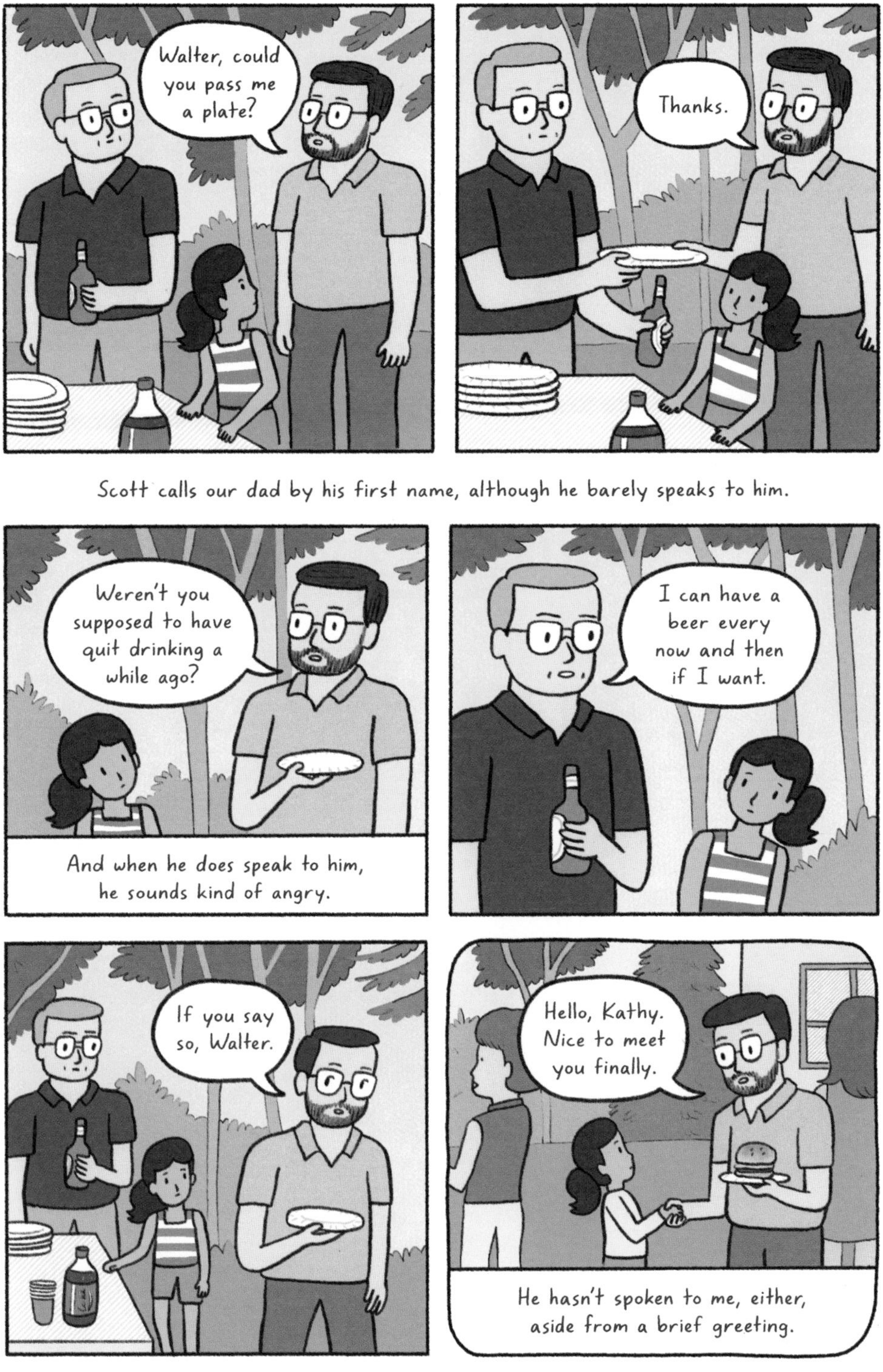
Walter, could you pass me a plate?
Thanks.
Scott calls our dad by his first name, although he barely speaks to him.
Weren't you supposed to have quit drinking a while ago?
And when he does speak to him, he sounds kind of angry.
I can have a beer every now and then if I want.
If you say so, Walter.
Hello, Kathy. Nice to meet you finally.
He hasn't spoken to me, either, aside from a brief greeting.

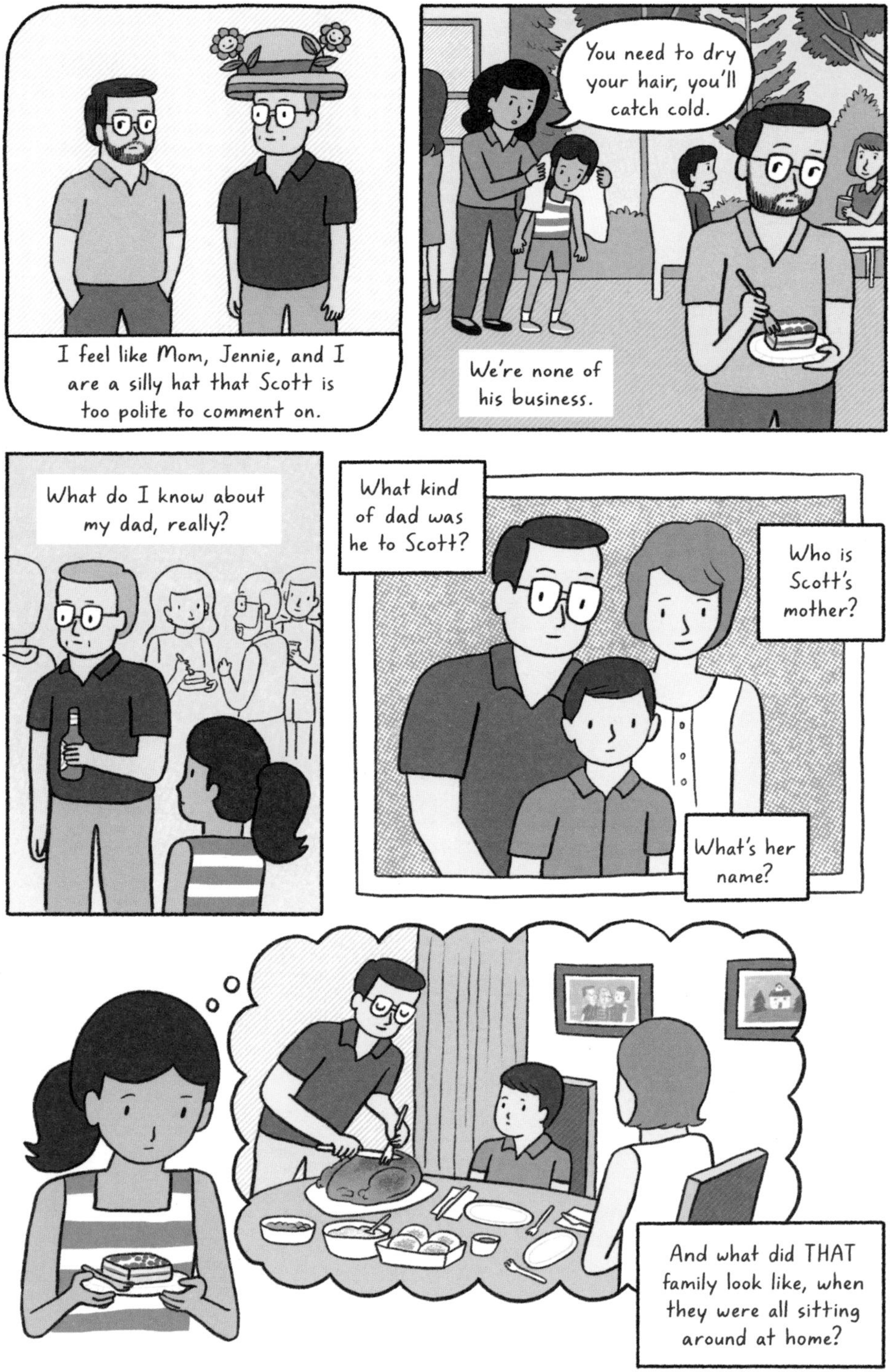
I feel like Mom, Jennie, and I are a silly hat that Scott is too polite to comment on.
You need to dry your hair, you'll catch cold.
We're none of his business.
What do I know about my dad, really?
What kind of dad was he to Scott?
Who is Scott's mother?
What's her name?
And what did THAT family look like, when they were all sitting around at home?

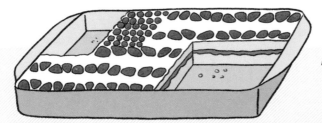

And how does it make Dad feel, to come back to the country where he grew up?

There's so much I want to know, but I can't imagine my parents sharing these things with me.

It was so long ago.

The past should stay in the past.

Maybe one day, when I'm older, I'll be brave enough to ask.

There's a man at the table with us, a neighbor of Aunt Louise's.

He seems to take a special interest in Jennie and me once he finds out we're from Thailand.

How...do...you... like...the... United...States?

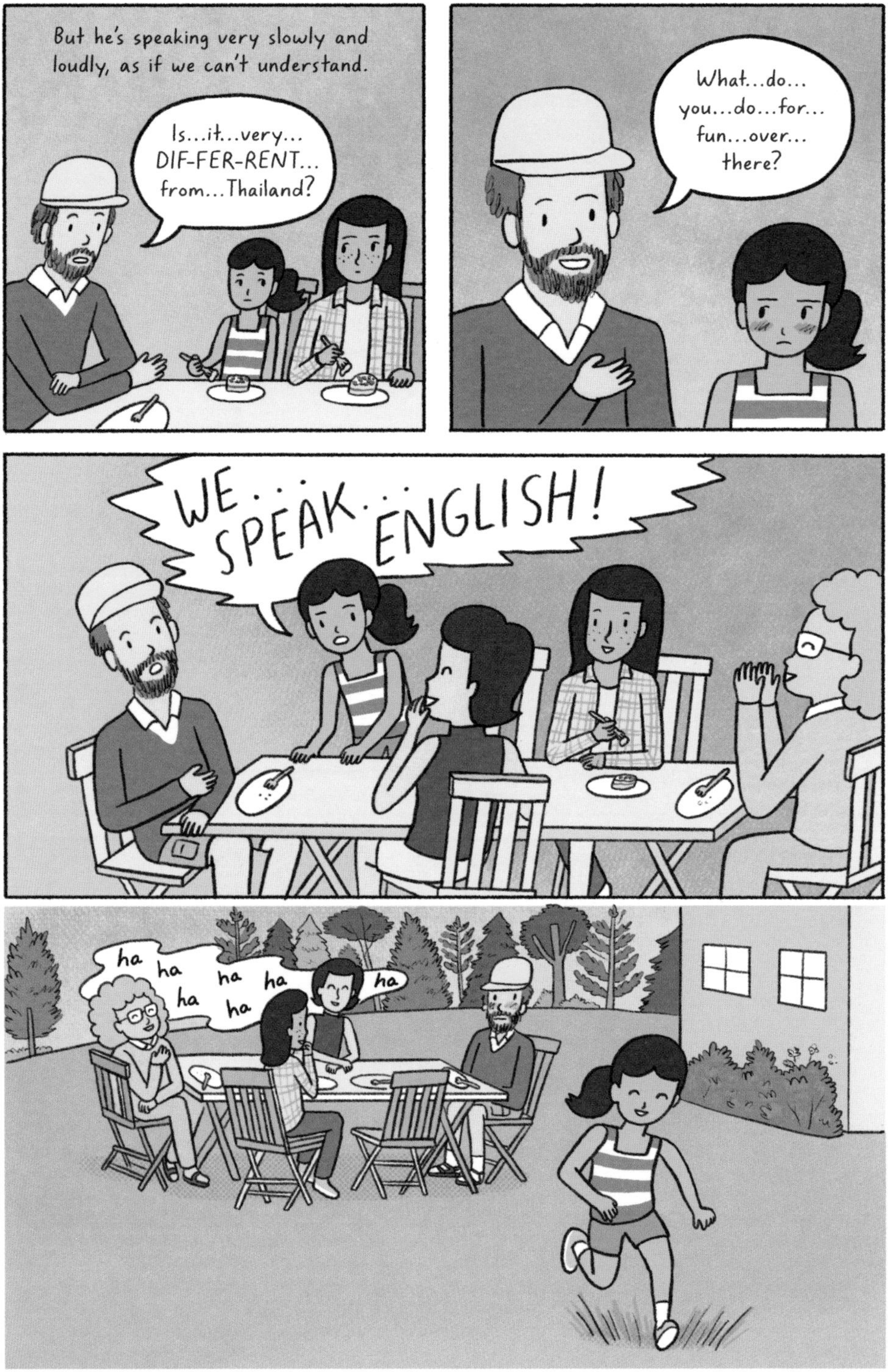
But he's speaking very slowly and loudly, as if we can't understand.
Is...it...very... DIF-FER-RENT... from...Thailand?
What...do... you...do...for... fun...over... there?
WE... SPEAK... ENGLISH!
ha ha ha ha ha ha ha

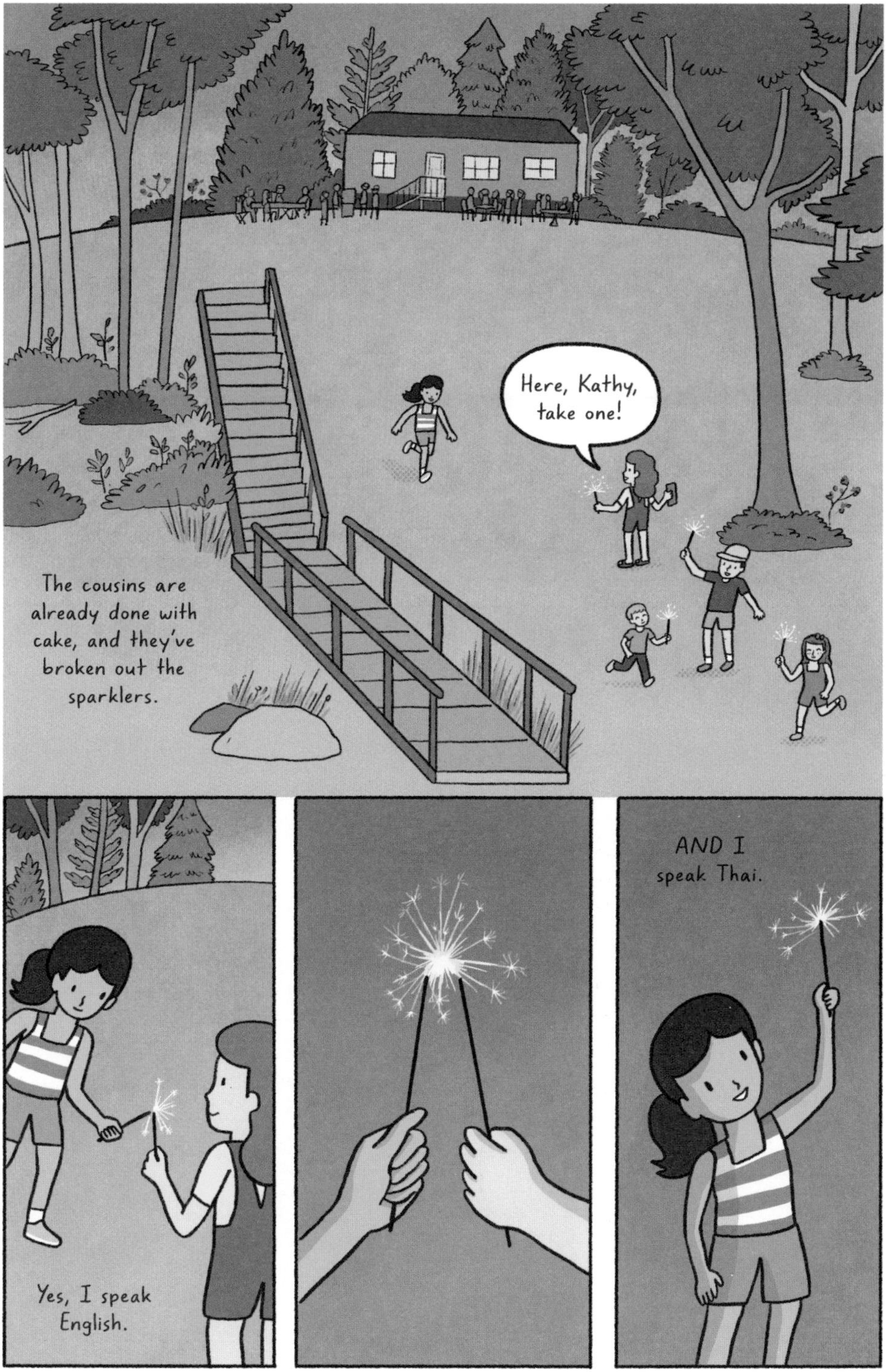
The cousins are already done with cake, and they've broken out the sparklers.
Here, Kathy, take one!
Yes, I speak English.
AND I speak Thai.

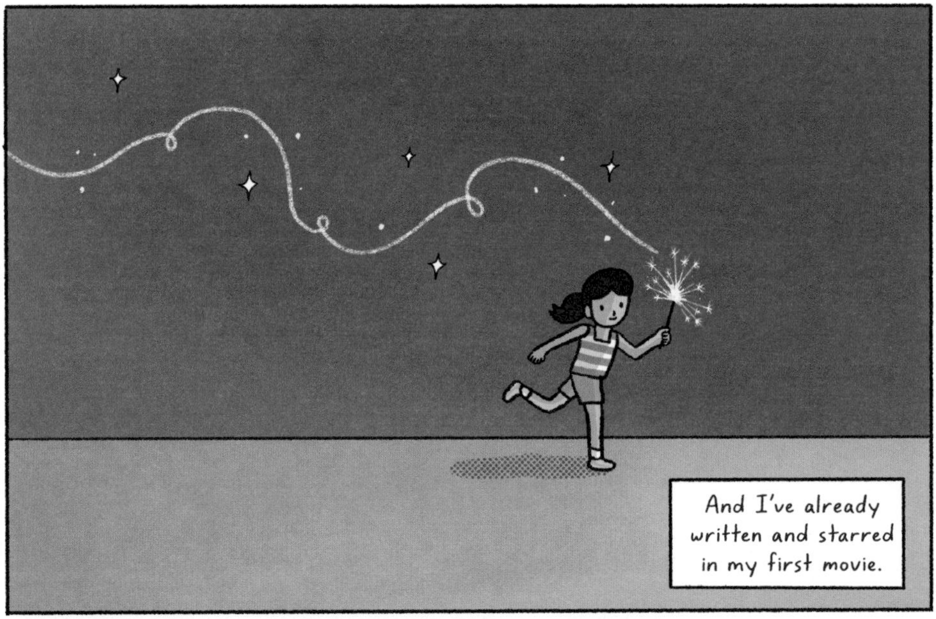
And I've already written and starred in my first movie.

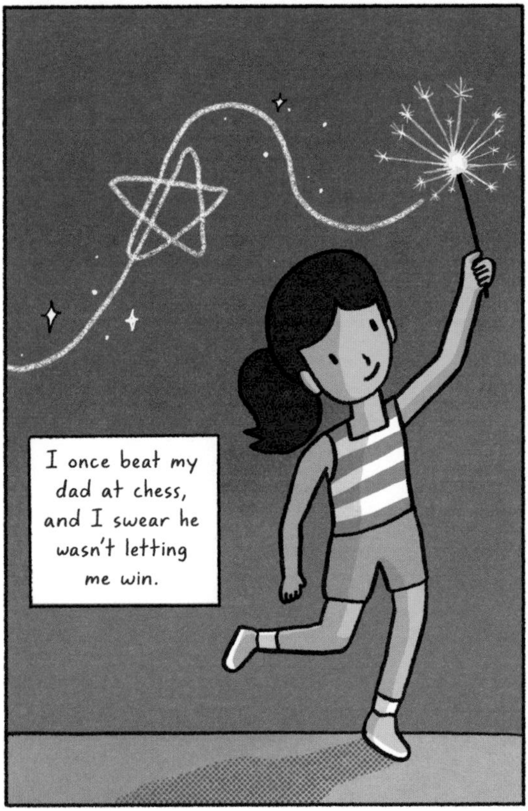
I once beat my dad at chess, and I swear he wasn't letting me win.

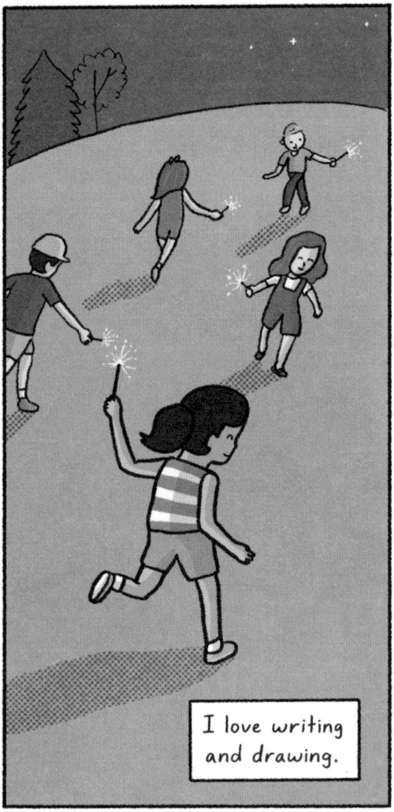
I love writing and drawing.

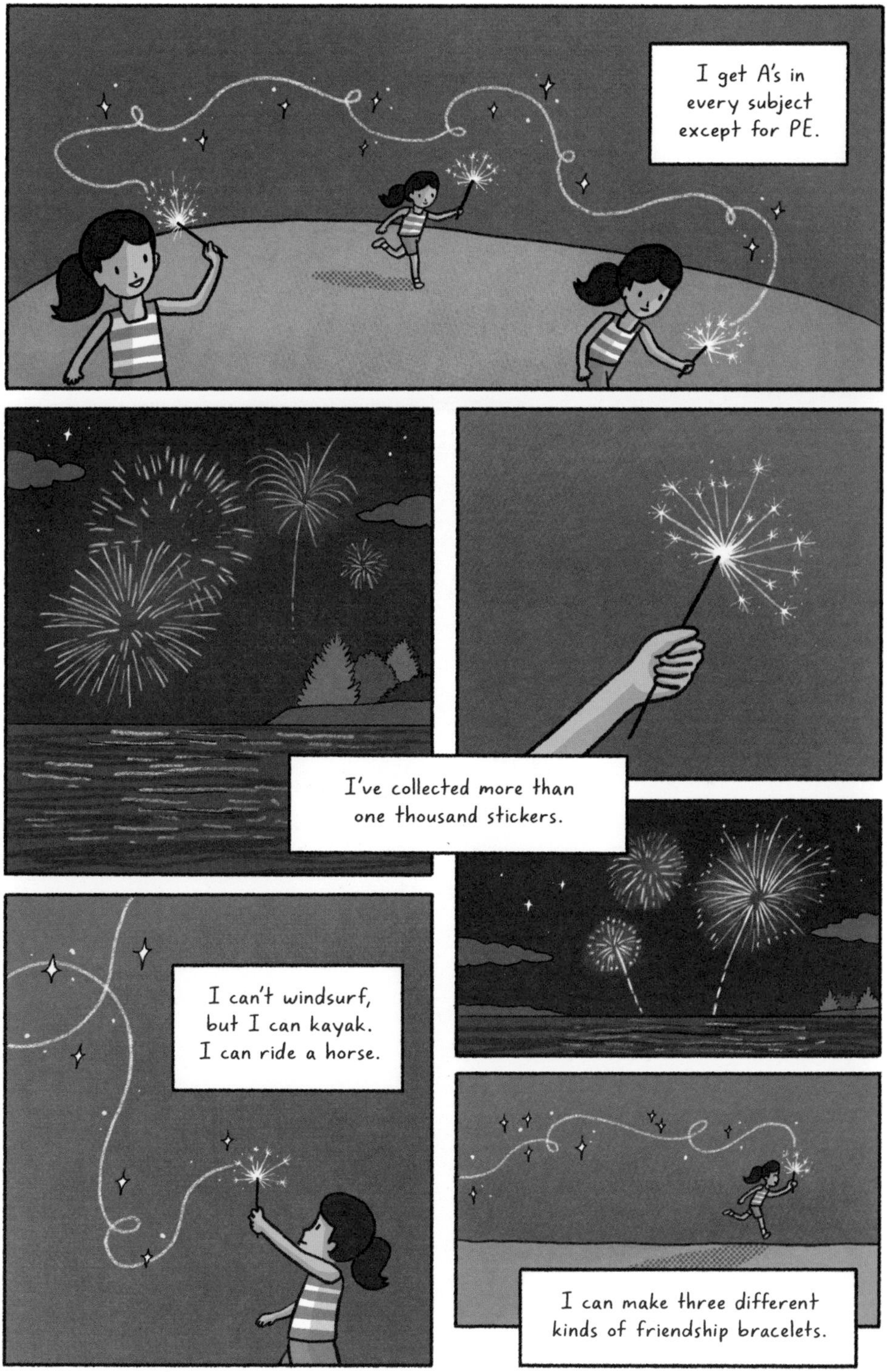
I get A's in every subject except for PE.
I've collected more than one thousand stickers.
I can't windsurf, but I can kayak. I can ride a horse.
I can make three different kinds of friendship bracelets.

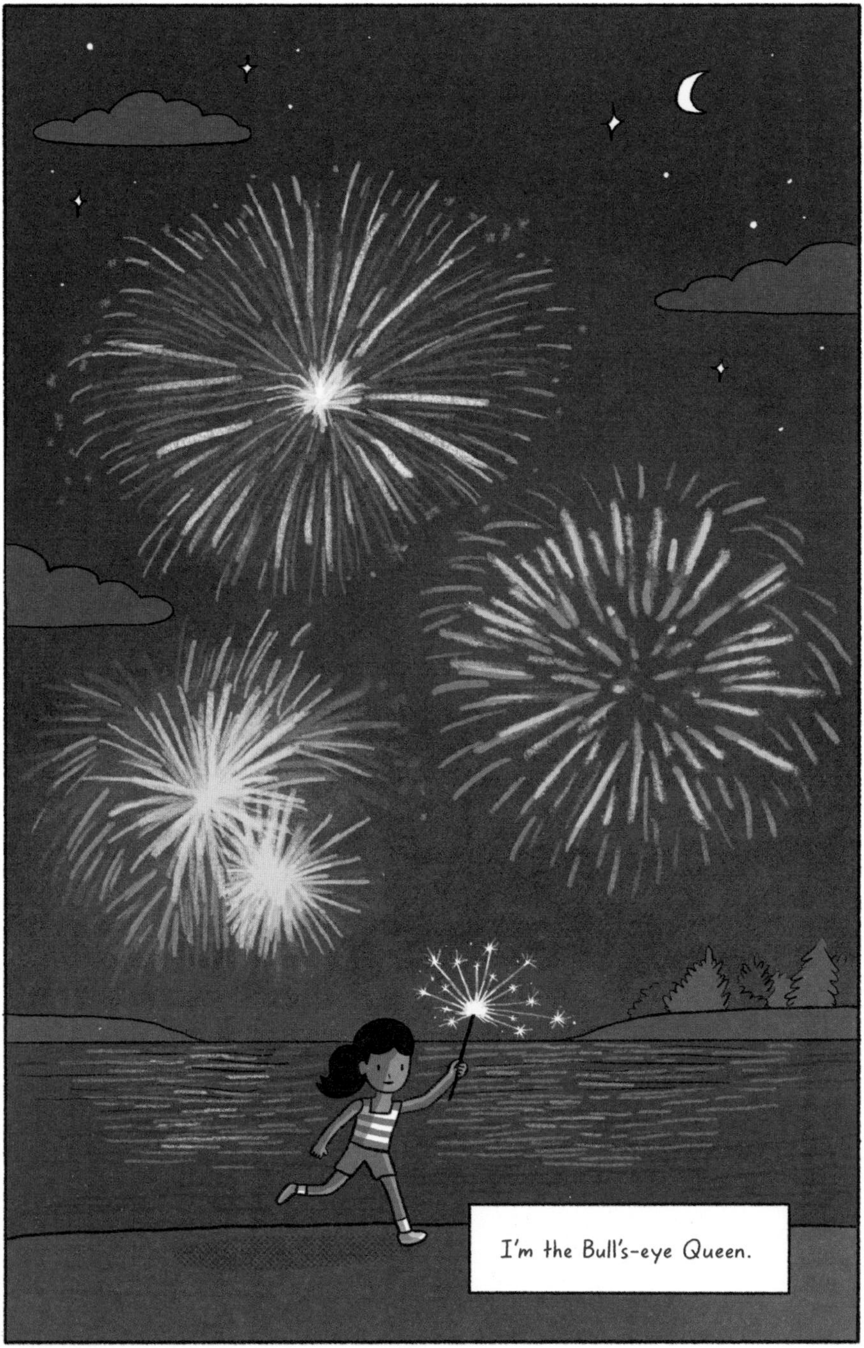
I'm the Bull's-eye Queen.

12

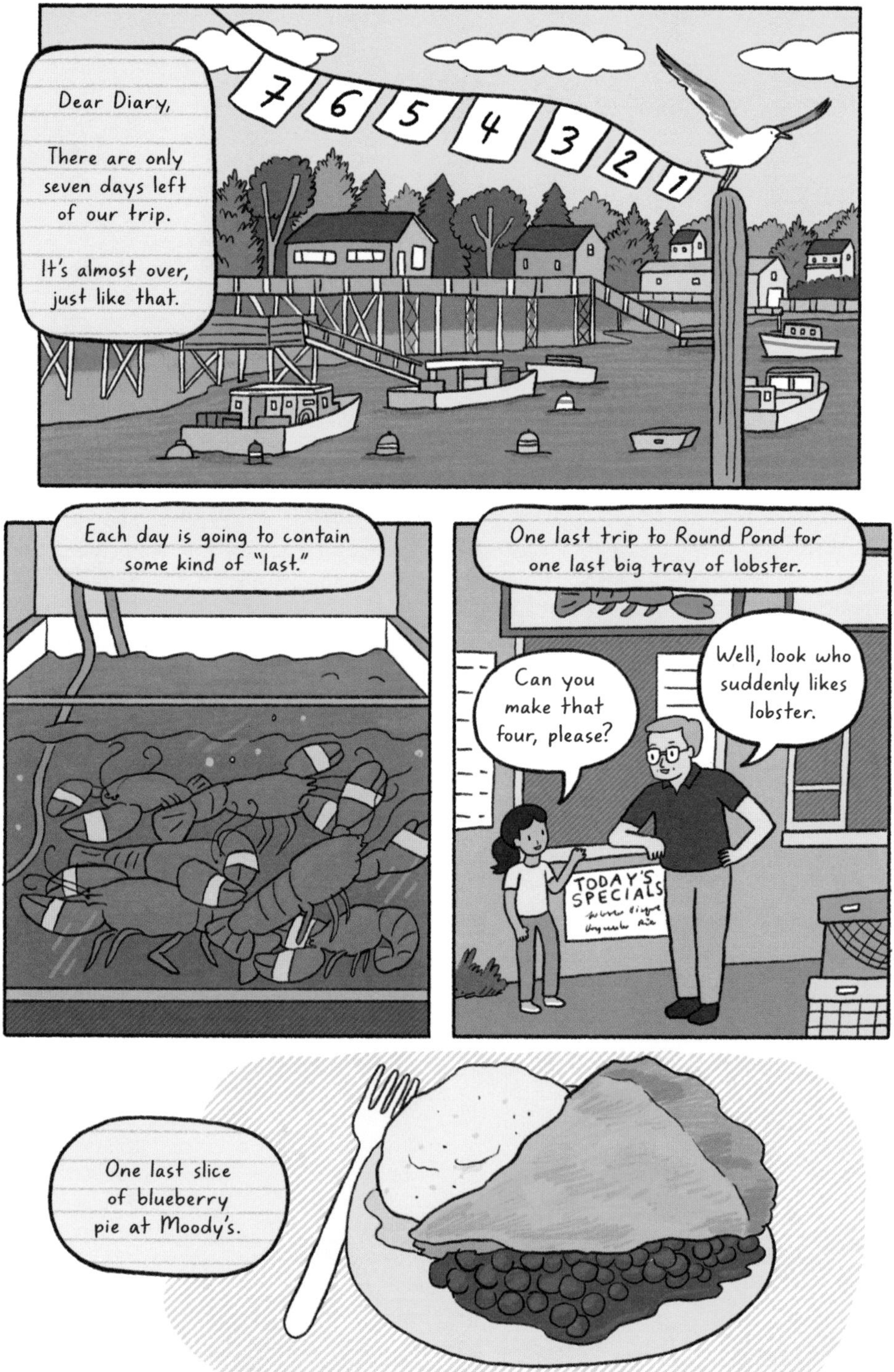
Dear Diary,
There are only seven days left of our trip.
It's almost over, just like that.
7 6 5 4 3 2 1
Each day is going to contain some kind of "last."
One last trip to Round Pond for one last big tray of lobster.
Can you make that four, please?
Well, look who suddenly likes lobster.
TODAY'S SPECIALS
One last slice of blueberry pie at Moody's.

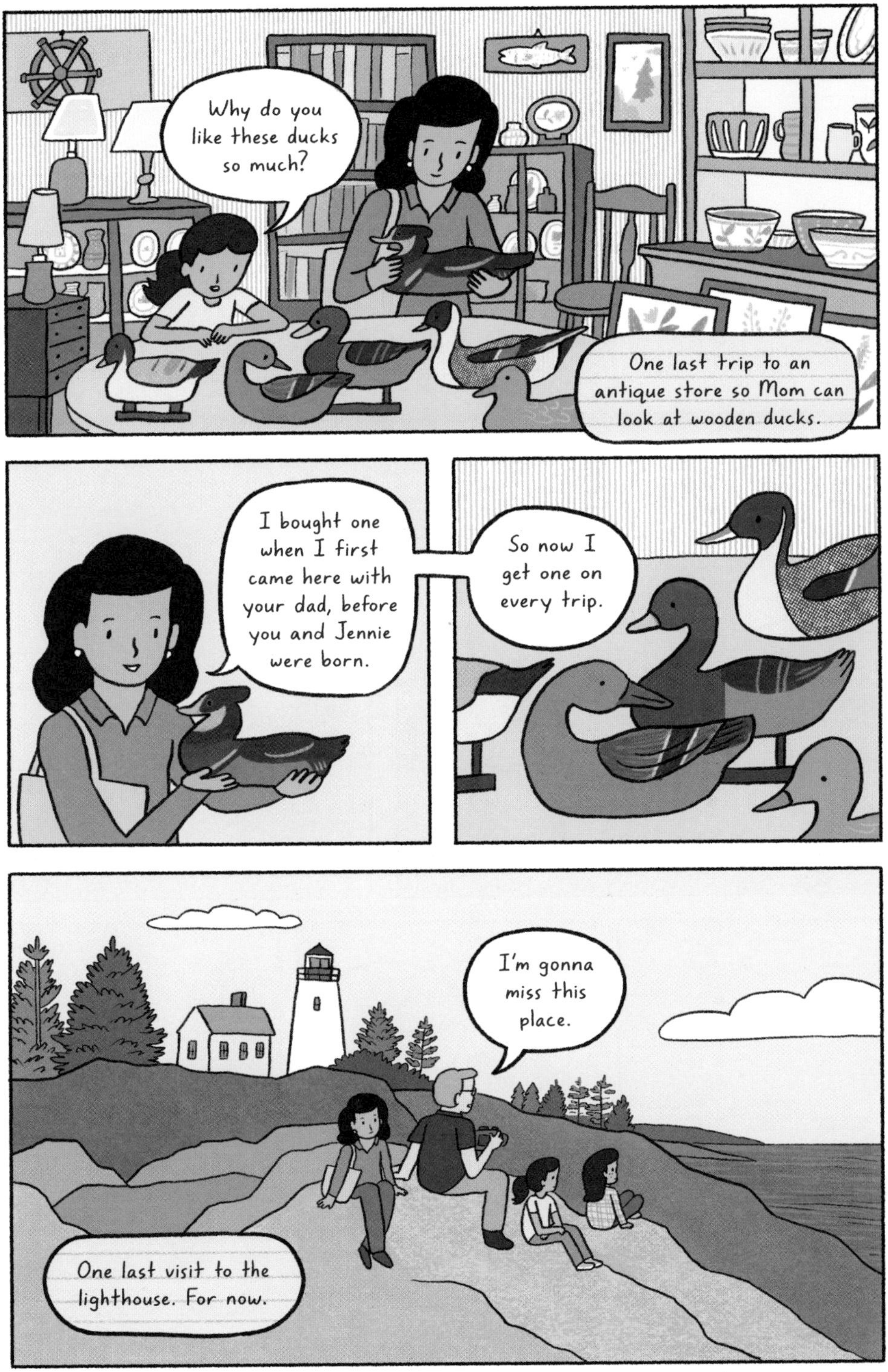
Why do you like these ducks so much?
One last trip to an antique store so Mom can look at wooden ducks.
I bought one when I first came here with your dad, before you and Jennie were born.
So now I get one on every trip.
I'm gonna miss this place.
One last visit to the lighthouse. For now.

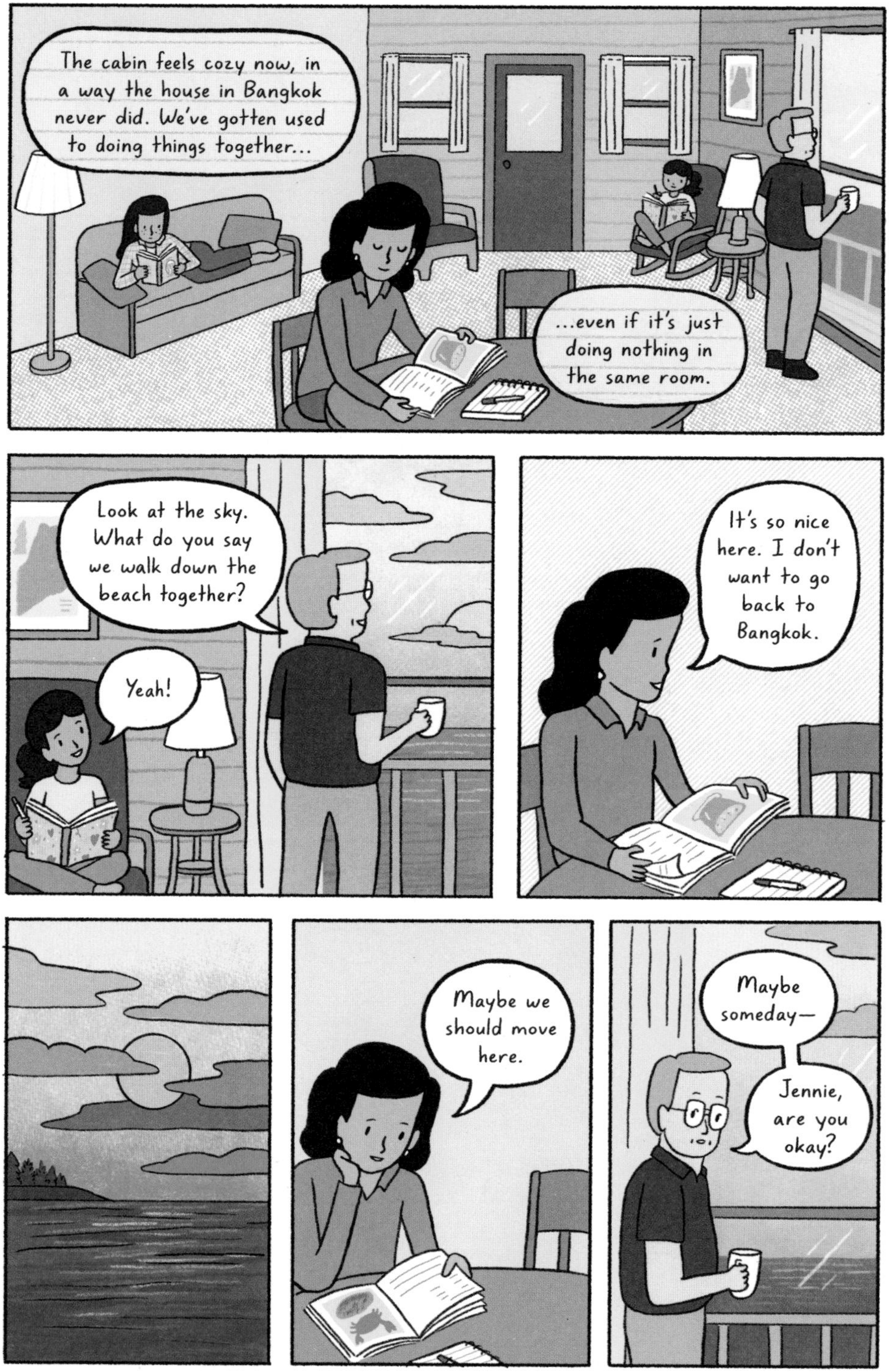
The cabin feels cozy now, in a way the house in Bangkok never did. We've gotten used to doing things together...
...even if it's just doing nothing in the same room.
Look at the sky. What do you say we walk down the beach together?
Yeah!
It's so nice here. I don't want to go back to Bangkok.
Maybe we should move here.
Maybe someday—
Jennie, are you okay?

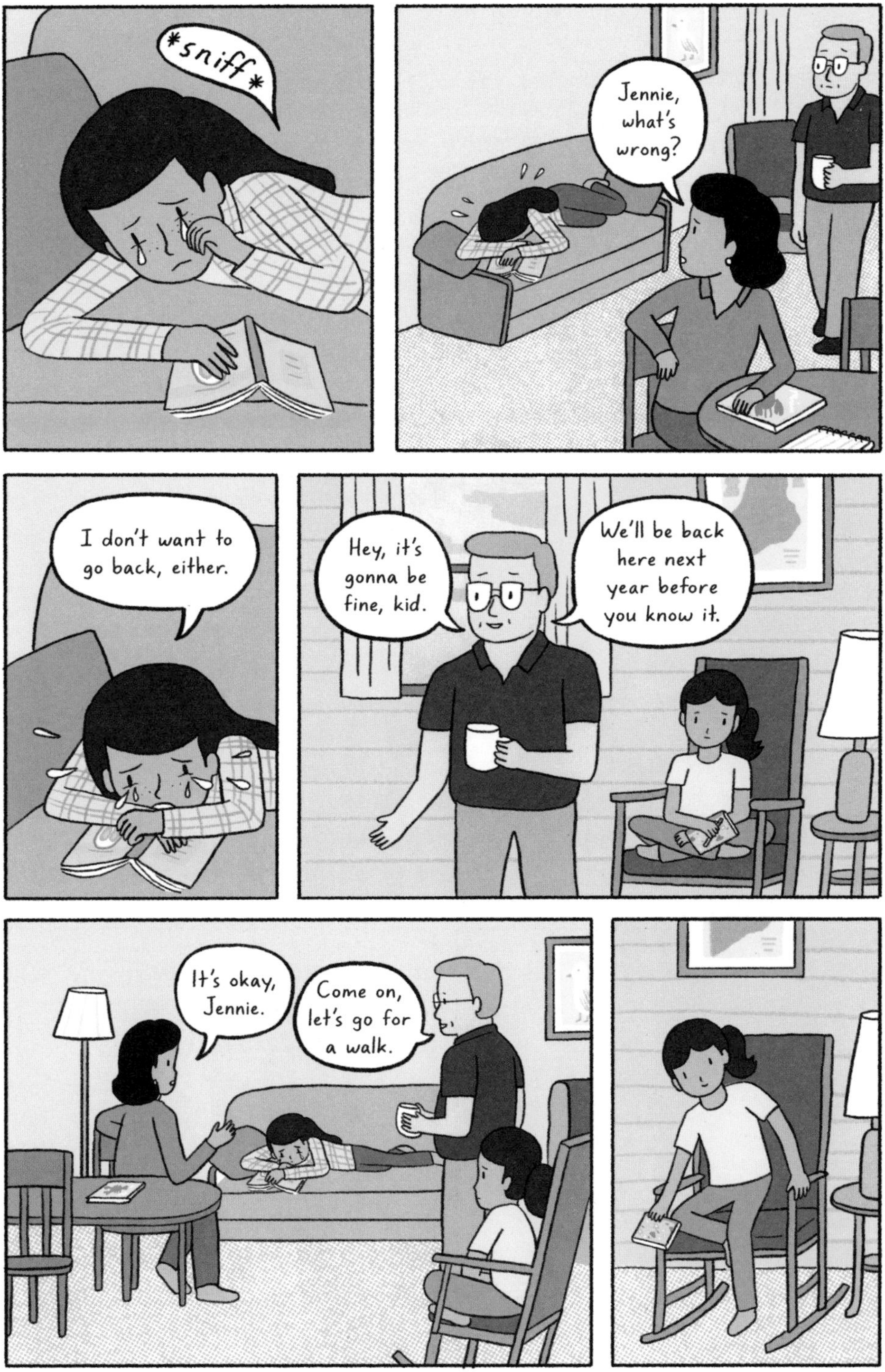
sniff
Jennie, what's wrong?
I don't want to go back, either.
Hey, it's gonna be fine, kid.
We'll be back here next year before you know it.
It's okay, Jennie.
Come on, let's go for a walk.

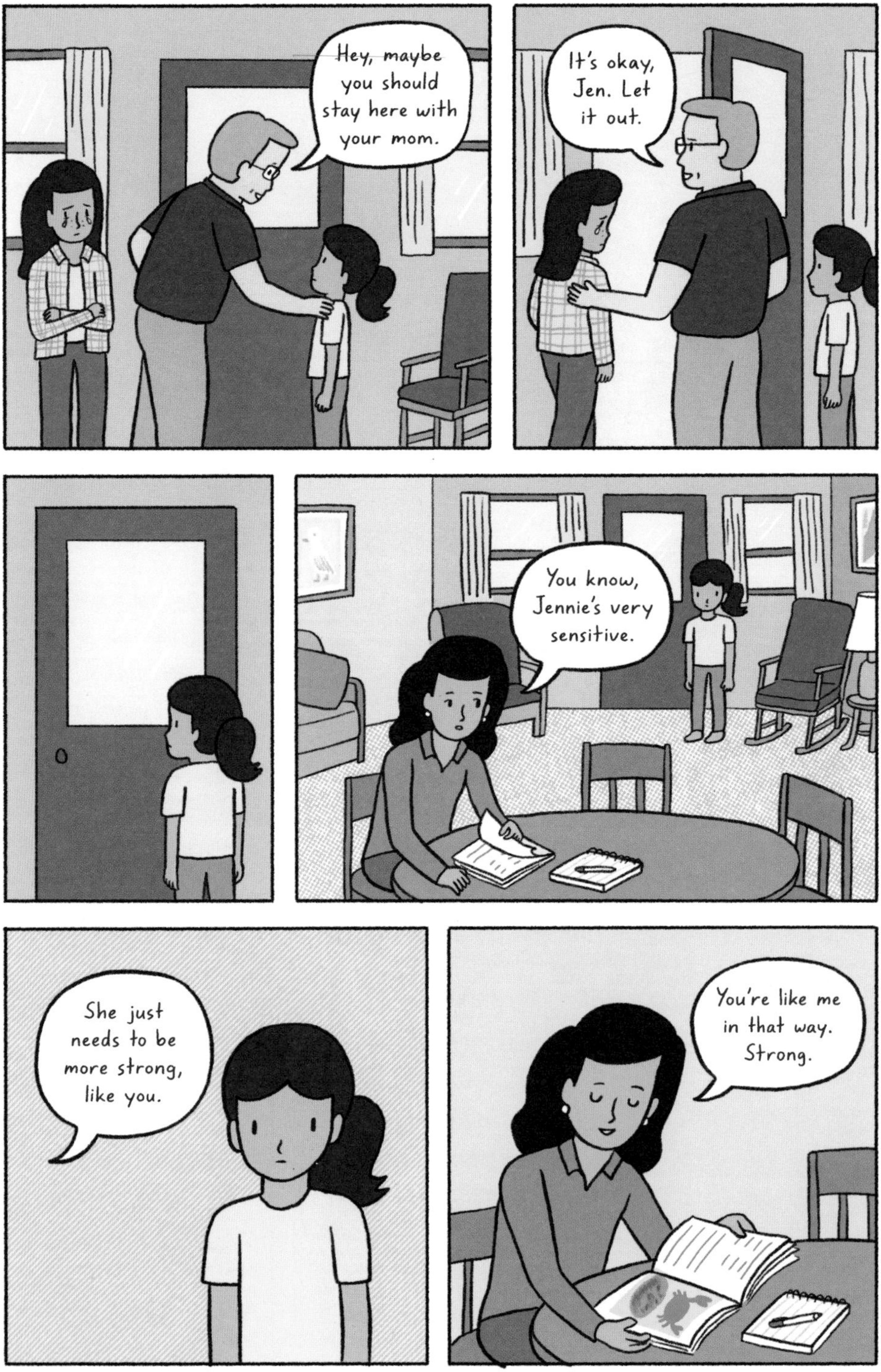
Hey, maybe you should stay here with your mom.
It's okay, Jen. Let it out.
You know, Jennie's very sensitive.
She just needs to be more strong, like you.
You're like me in that way. Strong.

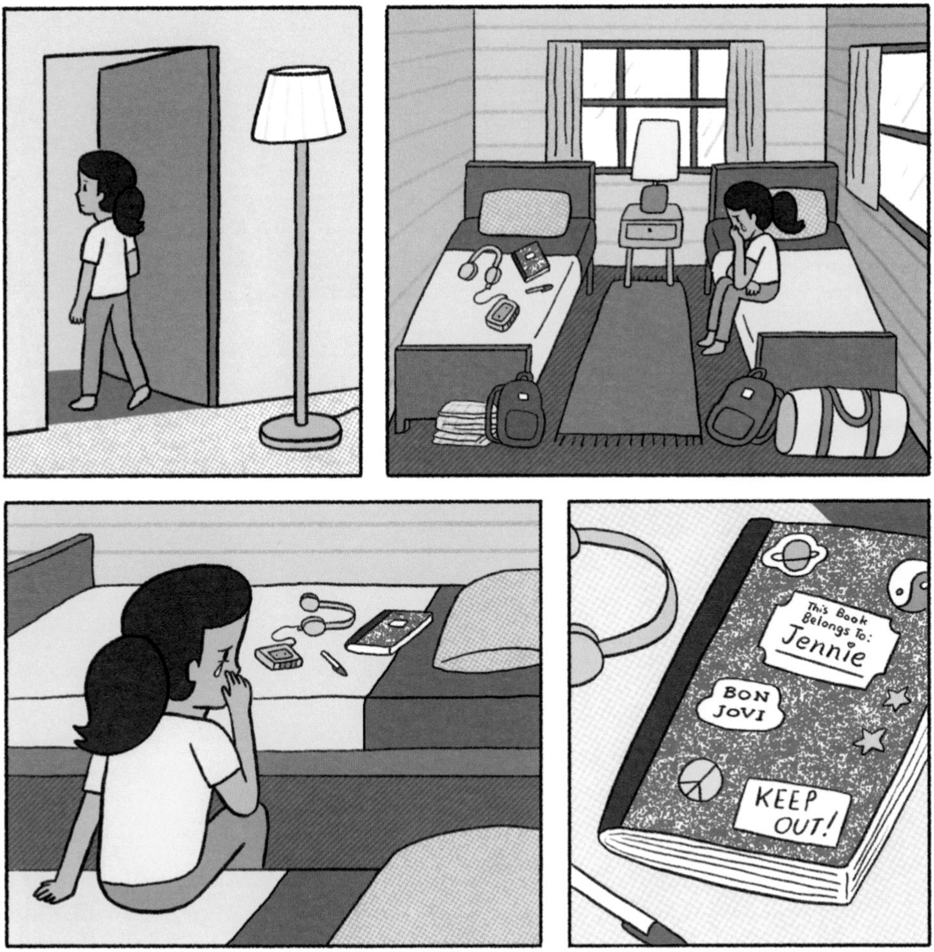
This Book Belongs To:
Jennie
BON JOVI
KEEP OUT!

I know it's wrong, but once the thought entered my head, I knew I was going to do it.

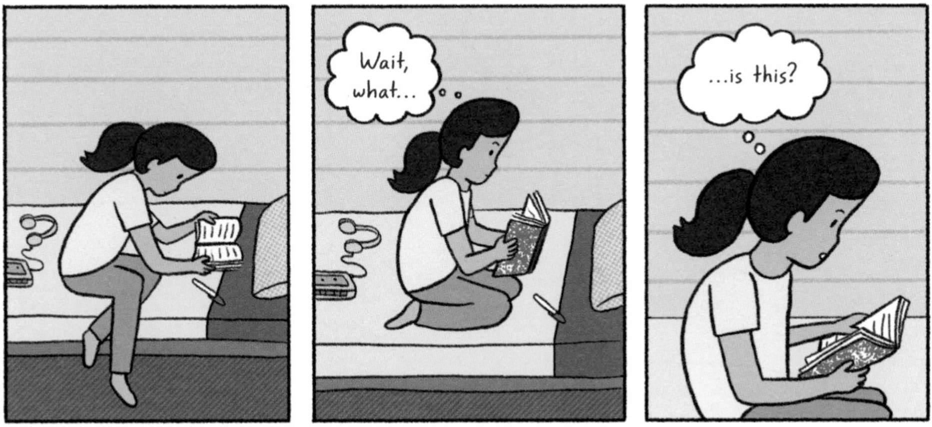
Wait, what...
...is this?

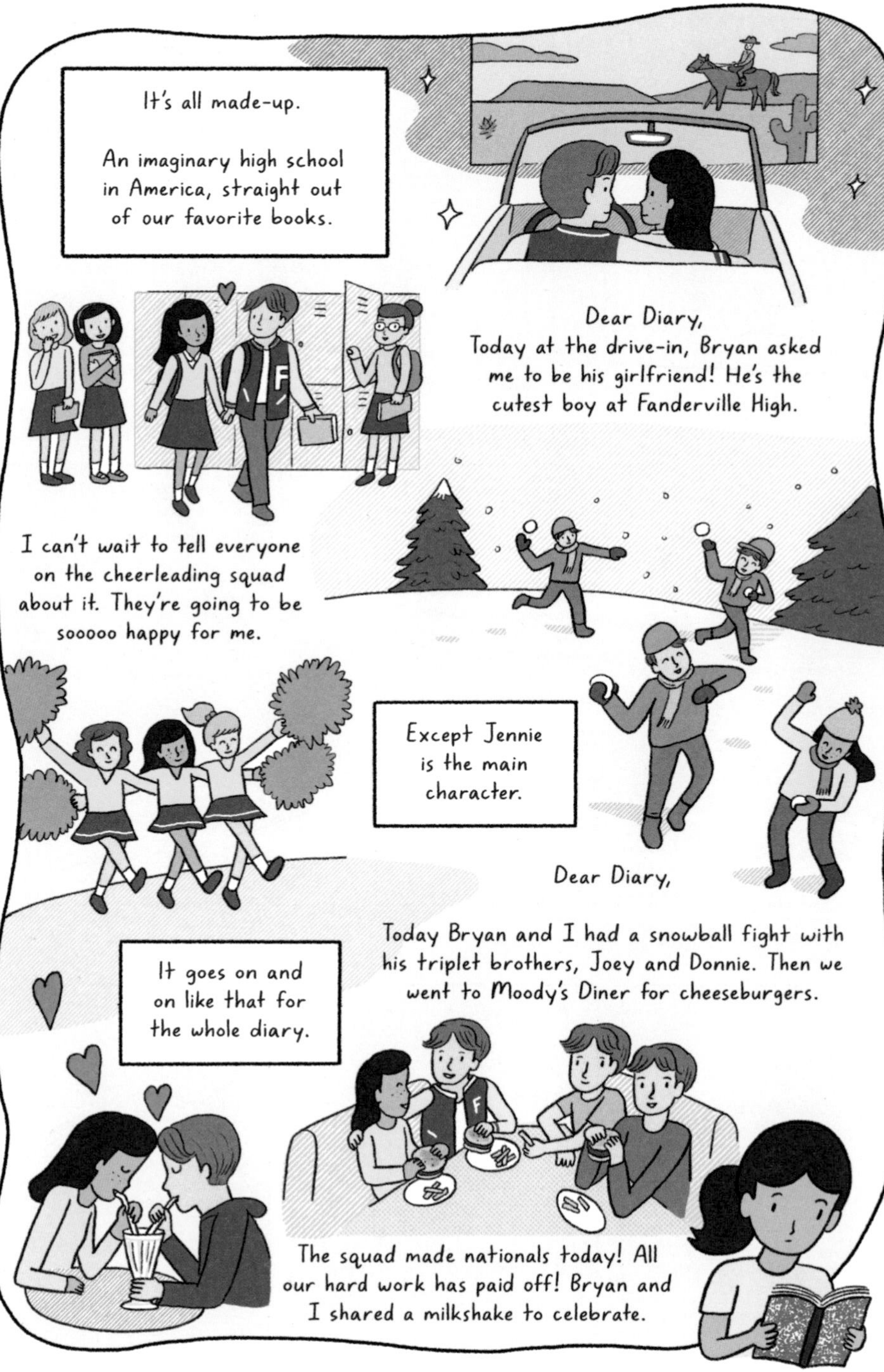
It's all made-up.
An imaginary high school in America, straight out of our favorite books.
Dear Diary,
Today at the drive-in, Bryan asked me to be his girlfriend! He's the cutest boy at Fanderville High.
I can't wait to tell everyone on the cheerleading squad about it. They're going to be sooooo happy for me.
Except Jennie is the main character.
Dear Diary,
Today Bryan and I had a snowball fight with his triplet brothers, Joey and Donnie. Then we went to Moody's Diner for cheeseburgers.
It goes on and on like that for the whole diary.
The squad made nationals today! All our hard work has paid off! Bryan and I shared a milkshake to celebrate.

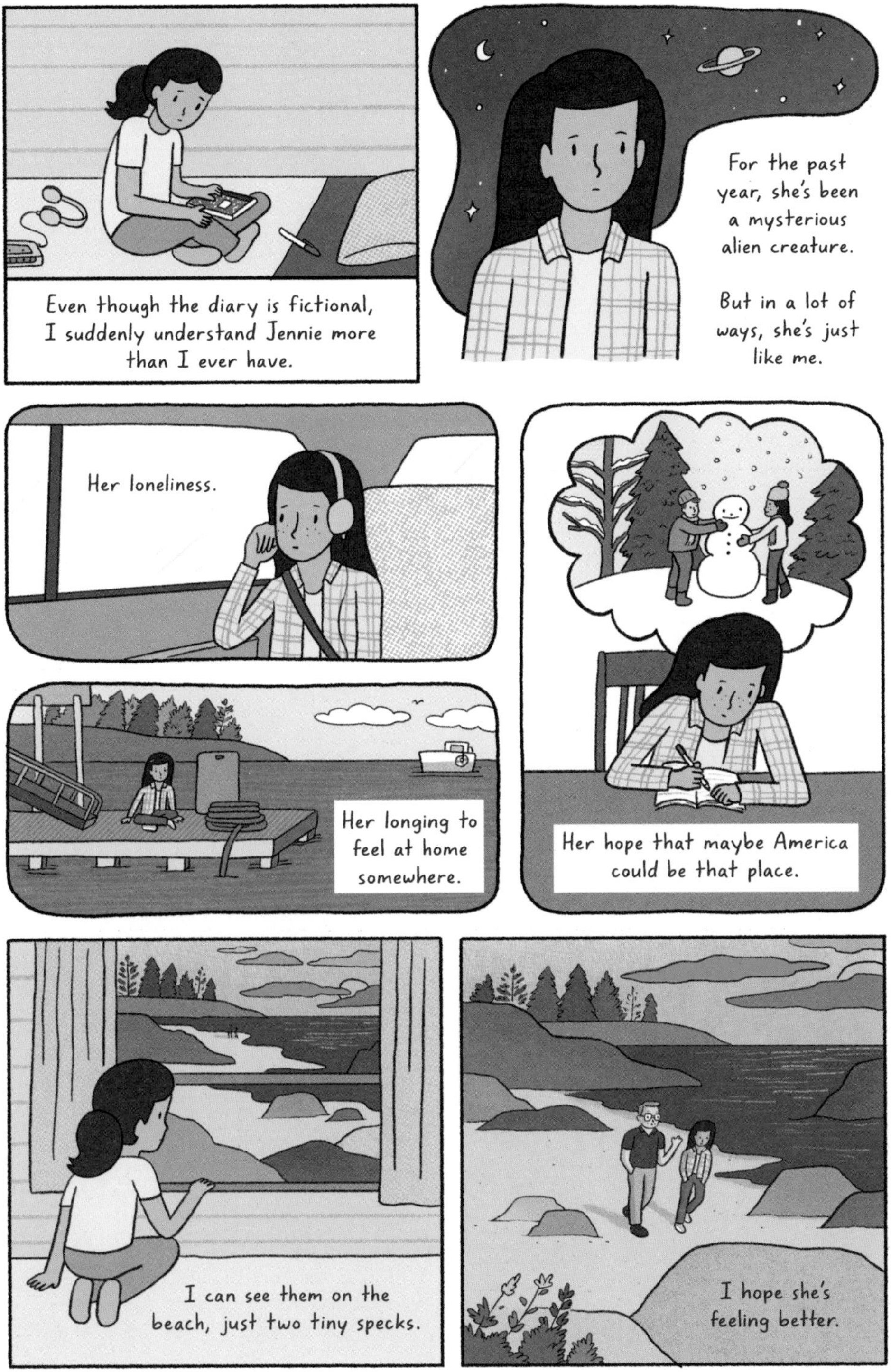

Even though the diary is fictional, I suddenly understand Jennie more than I ever have.
For the past year, she's been a mysterious alien creature.
But in a lot of ways, she's just like me.
Her loneliness.
Her longing to feel at home somewhere.
Her hope that maybe America could be that place.
I can see them on the beach, just two tiny specks.
I hope she's feeling better.

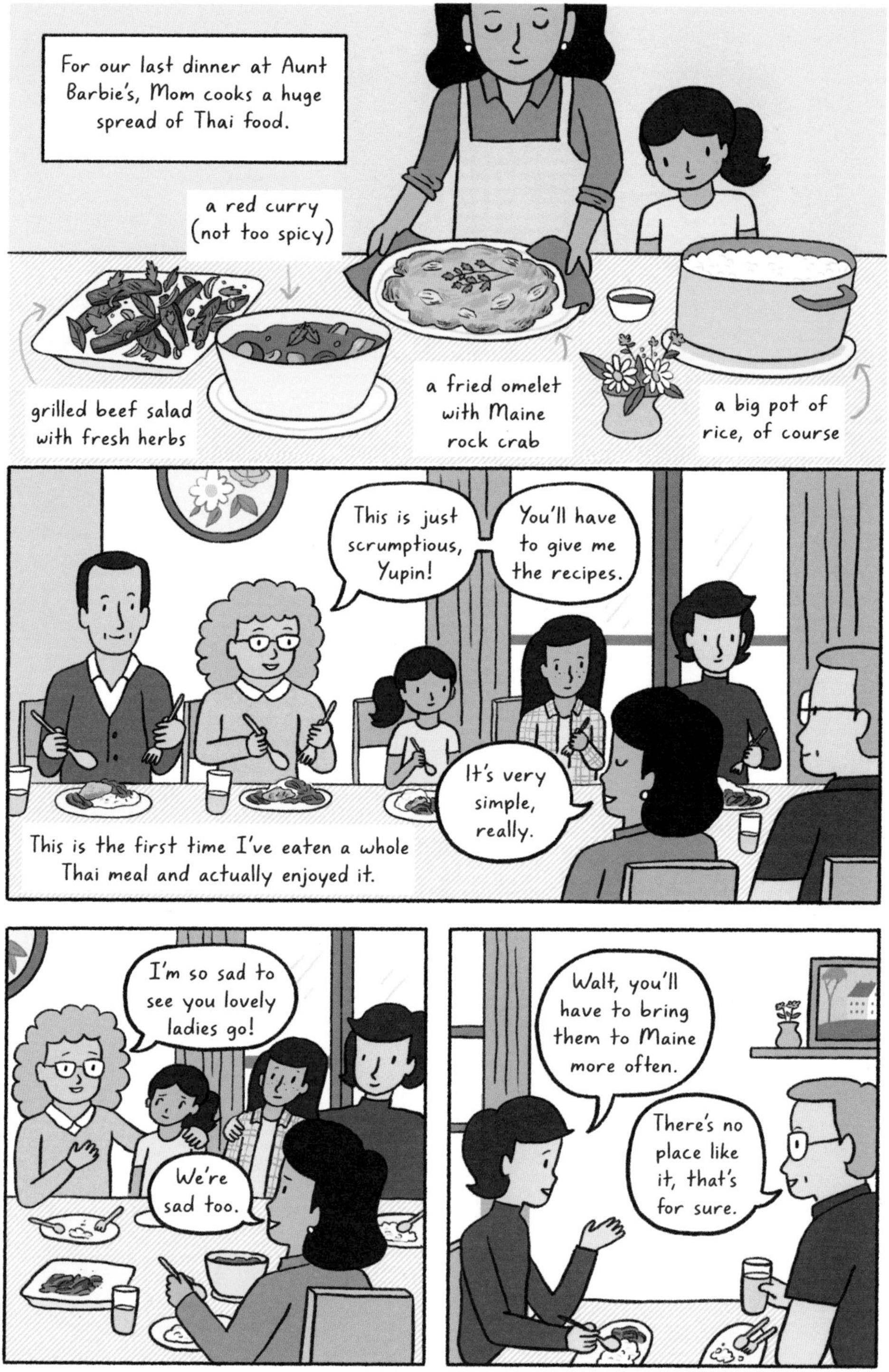
For our last dinner at Aunt Barbie's, Mom cooks a huge spread of Thai food.
a red curry (not too spicy)
grilled beef salad with fresh herbs
a fried omelet with Maine rock crab
a big pot of rice, of course
This is just scrumptious, Yupin!
You'll have to give me the recipes.
It's very simple, really.
This is the first time I've eaten a whole Thai meal and actually enjoyed it.
I'm so sad to see you lovely ladies go!
We're sad too.
Walt, you'll have to bring them to Maine more often.
There's no place like it, that's for sure.

I start to think about the things that connect me to my family, through all the distance.

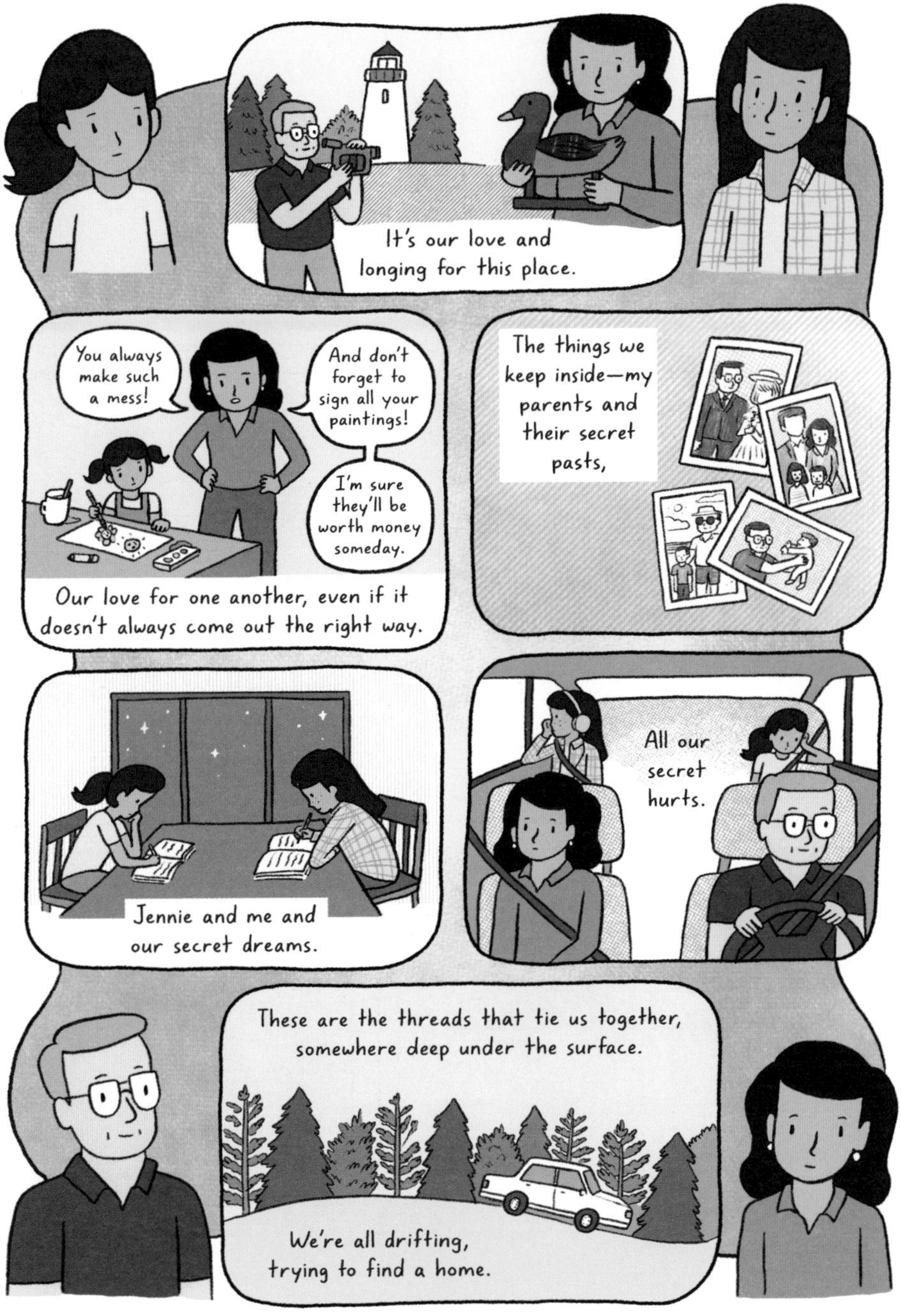
It's our love and longing for this place.
You always make such a mess!
And don't forget to sign all your paintings!
I'm sure they'll be worth money someday.
Our love for one another, even if it doesn't always come out the right way.
The things we keep inside—my parents and their secret pasts,
Jennie and me and our secret dreams.
All our secret hurts.
These are the threads that tie us together, somewhere deep under the surface.
We're all drifting, trying to find a home.

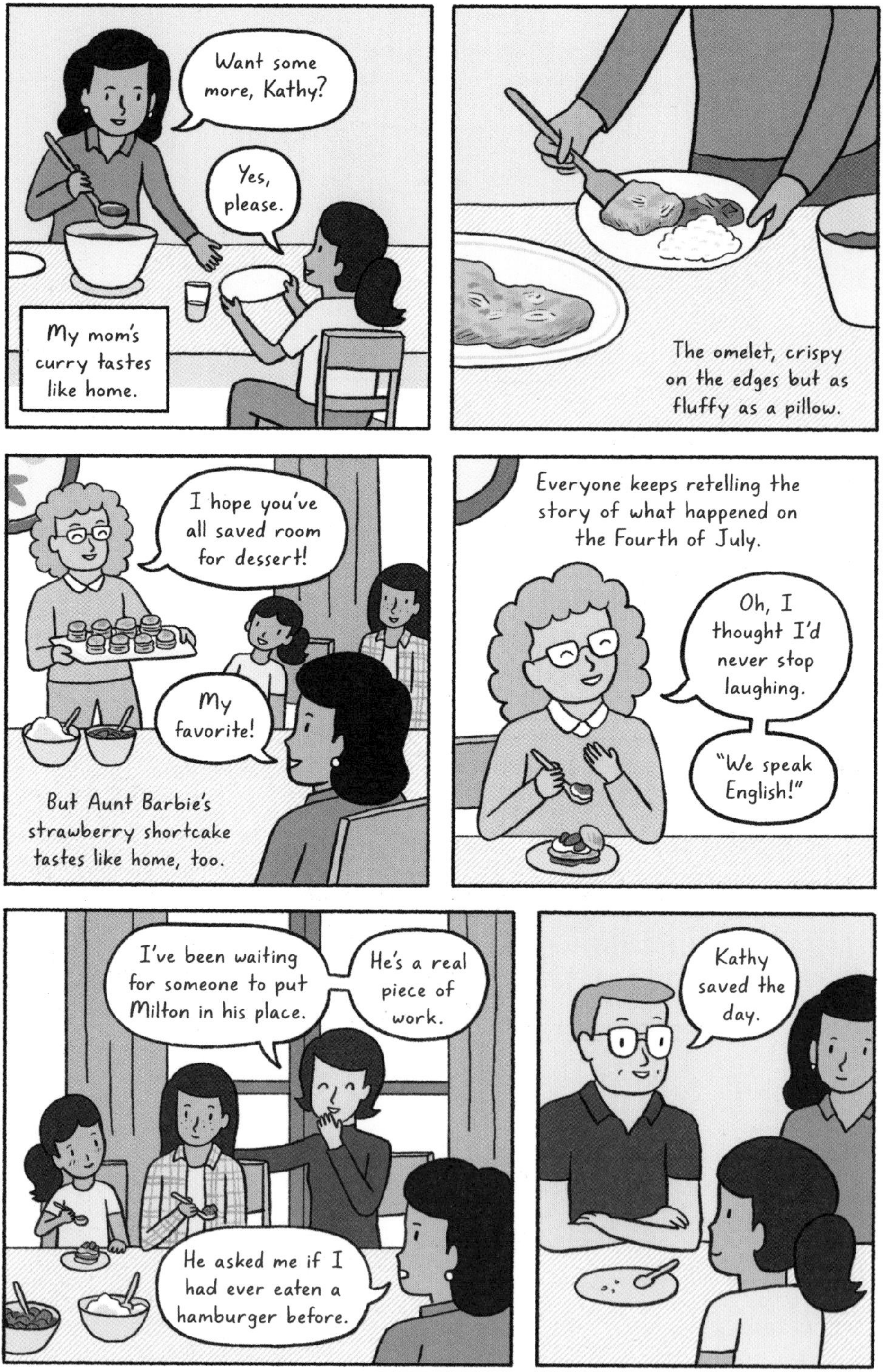
Want some more, Kathy?
Yes, please.
My mom's curry tastes like home.
The omelet, crispy on the edges but as fluffy as a pillow.
I hope you've all saved room for dessert!
My favorite!
But Aunt Barbie's strawberry shortcake tastes like home, too.
Everyone keeps retelling the story of what happened on the Fourth of July.
Oh, I thought I'd never stop laughing.
"We speak English!"
I've been waiting for someone to put Milton in his place.
He's a real piece of work.
He asked me if I had ever eaten a hamburger before.
Kathy saved the day.

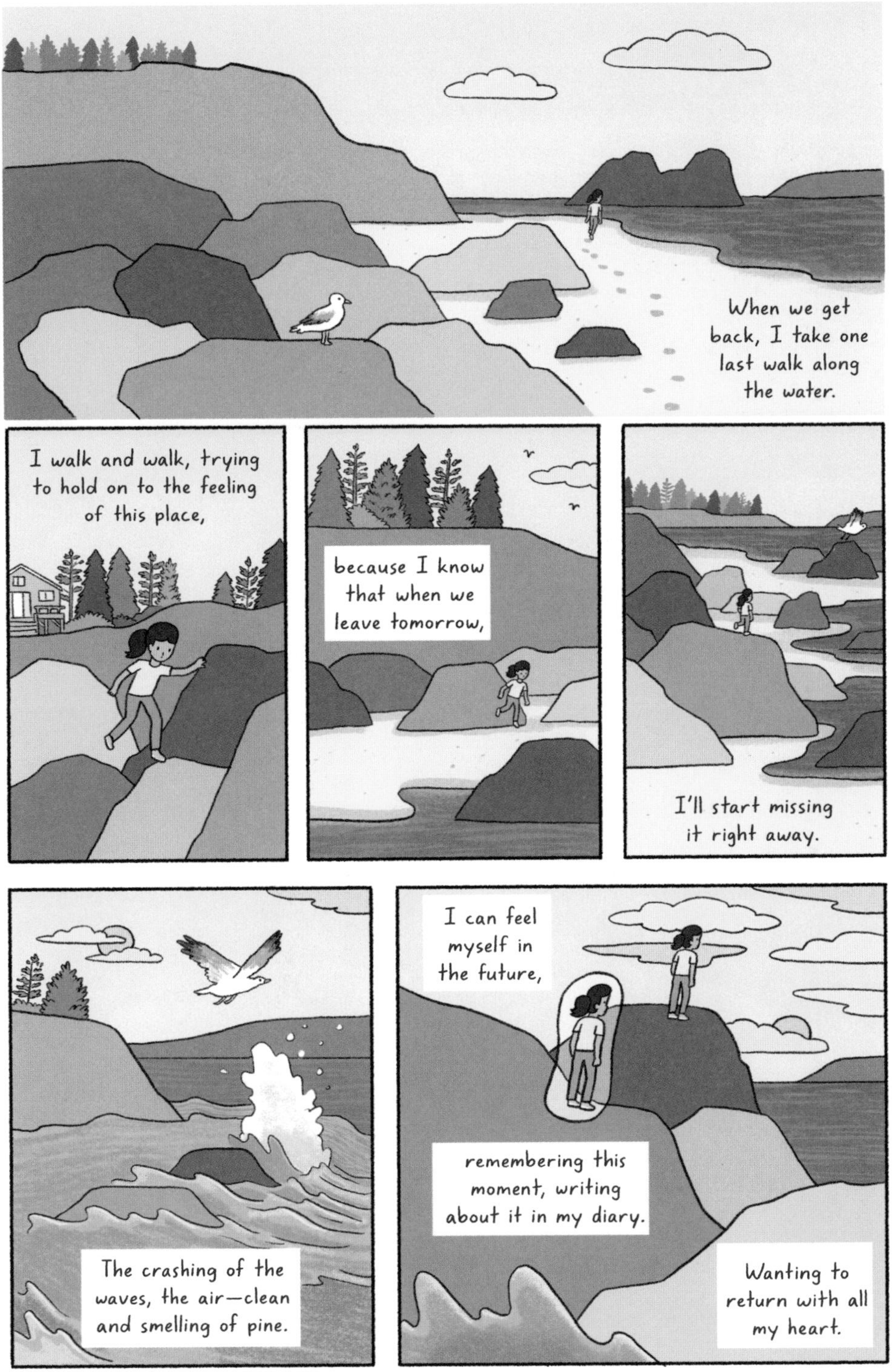
When we get back, I take one last walk along the water.
I walk and walk, trying to hold on to the feeling of this place,
because I know that when we leave tomorrow,
I'll start missing it right away.
The crashing of the waves, the air—clean and smelling of pine.
I can feel myself in the future,
remembering this moment, writing about it in my diary.
Wanting to return with all my heart.

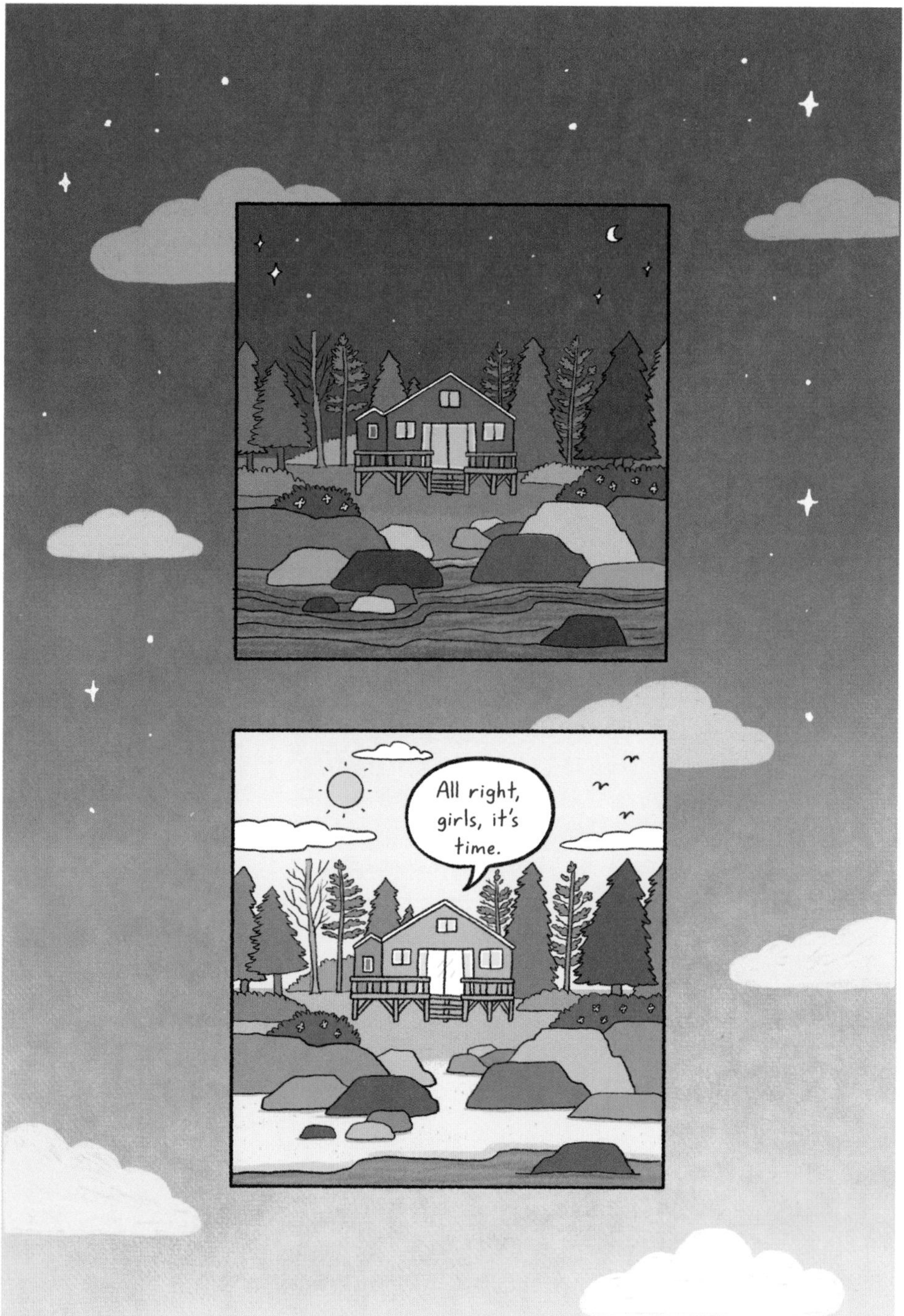
All right, girls, it's time.

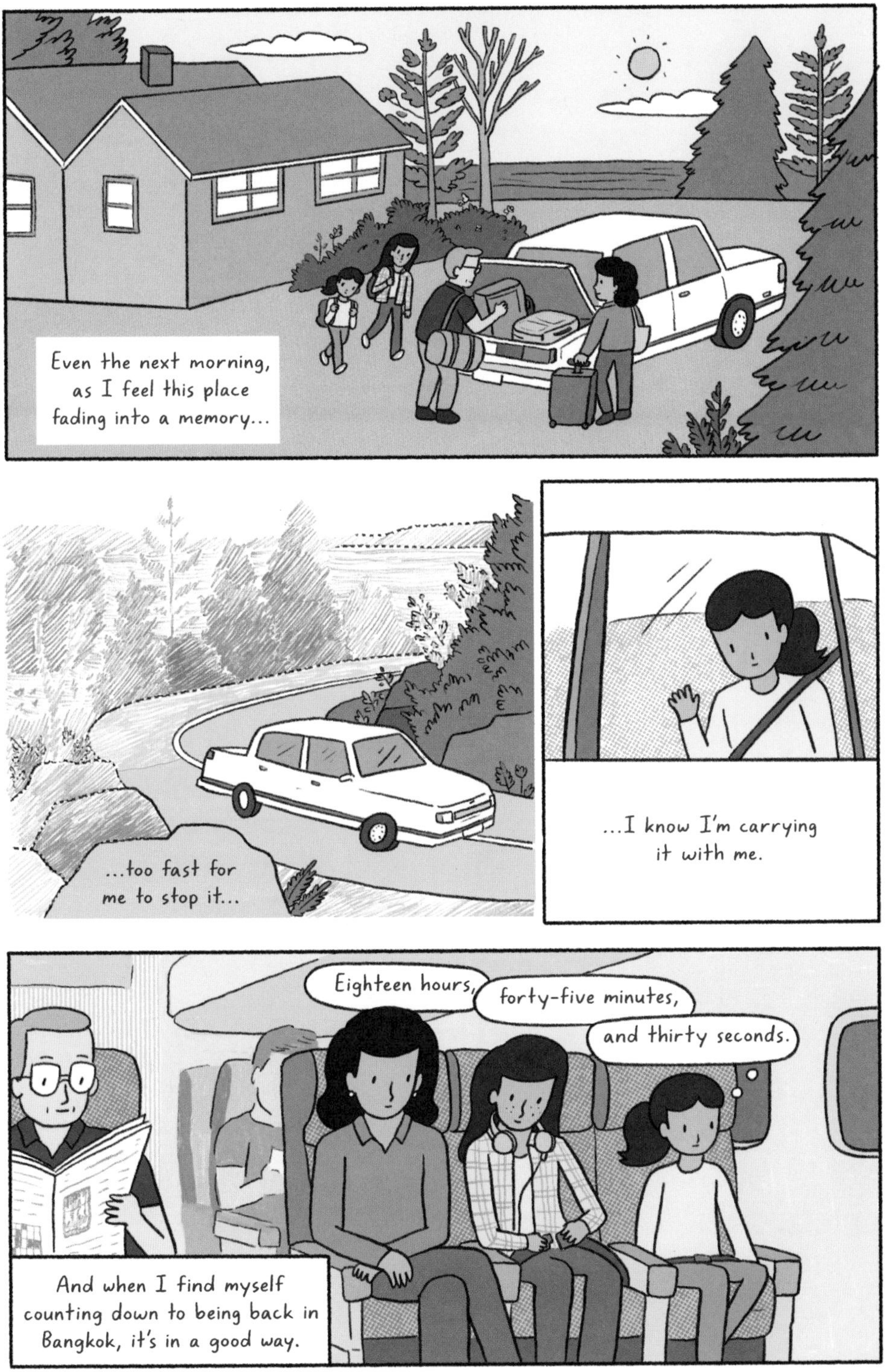
Even the next morning, as I feel this place fading into a memory...
...too fast for me to stop it...
...I know I'm carrying it with me.
Eighteen hours,
forty-five minutes,
and thirty seconds.
And when I find myself counting down to being back in Bangkok, it's in a good way.

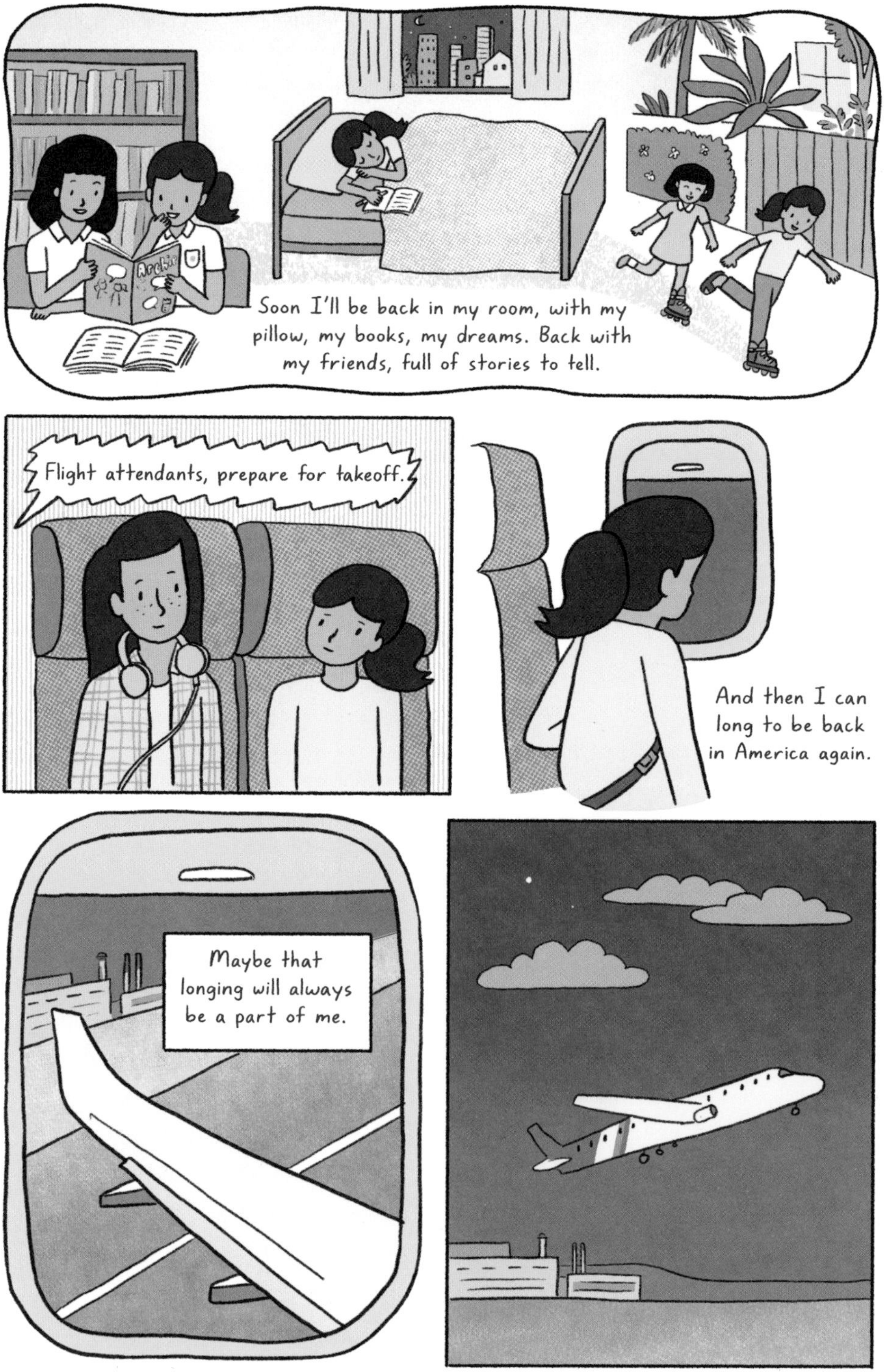
Archie
Soon I'll be back in my room, with my pillow, my books, my dreams. Back with my friends, full of stories to tell.
Flight attendants, prepare for takeoff.
And then I can long to be back in America again.
Maybe that longing will always be a part of me.

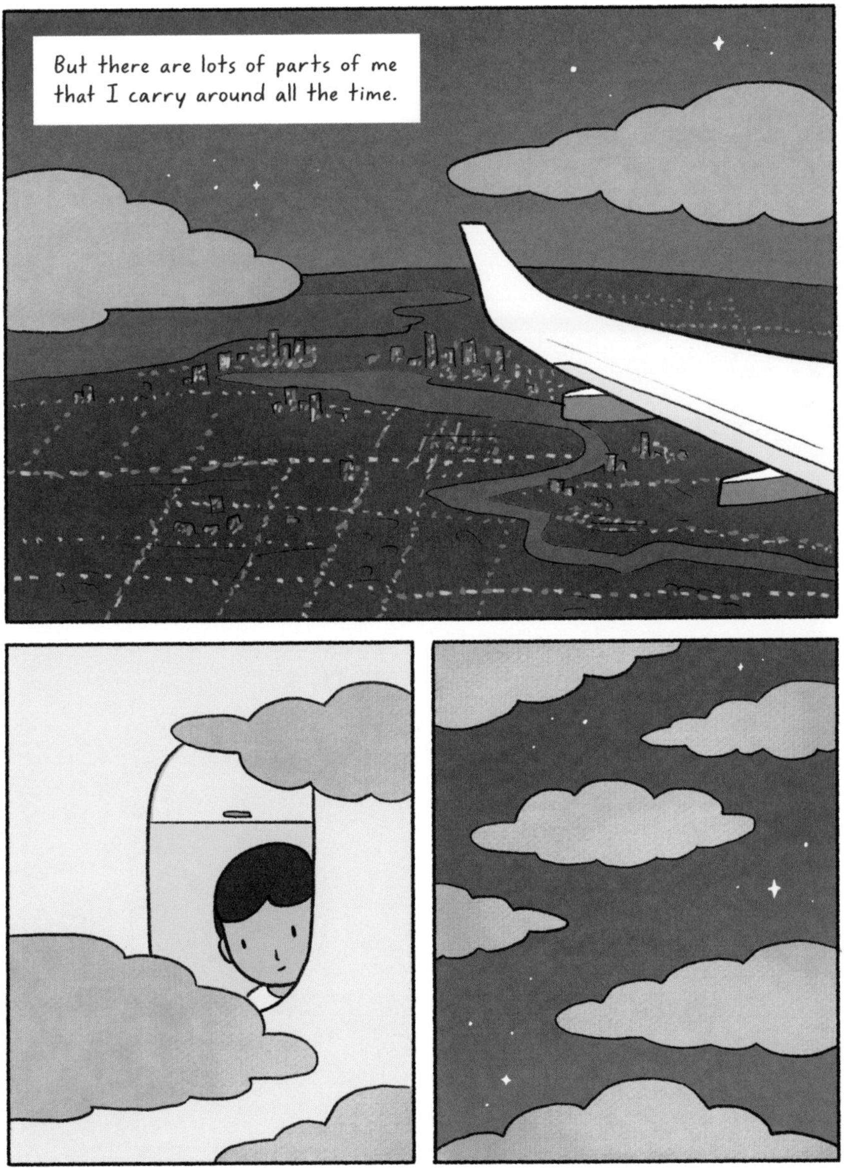
But there are lots of parts of me that I carry around all the time.

So many feelings.

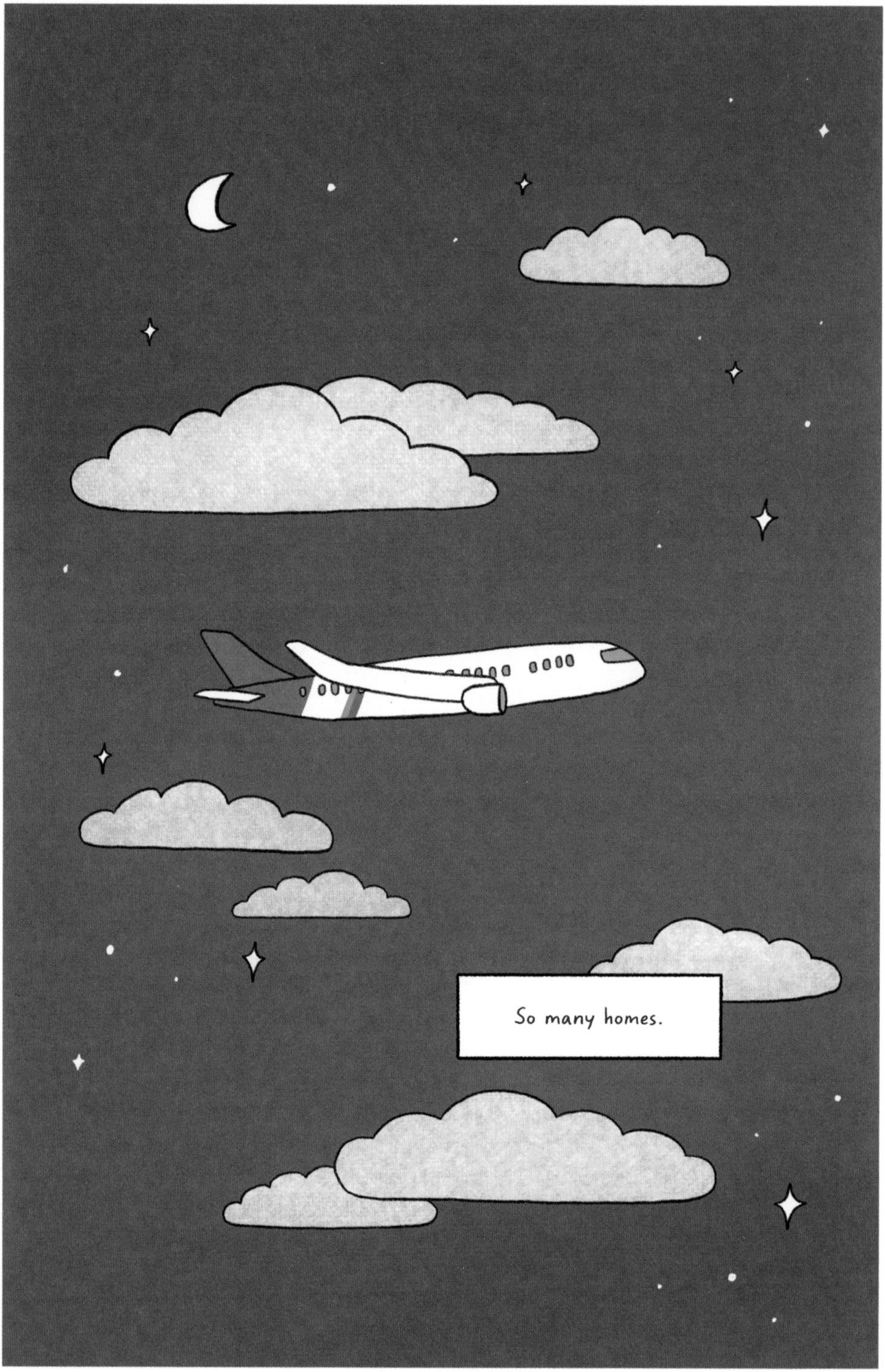
So many homes.

the
end

AFTERWORD

The events in the book take place over a single year, and mostly one summer. But in reality, they took place over many years, many summers. I pieced them together in a way that felt true. Wendy and I did skate down the street together, I did go over to her house on Christmas, we did have a neighbor with a cute dog, Wendy's brother did tell me I wasn't American because I didn't have blue eyes. Did all those things happen in the same afternoon? I don't know if they even happened the same year. But memories don't always exist in a straight line; they get tangled and knotted up. In a way, making this book felt like time travel—transporting myself back to a confusing past, untangling those knots, and making them make sense for you.

Writing and drawing all the scenes with my family felt like time travel too. It was easy to slip back into the family dynamic and the rhythms of our conversations, even though we haven't been a family like that in a very long time. My dad passed away in 2003, and now my mom, sister, and I all live on different continents. Mom is still in Bangkok, Jennie is in the United States, and I live in Germany. But when I sat down at my desk to make this book, we were all together again.

This book took me about a year to write, and another year to draw. During that period, the past and the present got blurred together. I was putting myself back in the shoes of my eleven-year-old self, trying to speak in her voice, trying to remember how the world looked through her eyes. When I drew her sitting alone and sad, or throwing a Rollerblade in anger, or jumping for joy, I would feel those things too. For two years, eleven-year-old Kathy was always with me.

Sometimes it got confusing and painful. There were a lot of times, as a kid, that I really didn't like myself, or I didn't feel good enough. I know now that this feeling is pretty common, but at the time it could get incredibly lonely. I didn't know how to be nice to myself. As

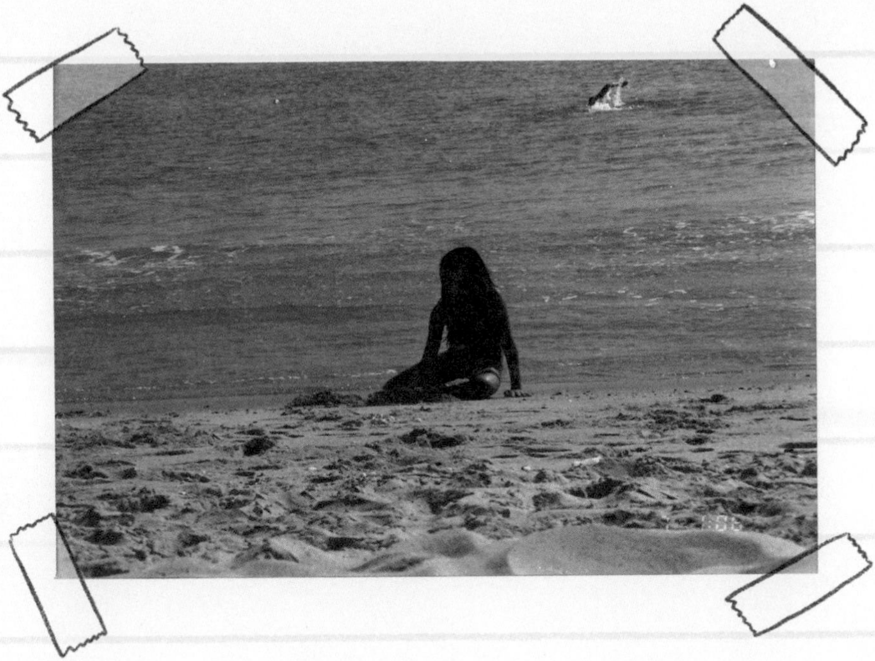

an adult, it still takes some effort! I had to keep reminding myself, while working on this book, to be gentle with eleven-year-old Kathy. After a while, I grew to love her, and wished I could travel back in time to just give her a hug.

There are a lot of things I wish I could tell her. Like, you may think you want blue eyes and blonde hair, or to be accepted by those who do, because you think that's what's going to make you like yourself. But everything about you is already enough. There is nothing wrong with you. What you're longing for—to be loved, to be seen—already exists within you.

My biggest hope for this book is that it will reach someone who feels the same way I did as a kid, someone who might need a hug right now. Maybe you're feeling bad about yourself for something you can't control. Maybe you're being extra-hard on yourself, thinking you need to be punished for something. But maybe what you need is to be nice to yourself. Be friends with yourself. Maybe your future self is looking back at you right this second, making a book about you, hoping you know just how fantastic you are.

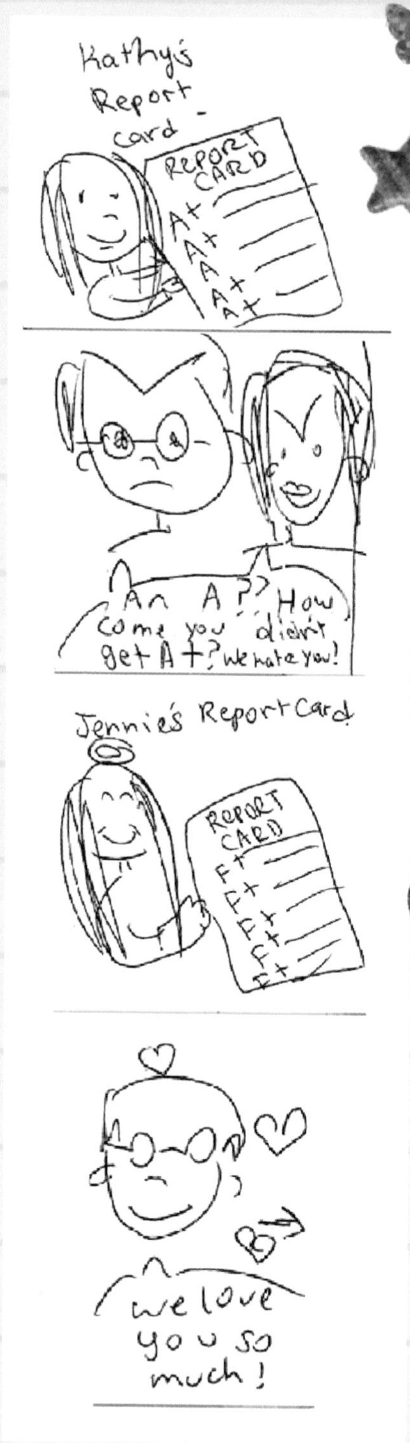
Kathy's Report card -
REPORT CARD
A+
A+
A
A+
A+
An A?? How come you didn't get A+? We hate you!
Jennie's Report Card
REPORT CARD
F+
F+
F+
F+
F
F+
we love you so much!

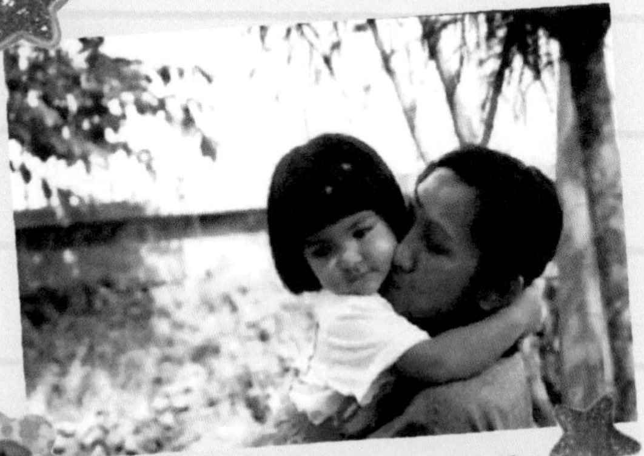

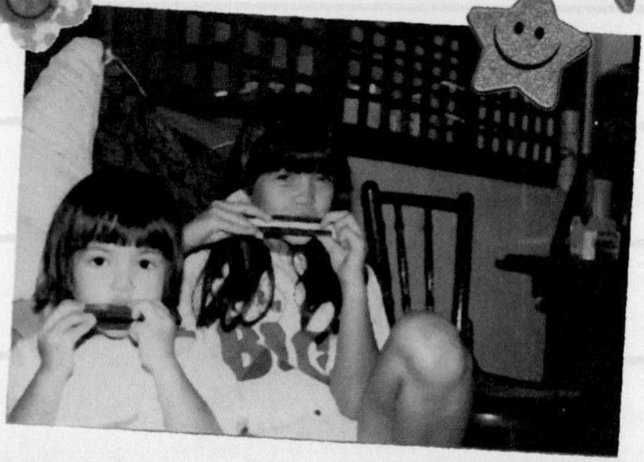

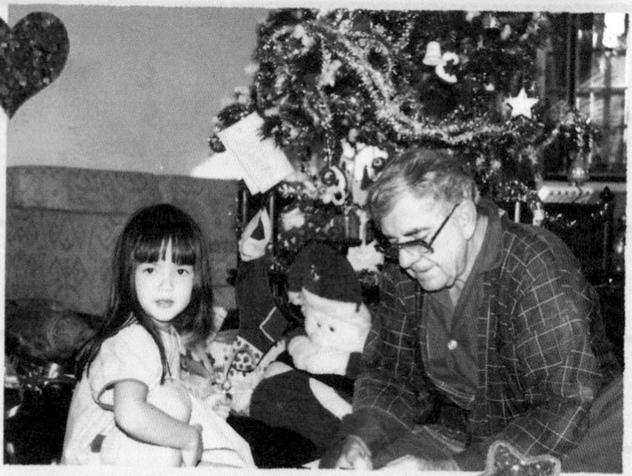

A comic I made for my dad when I was nine or ten years old

Mom and her famous Thanksgiving turkey

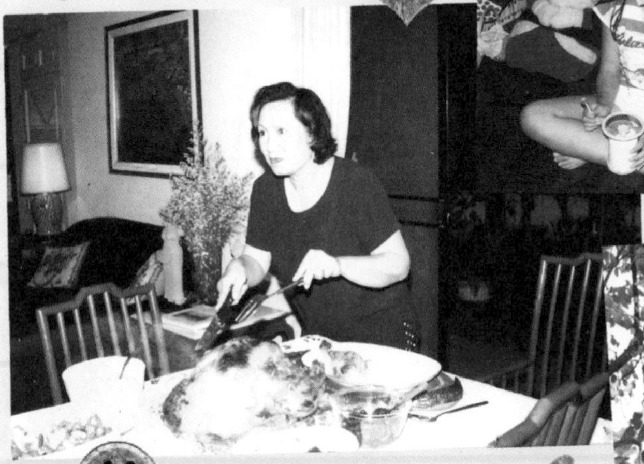

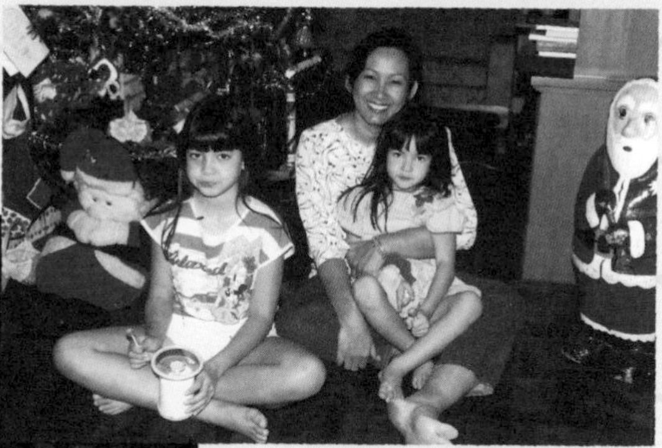

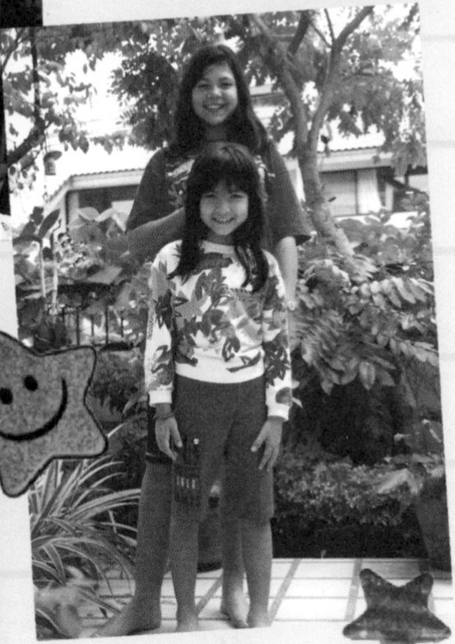

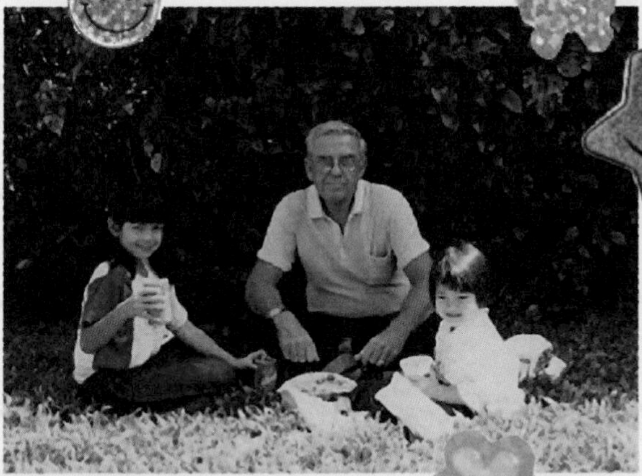

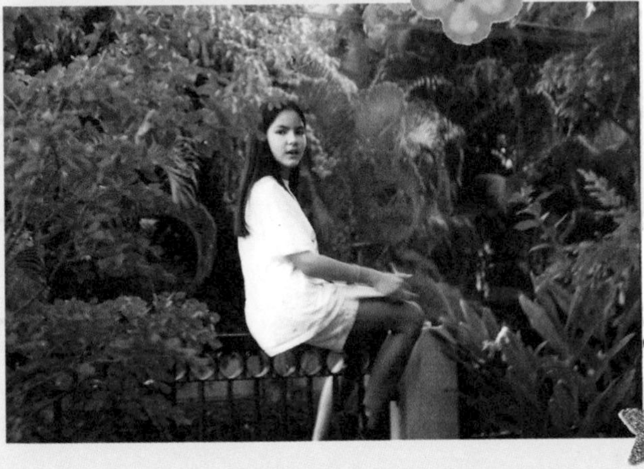

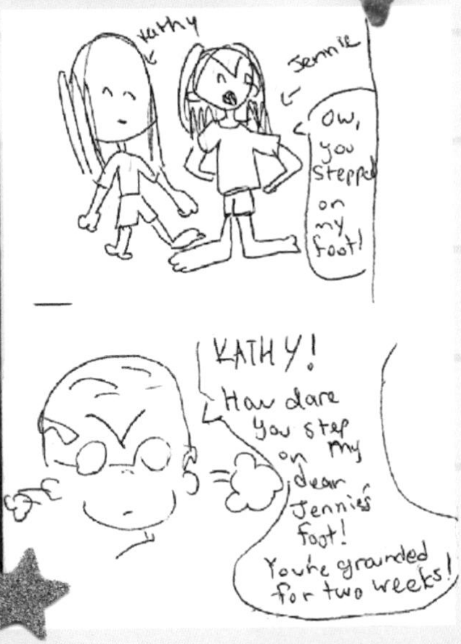
Kathy
Jennie
Ow, you stepp on my foot!
KATHY!
How dare you step on my dear Jennie's foot! You're grounded for two weeks!

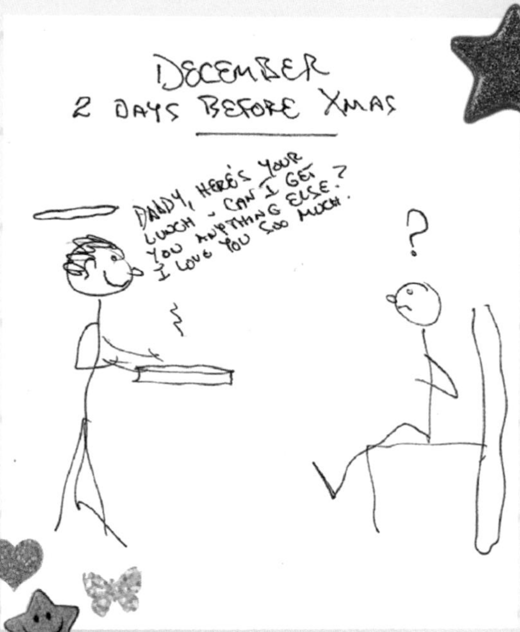
DECEMBER
2 DAYS BEFORE XMAS
DADDY, HERE'S YOUR LUNCH - CAN I GET YOU ANYTHING ELSE? I LOVE YOU SOO MUCH.
?

A comic my dad made in response to mine. Touché!

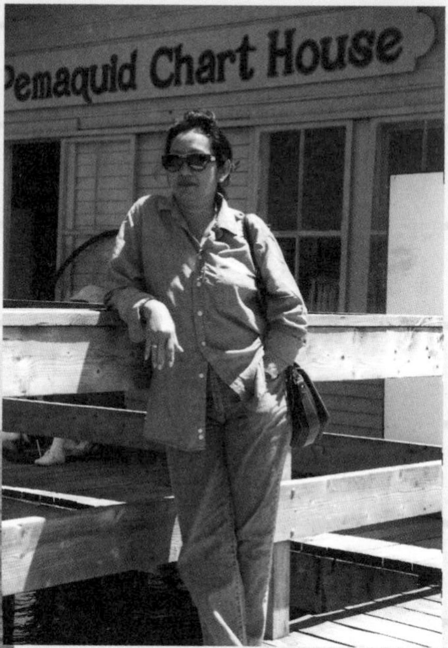
Pemaquid Chart House

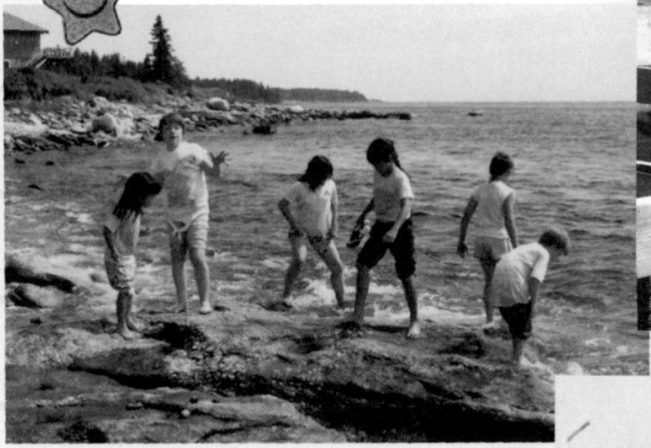

At the beach with the cousins

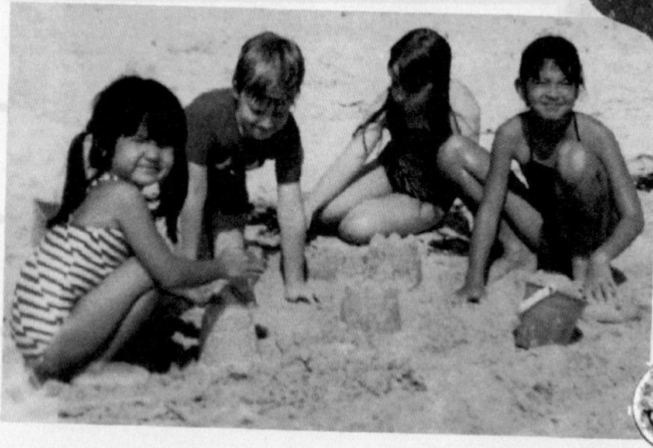

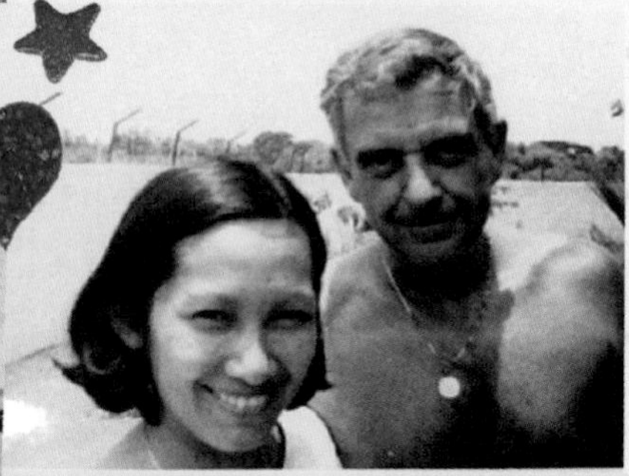

Mom and Dad before Jennie and I were born

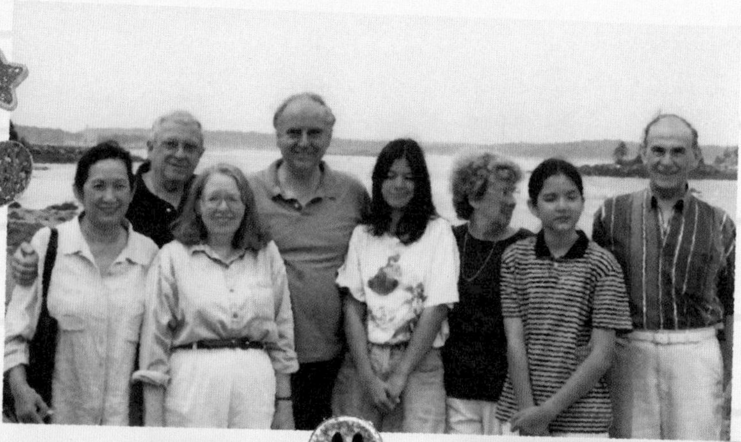

Dad and
his siblings

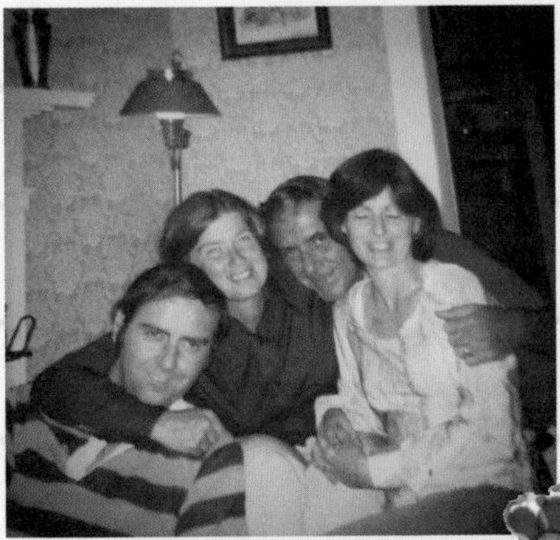

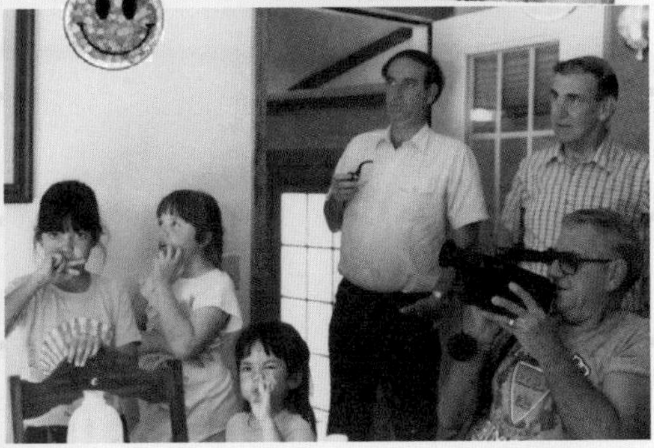

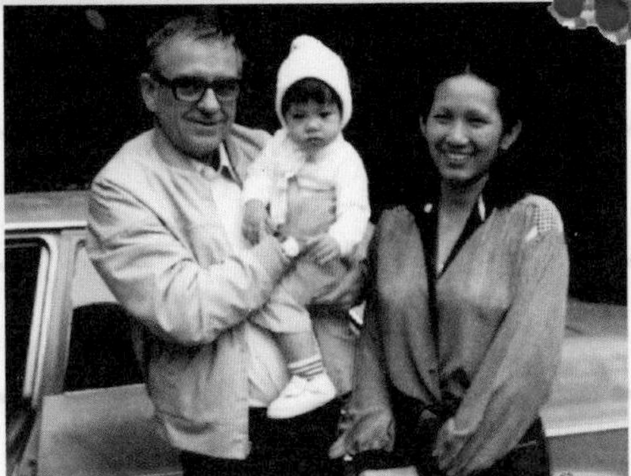

Jennie's first trip to
the United States

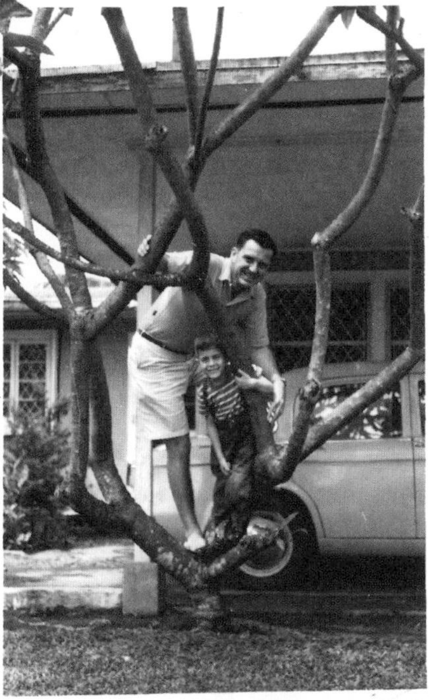

Dad and
Scott in 1961

ACKNOWLEDGMENTS

This book is for my family—for my mom, who taught me how to be strong; for my dad, who was my earliest fan and supporter; for my sister, whose weird and wild imagination helped bring mine to life. (Jennie, I would like to publicly apologize for reading your diary.) For Scott, who helped me understand why we are the way we are.

I'd also like to thank the friends who helped me understand family in a different way, the friends whose houses I'd go to after school, the college friends who brought me home for the holidays, the friends who now have families of their own who invite me over for dinners and cozy movie nights, and the friends I've made new traditions with. They've taught me a lot about love, and I can't believe my luck at having so much of it in my life.

I want to give enormous thanks to my agent Chad Luibl, to Robyn Chapman, and the rest of the amazing team at First Second. To my friends Bob Halliday and David Heatley, and to Anna Kaufman for seeing something in me and piercing through my self-doubt. To PJ Vogt for chanting, "Do it! Do it!" over the phone, incessantly, until I hit send on that first email just to shut him up. You were all major stepping stones towards making this book happen, and I didn't even realize it at the time.

:01

First Second

Published by First Second
First Second is an imprint of Roaring Brook Press,
a division of Holtzbrinck Publishing Holdings Limited Partnership
120 Broadway, New York, NY 10271
firstsecondbooks.com
mackids.com

© 2024 by Kathy MacLeod
All rights reserved

Library of Congress Control Number: 2023937817

Our books may be purchased in bulk for promotional, educational, or business use.
Please contact your local bookseller or the Macmillan Corporate and Premium Sales Department
at (800) 221-7945 ext. 5442 or by email at MacmillanSpecialMarkets@macmillan.com.

First edition, 2024
Edited by Robyn Chapman with help from Samia Fakih
Cover design and interior book design by Molly Johanson and Kathy MacLeod
Production editing by Sarah Gompper

Penciled and inked on an iPad Pro with Procreate. Colored digitally in Procreate and Photoshop.
Lettered with a custom font created from the artist's handwriting.

Printed in China by 1010 Printing International Limited, Kwun Tong, Hong Kong

ISBN 978-1-250-81374-9 (paperback)
1 3 5 7 9 10 8 6 4 2

ISBN 978-1-250-81373-2 (hardcover)
1 3 5 7 9 10 8 6 4 2

Don't miss your next favorite book from First Second! For the latest updates go
to firstsecondnewsletter.com and sign up for our enewsletter.